VISION IN VEHICLES – V

VISION IN VEHICLES – V

Edited by

A.G. GALE
University of Derby
Derby, U.K.

Co-edited by

I.D. BROWN
Cambridge, U.K.

C.M. HASLEGRAVE
University of Nottingham
Nottingham, U.K.

S.P. TAYLOR
Bournemouth, U.K.

N·H

1996

ELSEVIER
AMSTERDAM • LAUSANNE • NEW YORK • OXFORD • SHANNON • TOKYO

ELSEVIER SCIENCE B.V.
Sara Burgerhartstraat 25
P.O. Box 211, 1000 AE Amsterdam, The Netherlands

ISBN: 0 444 81477 9

This book is printed on acid-free paper.

Transferred to digital printing 2006

Preface

The Fifth International Conference on Vision In Vehicles was held at the Kelvin Conference Centre, University of Glasgow, Glasgow, Scotland in the autumn of 1993. The conference series is organised by a group of Societies with differing interests in driving and vision, these are The Applied Vision Association, The Ergonomics Society and the Association of Optometrists.

The aim of the conference series is to enable international researchers from different disciplines to come together and exchange ideas on the current state of the art on all aspects related to vehicles and vehicle controllers. This is perceived as encompassing the internal and external design of a vehicle, the environment in which vehicles move, as well as the visual, perceptual and cognitive limitations of the vehicle controller. Whilst the conference organisers interpret the term 'vehicles' in a very wide sense the papers submitted to the conference tend to focus on the automobile. Thus it is heartening to see some work here on other forms of transport including underground mining vehicles, helicopters, trains and motorcyclists.

The order of the chapters loosely mirrors the order of the papers at the conference. As in previous years equal weight has been attached to both oral and poster presentations and the poster chapters are intermingled appropriately with the papers.

The conference organising committee included I.D. Brown, C.M. Haslegrave, P.A. Smith and S.P. Taylor. The conference scientific committee included Lloyd Avant, Viola Cavallo and Michael Sivak to whom we are indebted for help in refereeing the presentations.

We thank John Bloomfield who presented the conference keynote address on 'Automated Highways: a Vision for the Future', which set the tone for the meeting. The proceedings here begin in similar vein with chapters considering Simulation Studies of Driver Performance, followed by a section on Visual Processing and Collision Avoidance. Cognitive issues are then addressed through several chapters detailing recent work on Cognitive Aspects of Visual Information Processing. The growing use of information technology is covered in two subsequent sections concerning firstly, the Visual Requirements of In-Vehicle Guidance Systems and secondly, Driver Support Systems. Environmental factors are discussed in the section on Visual Performance in Degraded Visibility. Drivers' own Visual Impairment is then considered and the final section concerns Arousal and Performance and discusses alcohol effects on driving ability.

The conference organisation was, as ever, ably handled by Sarah Rivington with additional assistance at the meeting given by Evelyn Pawley. These proceedings were prepared with the enormous help of Sarah Rivington with additional assistance given by Kirstin Wass,Vikki Taylor and Vikki Gould to whom I express my deep gratitude.

Previous conferences in the series have been published by North Holland / Elsevier and I thank Kees Michielsen for his enormous help and patience.

For information on future Vision In Vehicle conferences please contact the address below.

Prof. Alastair Gale
Applied Vision Research Unit
University of Derby
Derby DE3 5GX
UK
email: avru@derby.ac.uk
www: http://www-hcs.derby.ac.uk/avru.html

CONTENTS

1: SIMULATION STUDIES OF DRIVER PERFORMANCE

VISION IN VEHICLES - V
A.G. Gale et al. (Editors)

Applications of Appropriate Simulator Technology for Driver Training, Licensing and Assessment

J. A. Wachtel

The Design Eye Group, 226 East Montgomery Street, Baltimore, Maryland 21230, USA

1. INTRODUCTION AND OVERVIEW

Interactive driving simulators can be broadly clustered in three groups along a price continuum. At one extreme is the "home-grown" device, typically designed and built in university engineering laboratories, and used to support faculty and student research. At the other are devices, also one-off designs, which may be considered "high fidelity, full scope" simulators. These systems, of which there are but a handful in the world, cost tens of millions of dollars, and are patterned after simulators originally developed for the aviation industry. These high end devices typically include projected computer-generated imagery (CGI) displays which provide fields of view from the driver's eye position of 180 to 360°. In addition, they incorporate sophisticated motion systems which permit angular rotation as well as longitudinal and lateral translation to simulate vehicle movements. Although these two classes of simulators are quite different in capability, each has been successful over many years at supporting important research that has contributed to our understanding and improvement of the daily interaction between driver, vehicle, and environment (1).

Between these extremes, what has been absent from the marketplace is a class of device which would permit the benefits of driving simulation to be extended to highway safety applications on a broad scale, such as the training, licensing and assessment of vehicle operators. Simulators with this potential have begun to emerge in the past few years.

This paper will focus on the development, application and validation of an affordable, moderately high fidelity simulator using *appropriate technology* for driver training, licensing and assessment, issues of increasing concern as our roads become more crowded, our vehicles more laden with complex technology (intentional and otherwise), and our driving population older. After introductory remarks about the use of simulation for training and testing in other industries, and why simulation has not heretofore been successful in the automotive community, the paper will report on a series of diverse, loosely coordinated research projects underway at several institutions in North America. These projects, taken individually, are evaluating the viability of simulation for diverse applications. Despite this diversity, however, and despite the breadth of the organizations performing this research (including universities, hospitals, motor vehicle agencies, law enforcement training academies and standards-setting bodies), there is a common thread that binds these programs together. That is, they are each part of an integrated effort to develop, refine, test and validate a particular simulator technology, one which could eventually see widespread application.

2. AN OPERATIONAL DEFINITION OF "APPROPRIATE TECHNOLOGY"

Simulators are generally thought of as "high-tech" devices. At the annual meeting of the Committee on Simulation and Measurement of Vehicle and Operator Performance of the National Academy of Science's Transportation Research Board, the conversation reverberates with terms like: refresh rate, raster scan, polygon count, collimated imagery, rotational degrees of freedom, horizontal field of view, texture mapping, and so on. There is less discussion of *results* and of applications to real world settings - driver test scores, training time, instructor workload, accident reduction, or reduced recidivism of DUI arrests, for example. Why is this? I believe that much of the driving simulator community, at least in the U.S., is so caught up with the technology and the need for ever better *simulator* performance, that we have lost the forest for the trees - we fail to realize that its not the simulator performance that counts - but the *driver* performance. Thus, I think that we ourselves are to blame for the bad press, however misguided, that we occasionally receive (2,3). In short, I believe that our seemingly endless fascination with the technology that drives simulators is misplaced.

A simulator is merely a tool to accomplish an objective such as better training or testing. High technology, and the never-ending race to expand it, may not be necessary, and is certainly not sufficient to achieve that objective (4,5,6). In my work to develop simulator requirements for training and licensing in the U.S. nuclear power industry a few years ago, I stressed *performance criteria* in support of training objectives and licensing requirements, and it didn't matter whether those criteria were achieved with CRAY Computers or rubberbands (7). For the title of this paper, I have co-opted the term "appropriate technology" from a classical economics book called *Small Is Beautiful*, by E.F. Schumacher (8). To me, when applied to driving simulators, the term means that the design of the system, and its resultant scope and fidelity, should be based on the technology empirically determined to be appropriate (neither too much nor too little) to accomplish the goals for which it has been specified, and that technological embellishments for other reasons may unnecessarily add to costs, complexity and downtime, and may even detract from the very goals of the training or testing program (9,10).

This is not to say that all work on simulators to date is for nought. Far from it. Over the years, there have been hundreds of articles in the literature on the application of driving simulation to training and licensing. But how many situations exist today in which simulators are in use for actual driver training or licensing? In the U.S., those people who are responsible for the driver licensing programs have known for years that the road test as currently administered is essentially useless as a predictor of who will be a "good" driver (11,12). They are constantly seeking better alternatives, and for years they have looked to simulation as the holy grail. Do you know how many simulators are in use today in the U.S. as part of a driver licensing program? None.

3. SIMULATION FOR TRAINING AND LICENSING IN OTHER INDUSTRIES

In the U.S. nuclear power industry simulators are routinely used for operator training and licensing. Essentially the same situation exists, worldwide, in the commercial aviation industry, and increasingly so in the maritime industry. Why are simulators *the* tools to use for training and testing in these fields, and virtually *ignored* in the highway community?

To answer this question, we must look at the basic reasons for choosing simulators. Although this argument has been made in many ways over the years, it boils down to something like this (13). Once you have identified your training objectives or licensing criteria, you must consider whether training on the actual equipment would be *possible*, *practical*, or *cost-effective*. If the answer to at least one of these three questions is no, then simulation might be a viable alternative. The question of possibility is straightforward. Either you can or you cannot use the actual equipment to perform a task. Practicality may be viewed as asking whether the use of the actual equipment to perform the task might have adverse financial, environmental, or legal ramifications. Cost-effectiveness looks at the impacts that the use of actual equipment for training or licensing in anything other than a normal operating mode might have on equipment downtime, consumption of raw materials (such as fuel), reduction of the expected life of the equipment, or lost opportunity costs - i.e. equipment unavailability for the purpose for which it was intended.

Obviously, when one thinks of emergency or accident scenarios, it is neither possible, practical, nor cost-effective to fulfill complete training or licensing requirements in the nuclear, aviation or maritime environments using the actual equipment. And this has led to a situation in which simulators are used for the great majority of training and licensing activities in these industries. Conversely, when it comes to road vehicles of all types, training and licensing continue to be performed almost wholly on the actual equipment. Why is this? Following the decision criteria above, it has been argued that it is possible, practical, and cost-effective to perform these activities on the actual equipment. I disagree. I think that, at least in the U.S., we have been misled because our traditional driver training and licensing programs are simply inadequate.

A typical driver education course consists of 30 hours of classroom experience and six hours behind the wheel. Many police officers, being trained in high speed pursuit, are given no in-car time at all - so all they "need" and all they get is about six hours of lecture before being given the keys to a patrol car. Our driver training programs pay little or no attention to the practice of emergency maneuvers such as skid control, off-road recovery, evasive skills, and controlled braking, or to driving under common but hazardous conditions such as night, fog, snow and ice. The reasons given are *safety* (for people and property) and *cost* (of equipment, facilities, and liability). The underlying reason may be that most driver training programs exist *not* to develop better drivers but to prepare novices to pass the State administered licensing test. Of course, the typical State road test avoids the same hazardous, but real world, conditions, and offers the same safety and cost argument for doing so. No wonder it is possible, practical and cost-effective to train and test on actual equipment.

There is emerging in the U.S. a series of demographic, cultural and societal changes that are acting like an invisible hand to force increased scrutiny to be paid to issues of driver performance measurement and the assurance of some acceptable level of such performance. These changes include: the aging of the population and a concern about the hazards of the older driver (14)*; the increased attention being paid to the novice driver's accident and fatality rate (14,15,16,17); the powerful influence of the anti-drunk driving lobby, as exemplified by MADD (Mothers Against Drunk Driving); the public concern about the

---

*Also see the Special Issue on Safety and Mobility of Elderly Drivers, Part I - *Human Factors, 33*(5), 1991.

qualifications and training of law enforcement and emergency response personnel and the increasingly harsh court judgments against such personnel resulting from accidents involving the public; and the growing belief among motor vehicle licensing officials that, despite our efforts over the years, we still don't know how to avoid committing a Type II error every time we license an unqualified person to drive. The former President of the American Association of Motor Vehicle Administrators, has said: "We give road tests and written tests with ... not a grain of statistical evidence about what works and what doesn't" (11). And the Chief of Research for the California Department of Motor Vehicles agrees. He has stated: "To date, no drive test has been shown to have any validity in predicting (or correlating with) accident involvement rates (12).

This increased recognition of the inadequacy of our driver training and testing programs is leading us to reconsider the viability of using actual equipment in support of such training and testing. At the same time, the price of moderate fidelity simulators is decreasing quickly while their fidelity, functionality, and performance is increasing. Whereas the traditional argument against simulation said, in effect:

> when a commercial airplane costs $150 million and an airplane simulator costs $30 million it makes sense to perform training and testing on the simulator; but when an automobile costs $20 thousand and the simulator representing it costs $30 million, it makes no sense to do so (2),

I believe that we must begin to challenge this argument with questions like these: What if, by simplifying the visual system and eliminating the motion system, we could get the cost of simulators down by more than an order of magnitude? What if we account for the fact that simulators can operate 24 hours per day, in all weather conditions, virtually unattended, and may cost only a few dollars per hour to operate? What if these simulators could support training and testing domains not currently supported, but widely recognized as necessary? And what if simulation could overcome subjectivity and low interrater reliability, which reduce the validity of our current methods? In my opinion, when these issues are considered, the viability of simulation for training and testing increases dramatically.

Is it heresy to contemplate simplifying the simulator's visual imaging and eliminating its motion platform? Clearly, these two systems and their subsystems are largely responsible for driving up the costs of the world's commercial aviation simulators and its few most sophisticated driving simulators, into the tens of millions of dollars. Indeed, it has been reported (18) that, in the tradeoff between the required complexity of the visual scene and transport delay, the automotive application demands twice the complexity at half the latency of the flight simulator.

Can we successfully implement programs of driver training and licensing, of assessment and screening, of rehabilitation and remediation, using less than our full arsenal of technology? In short, how much fidelity is enough?

4. A SIMULATOR VALIDATION PROGRAM

A U.S manufacturer of arcade games, never before in the simulator business, intends to find out. To do so it has entered into working relationships with law enforcement training academies, State motor vehicle licensing agencies, and hospital, university and consultant-based facilities evaluating elderly drivers and those with specific medical/physiological conditions. Through carefully developed loan and confidentiality agreements, the manufacturer has made its prototype driving simulator platform available to these organizations, which have been grouped into three Technical Advisory Councils (TACs). The organizations receiving the simulators on loan (and two which purchased units earlier) gain access to the manufacturer's expertise and resources for modifying the simulator within its design parameters in response to "lessons learned" during their use in this program. The users, in turn, offer expertise in their particular subject area; design and conduct empirical experiments to validate the technology for their applications; and share data, conclusions, and recommendations with their fellow TAC members and with the manufacturer, who convenes TAC meetings and maintains general oversight of the collective process.

Each TAC is organized around a particular simulator application - police pursuit training, driver licensing, and medical research and rehabilitation. (We anticipate that new TACs will be added to address novice driver education and on-the-job performance testing).

In some cases, TAC members are undertaking closely related activities; in others, the specific interests of the participants are quite different. The strength of the approach, I feel, is in the development of large scale baseline data across different subject populations, driving environments, criterion measures, and experimental designs; while the basic technology is validated against real world issues and concerns developed empirically by subject matter experts. The only thing that is "fixed" in this process is the basic system architecture, while the capabilities of the platform are being exercised and extended to their fullest potential. We intend to subject our findings to scrutiny, not only through the TACs themselves but through the publication and presentation of findings in peer-reviewed forums. Some such results have already been published. More will follow.

4.1 Law Enforcement

Most police agencies in the U.S. have a "pursuit policy" which dictates when a police officer may (or must) initiate, continue or break-off a high speed chase. Because of increases in serious accidents during pursuits, and the concomitant adverse press coverage and legal judgments, pursuit policies are being reconsidered, tightened, and made more uniform; and the police agencies and the State government bodies which oversee them are developing sophisticated, defensible training programs to better equip their officers for this activity. The law enforcement community has begun to develop a systematic approach to training - including the development of learning objectives, lesson plans, and feedback to students. (Current training typically involves classroom instruction only, although more jurisdictions are employing in-vehicle training on closed courses or test tracks under carefully controlled conditions). For obvious reasons, even with protected driving ranges available, training does not include very high speeds or interactions with realistic traffic, whether planned or spontaneous. In addition to the risk factors that have led the police to consider simulation, costs are dictating this move as well. A police car is a highly sophisticated device with expensive components. Aside from the cost of fuel, components subject to wear, such as tires and brake pads, often must be replaced after *each day* of pursuit training support. In short, the growing costs of in-vehicle training, coupled with the recognition that key challenges to judgment, decision making, and information processing in pursuit situations are lacking in such training, have led to cooperative agreements to place simulators into police academies in programs of empirical research with trainees. In a series of "before and after with controls" studies, the participants will assess the contribution of the simulator, inserted between the classroom and the on-the-road training, to the achievement of certain criterion levels of trainee performance which have been developed by each individual agency in accordance with its own training objectives.

4.2. Motor Vehicle Licensing

The organizations responsible for driver licensing in the U.S. have long been subject to criticism, some of it from within, over the inadequacy of the typical road test to discriminate safe from unsafe drivers. Further, licensing officials must deal with social issues such as the high violation/high accident driver, the recidivism of drunk drivers, accident overinvolvement by young novice drivers, and the emerging "problem" of the older driver. As discussed above, concerns about risk and cost have prevented the typical road test from adequately representing real world conditions, and so we continue to conduct such tests with little confidence that they accomplish much. Three States (California, Oregon and Washington) with the prospects of others joining, are working with the simulator developer through the TAC to create scenarios which generically represent the current road test plus traffic conditions and hazard situations which have been identified as relevant to the test by numerous sources over the years (19,20,21) but which, for obvious reasons, have not been included on actual road tests to date. Examples include: driving at night, merging onto high speed freeways, cresting a hill and encountering an oncoming vehicle in one's lane, facing opposing traffic turning across one's path without warning, and suddenly seeing pedestrians running into the road between parked cars. Scenarios such as these (and many others) are being developed and integrated into a driving test which includes urban, suburban and rural components that may require up to 30 minutes to administer. Practice scenarios for simulator familiarization and alternate forms of this test are also being developed. Scoring criteria and data analysis software development is underway, and we hope to begin pilot testing this fall.

Each State will conduct its own research, but all will utilize common simulator software and hardware. Scenarios and evaluation criteria will be extracted by each State from the overall database to reflect the specific needs of the participating organizations. California, for example, is interested in developing a pre-screening test for older drivers, whereas Oregon will concentrate on young novice drivers and Washington will address "problem" drivers. The overall study will last up to two years, and include perhaps 10,000 subjects.

4.3. Medical Research/Rehabilitation

This most diverse TAC includes organizations performing applied research, typically funded by grant or contract, using an earlier version of the simulator to look at medical and physiological factors that may relate to driving performance. Again, hardware and software are consistent across participants, but all aspects of research design are unique. To date, studies have been completed in the several areas. The University of Illinois at Chicago Eye Institute has assessed driving performance in patients with retinitis pigmentosa (22), and in those with juvenile macular dystrophies (23). The University of Virginia Health Sciences Center has reported on a study of driving decrements and self-recognition of such decrements during and after diabetic hypoglycemia (24). Research will soon begin in the following areas:

(a) at the Stein Gerontological Institute researchers will attempt to identify those characteristic driving behaviors of the elderly that are susceptible to improvement through training, and, if successful, will develop training strategies to address them; (b) a team at Victoria Hospital in London, Ontario, Canada, will examine the effects of sleep apnea on driving performance; and (c) at the National Public Services Research Institute outside Washington, DC, a study will evaluate degradations in driving performance under alcohol consumption as part of their development of a "Standardized Field Sobriety Test" for law enforcement personnel.

Again, the researchers come together in TAC meetings to share ideas, problems and findings; provide help to one another in programming, scenario development, and data reduction and analysis; and, of course, add to the baseline which we feel is required before we can have confidence in the simulator's validity for any of these intended applications.

5. SUMMARY

Despite powerful technological advances and cost reductions, simulation is still looked on disparagingly by the community of driver trainers, examiners, rehabilitation therapists, and insurance executives. While some simulationists seem to believe that the only path to acceptance is via the achievement of very high levels of simulator fidelity, it is my opinion that this is an empirical question. That is, I believe, the only way to know how much fidelity is necessary and sufficient to measurably increase our predictive validity in the licensing process, to dramatically improve the level of preparation for licensure achieved through the training process, and to make accurate, reliable judgments of who should drive and who should have their driving privileges restricted or revoked - is to get out and try it in the most rigorous, comprehensive manner possible.

In this paper I have tried to outline why I think this is necessary, and how one organization has set out to do it. We are in the early stages of an exciting project. I hope to report back to a future Vision in Vehicles Conference that we have succeeded.

REFERENCES

1. *Driving Simulation Review.* L. Marowitz. State of California Department of Motor Vehicles, January, 1991.
2. *Traffic Safety and the Driver.* L. Evans. New York: Van Nostrand Reinhold, 1991.
3. "Simulators: Tools or Toys?" by K. Stadden. *Heavy Duty Trucking*, June 1991.
4. *Simulation Fidelity in Training System Design.* R.T. Hays & M.J. Singer. New York: Springer-Verlag, 1989.
5. "Training Simulators," R.E. Flexman and E.A. Stark. In G. Salvendy, Ed. *Handbook of Human Factors.* New York: John Wiley & Sons, 1987.
6. "Quality Criteria for Simulator Images: A Literature Review," P. Padmos and M.V. Milders. *Human Factors, 34*(6), 727-748, 1992.
7. "The Future of Nuclear Power Plant Simulation in the United States," J.A. Wachtel. In *Proceedings of the International Conference on Simulation for Nuclear Reactor Technology.* Cambridge, England: Cambridge University Press, 1984.
8. *Small is Beautiful: Economics as if People Mattered.* E.F. Schumacher. London: Blond and Briggs, 1973.
9. "Are We Training Operators Upside Down?" J. Wachtel. *Proceedings of the Ninth*

Symposium on the Training of Nuclear Facility Personnel, April 14-18, 1991. Oak Ridge, TN: Oak Ridge National Laboratory Report No. CONF-9104135.

10. "The Influence of Complex Systems on Motion Sickness," M. Wells. (Review of presentation by M. Griffin in Armstrong Laboratory Colloquium Series). *Gateway, IV*(1), 9-11, 1993.
11. "Trends: A look at the future of driver training and education." *Driver/Education, 1*(3), December, 1991.
12. "New Technology for an Old Problem: A Report on a Prospective Study to Evaluate a Simulator-Based Approach to Driver Licensing," R.C. Peck and J. Wachtel. Paper presented at the 72nd Annual Meeting of the Transportation Research Board. Washington, DC: January, 1993.
13. "Using Training Hardware to Accelerate Learning," J. Latham. *General Physics Report*, August, 1991.
14. "High Risk Drivers Act of 1993," Senate Bill S-738. *Congressional Record,* S4400-S4404, April 2, 1993.
15. "An Improved Driver Entry System for Young Novice Drivers," *NHTSA Technology Transfer Series*, No. 5. Washington, DC: U.S. Department of Transportation, August 1990.
16. *New to the Road: Prevention Measures for Young or Novice Drivers (Key Findings and Implications from an International Symposium)*. Ottawa: Traffic Injury Research Foundation of Canada, February 1991.
17. "Young Drivers at Risk: A Survey of State Programs," J.D. Jernigan, C.B. Stoke & J.V. Alcee. Paper presented at the 71st Annual Meeting of the Transportation Research Board. Washington, DC: January, 1992.
18. "Driving Simulators: Six Years of Hands-On Experience at Hughes Aircraft Company," C.M. Hein. Paper accepted for presentation at the 37th Annual Meeting of the Human Factors and Ergonomics Society. Seattle: October, 1993.
19. *Development of a Competency Based Driver License Testing System,* A.J. McKnight and M.A. Stewart. Report prepared under contract to California Dept. of Motor Vehicles. Landover, Maryland: National Public Services Research Institute, 1990.
20. *Tri-Level Study of the Causes of Traffic Accidents: Volume I - Causal Factor Tabulations and Assessments*. J.R. Treat, N.S. Tumbas, S.T. McDonald, D. Shinar, R.D. Hume, R.E. Mayer, R.L Stansifer and N.J. Castellon. (NTIS No. DOT-HS-805-085). Washington, DC: US Department of Transportation, 1979.
21. *Road User Behaviors Which Contribute to Accidents at Urban Arterial/Local Intersections*. P.T. Cairney and J.E. Catchpole. (Report ARR No. 197). Melbourne: Australian Road Research Board.
22. "Assessment of Driving Performance in Patients with Retinitis Pigmentosa," J.P. Szlyk, K.R. Alexander, K. Severing and G.A. Fishman. *Archives of Ophthalmology, 110*, December, 1992, 1709-1713.
23. "Evaluation of Driving Performance in Patients with Juvenile Macular Dystrophies," J.P. Szlyk, G.A. Fishman, K. Severing, K.R. Alexander and M. Viana. *Archives of Ophthalmology, 111*, February, 1993, 207-212.
24. "Driving Decrements in Type I Diabetes During Moderate Hypoglycemia," by D.J. Cox, L. Gonder-Frederick and W. Clarke. *Diabetes, 42*, February, 1993, 239-243.

VISION IN VEHICLES - V
A.G. Gale et al. (Editors)

The Leeds Driving Simulator: A New Tool For Research In Driver Behaviour

O.M.J. Carsten and S. Gallimore

Institute for Transport Studies, University of Leeds, Leeds LS2 9JT

1. OVERALL DESCRIPTION OF THE FACILITY

The new driving simulator at the University of Leeds is one of a new generation of simulators which can be termed "medium cost". They fall in between the very expensive moving base simulators which can cost tens of millions of pounds (e.g. the new U.S. national driving simulator in Iowa) and the relatively cheap units that have been developed using video-disks or arcade game technology. The typical features of the medium-cost simulators are:

- the provision of a full-sized and complete vehicle, with all the normal controls operational;
- the use of real-time animation to create a scene that is projected in front of the driver;
- construction of the simulator around a specialized visual simulation workstation (costing perhaps £100,000);
- the lack of a moving base to subject the driver to gravitational and inertia forces.

The Leeds simulator, whose development has been funded by the Science and Engineering Research Council (SERC), to provide a tool to the UK research community, conforms to this specification. At the moment it is a "rural simulator", in that it has been designed to create a wide range of rural driving scenes, but it is hoped in the future to develop it into a simulator that can also present urban conditions.

2. HOW IT WORKS

The vehicle in which the subject drives is a full car, a Rover 216 GTi donated by Rover cars. This sits in front of a curved projection screen which fills approximately 120° of the driver's view. A Sony video projector hangs above the car to project animated images generated by a Silicon Graphics 210/VGX computer. This single projector gives a 50° field of view directly in front of the driver, but there is provision for two further projectors to be placed either side of the current one so that an image covering the whole screen can be created. Figure 1 shows the car, projector and screen.

Figure 1. Car, projector and screen

The Rover has been extensively modified for use in the simulator. The engine and fuel system have been removed, but the gearbox has been reinstalled with new bearings on the end of the flywheel drive shaft. An electric motor now drives the gearbox at a constant speed so that gear changes feel natural. Having the clutch cable attached to the gearbox makes the clutch pedal feel normal as well, although there is currently no sense of a clutch `biting point'.

The cabin controls remain operational, including items such as the stereo system and the ventilation. The main driving controls, that is the steering position, accelerator, clutch, brake, gear selection, hand brake and ignition position, are sensed and this data is collected by a PC fitted with analogue and digital I/O expansion cards. Other controls, for instance the lighting system and indicators, control their dashboard lights but have no other effect. These may be detected by the computers, if needed, in the future.

Several types of feedback are given to the driver while driving the simulator, apart from the graphical display. A high powered servo motor, purchased from GEC Alsthom, is connected to the steering column to simulate both the static friction between the tyres and the road when the car is stationary or travelling at low speed and to imitate the self centring forces on the wheels while cornering.

The eddy current speedometer is also driven by a small electric motor, its speed controlled by a voltage from the PC. This gives an accurate speed reading to the driver and also drives the odometer. A simple voltage controlled oscillator and loudspeaker provides sound at a frequency linked with engine revs. While this is a crude temporary measure, when put together with the noise and vibration of the gearbox rotating it gives valuable cues to the driver. Eventually we will use high quality sampled sound to provide engine, road and wind noise. Finally the dashboard warning lights, for instance oil pressure and battery, are also controlled by the computers.

The signals from the car are transmitted to the Silicon Graphics machine by the PC over Ethernet. The Silicon Graphics machine runs a vehicle dynamics model using this information. The dynamics model is a real time simulation of a Rover 216 GTi, the same car the driver sits in. The model simulates both longitudinal (performance and ride) and lateral (handling and cornering) modes of motion. This forms a full, large amplitude, six degree of freedom simulation. The longitudinal simulation uses an engine model based on performance data and gearbox, braking and clutch specifications provided by Rover. The suspension model assumes the vehicle is a twin mass, one sprung and one unsprung. The lateral simulation is based on a mathematical model originally developed by Segel (1956). This uses equations of motion, dependent on the forces and moments calculated from a tyre model that mimics the contact between the road and wheels.

At low speeds simple Ackermann steering is assumed to take place. This model allows drivers to skid in extreme conditions and simulates understeer while cornering at high speed. The output from the model is the vehicle's position and orientation which the rendering code uses to generate the view projected in front of the driver. Figure 2 shows a projected scene.

Figure 2.Car and projected image

The model also generates and sends back to the PC values which are used to control the steering motor, speedometer, sound and dashboard lights.

This process runs in a continuous loop in real time and provides us with an average frame rate of between 25 and 28 frames per second during an experimental run. This gives consistently smooth animated images projected to the driver with no perceptible effect from the frame rate coinciding with, for example, the repetition of white lines on the road, so that the lines might appear to be going backwards. This is for a scene containing 5km of single lane rural road made up of over four thousand graphical objects, mostly pieces of landscape and the land horizon set at 1.5km. There are also ten autonomous cars in the scene, of which up to four are moving at any one time. The system also stores to disk, at each frame, telemetry from the car model and the `drone' cars.

3. SOFTWARE TOOLS

When work started at Leeds, there was no ready-made driving simulator software on the market. All the software used in the system has therefore been purpose-built.

A large amount of the development effort has been devoted to generating various tools which will allow experiments to be created with a minimum of effort. This work has been particularly directed to the building of a tool for creating the scene. Scene databases used in the simulator are created from a text description of the road network (Gallimore, 1993) which also includes the specification of the road markings and roadside furniture. Roads are created from three basic types of road segment:

- fixed width straights;
- fixed width, constant radius curves;
- straights that vary in width by a constant amount along their length.

Road segments follow on from each other to form a path. The program that compiles the database keeps track of the current position and direction the road is being built in so that road segments are automatically placed after each other. The path the road takes can temporarily be diverted, for instance by turning ninety degrees, to create an intersection.

A logical road network is created by numbering path ends and junctions, a logical connection is made between two points. A connection can either be made in both or in just one direction. For each connection an ordered list of road segment descriptions corresponding to the graphical description of the road is created. These are used by other autonomous vehicles to travel through the road network. The database compiler also creates a cyclic graph of the road network which can be used by autonomous vehicles to make arbitrary route choices. This network currently holds the total length of each path, however other information such as maximum speed or traffic flow rate could be added. The network could then be analyzed to find the best routes between particular points and to compare these with the actual route taken by a driver.

White lining and other road furniture is placed relative to a road segment. Any number of solid or dashed white lines may be placed on a particular segment. The width, length, length of the gaps for dashed lines, the distance from the centre of the road at both the start and end of a line and the distance along the road to the start of the line is specified. This is very flexible and allows us to create a large variety of road markings. Sign posts can be placed along a road section with any number of actual signs attached to them. The length along the road, distance from the centre of the road, thickness and height of the post can be defined. The posts can be square, round or a two stage round post with a thicker `lighting box' at the bottom. By default the signs are oriented so they would face a driver travelling along the road in the direction it is being built, however the signs can be rotated around the post relative to this direction. The height of the sign up the post is also specified. Other fixed objects can be placed along a road segment and are positioned and oriented in the same way as sign posts.

Signs and objects are referred to by a name which identifies an object defined in a separate database of graphical objects. This makes it very easy to add new objects to the system as they are needed by experimenters. Once the code to draw a new object has been added to the simulator graphics library and the object has been created in the object database, it is necessary only to re-link the applications with the new library. The object is then available for use by both the compiler and the simulator.

Before the file containing the road description is compiled it is passed through the `C' language preprocessor. It is therefore possible to use the features of this program which include:

- the inclusion of other files into the file being processed;
- `C' style comments;
- macro definitions;
- conditional compilation.

File inclusion allows us to create libraries of pre-defined road sections in separate files and use them in different scenes. Conditional compilation allows us to selectively use parts of the given file, depending on the definition of particular identifiers. This gives us the ability to specify small changes to the scene while keeping the same basic road network. For instance it would be possible to create a database with or without white lining or have several different sets of road signs available on the same network in order to judge their relative effectiveness.

After the scene has been compiled the program automatically generates landscape around the road network. This uses a fourier synthesis algorithm as described in Watt (1989) to create hilly terrain and changes of terrain colour. The current parameters create landscape very similar to areas of moor land.

Other autonomous cars can be placed into a scene using a separate program. For each car it is necessary to stipulate both a path, specified by referring to the logical road network, and its maximum speed. A car does not start to move until the driver or another `drone' car moves into a zone around it ¾ the distance at which a car is triggered can be specified. Using this program, we can add different car behaviour to the same scene database or add the same car behaviour to slightly different scenes, created using the conditional compilation technique described above.

A scene database preview program has been created to aid the building of scenes, showing two consecutive views of the simulated world. The first is a plan view where the height above the road can be varied from 5m to 10km which allows you to see the overall structure of the road system as well as being able to zoom in on any part of the road. The second is a three dimensional perspective `fly through' which gives a driver's eye view of the scene. The two views can be linked so that clicking the mouse on the plan view will move the three dimensional view to that position in the world.

At the start of each simulated run, a scenario is entered by the experimenter. This currently consists of the name of a scene database, a logical road path and the position along it from which the simulation will start. Optionally fog can be added to the scene and a filename and identification note for a data dump file can be specified. If a dump filename is given then the position, direction, speed and gear selection of the simulated car is stored to that file along with a time stamp every frame. Similarly any `drone' cars that are moving also store their position and direction. If an experimenter requires further information about the driver's performance, that is already available within the system, it can be easily added to the dump. The scenario parameters can be saved to a file and re-loaded when needed. This allows a configuration for each run to be created before the experiment starts.

An extension to the preview program is currently under way to allow it to read dump files and replay an experiment. This will allow the experimenter to interpret the raw data more easily.

Measurements that can be captured directly from the system include:

- the time between two events;
- the actual speed of the driver at any point;
- the average speed of the driver between two points;
- the distance between the centre of the car and the centre of the road;
- the distance between the car and other vehicles.

It is anticipated that this list will become more extensive as we are required to meet the specific demands of different experiments.

4. APPLICATIONS

The simulator provides the capability to create an artificial virtual world under laboratory conditions. Like any other laboratory facsimile, it will never replicate the real world. That constitutes both its strength and its weakness. The strength arises from the ability to control the environment as desired by the experimenter and to control it in systematic ways. An additional strength is that this is done while the driver is performing the driving task, and from the fact that drivers do not need to be trained extensively to drive on a simulator (although they may require a small period of adjustment).

The capability to study drivers while they are engaged in a proper driving task is the major advantage of simulators over other laboratory techniques, such as the use of simple video. This capability means not only that the results obtained should be more realistic than is possible with simpler equipment, but also that the simulator can play the role of a fully equipped test vehicle in an on-road trial, and provide data about vehicle position, vehicle speed, driver steering inputs, etc. A polygraph machine is available for use with the simulator, so that physiological measurements from the driver can also be recorded.

The weakness of simulators is that the real world will never be replicated in all its complex reality. It follows that a simulator is not appropriate for all research, but is the best tool under certain conditions, e.g.:

- Where the tests might endanger the drivers or other road users if conducted on the street;
- Where systematic variation in road, vehicle or traffic conditions is difficult to achieve in the real world;
- Where the test situation is difficult to create on the road (for example when investigating in-car or roadside technology that is in the development phase);
- Where approval for an on-road experiment is unlikely to be forthcoming from the relevant authorities without some prior evidence on behavioural and safety issues.

Work is currently under way at Leeds to investigate the potential for using double white lines on straight single-carriageway roads to prevent undesirable overtaking and curtail vehicle speed. A more extensive investigation of the interplay between road layout and driver behaviour on single carriageway rural arterial roads, funded by SERC, will begin in the autumn.

5. CONCLUSION

Perhaps the greatest barrier to more extensive use of driving simulators for research in driver behaviour and road safety is the issue of reliability, i.e. to what extent behaviour in a simulator corresponds to that in the real world. Even with the latest technology, simulators cannot reproduce the complexity of the real world. It is a comparatively well-known phenomenon that drivers drive faster on simulators than on real roads, in part due to the lack of visual cues to provide feedback about speed. On static simulators, this is compounded by the absence of any acceleration or deceleration forces. On the whole, this issue of reliability has been neglected or ignored, even as regards well-established simulators. Some limited validation of driver behaviour has been carried out for moving base simulator at VTI in Sweden (Nilsson, 1989) and, for one experiment carried out on the Daimler Benz moving base simulator in Berlin, a comparison was made between results on the simulator and those obtained in the real world (Riemersma, van der Horst and Hoekstra, 1990). We intend to conduct our own tests of the validity of the Leeds simulator, but there is an urgent need for a standard test suite that could be applied to any simulator for checking its suitability for a range of tasks.

REFERENCES

Gallimore, S. (1993) A road description language for the Leeds driving simulator: user guide (V1.0). Working Paper 389, Institute for Transport Studies, University of Leeds.

Nilsson, L. (1989) The VTI driving simulator: description of a research tool. Swedish Road and Traffic Research Institute (VTI), Linköping.

Riemersma, J.B.J., van der Horst, A.R.A. and Hoekstra, W. (1990) The validity of a driving simulator in evaluating speed-reducing measures. *Traffic Engineering and Control*, 31, 7/8.

Segel, L. (1956) Theoretical prediction and experimental substantiation of the response of the automobile to steering control. Proceedings of the Automobile Division of the Institute of Mechanical Engineers, 7: 310-330.

Watt, A. (1989) *Fundamentals of Three-Dimensional Computer Graphics*. Addison-Wesley.

VISION IN VEHICLES - V
A.G. Gale et al. (Editors)

Driving Performance on a Real Road and in a Driving Simulator: Results of a Validation Study.

Lisbeth Harms

Swedish Road and Transport Research Institute (VTI), 58101 Linkoping, Sweden.

Abstract

This paper presents some first results of an investigation of the behavioural validity of the VTI Driving Simulator. Subjects' driving speed and lateral position were measured continuously during driving on a real road section and on a simulation of that same road section. The two factors, driving conditon (simulator vs. road) and training, accounted for only a small proportion of the variance in driving speed, whereas mean driving speed differed considerably between subjects. Also the mean lateral position differed between subjects, but the distance to the centreline was generally smaller in the driving simulator than on the real road section. A comparison of the variation in driving speed and lateral position along the road section indicated a highly consistent driving pattern within each of the driving conditions, whereas less consistency was found between the conditons. In particular the variation in subjects' lateral position along the road differed between the real and the simulated road section. This finding suggested that both absolute and relative measures of lateral position in the driving simulator differed from the same measures during driving on the real road. This result may be due to fact that subjects' lateral position during driving on the real road was sensitive to the presence of other road users. Subjects' curve negotiation performance is another source of variance, which may account for some of the difference in lateral variation between the driving conditions. The influence of these two factors, traffic and road curvature, in order to examine their importance to the observed "simulator" effect reflected in the subjects' lateral position, will be reported in a later paper.

1. INTRODUCTION

'Driving simulator' is a common term for a wide variety of devices designed for experimental research on the relationships between the driver, the vehicle and the driving environment. Despite their common purpose, driving simulators differ considerably with respect to basic design and technical specifications.

1.1. Design Characteristics of the VTI Driving Simulator

The design of the VTI Driving Simulator has been focused on vehicle dynamics, and much effort has been devoted to the construction of a moving base sysem, which would provide experimental subjects with a realistic impression of vehicle motion. The visual references required for turning this impression into an experience of driving are provided by a wide angle visual system, mainly representing the road surface and the road layout. The visual system is based on computer graphics and was developed exclusively for this Simulator.

A distinguishing feature of the VTI Driving Simulator is the spatio-temporal coordination of the movement system and the visual system in accordance with a subject's monitoring activity and, in fact a convincing illusion of driving is experienced by anybody who operates it. This experience and the general absence of simulator sickness may be taken as simple but strong indications of a successful construction, but they do not necessarily imply a strong behavioural validity of the driving simulator (for technical descriptions of the VTI Driving Simulator see Nordmark et al., 1986, Nilsson, 1989 and Nordmark, 1990).

1.2. The Behavioural Validity of Simulator Studies

Usually simulator studies of driving performance are based on the assumption that experimental subjects operating a driving simulator will behave like car drivers during driving. There are two main reasons for questioning this assumption. The first one is that experimental methodology may be thought to influence subjects' actual driving behaviour. The other one concerns the use of a driving simulator as a research tool. Obviously a subject performing in a driving simulator is presented with a artificial driving environment, which differs in many respects from that of real driving. These differences might be expected to influence subjects driving performance, and any performance measures observed in a driving simulator may be suspected to differ from the same measure observed during real driving, although it is not clear how it might differ or exactly for what reasons.

Although the behavioural validity of simulator studies can hardly be estimated, generally a driving simulator may be validated simply by estimating the difference between performance measures observed during driving and during simulated driving. A valid driving simulator should allow at least the transfer of basic driving skills from a real driving environment to a simulated one. Absolute behavioural validity of a driving simulator is reflected in the numerical correspondance between a performance measure observed in that driving simulator and during real driving. Another relevant measure of simulator validity is the variation in the measures. Relative validity of simulator measures of driving performance would imply that more or less specific variations of the driving task would have the same impact on driving performance during simulated driving and during driving on a real road (Blaauw, 1982).

This paper presents some first results of an investigation of the behavioural validity of the VTI Driving Simulator. Subjects' driving speed and lane position was measured continuously during driving on a rural road and on a simulation of that same road. The numerical correspondance between the mean values of those variables was used for estimating the absolute validity of subjects' simulator performance whereas the correspondance between the variation of the those along the road section was used for indicating the relative validity of simulator performance.

2. METHOD

2.1. Apparatus

The VTI Driving Simulator and an instrumented car (Volvo, 240 Sedan, 1984) were used for the experiment. The car was equipped with an apparatus for recording both the driving speed and the lateral position i.e. the distance between the left front wheel of the car and the centreline of the road during driving. The presence of other road users was recorded manually during driving by a research assistant present in the car, who pressed a button on a control panel to indicate the presence of traffic. A total of 6 predelined traffic situations could be registered simultaneously. All measures: lateral position, driving speed and traffic situations were recorded for each 5-metre interval of driving and stored for subsequent analysis .

In the driving simulator the corresponding measures were recoreded automatically, except the presence of traffic, since traffic could not be presented in the driving simulator at the time of the experiment .

2.2. The Road Section

The road section used for the experiment was an 8 kilometre long and 7 metre wide rural road. In accordance with Swedish design standards the road was painted with 10 cm wide intermittent center- and edgelines. The road environment was an agricultural landscape with few buildings and little traffic. No road crossings and few traffic-signs were present, including a sign indicating a change from 70 km/h to 90 km/h located 3.000 metres from the starting point. The road section included a total of 12 curves (i.e., road sections with a radius < 600 m).

The road was measured by the VTI Road Surface Tester, which continuously measures horizontal and vertical curvature (i.e., angles) during driving. Those measures were transferred to a simulator programme and used for generating an identical road layout in the driving simulator. The design of the visual characteristics of the road surface in the driving simulator was based on a video-tape of the road section. It was not possible at the time of the experiment to simulate the road environments, but the change in speed limit was presented to subjects during simulated driving.

2.3. Subjects and Instruction

Seven subjects participated in the experiment. Their age varied between 24-54 years with a mean age of 29.8 years. According to the subjects reports, their driving varied between 10.000-35.000 km/year with a mean of 14.000 km. The subjects were informed about the general purpose of the experiment and instructed to drive "as they would usually do" on a similar road, both during simulator driving and during driving on the real road section.

2.4. Procedure

Subjects participated in 6 experimental sessions, with 1 session per day, including 8 trials (drives along the road section) either on the road or in the driving simulator. Driving conditions (simulator or road) alternated betwen consecutive sessions. Before participating in the experiment the subjects received 2 full sessions of simulator training. In field conditons subjects drove from a predefined starting point, where the research assistent started the automatic recordings, to a predefined endpoint, where the recordings were stopped. The subjects returned to the starting point between the trials without any recordings being made.

The same procedure was used in simulator sessions, except that threw research assistent was placed outside the simulator and that subjects did not 'drive' to the starting point between trials.

Data were obtained for a total of 336 trials (7 subjects, 24 trials, 2 driving conditions). The first and the last 400 metres of driving were excluded from analysis and each trial thus included 1440 measurements of speed and lateral positon, corresponding to a route length of 7.2 km. The present analysis deals with subjects' driving speed and lateral position in the two different conditions of driving. The influence of traffic and road curvature on the subjects driving performance is not considered in this paper.

3. RESULTS

3.1. Absolute Measures of Simulator Validity

According to previous defintions of simulator validity (Blaauw, 1982) an absolute measure of the behavioural validity of a driving simulator is the numerical correspondence between variables observed during simulated driving and those same variables observed during driving on a real road section. The present analysis is based on individual subjects' mean speed in each driving session and driving condition. As can be seen in Table 1 driving speed differed considerably between subjects. Generally driving speed was somewhat higher in the simulator than on the real road and a slight increase in driving speed between early and late driving sessions within each the two conditions may also be noticed. However, considering the between-subject variation in driving speed as an error term in the analysis of variance the factors, driving condition, and, driving session, accounted for only 15 percent ($r2 = .15$) of the variance and neither the effect of driving condition ($F(1,36)=3.67$, $p>.06$) nor the effect of practice (driving session), ($F(2,36)=1.44$, $p>.25$) were significant.

Table 1
Mean driving speed of individual subjects in different sessions and driving conditions.

	SIMULATOR SESSIONS				**ROAD SESSIONS**			
Subj.	1st	2nd	3rd	Across Sess.	1st	2nd	3rd	Across Sess.
sl	75.5	76.5	78.4	76.8	74.7	74.2	76.4	75.1
s2	80.3	81.6	90.7	84.2	80.9	83.3	84.5	82.6
s3	85.7	88.5	91.8	88.6	79.0	85.3	86.0	83.4
s4	80.1	80.8	79.4	80.1	76.3	76.1	76.0	76.1
s5	79.1	80.2	80.0	79.8	73.5	75.6	75.7	74.9
s6	77.9	79.4	78.6	78.6	81.3	83.2	80.7	81.7
s7	81.3	85.4	82.0	82.9	78.1	80.1	80.0	79.4
group mean	80.8	81.8	83.0	**81.7**	77.7	79.6	79.9	**79.0**

Analysis of the subjects' mean lateral position showed a somewhat different result. Although considerable individual differences were again observed also for the lateral position, the distance to the centreline was generally much smaller in the simulator than during driving on the real road section. On average, this difference was about 20 centimetres, but it varied considerably between subjects and could hardly be due to a constant error in the measurements. Taken together the two factors, driving session, and, driving condition, accounted for about 50 percent ($r2= .52$) of the variation in lateral position, but only the effect of driving condition was significant ($F(1,32)=741.44$ $p<.001$).

Table 2Mean lateral position of individual subiects in different sessions and driving conditions.

	SIMULATOR SESSIONS				**ROAD SESSIONS**			
Subj.	1st	2nd	3rd	Across Sess.	1st	2nd	3rd	Across Sess.
s1	79.8	83.0	85.0	82.6	105.9	100.1	102.3	102.7
s2	53.3	56.3	57.9	55.8	91.0	101.1	88.5	93.7
s3	66.4	68.0	68.8	67.7	96.7	95.6	83.5	91.9
s4	70.4	71.7	69.3	70.4	90.1	95.2	95.3	93.5
s5	62.4	59.6	70.1	64.0	79.8	83.2	84.7	82.5
s6	93.8	100.0	90.2	94.6	96.0	90.8	102.1	96.3
s7	60.4	56.7	61.4	59.5	84.6	86.8	87.5	86.3
group mean	69.5	70.7	71.8	**70.6**	92.0	93.3	91.9	**92.4**

3.2. Relative Measures of Simulator Validity

The spontaneous transfer of a certain driving pattern from a real road to a simulated one by experimental subjects may be a strong indicator of the relative validity of the simulator measures. However, since a certain driving pattern may not be replicated perfectly within a driving condition, the consistency in the driving pattern between different driving trials within each of the driving conditions was first estimated.

The relationship between observed driving speed in successive5-metre intervals of the road in the two different driving trials within the same driving condition was estimated by calculating the product-moment correlation between observations in first 12 trials (the first half of the sample) with the same observarions in the last 12 trials (the last half of the sample) for each driving condition.

The mean correlation based on the correlation coefficients of individual subjects can be seen in Table 3 (upper panel). As may have been expected both from the number of observations in each driving trial and from the aggregation of those across 12 trials, the correlations were extremely high and also they were at the same level in both driving conditions.

Table 3
Correlations between driving speeds in successive 5-metre intervals of the road within and between conditions of driving.

Subjects	s1	s2	s3	s4	s5	s6	s7	Ss
WITHIN DRIVING CONDITIONS								
Simul1/ Simul2	.98	.98	.95	.99	.98	.97	.97	**.97**
Field1/ Field2	.97	.98	.91	.98	.98	.97	.98	**.97**
BETWEEN DRIVING CONDITIONS								
Simul1/ Field2	.88	.87	.87	.90	.89	.86	.90	**.88**
Field1/ Simul2	.88	.86	.84	.87	.88	.81	.90	**.86**

The corresponding correlations calculated between the conditions of driving can be seen in the lower panel of Table 3. As can be seen, the correlations between driving speeds in 5-metre intervals of the road section were strong also between conditons of driving, but generally the coefficients were lower between than they were within driving conditions.

A corresponding analysis of the variation in lane position along the road section was carried out and product-moment correlations calculated within driving conditions can be seen in Table 4 (upper panel). Like for driving speed, the correlations *within* each of the two driving conditions were high and at the same level both for simulator trials and field trials. However, as can be seen in Table 4 (lower panel) the correlations calculated *between* driving conditions were much lower and, although the correlations were still positive, they demonstrated a less consistent driving pattern between the two driving conditions than within each conditon.

Table 4
Correlations between lateral positions in 5-metre intervals of the road within and between conditions of driving

Subjects	s1	s2	s3	s4	s5	s6	s7	**Ss**
WITHIN DRIVING CONDITIONS								
Simul1/ Simul2	.86	.91	.96	.94	.95	.90	.97	**.93**
Field1/ Field2	.90	.95	.91	.91	.94	.93	.93	**.92**
BETWEEN DRIVING CONDITIONS								
Simul1/ Field2	.19	.66	.64	.48	.62	.47	.52	**.51**
Field1/ Simul2	.20	.49	.48	.51	.62	.47	.55	**.47**

In summary, the mean driving speed measured in the VTI Driving Simulator showed a good correspondance with the mean driving speed measured during driving on the real road section with the same road layout. Although a slightly higher driving speed was observed in the simulator than during driving on the real road, this difference was completely overshadowed by the variation in driving speed among individual subjects.

The variation in driving speed along the road showed a highly consistent pattern both within and between driving conditions, although higher correlations were generally obtained within the driving conditions than between those. Taken as a whole the results suggested a good correspondance both between absolute measures and between relative mesures of driving speed in the VTI Driving Simulator and on the road.

The absolute validity of the simulator measure of subjects' lane position was less convincing. In general, subjects drove nearer to the centreline in the simulator than they did on the real road. Lateral variation along the road section showed a consistent driving pattern within each of the driving conditions, whereas much weaker correlations were obtained between the two conditions of driving.

4. DISCUSSION

The results of the present study demonstrate that lateral position is more sensitive to variation in driving conditions than is driving speed, and the validity of simulator measures of this variable is not convincing. This is consistent with previous findings from a validation study of a fixed-base driving simulator by Blaauw (Blaauw, 1982). He suggested that the lack of absolute validity and the limited relative validity of simulator observations of lateral position might be due to the absence of kinesthetic feed-back in the fixed-base driving simulator. The results of the present investigation suggest that other factors than the simulation of vehicle motion may be important to the lack of correspondance in lateral position and lateral variation between simulated driving and real driving.

It may be assumed that the presence of other road users is a major source of variation in subjects' lane position during field driving. The absence of particular oncoming vehicles, in the driving task might lead subjects to drive closer to the centreline. Where no traffic appears in the opposite lane, it may be more safe and less demanding to keep a convenient distance to nearest edge line. However, assuming that the presence of other road users is a major source of variation in subjects' lane position, a less consistent pattern of variation in lane position should actually be expected in field trials than in simulator trials, and this was not found in the present study. The pattern of variation was consistent in both driving conditions, it was less consistent only between conditons.

Another possible explanation of the difference in lateral variation between driving conditions is that subjects may use different cues in cues for their lateral control in a driving simulator than they during field driving. This assumption is consistent with findings from a previous simulator validation study by Laya (1992). He found that subjects' viewing strategy in the approach to road curves differed between a real road and a simulation of that same road - at least for experienced drivers. This difference in viewing strategy between driving conditions might lead also to a difference in curve negotiation performance. However, more comprehensive analysis of the present data is necessary to elucidate the influence of road curvature on subjects lateral position in each of the two driving conditions. The influence of traffic on subjects' lateral variations during driving on the real road also needs be analysed in order to distinguish this effect from effects of the simulator device.

REFERENCES

1. Blaauw, G.J. (1982). Driving Experience and Task Demands in Simulator and Instrumented Car: A Validation Study. Human Factors no. 4 pp 473-487.
2. Laya, O. (1992) Eye Movements in Actual and Simulated Curve Negotiation Tasks. IATSS Research no 1 pp 9-15.
3. Nilsson, L. (1989) The VTI Driving Simulator. Description of a Research Tool. Drive Project V1017 Bertie. Deliverable Number 24.
4. Nordmark S., H. Junction, M. Lidström and G. Palmkvist (1986) A Moving Base Driving Simulator with a Wide Angle Visual System. Paper prepared for the TRIBE Conference Session on "Simulation and Instrumentation for the 80s". 64th Annual Meeting, Transportation Research Board, 1985. VTI-reprint no 106 A.
5. Nordmark, S. (1990) The VTI Driving Simulator - Trends and Experiences. Proceedings of "Road Safety and Traffic Environment in Europe" in Gothenburg.

VISION IN VEHICLES - V
A.G. Gale et al. (Editors)

Computer Simulation of Some Visual Aspects of the Driving Situation: A Preliminary Report

Isabel Cristina Bichao[a], Dean Yager[a] and Alan Lewis[b]

[a]State College of Optometry, State University of New York,
100 E 24th St.., New York, NY 10010, U.S.A.

[b]College of Optometry, Ferris State University,
Big Rapids, MI 49307, U.S.A.

1. INTRODUCTION

Driving in reduced visibility conditions at night is one of the most difficult visual tasks; both detection and recognition of objects are necessary for successful performance. What are the stimulus requirements for these visual discriminations?

The current illuminance method of specifying lighting standards for roadways in the United States (IENSA, 1983) is both inadequate and inappropriate (Baldrey, 1988; Campbell, *et al.* 1987; Gallagher, 1975; Janoff, 1990). A better way would be to determine the appropriate visibility level for commonly occurring driving tasks taking place in a realistic environment.

Much of the controversy over this new approach to roadway lighting centres on the choice of the targets that are best suited to be used as a visibility standard. What are the targets that are best suited as standards against which actual installations could be evaluated? How do different conditions (blur, glare, darkness) affect the visibility of these targets? What are the demands of the driving task on vision? How do they affect the way those targets must be viewed by the driver?

In this paper we studied the effect of luminance, visual field position, and blur (up to two diopters), on the ability to discriminate between a simulated common potential hazard (a pedestrian who is about to cross the street) and a situation that is visually very similar, but that *a priori* does not involve danger (a pedestrian on the side of the street, facing away from it). We used, as targets, real-life video images of a pedestrian surrounded by a background of trees and a wooden fence, on the side of a road. Throughout the experiment the subjects viewed this same scene under different conditions; with foveal or 10 deg fixation, with non-blurred or blurred images, and at several mean luminance levels in the mesopic and scotopic range.

2. METHODS

2.1 Stimuli

The stimuli were images of a pedestrian about to cross a road, and the same pedestrian just after crossing the road, at the same spot. The images were recorded with a VHS video camera, and imported into a Macintosh graphics file using the QuickCapture Frame Grabber System. This hardware-software system captures an 8-bit gray scale image from a video source and stores it as a PICT file. The dimensions are 640 pixels horizontal and 480 pixels vertical.

2.2 Simulation of Blur

The pictures were blurred by convolving them with Gaussian filters, using Image 1.29 software. The filters were first constructed in the Matlab program. The parameters of the Gaussians were calculated from Glenn Fry's book "Blur of the Retinal Image" (1955), for 1.0 and 2.0 Diopters of refractive error. Figure 1 gives examples of two blurred images: a left- and right-facing pedestrian blurred by two diopters.

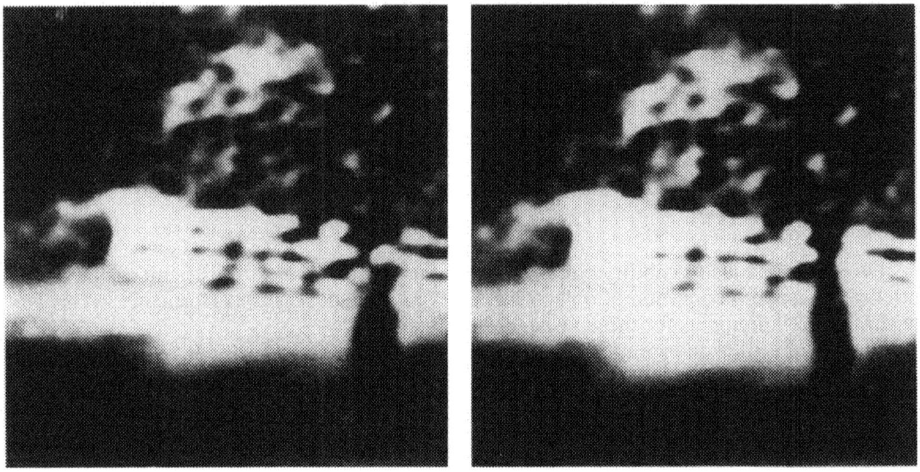

Figure 1.

We used six images as stimuli: three blur conditions (0, 1 and 2 Diopters) for each of the two pedestrian positions (looking left- facing the street, or looking right- away from the street). The pedestrian in the images subtended an angle of 2 degrees and 24 minutes, and the apparent distance was 42 metres. The experiment was run at three different mean luminance levels, using neutral density filters in front of the monitor to reduce the original luminance of the screen. The three levels used were 0.55, 0.069, and 0.0086 candelas per square meter. At each of three luminance levels we collected data at zero degrees (foveal fixation) and at 10 degrees to the right, in the periphery. This gave a total of 18 different conditions: blur (3), retinal position (2), and luminance (3).

2.3 Subjects

Subjects were ten adults aged 23 to 51, 7 female and 3 male, with no known ocular pathology, recruited from the student body and faculty of the College of Optometry. They wore their normal optical correction in the experiment.

2.4 Experimental Procedure

The subjects viewed the screen binocularly from 1.0 metre away, with their head positioned with a chin rest. They could rotate their head and eyes, but were asked to look at the fixation point on the screen. The only light source in the room was the monitor. They were told to pay attention to the human image that would show up very briefly on the screen, without moving their gaze from the fixation point. Before data collection began, we showed the pictures of the pedestrian on the screen, allowing the subjects to look at them foveally, with no blur, at maximal luminance and for as long as necessary so they would know how the pedestrian looked both when facing the street or looking away from it.

To start each trial the subject pushed a button, and one of the six images would appear, in random order, for 17 milliseconds. In three of these images the pedestrian was facing to the left, towards the street, each of them with a different blur; in the other three, the subject was facing to the right, and each of them had a different blur. The subjects task was to report if the pedestrian was facing left or right, by pushing a joy-stick to the left or to the right, respectively, in a two-alternative forced-choice (2AFC) method. A single luminance level and a single retinal position were used for each block of 500 trials. Feedback was given after each trial as to whether the response was correct or not. We used SuperCard software both to control the experiment and collect the data. Each of the 18 conditions was presented for average of 167 trials. All conditions were run in random order. The proportion of correct answers for each condition was computed and the arcsin transform was used to normalize the data for parametric statistical analysis.

3. RESULTS

The graph in figure 2 is a plot of the data obtained for the 10 subjects in the study: the proportion of correct answers as a function of mean luminance, for different viewing eccentricities, and different blurs.

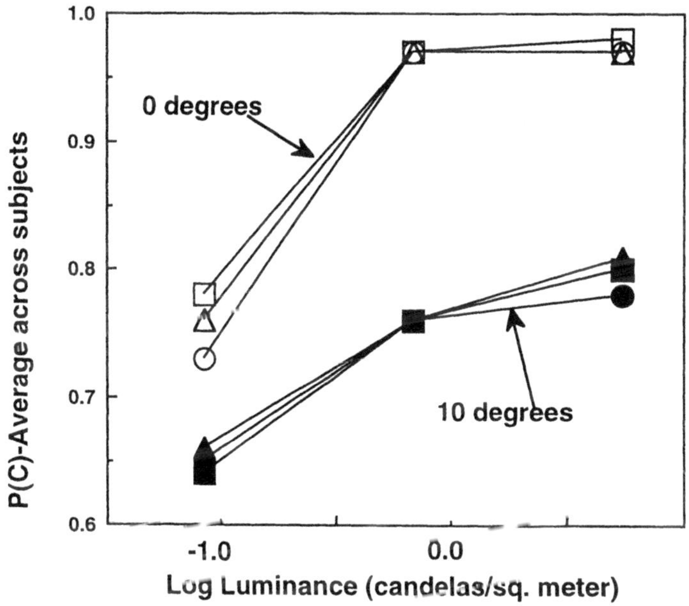

Figure 2. Proportion correct as a function of mean luminance. Squares: no blur; triangles: one diopter; circles: two dipoters

3.1 Effect of Eccentricity

There was a clear difference in performance between foveal fixation and 10 degrees in the periphery, for all blurs and all the three levels of luminance. This difference increased as the luminance increased.

3.2 Effect of Luminance

As the luminance increased the performance of the subjects improved. This effect was more accentuated in the first luminance increment in both the centre and periphery. After this first increment the performance of the subjects in central vision did not improve, showing a ceiling effect at around the 0.97 correct level. In the periphery, the rate increased further with the second luminance step, but at a slower rate than the previous step.

3.3 Effect of blur

There was no effect of blur on the performance of the subjects, at any of the luminance levels or eccentricities.

4. STATISTICAL ANALYSIS

The arcsin transform was used to normalize the proportion data. Quick ANOVA, in the CSS statistical package, was used to perform a 3-way analysis of variance.

The statistical significance of the eccentricity and luminance effects is very high: $p<0.0001$ for both effects. There was also a significant interaction between these two variables.

There was no statistically significant effect of blur on performance ($p=0.738$), and there were no significant interactions of blur with the other two variables.

5. DISCUSSION

We have studied a method that has promise for simulating certain driving conditions. Real-life video images were used so that the stimuli presented to the subjects were as similar as possible to the real visual environment that they may face when driving a car. By using digitized images we could manipulate various parameters, as well as easily set up the experimental routine in a way that is practical to present several thousands trials in the same experiment. Doing the same study in a real driving situation would enormously escalate its costs.

We focused on driving at night and particularly on a common problem, that is, the driver's ability of to discriminate promptly if a pedestrian is facing the street or away from it. We studied how the performance for this discrimination task in the periphery would compare to the performance with foveal fixation. We found that it is much more difficult to discriminate the pedestrian's orientation when she is at 10 deg horizontal in the visual field rather than at the fovea. According to our data, a luminance increment of a log unit or more is needed to achieve a comparable performance in the periphery. The point is that one has to be rather careful in making assumptions in assessing visual performance when testing foveal targets and generalize these results for the whole visual field. This must be taken into account when designing and testing highway lighting: to perform equally well in the periphery we need considerably higher levels of luminance.

The stimuli in this experiment were very complex, and so they were analyzed in terms of the simple elements classically used in vision science: the pictures were subjected to a 2D Fast-Fourier-Transform, using IPLab software, on the Macintosh. (See Figure 3) We verified that there was a marked difference between the high spatial frequency content of the no-blur pictures and the blurry ones: the higher the blur the lower the content of the high spatial frequencies. All of the pictures are very rich in medium and low spatial frequencies. This is consistent with findings of experiments on a related task--the recognition of faces (Owsley and Sloane, 1987). Medium spatial frequencies are most important in making these kinds of discriminations, and moderate blur of the retinal image has little effect on performance.

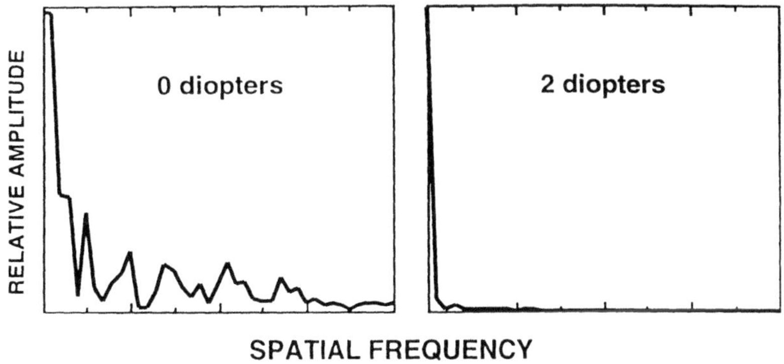

Figure 3. Horizontal slices of two dimensional FFT's for an original stimulus (left) and a two-diopter blurred stimulus (right). Low spatial frequencies are to the left and high spatial frequencies to the right.

6. CONCLUSION

We have presented here a *preliminary* investigation of a method that may be developed to be used in research on road safety. The method has the potential to simulate several conditions necessary to this kind of research, such as changes in luminance, blur, and visual field position. Data collection is easy and accurate. This makes it possible to design experiments involving many trials and various conditions, easily and inexpensively. Unlike the usual methods involving computer graphics (e.g., Guyard, 1993; Brouwer, *et al.*, 1991; Ball, *et al.*, 1990; Lovsund and Hedin, 1986), it uses images of real scenes instead of computer-generated drawings and stylization's which use techniques similar to video game graphics. The video images used here reproduce the scenes accurately, including natural shadows, backgrounds, and their interactions, which affect the visibility of the stimuli that are being studied. These images can also be animated and used to make video movies, and therefore be used in studying situations involving movement.

Realism of the visual testing conditions seems to be regarded by many researchers as desirable, as stated in published work (*e.g.*, Shinar and Schieber, 1991; Yonemura and Kohayakawa, 1976). So much so that some even venture to do their research in actual driving conditions in spite of its limitations and costs (*e.g.*, Bartmann and Reiffenrath, 1991; Osaka, 1988; Sato and Kondo, 1969; Probst, 1986). The present study suggests a reasonable compromise, between the desired realism of the experimental setting and the advantages in-lab computer-controlled psychophysical experiments: flexibility, easy access, high accuracy and reproducibility of data, and low costs.

ACKNOWLEDGEMENTS

Dr. Bichao was supported by a graduate fellowship from INVOTAN. Research support was provided by the Schnurmacher Institute for Vision Research. We thank Hal Sedwick, Harold Solan and Jeffrey Cooper for their valuable comments on an earlier version of this paper.

REFERENCES

Baldrey, P. A. (1988) Road Lighting. In "Vision in Vehicles II." A.G. Gale et al. (editors) Elsevier Science Publishers B. V. (North-Holland), pp. 163-165.

Ball K.K., Roenker D.L. and Bruni J.R. (1990) The use of Functional Vision Assessment in Predicting Mobility Problems in Older Adults. Noninvasive Assessment of the Visual System, 3, 138-141.

Bartmann A. and Reiffenrath D. (1991) Visibility under Night Driving conditions. In "Vision in Vehicles III." A.G. Gale et al. (editors) Elsevier Science Publishers B. V. (North-Holland), pp. 361-368.

Brouwer W.H., Waterink W., Van Wolffelaar P.C., Rothengatter T. (1991) Divided Attention in Experienced Young and Older Drivers: Lane Tracking and Visual Analysis in a Dynamic driving Simulator. Human Factors, 33, 573-582.

Campbell F.W., Rothwell S.E. and Perry M.J. (1987) Bad light stops play. Ophthalmic & Physiological Optics, 7, 165-167.

Fry, G. (1955) Blur of the Retinal Image. The Ohio State University Press, Columbus, Ohio.

Gallagher, V.P. (1975) The Specification of Street Lighting Needs. FHWA Report No. Dot-TST-72-1.

Guyard, I. (1993) The driving simulator: an aid for ergonomic design of car interiors. In "Vision in Vehicles IV." A.G. Gale et al. (editors) Elsevier Science Publishers B. V. (North-Holland), pp. 311-320.

IESNA. RP-8: American National Standard for Roadway Lighting (1983).

Janoff, M.S. (1990) A Standard Practice for Roadway Lightning based on Driver Performance. Journal of the Illuminating Engineering Society, winter, 47-51.

Lovsund P. and Hedin A. (1986) Effects on driving performance of visual field defects. In "Vision in Vehicles" A.G. Gale et al. (editors) Elsevier Science Publishers B. V. (North-Holland), pp. 323-329.

Osaka N. (1988) Speed Estimation through restricted visual field during driving in day and night: Naso-temporal hemifield differences. In "Vision in Vehicles II" A.G. Gale et al. (editors) Elsevier Science Publishers B. V. (North-Holland), pp. 45-55.

Owsley C. and Sloane M.E. (1987) Contrast sensitivity, acuity, and the perception of "real-world" targets. British Journal of Ophthalmology, 71, 791-796.

Probst T. (1986) Thresholds for detection of changes in headway are elevated during car ride. In "Vision in Vehicles" A.G. Gale, et al. (editors) Elsevier Science Publishers B. V. (North-Holland), pp. 157-166.

Sato M. and Kondo M. (1989) Measurement of gaze movements while driving. Perceptual and Motor Skills, 6, 19-25.

Shinar D. and Schieber F. (1991) Visual Requirements for Safety and Mobility of Older Drivers. Human Factors, 33, 507-519.

Yonemura, G.T. and Kohayakawa, Y. (1976) A New Look at the Research Basis for Lighting Level Recommendations. National Bureau of Standards, NBS-BSS-82, March.

VISION IN VEHICLES - V
A.G. Gale et al. (Editors)

The Role Of General Attentional Resources In Simulated Driving Performance

G. Matthews and T.J. Sparkes

Department of Psychology, University of Dundee, Dundee DD4 1HN, Scotland

1. INTRODUCTION

A recognised problem during driving performance is overload of information-processing capacity. At a busy intersection, for example, the driver may be unable to process the visual attributes of all the vehicles within the field of view, leading to a risk of error in perception, attention or judgement. The problem is exacerbated by components of the task additional to the primary task of controlling vehicle speed and direction. The driver may have to encode and act upon information on road-signs, for example. Technological advances, such as provision of visual or auditory route-finding devices, are likely to increase the amount of information to be processed. Hence, it is important to test whether overall assessments of the cognitive load on the driver are likely to be predictive of performance impairment.

Existing research provides a number of demonstrations of overload. Brown, Tickner and Simmonds (1969) showed that concurrent performance of an auditory reasoning task impaired judgements of whether the car could be driven through a narrow gap. Harms (1991) used mental arithmetic performance as an index of cognitive load, and showed that calculation speed was sensitive to the demands of the driving task. Each of these secondary tasks, reasoning and calculating, would seem to use rather different specific processes to the main, visual-motor driving task. Hence, it is plausible that driving performance is limited by availability of some general attentional capacity or resource (Norman and Bobrow, 1975). Much of the time, the driver has sufficient resources for the various components of the task, and performance is *data-limited*. With increasing demands, performance becomes *resource-limited*, and one or more task components will be performed with reduced efficiency. The precise impact of resource shortfalls on performance depends on the driver's strategy for allocating resources across task components. For example, the breadth of attentional focus shifts dynamically in response to task demands (Miura, 1987). Normally, low-priority components, such as listening to the car radio, would be impaired first, but if demands are very high, then essential task components such as controlling speed and direction are likely to deteriorate in efficiency also. Although general resource theory is intuitively appealing, it cannot be accepted uncritically. One difficulty is that resources may be *multiple*: qualitatively different kinds of processing, such as encoding visual or auditory stimuli, may draw on different pools of resources (Wickens, 1984). A second difficulty is that combining performance of multiple concurrent tasks may be a *skill*, which has to be learnt for each task combination performed (Hirst, 1986). Wickens (1984) points out that dual-task performance often shows a fixed *cost of concurrence*, related to the intrinsic difficulty of combining task components, rather than to the difficulty of the individual tasks. For example, monitoring the road ahead and the mirror simultaneously would have a high cost of concurrence because both sources of stimuli cannot be fixated simultaneously. The role of skill in dual-task performance is not simply a question of the degree of proceduralisation or automatisation of performing the combined task. As Duncan (1979) points out, task pairings often have 'emergent' properties which cannot be predicted from performance of the single tasks individually.

Hence, a simple test for dual-task interference is insufficient to establish that general resource limitations play a role in driving performance. Apparent instances of overload of capacity may in fact be instances of task combinations with a high cost of concurrence. Conversely, tasks may fail to interfere because they draw on different multiple resources. The present research aimed to test the role of general attentional resources in driving performance against two criteria for resource-limitation which are said to be more rigorous than dual-task interference alone (Wickens, 1984). The first criterion is *difficulty-sensitivity* of interference: performance is resource-limited if the amount of interference increases with the difficulty of one or both of the tasks performed. The second criterion is a *smooth tradeoff* of performance in the Performance Operating Characteristic (POC) for the tasks. The two tasks are performed under a variety of priority instructions, assumed to affect the proportions of resources allocated to each task. The POC is the graph plotting performance levels on the two tasks against one another. If performance depends on the transfer of resources between tasks, any performance gain on one task should be achieved at the expense of performance loss on the other. If the POC shows independent changes in performance of the two tasks, rather than a tradeoff, it is assumed that performance is data-limited.

These criteria were tested with the Aston Driver Simulator (ADS: Taylor, Dorn, Glendon, Davies and Matthews, 1991), a microcomputer-controlled fixed-base simulator of moderate fidelity. In the present study, the main performance measure was *heading error*, the driver's mean deviation from the direction of the road. The concurrent secondary task was a logical reasoning task similar to that of Brown et al. (1969). Difficulty-sensitivity of dual-task interference was assessed by comparing performance on straight and curved sections of the track followed. The resource model predicts that interference should be greater on curves than on straights, even if there is a cost of concurrence influencing the magnitude of interference. To construct POCs, subjects performed the dual-task in three different priority conditions. The resource hypothesis predicts that changes in performance in the two tasks should tradeoff against each other. Testing for multiple resources is difficult because the number and nature of multiple resources is unclear. The study compared auditory and visual input modalities for the secondary task, manipulated between-subjects, because there is some evidence for separate resources for auditory and visual encoding (Wickens, 1984). The general resource hypothesis predicts that the two criteria for resource-limitation should be satisfied irrespective of input modality (although modality may affect cost of concurrence).

2. METHOD

2.1. Subjects

80 young drivers participated in the study. Mean age was 20.9 (range: 18-24).

2.2. The Aston Driver Simulator

The driver of the ADS views a 22" monitor at a distance of 1 m, displaying a scaled 3-D view of the road ahead, including other traffic, occasional trees by the road-side, and curve signs. The car is controlled with a wheel and brake and accelerator pedals. A speedometer is provided. Every 80 ms, the velocity and position of the car and other traffic is updated, and the screen re-drawn accordingly. The state of the controls and the traffic environment are also logged every 80 ms. Validity of the simulator is indicated by its ability to reproduce age and sex differences obtained in studies of real driving (Dorn, Glendon, Hoyes, Matthews, Davies and Taylor, 1992). It has also been successful in eliciting realistic emotional and behavioural stress reactions (Matthews, Dorn, Hoyes, Glendon, Davies and Taylor, in press). Its main shortcomings are the lack of kinesthetic feedback while steering, compression of the field of view, and the limited screen resolution (Taylor et al., 1991).

2.3. The reasoning task

Reasoning items required subjects to judge whether simple sentences followed by a letter pair were true or false. An example is: "A precedes B. AB" (True). Subjects said "True" or "False" aloud into a microphone, which stopped a timer initiated by presentation of the item, allowing response times (RTs) to be measured. In the auditory version of the task, items were generated as computer speech. In the visual version, items were presented on roadside 'billboards', so that the text increased in size as the driver approached. Stimulus exposure times were similar across the two task versions.

2.4. Procedure

First, subjects performed three practice tasks: two simulator drives and practice reasoning items. On the first practice drive, subjects were asked to drive at about 30 m.p.h. On the second practice run, subjects were instructed to follow a lead vehicle in front of the driver's car at a constant distance and speed. Subjects then performed three dual-task runs with a similar instruction. Priority was manipulated across the runs, such that driving was designated the main task on one run, reasoning the main task on a second run, with the tasks assigned equal priority on the third run. Order of priorities was counterbalanced across subjects. The track followed comprised alternate straight sections, and sequences of four alternating left and right hand curves (radius 76 m) . On each run, 8 of the reasoning items were presented while the driver was on a straight section, 8 on a curved section. Simulator variables were logged and averaged across three successive time-blocks associated with each reasoning item: (i) the 10 s preceding item presentation, (ii) the interval in which the item is presented, and (iii) the interval between termination of item presentation and response. Mean and variability of the variables of interest, heading error and distance from the lead car, were calculated for each time-block.

3. RESULTS

Initially, data were analysed with modality of reasoning task as a between-subjects factor. These analyses showed a number of significant interactions between modality and task factors, so results from the two task versions are reported separately.

3.1. Auditory reasoning task

3.1.1. Difficulty-sensitivity of interference

To test whether interference between driving and reasoning tasks increased on the more difficult curved sections of the driver, data from the equal-priority condition only were analysed. Heading error was the dependent variable, and there were two within-subjects factors of curvature (straight vs. curved) and task demands (driving only, driving + reasoning item encoding, driving + formulating response to reasoning item). Results showed a main effect of curvature ($F(1,39) = 170.6$, $p <.001$), and a significant curvature × task demands interaction ($F(2,78) = 7.32$, $p <001$). As expected, heading error was greater on the curved road sections. More importantly, heading error increased in the two dual-task conditions, compared to single task driving, only when the road was curved. Accuracy of steering actually increased during reasoning when the road was straight. These effects are shown in the left-hand panel of Figure 1. Mean RT on the reasoning items was also sensitive to driving task difficulty: RT was significantly slower ($t(39)=3.1$, $p <.01$) on the curves than on the straights (means: 1202 and 1023 ms). Accuracy was non-significantly lower on the curves (means: 82.9% and 86.1%). In general, these data meet the difficulty-sensitivity criterion for resource-limitation: dual-task interference was greater on the curves.

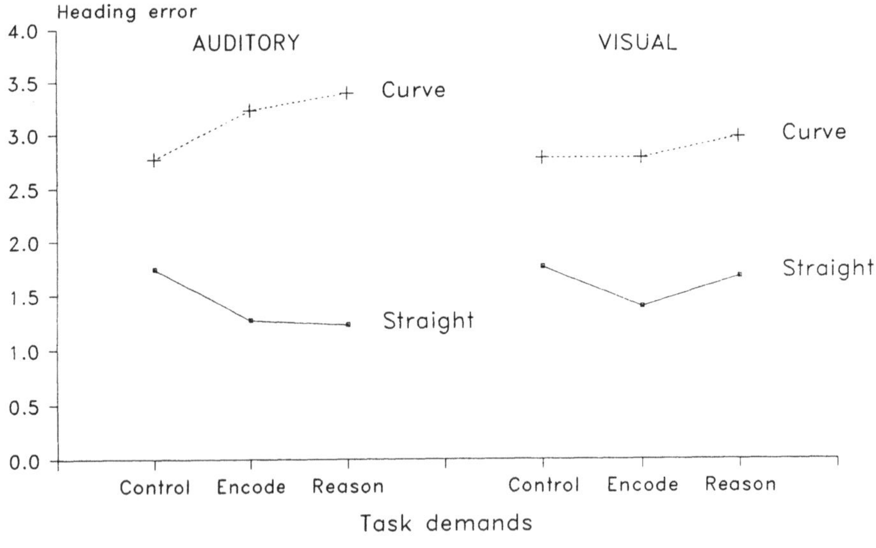

Figure 1. Heading error (degrees) as a function of task demands, driving difficulty (curve vs. straight), and modality of reasoning task (auditory vs. visual).

3.1.2. Performance Operating Characteristics

To test the role of task priority, analyses were repeated with priority (3 levels) as an additional within-subjects factor. In fact, there were no significant main or interactive effects of priority on heading error. There was a significant priority effect on accuracy of reasoning ($F(2,78)=5.53$, $p <.01$), but no significant priority × curvature interaction. Subjects became more accurate as increasing priority was assigned to reasoning. Priority had no effects on RT. Figure 2 shows the POC for tradeoff between reasoning accuracy and heading error. The horizontal form of the POCs is indicative of data-limitation: there is no performance tradeoff between the two tasks.

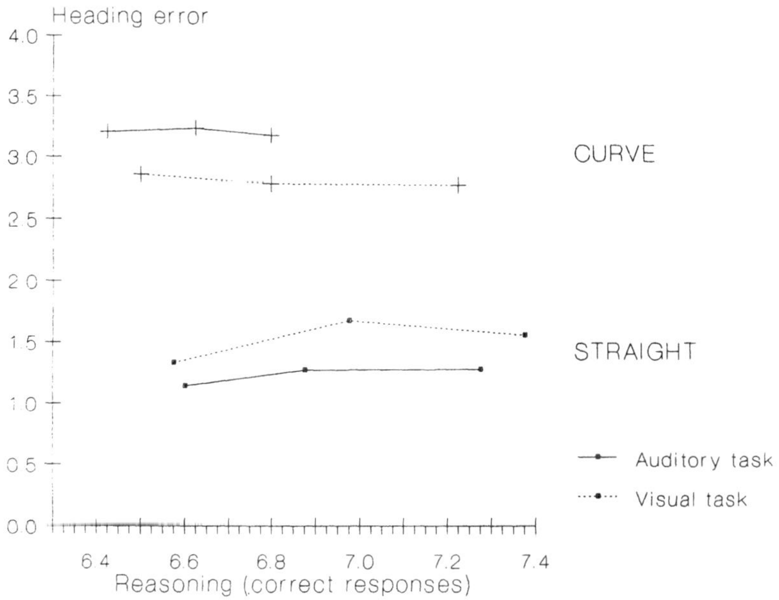

Figure 2. Performance Operating Characteristics for the relationship between heading error (degrees) and accuracy of reasoning (correct responses), as a function of driving difficulty (curve vs. straight) and modality of reasoning task (auditory vs. visual).

3.1.3. Other analyses of driving performance

Because the driver must control the longitudinal distance to the lead car, as well as lateral position, we tested for effects of task and curvature on mean distance, and mean variability of distance within each of the three data sampling intervals. The main results from these analyses were that both mean distance, and variability of distance tend to decline during secondary task performance ($p <.001$), with the effect being somewhat stronger during curve driving. We interpret these results as indicative of a strategy change during dual-task performance: drivers may react to the increased workload by postponing any adjustment of distance until after response to the reasoning task.

3.2. Visual reasoning task

There was little evidence for any dual-task interference on the visual task. In the test for difficulty-sensitivity, the main effect of curvature reached significance ($p < .001$), as before. The main effect of sample was also significant ($p < .05$), but there was no interaction between the two factors. As Figure 1 (right panel) shows, heading error tended to be lower while encoding the problem than in the other two task conditions. Curvature failed to influence either speed or accuracy of reasoning significantly. Priority affected accuracy of reasoning as with the auditory task, but, again, heading error was indifferent to priority at both curvatures. POCs for the visual reasoning task are shown in Figure 1, and again tended to indicate data- rather than resource limitation. Distance and distance variability also varied with task demands much as in the auditory task condition.

4. DISCUSSION

The data imply that concurrent performance of reasoning and controlling lateral position on the road is not limited by a common resource. With an auditory reasoning task, evidence was found for dual-task interference when the driving task was sufficiently difficult. However, although the priority manipulation influenced accuracy of reasoning as expected, there was no tradeoff between reasoning and driving task performance, a finding inconsistent with a resource theory explanation. An alternative explanation for the dual-task interference obtained is that, in curve driving, there is conflict between the specific strategies required for regulation of the two time-shared processing activities. Driving on a straight road may be relatively automatic, whereas driving on the curves requires frequent strategic intervention to correct the course followed. In other words, curve negotiation changes the qualitative nature of the task. Duncan (1990) points out that dual-task interference may be generated by difficulties in weighting the multiple goals which must be activated to perform the driving task, rather than by resource limitations. Hence, the extra goals associated with curve driving may render the driver more vulnerable to interference of this kind.

It appears too that drivers have some ability to compensate for the increased demands imposed by the reasoning task, such that lateral control during task encoding actually tended to improve in the straight driving condition. Possibly, subjects are able to improve performance efficiency through mental effort. Kahneman (1973) has proposed that additional processing capacity may be mobilised through increased effort, although Kahneman's resource model does not seem well-suited to explaining the current data. Alternatively, subjects may reduce non-essential strategic processing during dual-task performance, by postponing adjustment of distance from the lead car, for example.

Multiple resource theory might predict greater dual-task interference with visual-motor tracking from an additional visual task. In fact, no evidence for any dual-task interference was found in the visual condition, with heading error actually decreasing during encoding of reasoning items. The lack of interference in the more difficult, curve-driving condition implies that dual-task interference found with the auditory task may be specifically associated with a deficit in dividing attention across two sensory modalities. Concurrent strategies of 'looking' and 'listening' may be harder to combine than two 'looking' strategies.Duncan (1990) indicates that unpractised performance is particularly sensitive to goal weighting, because, in expert drivers, an efficient sequence of goal states tends to be strongly activated by task stimuli. The difference in levels of interference generated by auditory and visual tasks in the current study may relate to drivers' familiarity with processing stimuli from the two modalities in combination with the driving task. Driving typically requires weighting goals associated with off-road stimuli such as road-signs and pedestrians with the dominant car control goals. Hence, the division of attention required by the visual reasoning task may be relatively familiar to drivers, and so the goal weighting necessary does not generate interference. Conversely, auditory stimuli are usually of minor importance in driving, so that combining goals related to auditory and visual processing is unfamiliar, and more likely to impair dual-task performance.

Resource theory may well be applicable to aspects of driving other than those investigated here. Real driving typically involves richer visual environments than the simulator display, and it may be that real-life performance is more constrained by resource limitations. However, it should be noted that demands for attentional resources are likely to have been elevated in the experiment by (i) the use of relatively unskilled, novice drivers, and (ii) the unfamiliarity to subjects of the control characteristics of the simulator. Furthermore, the two visual tasks of reasoning and lateral tracking may have been too dissimilar to overload a common resource when combined. Wickens (1984) has proposed several dimensions of multiple resources, with interference between tasks varying with the number of shared dimensional attributes. On this model, visual reasoning and tracking tasks would share modality and processing stage resources, but might differ in the type of processing code used, in that reasoning is more likely to be verbally mediated. Greater interference might be found if the additional visual task was spatially coded, such as processing information from a navigation display system, or Brown et al.'s (1969) gap judgment task.

At a practical level, the data suggest caution is necessary in trying to use measurements of 'cognitive load' as a guide to dual-task interference. As we have seen, difficulty-sensitivity of interference is not a guarantee that performance is actually resource-limited. Designers of in-car information systems such as navigation aids should perhaps be primarily concerned with the costs of specific combinations of tasks. The present data suggest, somewhat unexpectedly, that auditory systems may be more difficult to combine with driving than are visual systems, although more work is necessary to establish the generality of this conclusion. Drivers may be able to acquire the skill of combined auditory and visual encoding with relatively little practice. On a more positive note, the data also demonstrate that drivers are often able to compensate for increased task demands by strategy change, reducing vulnerability to performance failure due to overload. Wierwille, Hulse, Fischer and Dingus (1991) arrived at a similar conclusion from a study showing that drivers flexibly shift their attention between a navigation display and the driving scene in response to task demands. System designers may be able to capitalise most effectively on drivers' flexibility of control by presenting stimuli in a form familiar within the driving context.

ACKNOWLEDGEMENTS

We gratefully acknowledge the support of the University of Dundee Research Initiatives Fund. We also thank Helen Bygrave for her assistance with the visual reasoning study.

REFERENCES

Brown, I.D., Tickner, A.H., and Simmonds, D.C.V. (1969) Interference between concurrent tasks of driving and telephoning. Journal of Applied Psychology, 53, 419-424.

Dorn, L., Glendon, A.I., Hoyes, T.W., Matthews, G., Davies, D.R., and Taylor, R.G. (1992) Group differences in driving performance. In G.B. Grayson (Ed.), Behavioural research in road safety II (pp. 68-78). Crowthorne: Transport and Road Research Laboratory.

Duncan, J. (1979) Divided attention: The whole is more than the sum of its parts. Journal of Experimental Psychology: Perception and Performance, 5, 216-228.

Duncan, J. (1990) Goal weighting and the choice of behaviour in a complex world. Ergonomics, 33, 1265-1279.

Harms, L. (1991) Variation in drivers' cognitive load. Effects of driving through village areas and rural junctions. Ergonomics, 34, 151-160.

Hirst, W. (1986) Aspects of divided and selective attention. In J. LeDoux and W. Hirst (Eds.), Mind and brain (pp. 105-141). New York: Cambridge University Press.

Kahneman, D. (1973) Attention and effort. Englewood Cliffs: Prentice Hall.

Matthews, G., Dorn, L., Hoyes, T.W., Glendon, A.I., Davies, D.R., and Taylor, R.G. (in press) Driver stress and simulated driving: Studies of risk taking and attention. In G.B. Grayson (Ed.), Behavioural research in road safety III. Crowthorne: Transport Research Laboratory.

Miura, T. (1987) Behavior oriented vision: Functional field of view and processing resources. In J.K. O'Regan and A. Levy-Schoen (Eds.), Eye movements: From physiology to cognition (pp. 563-572).

Norman, D.A., and Bobrow, D.G. (1975) On data-limited and resource-limited processes. Cognitive Psychology, 7, 44-64.

Taylor, R.G., Dorn, L., Glendon, A.I., Davies, D.R., and Matthews, G. (1991) Age and sex differences in driving performance: Some preliminary findings from the Aston Driver Simulator. In G.B. Grayson and J.F. Lester (Eds.), Behavioural research in road safety (pp. 30-38). Crowthorne: Transport and Road Research Laboratory.

Wickens, C.D. (1984) Processing resources in attention. In R. Parasuraman and D.R. Davies (Eds.), Varieties of attention (pp. 63-101). New York: Academic Press.

Wierwille, W.W., Hulse, M.C., Fischer, T.J., and Dingus, T.A. (1991) Visual adaptation of the driver to high-demand driving situations while navigating with an in-car navigation system. In A.G. Gale, I.D. Brown, C.M. Haslegrave, I. Moorhead and S. Taylor (Eds.), Vision in vehicles - III (pp. 79-88). Amsterdam: Elsevier Science Publishers (North-Holland).

VISION IN VEHICLES - V
A.G. Gale et al. (Editors)

The Influence Of Vestibular Disorder On Driving Behaviour

A.H. Clarke, M.C. Clarke & H. Scherer

Vestibular Research Laboratory, ENT Clinic, Benjamin Franklin Medical Center, Free University of Berlin, 12200 Berlin, FRG.

1. INTRODUCTION

Human spatial orientation is facilitated predominantly by sensory information from the visual and vestibular systems. Any disorder in these sensory organs or associated neurophysiology may lead to loss or distortion in orientation. In normal human locomotion, such disorders are often noticeable in unsteady gait or ataxia. In the automobile driving situation, there is some evidence to indicate that even minor disorders in the visual-vestibular system may cause inadequate movement perception, which can induce incorrect vehicle control and increase the risk of serious accident (Page & Gresty, 1985; Moser , 1985).

The medico-legal assessment of driving performance, particularly of professional vehicle drivers or pilots, after the occurrence of vestibular disease therefore requires more objective criteria than have been employed to date. In most cases, standard clinical testing of the visual-vestibular function is based on examination of vestibulo-oculomotor responses, i.e. measurement of eye movement responses to visual and/or vestibular stimulation. Such testing does not provide adequate information for the more complex visual and sensorimotor tasks involved in vehicle driving. In this situation, any inappropriate eye movement will cause a transitory visual illusion, which in turn is likely to elicit inappropriate compensation in steering. Thus, for example, if the eyes are deflected (involuntarily) to the left, the visual environment is perceived as moving to the right, and this is likely to induce an inappropriate steering correction to the right. Due to the obvious difficulties of testing such effects in a real driving situation, our knowledge of the influence of visual vestibular disorder on vehicle control has remained limited.

The purpose of the present study was to examine the direct influence of vestibular disorder on vehicle driving performance in the safety of an automobile simulator facility[1].

2. METHODS

In order to determine the influence of visual, or optokinetic flow, driving performance was evaluated for three visual conditions - namely daylight with clear vision, darkness with

[1]Courtesy of Daimler-Benz AG, Berlin Division. All trials were performed in co-operation with the Daimler-Benz simulator research group.

headlights and fog with 70 metres visibility. In addition, vestibular imbalance was induced by presenting unilateral caloric stimulation[2] to the right ear.

A group of 30 normal, healthy test subjects (15 female of average age 28, 15 male with average age 33) was tested. Each subject performed trials in each of the three visual conditions, once with normal vestibular function and once with induced vestibular imbalance. The sequence of the three visual conditions was randomised across the group. With each subject, the same order of visual conditions was employed for the two vestibular conditions.

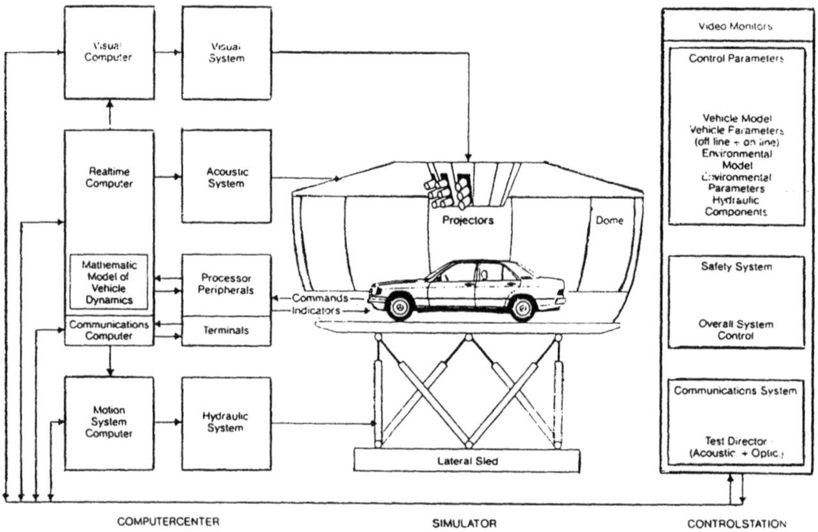

Fig. 1 Layout of Daimler-Benz vehicle simulator facility. A realtime visual surround of 180° horizontal x 60° vertical is projected by a set of six computer generated video graphics displays. Six degree-of-freedom motion is simulated by means of a hydraulic pedestal with a translational displacement of +/- 1.5 metres and approx. +/- 45° tilt range . A computer generated acoustic surround is also provided. For details see Drosdol et al (1985).

Each trial involved driving a saloon car (Mercedes 350S) over a 4.5 kilometre stretch of winding country road (see Fig. 2) and random occurrence of oncoming traffic. The subjects were instructed to drive briskly, but carefully, paying attention to lane position by pursuing the centre line. Previous to the experiment trials, each subject was given the opportunity to familiarise her/himself with the vehicle by driving along a stretch of motorway and a section of strongly curved hill road.

From the point of view of the test subject, the operation and appearance of the vehicle is identical to that of a normal automobile. To ensure the naivety of the test subjects, they were neither given access to, nor familiarised with any parts of the simulator facility other than the test vehicle itself.

[2]Caloric stimulation is widely used in clinical testing of the vestibular function. The irrigation of warm/cold water or air into one external ear canal presents a unilateral stimulus to the vestibular labyrinth in the inner ear. Via the vestibulo-ocular pathways characteristic (non-voluntary) eye movements (nystagmus) are elicited, and unsteadiness resp. ataxia is induced via the vestibulo-spinal pathways.

The discrepancy between the simulator and the real driving situation becomes most obvious in the translational acceleratory behaviour. In the simulator, translational displacements are limited to +/1.5m, so that translational accelerations are largely 'realised' by tilting with respect to the vertical gravity vector. The visual flow presented by the computer-generated graphic surround is effectively realtime with a repetition rate of up to 30 frames/s. The general psychological effect on the driver/subject was consistently estimated as being very authentic. Of the 30 subjects tested, only two experienced 'simulator sickness', which is generally attributed to the particularly high sensitivity in those individuals to slight discrepancies in the mechanical/visual movement of the simulator with respect to the real driving world.

2.1 Data recording and evaluation

During all trials the following simulator parameters were recorded on multichannel analogue tape: *road curvature*, *vehicle speed*, *steering wheel angle*, *deviation of vehicle from centre line*.

As a physiological measure of the vestibulo-oculomotor response, the *vertical* and *horizontal eye movement components* were recorded by electrooculography (EOG). Performance measures were obtained by calculating *average speed* over each trial, *average lane position*, and *average course of deviation* whilst passing oncoming vehicles. Further measures of general physiological and motor activity of the driver, defined as *ocular motility* and *steering activity*[3] were estimated for each trial.

In contrast to previous studies on eye movements during driving behaviour (e.g. Cohen & Hirsig, 1979; Luoma, 1988) in which saccade behaviour and fixation evaluation were of primary interest, the eye movement recordings were scored here for nystagmus activity. This was regarded as the most efficient means of obtaining an objective measure of any vestibular imbalance (induced by caloric irrigation). A nystagmus event was scored when a slow phase velocity greater than 1.5°/s and a minimum duration of 0.1s was measured. Only those nystagmus events observed in the horizontal component of eye movement were taken into consideration.

The relationship between vestibulo-oculomotor activity and driving behaviour was examined on the basis of the scored nystagmus beats. Thus parameters such as *nystagmus frequency* and *slow phase velocity* versus road curvature, and *distribution of nystagmus events* in relation to road curvature were evaluated.

[3]Measures of ocular motility and steering activity were defined as the integration path of the horizontal eye component resp. steering wheel angle over the trial interval. These were obtained by integrating the absolute differences across the sampled interval (sampling rate 150 Hz). This yields a measure of degrees/second, i.e. $\frac{1}{T}\sum^{N}|x_i - x_{i-1}|$.

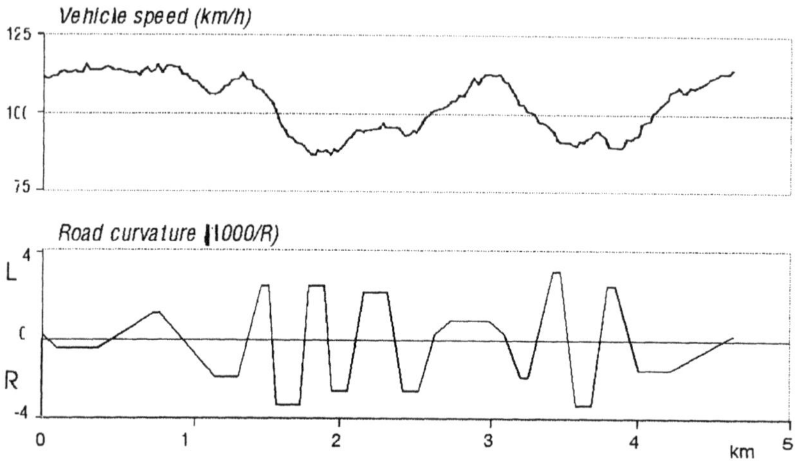

Fig. 2 Road curvature along the 4.5 kilometre section of simulated road, as employed for each trial. The upper plot illustrates a typical vehicle speed profile during the trials performed.

In addition, analysis was performed to determine the extent to which involuntary eye movements were accompanied by (involuntary) steering behaviour. Classical averaging was employed for this purpose. Thus, a time window of +/- 1 second was defined around each nystagmus event (apex[4] of nystagmus beat set to t=0), and the corresponding steering activity extracted and time-averaged.

3. RESULTS

3.1 General parameters

The average speed and the ocular motility did not differ significantly among the three visual conditions. The results from the trials with induced vestibular imbalance indicate that, for all three visual conditions, driving speed was reduced. These reductions were however, not statistically significant (Wilcoxon paired test, <0.05) .

Comparing results between trials with normal vestibular function and induced vestibular imbalance, the amount of steering activity was found to be increased significantly for the low-visibility visual condition in those trials with vestibular imbalance, whereas for the other two visual conditions it was found to be significantly reduced during those trials with vestibular imbalance.

[4]A nystagmus event is defined as a sawtooth-like eye movement, consisting of a slow phase component (minimum velocity 1.5°/s) followed by a second compensatory fast phase. The apex or peak of the nystagmus is the point of transition between slow and fast phases.

Regression analysis indicated that the ocular motility was correlated with average driving speed with both normal vestibular function and with induced imbalance. No significant correlation was found between average speed and steering activity.

In Fig.3 these three parameters are presented for each of the tested individuals, both with normal function and induced imbalance. The data from the low-visibility visual visual trials are illustrated. Average speed is thus plotted against ocular motility and steering activity for each subject in each of the two trials. The positive correlation between individual average speed and ocular motility can be recognised; and the significant increase in steering activity after vestibular imbalance has been induced, can be observed in the majority of the tested individuals.

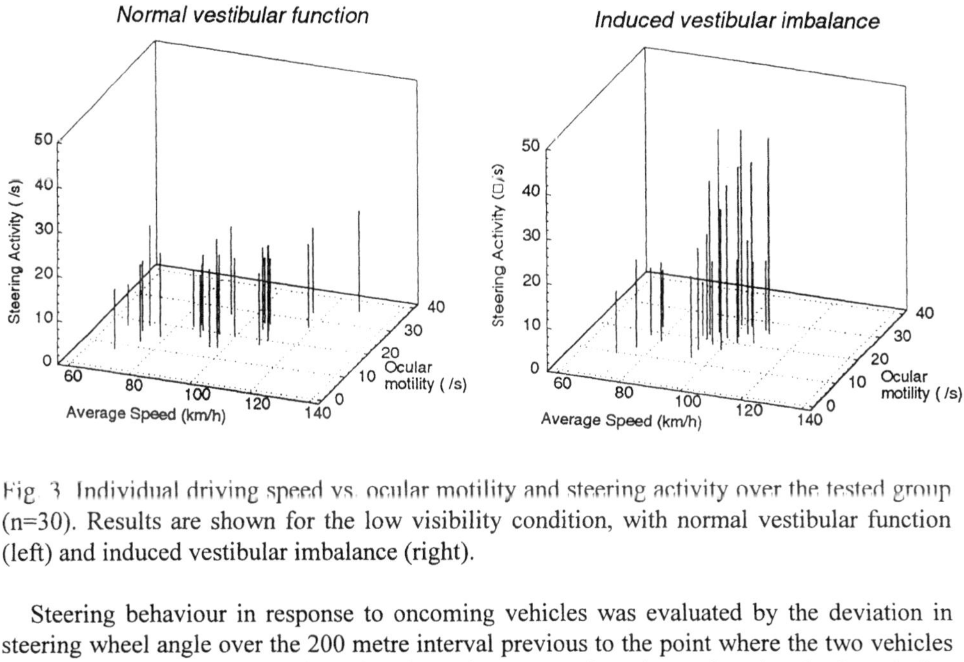

Fig. 3 Individual driving speed vs. ocular motility and steering activity over the tested group (n=30). Results are shown for the low visibility condition, with normal vestibular function (left) and induced vestibular imbalance (right).

Steering behaviour in response to oncoming vehicles was evaluated by the deviation in steering wheel angle over the 200 metre interval previous to the point where the two vehicles were adjacent. The average deviation from the centre of road was found to be less during trials with induced vestibular imbalance. The course of deviation over the 200 metre interval was found to be analogous for trials with and without vestibular imbalance. The average response during trials with low visibility (fog, 70m visibility) indicated that the deviation manoeuvre was notably lower and later than under daylight and darkness (with lighting) conditions.

3.2 Nystagmus-related steering response

Event-related time averaging of steering angle was performed separately for right and left nystagmus beats, during right going and left going road curvatures. Control data were obtained by sampling equivalent time windows at random from right-going and left-going curvatures.

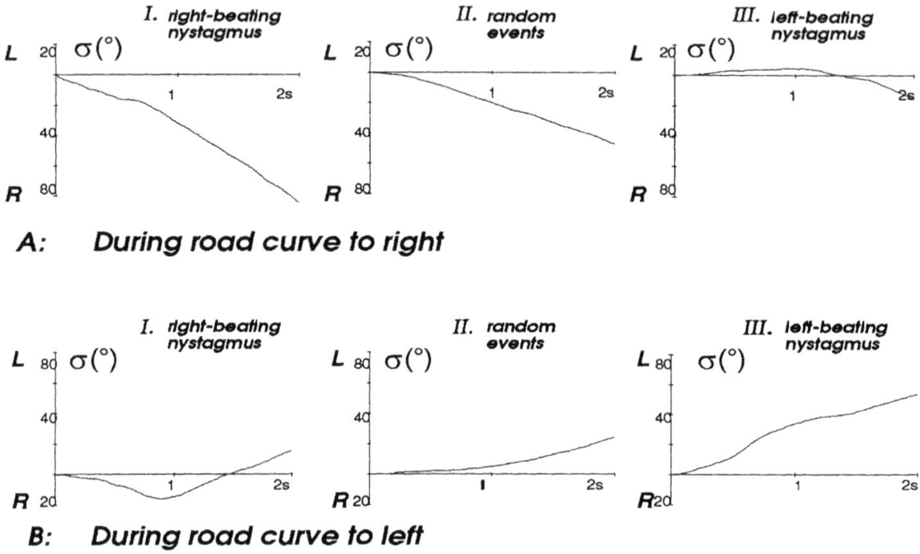

Fig. 4 Illustration of nystagmus-related steering behaviour, (σ) in degrees, averaged over a time window of 2 seconds.

A. Road curvature to the right:- I. Averaged steering response related to right-beating nystagmus; II. Averaged response for random, non-nystagmus events; and III. Averaged steering response related to left-beating nystagmus. B. Road curvature to the left:- I. Averaged steering response related to right-beating nystagmus; II. Averaged response for random, non-nystagmus events; and III. Averaged steering response related to left-beating nystagmus.

In this report, only those data from the trials performed in low visibility and with induced vestibular imbalance are presented (Fig.4). Over the 30 tested subjects, this yielded a count of 721 left-beating nystagmus events for left curvatures and 524 for right curvature, resp. 255 right-beating nystagmus events for left curvatures and 185 during right curvatures.. For the control data, 940 events were extracted and averaged for left curvatures and 551 for right curvature.

This time averaging analysis yielded the following results:

The control results (Fig. 4A II, 4B II) demonstrate that, as expected, steering wheel angle corresponded to the given road curvature, i.e. steering right on right curves, and steering left on left-going curves. The nystagmus-defined time averaging (Fig. 4A I, III & 4B I, III) yielded results that indicate systematic deviations from this expected behaviour.

For road curvature to the left and nystagmus to the right (Fig. 4B I), the vehicle is initially steered to the right before being corrected to the appropriate direction (left). According to the course of the nystagmus event (as indicated by the dotted line), this incorrect steering behaviour occurs during the slow phase of nystagmus and is corrected only after the occurrence of the compensatory fast phase. In Fig. 4A III, the reverse pattern can be observed during road curvatures to the right and nystagmus to the left.

For left curvature and left-beating nystagmus (Fig. 4B III) the steering response is (correctly) to the left, but in comparison to the control data ((Fig. 4B II) appears overcompensated. Again the reverse pattern can be observed for right curvature and right-beating nystagmus in Fig. 4A I).

4. DISCUSSION

The simulator environment represents - as does the real driving situation - a multisensory stimulus constellation, which elicits a complex response from the central nervous system. Ongoing eye movements will therefore be the result of both higher-order cortical processes and brainstem reflex mechanisms. For this reason some caution must be exercised when interpreting the findings of the evaluation of the recorded eye movements.

In this study, particular attention has been given to the influence of afferent information from the visual and vestibular senses and their interaction in the central vestibular system. This visual-vestibular interaction is essential for the adequate CNS processing of the individual's own movement and that of his environment (Dichgans & Brandt, 1978).

While these perceptual mechanisms possess some intrinsic tolerance to perturbations, any misinformation, either experimentally induced or caused by some disease, will potentially lead to a decrement in the individual's spatial orientation. In this study the application of caloric stimulation was intended to induce such a sensory misinformation by way of the peripheral vestibular organ. Thus, the subjects' performance, as reflected by driving speed, steering behaviour and lane position, was compared for conditions with normal vestibular function and with induced vestibular imbalance.

It was observed that driving speed was reduced during all trials with induced vestibular imbalance. In addition, it was found that during trials with induced vestibular imbalance the test subjects drove more closely to the centre line of the road. These observations can be interpreted as evidence that the caloric stimulation did indeed influence the CNS processing of visual-vestibular information during vehicle motion. In general, it must be presumed that the observed increase in nystagmus activity reduced the stability of the visual field which, in turn, led to the more cautious driving behaviour.

Similar adherence to the centre line was observed during those trials with low visibility and normal vestibular function. The practical relevance of such behaviour becomes more obvious when the consequences of such adherence to the centre line in the presence of oncoming vehicles is considered, i.e. the likelihood of collision is increased.

In contrast, the event-triggered evaluation of steering behaviour (i.e. contingent on occurrence of nystagmus) demonstrated a systematic interaction between involuntary eye movements and corrections to steering position. Thus, it appears that a vestibulo-motor response - manifested as a manual movement of the steering wheel - is elicited by the involuntary shift of the visual environment on the retina during nystagmoid eye movements. This finding represents an important objective relationship between visual-vestibular disorder and decrement in vehicle-driving performance.

Whereas it appears that the inappropriate steering responses detected here are solely contingent on the occurrence of nystagmus, the phenomenon signals a fundamental disorder in the vestibular system, such as is otherwise manifested as postural instability in many patients suffering from vestibular disorder.

REFERENCES

1. Page NGR, Gresty MA (1985) Motorist's disorientation syndrome. Journal of Neurology, Neurosurgery and Psychiatry 48, 729-735.

2. Moser M (1985) An objective testing method to determine driving ability. Acta Otolaryngolica (*Stockholm*) 99, 326-329.

3. Drosdol J, Käding W, Panik F (1985) The Daimler-Benz driving simulator: new technologies demand new instruments. Proceedings of the 9th IAVSD Symposium Linköping,.

4. Cohen AS, Hirsig R (1979) Causality between drivers' successive eye fixations. Perceptual and Motor Skills 48, 974.

5. Luoma J (1988) Drivers' eye fixations and perceptions. In: Gale AG et al (Eds) Vision in Vehicles II, Elsevier, Amsterdam.

6. Dichgans J, Brandt T (1978) Visual-vestibular Interaction: Effects on self motion perception and postural control. In: Held R, Leibowitz H, Teuber HL (Eds) Handbook of Sensory Physiology Vol VIII, 755-804, Springer, Berlin.

ACKNOWLEDGEMENTS

The authors wish to express their gratitude to the Daimler-Benz simulator research group for providing the opportunity to perform this study and for their technical support during the course of the experiments. We are also grateful to our colleagues W. Krzok, U. Spangenberg and W. Teiwes for their assistance and critical appraisal during the preparation and analysis of the data.

2: VISUAL PROCESSING AND COLLISION AVOIDANCE

VISION IN VEHICLES - V
A.G. Gale et al. (Editors)

An Alternative Source Of Time-To-Collision

Douglas L Stewart[1], J Rowland Lishman[2], and Christopher J Cudworth[3],

[1]Dept. of Engineering, [2]Dept. of Computing Science, [3]Centre for Continuing Education,University of Aberdeen, Aberdeen, Scotland

It is widely assumed that the basis for judging time-to-collision from optic flow is the algorithm $T_c=\theta/\dot{\theta}$, where θ and $\dot{\theta}$ are angular position and velocity respectively. The inherent difficulty of perceiving θ suggests, however, the use of the alternative algorithm $T_c=2\dot{\theta}/\ddot{\theta}$, $\ddot{\theta}$ being angular acceleration. This proposal is supported by experiment.

By removing the need for θ, the new algorithm facilitates rapid and reliable perception of time-to-collision, and automatically makes allowance for acceleration. Perception of $\ddot{\theta}$ can also control interception of a ballistic trajectory by means of the algorithm $\ddot{\theta}=0$.

1. INTRODUCTION

The concept of time-to-collision (T_c) is surprisingly recent. The reason may be that our response to an approaching object is so automatic that we have no awareness of the cognitive process which must be taking place.

There is still uncertainty about how we perceive T_c, despite extensive research. However the consensus seems to be that T_c is obtained in two ways; if it is long, from separate estimates of distance D and velocity V; if it is short, from direct interpretation of the optic flow caused by relative movement between observer and environment. For intermediate durations of T_c, both methods may be used [e.g.1,2].

A means by which optic flow could specify T_c was proposed by Lee [3]. He demonstrated that the optic flow relationship $\theta / \dot{\theta}$ specifies T_c if θ is small, θ being the visual angle subtended at the observer by an approaching point and the focus of expansion (or between two equidistant points), and $\dot{\theta}$ its angular velocity, the first derivative of that angle with respect to time. The elegant simplicity of this algorithm, which eliminates the need for any information about the speed, distance, size or even identification of an object, made a compelling case for it being the most effective source of T_c if optic flow is sufficiently fast. But it is perhaps because this hypothesis is so attractive that some potential problems in obtaining θ and $\dot{\theta}$ have tended to be ignored.

One of these was discussed by Stewart[4], who examined the role of T_c errors by drivers in causing child pedestrian accidents. It was suggested that drivers approaching pedestrians could have difficulty in applying $\theta / \dot{\theta}$ because the cyclic movement of limbs when walking

would cause optic flow to change rapidly in magnitude and direction. Drivers might therefore be forced to obtain T_C from D/V, but if D was based on familiar size of pedestrian, any overestimation of size of a child would then cause overestimation of T_C.
The proposal that this form of T_C error is a prime cause of child pedestrian accidents was supported by analysis of accident records, but a simulation of 'scrambled' optic flow failed to show any deterioration in judging T_C [5]. That research, however, produced the following explanation.

2. T_c ERROR DUE TO LONG TIME-TO-COLLISION

In an emergency, it can take drivers up to 2 s to start to brake, then several seconds to come to a stop. As a result, they are required to judge times-to-collision of up to about 7 s at normal traffic speeds to ensure that they can stop before hitting a hazard. Yet the 'ecological' requirements for interception or avoidance, for which our perceptual system is 'designed', probably do not exceed a T_C of 1 s; long enough to judge a catch or avoid a projectile.

That extension of time-to-collision would greatly reduce optic flow from an object at braking distance. If D is braking distance and T is time, assuming θ is small and ignoring response time before braking:-

$$\theta = \frac{k}{D} \quad \therefore \dot{\theta} \rightarrow \frac{d\theta}{dD} \times \frac{dD}{dT} \rightarrow \frac{kV}{D^2} \rightarrow \frac{k}{DT_c}$$

$$\text{but } D \propto T_c^2 \quad \therefore \dot{\theta} \propto \frac{1}{T_c^3}$$

This rapid decrease in optic flow with increase in T_C would be expected to degrade perception of $\dot{\theta}$ and cause a transfer from $\theta / \dot{\theta}$ to D/V. Recent research [6] identified such a transfer and its generation of T_C error due to misperception of familiar size. It also confirmed that the error is reduced by increasing driver eye level so that $\dot{\theta}$ of the road surface ahead of the driver increases, thus facilitating its estimation.

The practical consequences of these effects, as discussed previously [4], may be that the casualty rate for child pedestrians is very large, but that they comprise a far smaller proportion of total pedestrian casualties for lorries than for cars, a possibility reinforced in subsequent research [6]. It can be estimated that over half of all child pedestrian accidents in Britain would not occur if drivers did not misjudge distance to children. Hence there is an urgent need to review policy on child pedestrian safety, and to implement appropriate remedial measures.

3. PERCEPTION OF OPTIC FLOW

In addition to giving insights to the causes of road accidents, the research reported by Stewart et al (6) prompted a fundamental question about the derivation of T_C from optic flow. How could θ and $\dot{\theta}$ be judged with sufficient accuracy to compute $\theta / \dot{\theta}$?

The method of testing the "familiar size" hypothesis was to simulate the approach of an object on a computer monitor. The only other image on the screen was a fixed line near the bottom, which could be considered as the lower edge of a car's windscreen through which the subject was looking. When the space bar was pressed, the object began to decelerate at a constant rate. The experimental task was to stop the object as close to the fixed line as possible. By altering the size of the object, to give the illusion that it was closer or more distant, it was possible to examine errors due to misperception of familiar size.

If that simulation had been static the focus of expansion could not, of course, have been deduced. In the tests, the object approached at constant speed and direction, so the information necessary to find its focus of expansion would have been available from its expansion on the screen. Warren and Hannon [7] have demonstrated, however, that the accuracy of judging focus of expansion from optic flow is only in the order of 1°. A further difficulty is that whereas the focus of expansion was always at the same point on the screen, in reality a driver's focus of expansion must continually shift as he moves the steering wheel. It must therefore be concluded that the focus of expansion would normally be ineffective as a datum for θ.

The alternative source of θ, two points equidistant from the observer such as the tail lights of a preceding car [3] would avoid these limitations, but many objects are too small, featureless or irregular for this option. For example, a squash or rugby ball would be unsuitable, yet there is no special difficulty in judging T_C when intercepting them.

Similar problems should not, however, affect perception of $\dot{\theta}$. An important difference between θ and $\dot{\theta}$ is that whereas θ for any approaching point has to be related to another point, $\dot{\theta}$ could be related to a static background or obtained directly from the movement of the retinal image. To be able to do so for objects of any size or shape suggests, however, that the cognitive process integrates or averages $\dot{\theta}$ over the complete object, so that in effect the observer is judging the angular speed of its centroid. This basis for determining $\dot{\theta}$ will be termed 'whole body' optic flow.

4. AN ALTERNATIVE ALGORITHM FOR TIME-TO-COLLISION

Having rejected θ, there is no way in which $\dot{\theta}$ alone could provide T_C. Hence for optic flow to provide T_C directly there must be an alternative algorithm to $\theta / \dot{\theta}$.

During the simulation trials, subjects were asked how they thought they had made T_C judgements. Several said that they responded to the rapid expansion of the object as it approached them, the explosion of optic flow identified by Gibson [8] as characteristic of imminent collision. The optic flow parameter which would define such expansion is neither θ not $\dot{\theta}$, but angular acceleration $\ddot{\theta}$. How this might facilitate perception of T_C was first explored theoretically.

In Fig 1, object A at distance D from observer B is approaching at constant velocity V, and at angular distance θ from the focus of expansion. In time dT it travels a distance VdT, which subtends angle $d\theta$ at B.

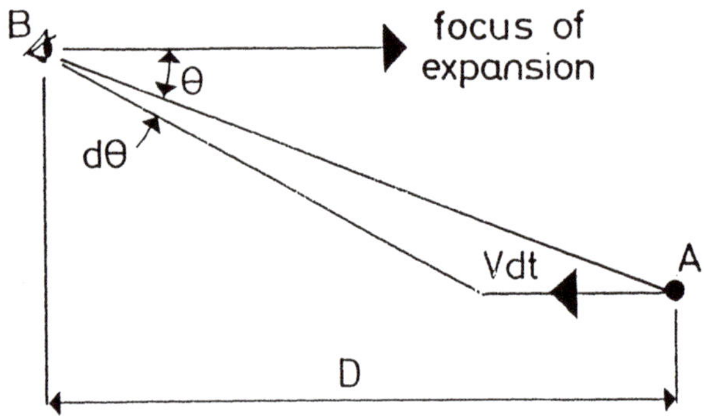

Figure 1. Optic flow from point A approaching observer B at constant velocity V

If θ is small:-

$$\frac{VdT\theta}{D} \approx d\theta$$

Time-to-collision $T_c = \frac{D}{V} \rightarrow \frac{\theta.dT}{d\theta} \rightarrow \frac{\theta}{\dot{\theta}}$ which is, of course, the original algorithm

If D/V and $\theta/\dot{\theta}$ are differentiated with respect to time:-

$$\frac{dD/dT}{V} = \frac{\dot{\theta}^2 - \theta\ddot{\theta}}{\dot{\theta}^2}$$

$$\frac{-V}{V} = 1 - \frac{\theta\,\ddot{\theta}}{\dot{\theta}^2}$$

$$\dot{\theta} = \sqrt{\frac{\theta\ddot{\theta}}{2}} \rightarrow \sqrt{\frac{T_c\dot{\theta}\ddot{\theta}}{2}}$$

$$T_c = \frac{2\dot{\theta}}{\ddot{\theta}}$$

A more general proof of this algorithm is provided by the standard kinetic relationships for plane motion [6].

T_C could therefore be obtained solely from angular speed $\dot{\theta}$ and angular acceleration $\ddot{\theta}$, with no need for θ. This would have great benefits. Because the problem of locating a datum for θ vanishes, the observer need only relate the angular velocity of an object to its angular velocity an instant earlier. Hence the ability to respond rapidly and accurately to a view of only a fraction of a second [e.g.9] becomes more understandable, especially if $\dot{\theta}$ is derived from 'whole body' optic flow. Also, the problem of judging T_C to an accelerating object is resolved, but before discussing that we have to establish that T_C could be judged from optic flow without using θ.

5. EXPERIMENTAL METHOD

To examine the perception of time-to-collision a subject is asked to respond to an approaching object. A standard method is to occlude the object and to ask the subject to judge when it would have reached him. He therefore has to respond not to a visible object, but to a memory of it. That interval between perception and response differs so much from reality that it was considered essential to devise a test in which the subject would respond directly to an approaching object.

The computer simulation of an approaching object met that requirement by replicating a braking manoeuvre. The object approached the subject at constant speed, as though moving along an invisible road. Response by the subject initiated a constant rate of deceleration which stopped the object in a predetermined period, the braking time. If the object stopped exactly at the subject then its T_C at application of braking, defined as the time it would take to reach the subject at constant speed, would be half the braking time because for uniform deceleration:-

$$\textit{braking time} = 2 \times \frac{\textit{braking distance}}{\textit{initial velocity}} = 2 \times \textit{time-to-collision}$$

To prevent the object expanding beyond the screen, however, the task was to initiate braking so as to stop not at the subject, but at a target line near the bottom of the picture, analogous to the bonnet of the vehicle which the subject was 'driving'. If we call the point at which the object actually stops the terminal point, then at the moment of braking:-

$$\textit{Time-to-collision} = \frac{\textit{braking time}}{2} + \frac{\textit{distance from terminal point to subject}}{\textit{initial velocity}}$$

$$\textit{Time-to-collision error} = \frac{\textit{distance from target to terminal point}}{\textit{initial velocity}}$$

The direction of that error would be positive if the object overshot the target, because that would imply overestimation of T_C. These equations were the basis for evaluating the test.

Several pictorial and dynamic parameters of the simulation could be varied according to test requirements, but it was always intended to appear in correct perspective, as thought the screen of the monitor was the windscreen of a vehicle. For this experiment the simulation comprised the 'driver' at an eye level of 1.8 m above the 'road', viewing the object approaching the target line 7 m ahead of him at a constant velocity of 13.9 ms^{-1} (50 km h^{-1}).

To ensure that T_C was obtained from optic flow rather than D/V, a brief braking time of 1 s was adopted. From the time-to-collision equation, therefore, T_C was also 1 s.

The object had two alternative forms. One was intended to encourage perception of θ, so that T_C might be obtained from $\theta/\dot{\theta}$. It was a solid square of side 3.6 m, whose focus of expansion was therefore its centre, which could provide a datum for θ. An alternative θ could be obtained from the angle subtended at the subject by the width, depth or diagonal of the square.

The other object had the opposite purpose, to make perception of θ difficult. It was a point - a single pixel - located where the centre of the bottom edge of the square would have been. In all trials, the pixel was always well below the focus of expansion so that it could not readily provide a datum for θ. Nor could θ or $\dot{\theta}$ be obtained from any linear dimension of the object, because it was tiny and did not expand. That also precluded judgement of distance from familiar size, making it very difficult to obtain T_C from D/V. The only practicable source of T_C, therefore, was $2\dot{\theta}/\ddot{\theta}$, both $\dot{\theta}$ and $\ddot{\theta}$ being available as the pixel accelerated down the screen.

The appearance of the resulting simulation is shown in Fig.2.

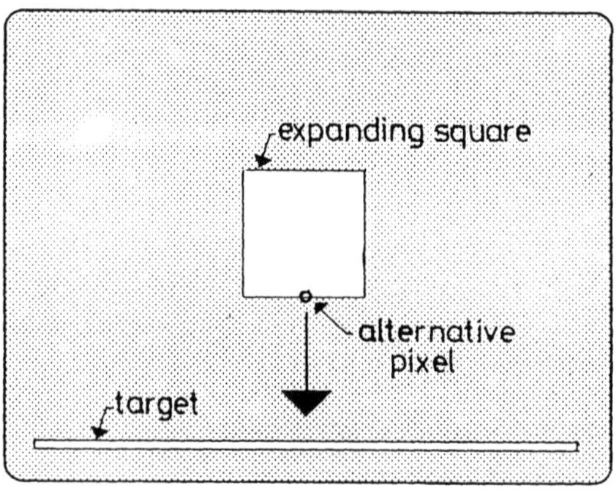

Figure 2. Computer display of square and alternative pixel approaching target. Focus of expansion for both objects is at the centre of the square.

5.1. Subjects

12 male volunteers participated in the experiment. All were students aged from 17 to 31, who held current driving licences and had normal vision.

5.2. Procedure

The subject was seated at the correct viewing distance from the monitor. He was told that the experiment was a driving simulation, in which he would see an object approaching the target line - the bonnet of his vehicle. It would always have the same speed, and would decelerate to a stop in 1 s when he pressed the space bar. His task was to stop the object as close to the target as possible.

Variation in initial distance from the subject was provided by viewing times of 2 s, 4 s and 8 s before the point at which the 1 s braking should be initiated. That gave a total of 6 variants for the square and the pixel together.

The subject was first presented with each of these 6 variants, in random order, to familiarise himself with the 1 s braking time. They were followed by 30 randomised trials, comprising 5 of each variant. The success of each trial was immediately apparent to the subject by noting the terminal position of the object relative to the target, but no other feedback was given. Terminal distances were recorded and converted to equivalent T_C errors.

5.3. Results

Each combination of object and viewing time provided 12 values of T_C error from which the means, standard deviation and standard error of the mean were calculated. They are presented in Fig.3.

For the square, T_C was on average underestimated by 0.154 s, whereas for the pixel it was overestimated by 0.064 s. This difference was significant ($p<0.001$) and showed that despite the availability of θ from the square, T_C estimates from it were less accurate than those from the pixel.

That evidence that subjects could respond more accurately to the pixel was reinforced by comparison of the standard deviations. They were significantly larger for the square than for the pixel ($p<0.001$), those for the square being more than twice as big as those for the pixel. The dilation of the square may therefore have been more of a distraction than an aid to perceiving T_C, a view expressed by some of the subjects after the experiment.

Both curves also show that as viewing time increased, subjects responded earlier. This is probably a regression effect, subjects tending to respond too early when viewing time is longer than average, and the converse when shorter than average.

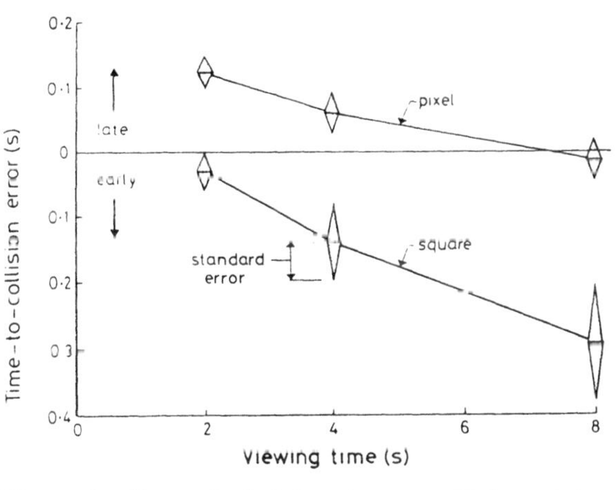

Figure 3. Errors in judging time-to-collision. Diamonds represent ± one standard error, which is the standard deviation $\div\sqrt{12}$

6. TIME-TO-COLLISION WITH AN ACCELERATING OBJECT

Time-to-collision is defined as the time it would take an object to reach collision point at constant velocity, which is the basis of the T_C algorithms D/V, $\theta / \dot{\theta}$ and $2\dot{\theta} / \ddot{\theta}$. In practice, however, velocity is variable. Of particular ecological importance must be judgement of T_C for a projectile falling under gravity, yet neither D/V nor $\theta / \dot{\theta}$ offer any correction for acceleration. Hence these algorithms would overestimate T_C, which must be ecologically undesirable because risk of collision would increase.

It is obvious from common experience, however, that we can judge T_C to accelerating objects, as has been demonstrated experimentally [e.g.10]. To do so would be facilitated by using $2\dot{\theta}/\ddot{\theta}$, because acceleration increases the value of $\ddot{\theta}$, with the result that $2\dot{\theta} / \ddot{\theta}$ automatically provides a smaller T_C. This effect can be calculated from plane motion kinematics [6] for an object in linear motion, with distance D and velocity V as variables and acceleration A as constant, to give:-

$$T_c = \frac{2\dot{\theta}}{\ddot{\theta}} = \left(\frac{A}{2V} + \frac{V}{D}\right)^{-1}$$

From inspection of the equation it is apparent that positive acceleration will always give a shorter T_C for $2\dot{\theta}/\ddot{\theta}$ than for $\theta / \dot{\theta}$. It can also be shown that $2\dot{\theta}/\ddot{\theta}$ is always less than the actual T_C, which from the Newtonian equations of motion is:-

$$T_c = \frac{\sqrt{V^2 + 2AD} - V}{A}$$

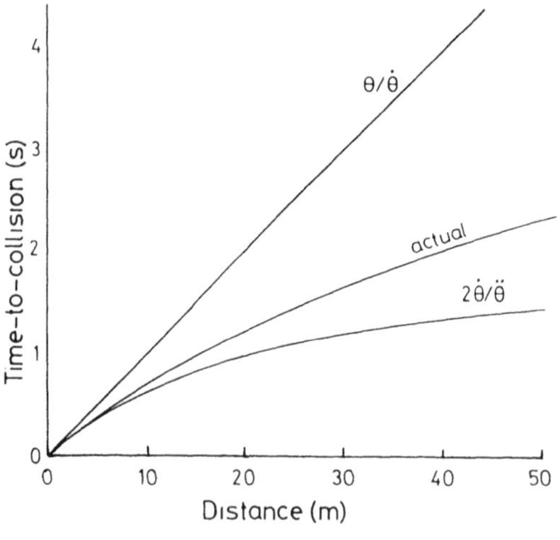

Figure 4. Times-to-collision for initial speed of 10 ms^{-1} and acceleration of 10 ms^{-2}

The difference between these alternative sources of T_c is demonstrated in Fig.4. T_c is plotted for an approaching object whose velocity is 10 ms^{-1} at any specified distance up to 50 m, accelerating with gravitational acceleration of 10 ms^{-2}. The underestimation of T_c from $2\dot{\theta}/\ddot{\theta}$ must be preferable ecologically to overestimation from $\theta / \dot{\theta}$, because of the safety margin it introduces. No single algorithm could, of course, fit the infinite variety of accelerating and curvilinear motions which occur naturally, but that problem would be resolved by the monitoring and updating of T_c estimates as an object approaches.

7. INTERCEPTING A TRAJECTORY

The value of $\ddot{\theta}$ for judging time-to-collision suggests that it could have other uses. One is to facilitate judgement of an approaching trajectory. If it has to be intercepted, as in catching a ball, then this could be achieved by keeping $\ddot{\theta}$ zero. For a circular trajectory, with constant speed, that condition exists relative to any fixed point on the trajectory. For other curvilinear trajectories, running to maintain $\ddot{\theta}=0$ would ensure interception. Absence of $\ddot{\theta}$ would, of course, preclude judgement of time-to-collision from $2\dot{\theta}/\ddot{\theta}$, but as the ball passes in front of the catchers eyes $\ddot{\theta}$ would briefly have a positive value, which could permit the use of $2\dot{\theta}/\ddot{\theta}$. The similar expression $d^2(\tan\theta)/dT^2 = 0$, proposed by McLeod and Dienes [11] as an algorithm for catching, poses difficulties which are resolved by $\ddot{\theta}=0$.

8. CONCLUSIONS

The long times-to-collision which can occur in traffic accidents require drivers to make judgements of distance and speed to supplement times-to-collision based directly on optic flow. The resulting errors due to overestimating familiar size for child pedestrians may cause over half of their casualties in Britain.

For imminent collision, however, when optic flow is an effective source of time-to-collision, the algorithm which provides time-to-collision is probably $2\dot{\theta}/\ddot{\theta}$, rather than $\theta/\dot{\theta}$ as generally assumed. By removing the need to judge angular position relative to a datum, the new algorithm helps to explain our ability to respond accurately to moving objects, and would also facilitate the rapid updating of time-to-collision necessary for motion which is accelerating or non-linear.

The developments reported in this paper serve more to highlight the amazing capability of visual perception than to explain it. But if they are as fundamental as they appear to be, then not only is there great potential for preventing accidents and for new research and development into the perception of collision, but previous research may also merit reassessment.

REFERENCES

[1] Cavallo V, Laurent M, 1988. Visual information and skill level in time-to-collision estimation, Perception 17 623-632

[2] De Lucia P R, 1991. Pictorial and motion-based information for depth perception, Journal of Experimental Psychology: Human Perception and Performance 17 738-748

[3] Lee D N, 1976. A theory of visual control of braking based on information about time-to-collision, Perception 5 437-459.

[4] Stewart D, 1991. Driver perceptual error and child pedestrian accidents, in Vision in Vehicles III Eds A G Gale et al (Amsterdam, North-Holland) 143-152

[5] Stewart D, 1993. PhD thesis, Safety implications of driver misperception in road accidents involving child pedestrians, University of Aberdeen

[6] Stewart D, Lishman J R, Cudworth C J, 1993. Misperception of time-to-collision by drivers in pedestrian accidents, Perception (1993) 22 1227-1244.

[7] Warren W H, Hannon D J, 1990. Eye movements and optical flow, Journal of the Optical Society of America 7 (1) 160-169

[8] Gibson J J, 1950. The perception of the visual world, (Boston, MA: Houghton Mifflin)

[9] Whiting H T A, Gill E B, Stephenson J M, 1970. Critical time intervals for taking in flight information in a ball-catching task, Ergonomics 13 265-272.

[10] Lee D N, Young D S, Reddish P E, Lough S, Clayton T M H, 1983. Visual timing in hitting an accelerating ball, Quarterly Journal of Experimental Psychology 35A 333-346

[11] McLeod P, Dienes Z, 1993. Running to catch a ball, Nature 362 23.

VISION IN VEHICLES - V
A.G. Gale et al. (Editors)

Driver Strategies In Car-Following Situations

Farida Saad

Laboratoire de Psychologie de la Conduite
INRETS, 2 avenue du Général Malleret-Joinville, 94114 Arcueil Cedex, FRANCE.

Abstract

Our research is aimed at making a contribution to the analysis of cognitive aspects of driver behaviour in car-following situations. It represents an in-depth qualitative investigation into driver behaviour in the context of the complex interactions at work in real situations. The methodology used consists of observing driver behaviour from within a specially equipped vehicle during an actual journey. To complement this observation, in-depth interviews were conducted with the subject after the drive. Our paper focuses mainly on the results of an analysis of these interviews. This analysis highlighted the diversity of cues that drivers take into account to gauge the critical nature of safety margins with respect to the preceding vehicle (speed, instability of the traffic situation, manoeuvres carried out by the driver or by other drivers, ...), as well as the temporal aspect and the anticipation mechanisms involved in the control of these margins.

1. INTRODUCTION

Car-following is an increasingly common situation, especially on urban motorways, urban freeways and high-volume ring roads around large cities. In this type of road situation, the driver's adaptation is crucially dependent on his controlling interaction with other users who could interfere with his driving, and on maintaining "safety margins" that are sufficient to enable him to deal with possible incidents. A specific feature of this margin is the headway he leaves between himself and the preceding vehicle. Several studies have stressed the critical nature of headways adopted by drivers and the implications of such practices for overall safety [1, 2]. A number of variables likely to explain these practices have been studied through external observations of behaviour from a fixed observation point [3, 4, 5]. This type of approach enables the frequency with which such behaviour occurs to be evaluated, and the effect of different variables to be estimated at a global level. On the other hand, it provides little information about the frequency with which a given driver is or is not involved in these critical situations, in what circumstances and for how long. Similarly, the mechanisms by which the driver monitors his driving and the regulating actions he carries out cannot be studied in depth.

While much experimental work has been conducted to analyse the perceptual mechanisms involved in performing this task, the decisional aspects of car-following have not been greatly investigated [6]. Our research is aimed at making a contribution to the analysis of these cognitive aspects. The approach chosen was to analyse behaviour in real driving conditions. This approach, based on broader functional units of analysis, should make it possible to analyse how drivers weigh and take into account the different demands associated with driving in this road situation, and the strategies they adopt to control their safety margins in the context of the complex interactions at work in real situations. To our knowledge, this type of approach has been only rarely developed. The most important work in this field was done by Fuller [7] and concerned drivers of heavy goods vehicles. Few analyses of car driver behaviour have been made using such an approach.

2. CAR-FOLLOWING SITUATIONS AND SITUATIONAL DEMANDS IN DYNAMIC ENVIRONMENTS

Car-following situations are generally defined as traffic conditions involving a number of users driving in line and whose behaviour is closely inter-dependent. Leutzbach [1] considers that car-following begins when a driver is no longer free to adopt the speed he wishes to drive at. This constraint varies, depending on the number of vehicles involved and the number of lanes available. Several different stages of traffic have been established. These range from free-flow traffic, through traffic with occasional or repeated constraints, to congested traffic [2]. Within these different stages, there may be, at certain times, significant and rapid changes in traffic flow. Driving in car-following situations thus consists of adapting to traffic constraints and variations, and detecting "critical" variations, i.e. those which demand regulating action to avoid collision.

Several authors have stressed the problems raised by detecting and controlling changes in dynamic environments [8, 9, 10]. In such environments, where the variations are continuous, a situation may be said to be "normal" as long as these variations remain within specified limits. The difficulty facing the individual is being able to detect the point where a variation is sufficiently significant for the situation in question to be no longer considered as "normal", thus requiring regulating action. To manage such dynamic situations, the individual must integrate the time dimension of the events to be controlled, take into account the variables that enable him to understand how the on-going situation is developing, and foresee the direction and extent of these variations. Detecting these "critical variations" and the regulating action taken depends, not only on the information available in the actual situation, but also on an individual's representation of what the "normal course of events" should be, and the variation limits acceptable to him.

3. OBJECTIVES AND METHODOLOGY

Our research represents an in-depth qualitative investigation into driver behaviour in car-following situations. It sets out to define the situational demands to which drivers have to adapt while driving in this road situation, as well as to analyse the psychological mechanisms underlying the behaviour adopted. On this basis, it should be possible to identify the difficulties specific to this situation and the type of assistance that could help drivers' adaptation. The methodology used consists of observing driver behaviour from within a specially equipped vehicle during an actual journey. To complement this observation, in-depth interviews were conducted with the subject after the drive. Our paper will focus mainly on the analysis of these interviews. Nevertheless, we will briefly describe the general procedure, to place this work in the context of the overall approach [11].

3.1. The experimental route and motorway characteristics

The route chosen for the experiment was a stretch of urban motorway in the Paris region, covering an overall distance of 20.7 kms. This type of motorway is a complex network comprising a number of slip-roads and points where drivers have to choose their direction. It generally carries a high volume of traffic, often resulting in car-following situations. The experimental drives were all made at the same time of day, between 2.00 and 3.00 pm on a weekday, so as to ensure as far as possible that the subjects encountered similar general driving conditions.

3.2. Procedure

All the drivers used the same car, which was equipped to record the following data: time taken, distance, speed, and use of the brake. It also made a video recording of the journey, and these four sets of data were superimposed on the video screen. By making this video recording it was possible to keep a record of events that took place along the road during the subject's drive. It also enabled us, by means of abacuses specially built for the purpose, to determine the apparent size of the vehicle in front and hence deduce the distance between it and the experimental vehicle. Two observers travelled with the subject to set the data-recording instruments in motion and guide him along the prescribed route.

Immediately after the journey was completed, the drivers were interviewed at length. The aims of this interview were to identify their objectives and strategies, their knowledge and their representations of the driving situation studied. The interview was based primarily on subsequent verbalization techniques [12]. It took place in a room where the subject was shown a recording of his journey on a television screen. The driver was asked to comment on his driving during the experimental drive (in particular the manoeuvres he carried out and the car-following situations he was involved in). The interviews lasted on average one hour and a half. They were recorded in full and transcribed for subsequent analysis.

Two groups of male drivers participated in the experiment - one of three experienced drivers (average age : 36 years; average total mileage : 356.000 Kms) and one of three novice drivers (average age : 21 years; average total mileage : 1067 Kms).

4. RESULTS AND DISCUSSION

In real driving situations, various activities are performed by the driver and multiple determinants may explain his behaviour. Different data analyses are needed to ascertain that a valid level of description and explanation will be achieved. As a first step, an analysis of the inteviews has been made in order to identify the range of conditions taken into account by the driver and the different strategies he applies when driving in car-following situations. This analysis is based on a categorisation of driver's comments with regard to the various traffic conditions encountered during the experimental drive.

4.1. General motives and priorities in car-following situations

In general, drivers attempt to avoid car-following situations, i.e. situations where their behaviour, and more particularly their speeds, are closely dependent on those of other drivers. There are two main motives for this. The first is the desire to maintain their preferred speed as long as possible. The second refers to the principle of minimizing effort when driving : it consists of minimizing the mental strain involved in controlling traffic situations and/or the adjustments to be realized, in particular when significant or frequent variations exist or are anticipated. When heavy traffic occurs, another motive would appear to be of importance to drivers: that of adapting to the behaviour of other drivers and, in particular, to the general traffic speed that may in some cases produce a slowing-down effect and in others an accelerating effect. The speeds adopted and the margins maintained in these situations may therefore differ significantly (in extent and/or in duration) from those which drivers would have preferred to maintain, had these constraints not been present. The first two motives are linked to drivers' personal standards and refer to the "self-paced" driver attribute, i.e. to the fact that drivers prefer to establish their own driving "rythm" comensurate with the representation they have of their ability to handle a given situation [13, 14]. The third emphasises the collective or social dimension of driving and how drivers account for the group norm. The choice they make depends, not only on their personal norms and objectives, but also on those of the group in which they are, more or less willingly, involved. When these traffic conditions are severe, they represent, to a certain extent, the "force-paced" aspect of driving.

These motives determine the way in which drivers adapt to the different traffic conditions encountered. They account for the choice of traffic lane, the manoeuvres performed and the margins maintained while driving.

4.2. Critical control in car-following situations

An optimal adaptation to this driving situation assumes that the driver monitors both near and distant traffic and predicts the variations that could influence his driving. The driver must monitor the area around him in order to manage immediate interactions with other users and the possible conflicts that could arise in the course of these interactions. Distant monitoring is also essential, in view of the high speeds on motorways : it should make it possible for the driver to detect any variation (in traffic or in the infrastructure) likely to influence his driving and enable him to anticipate the corrections to be made.

The drivers' comments on the different car-following situations (and on some incidents) encountered during the experimental drive enable us to identify a number of interactions and traffic conditions they thought to be particularly "critical". They illustrate the constraints and difficulties that drivers perceive in this type of driving and how they intend to cope with them.

4.2.1 Critical interaction with other drivers in the immediate vicinity

Drivers commented on certain types of "critical" behaviour they had to cope with during the experimental drive which contributed to making the management of the traffic situation difficult. Any behaviour of another user in the vicinity that introduces significant variability or creates "undue" instability in a traffic situation is considered to be a hindrance. This also applies to "unpredictable" users, whose behaviour is inconsistent with traffic demands, or drivers whose "atypical" behaviour leaves other drivers uncertain as to the actions they are about to perform. These types of behaviour increase the effort of controlling the traffic situation and/or the number of adjustments which need to be made to integrate the variations they introduce in driving. Finally, this also applies to users who pressurise the driver from the rear and thus restrict his freedom of choice with regard to speed, choice of traffic lane and/or manoeuvres to be performed. Although drivers think they are, for the most part, able to regulate their headways, they do not consider, on the other hand, that they have any control over the margin maintained by the driver following them and no (safe) means of influencing his behaviour.

4.2.2. Critical traffic conditions : overall context for the management of interactions

These different types of behaviour prove to be particularly critical in heavy traffic when associated with high speeds. Three main traffic conditions are considered by drivers to be particularly "critical":

- *Unstable traffic conditions within a lane*, qualified by drivers as driving "in fits and starts" where there are frequent changes in speeds and distances. In these conditions, drivers find it difficult to stabilise their driving, as these variations are considered to be essentially unpredictable. An extremely high level of attention is required to adequately integrate these variations. If this instability in the lane is expected to last for a long time and the conditions permit him to do so, the driver is prompted to leave this lane as soon as possible, to join another where traffic conditions appear to be more stable.
- *Unstable traffic conditions between lanes*, linked to speed differentials between the different lanes (very often determined by the number of HGVs in the traffic). In these circumstances, the likelihood of lane change manoeuvres is high, and this demands greater attention to the behaviour of other drivers in the different lanes. In heavy traffic, these lane changes are more likely to be "forced", without drivers giving any systematic indication of their intentions. In these situations, it also becomes more difficult for them to perform their own manoeuvres and to find a gap in the continuous traffic flow. Depending on the expected duration of this instability, drivers may be encouraged, either to reduce their margins (to prevent others from cutting in on their lane), or to increase them, waiting for this instability to lessen
- *Slow-downs that are unpredictable or more significant than expected* : this is thought to be the most "critical" traffic situation that can occur on the motorway. For drivers, changes in speed in motorway traffic are usually moderate and/or short-lived. The possibility of traffic coming to a complete standstill is relatively improbable. Their driving does not therefore take into account braking actions that go beyond such "standard" behaviour. In general, by anticipating the traffic situation ahead, "non standard" correction needs can be detected sufficiently in advance and the necessary adjustments made. However, these variations in speed may somctimes occur outside the "driver's possible field of control" and/or spread more rapidly than expected in the traffic flow. Greater changes in speed become necessary and the time available to make these adjustments is limited. In such cases, the driver is not only required to manage his own reduction in speed, but must also ensure that the variation has been noted by the vehicles following him, and make allowances for possible delays in speed reduction by these vehicles.

The various comments made with regard to the difficulty of managing such traffic situations are implicit proof of what drivers consider to be the standard behaviour in these cases. The interviews indicated that drivers (and particularly experienced drivers), when managing interactions with other road users, use a number of "reference situations" and base their decisions on a representation of the "typical behaviour" adopted in such situations. Any deviation from this standard encourages them to increase their monitoring of the situation and/or perform regulating action, by seeking to escape the situation in question or adapting their safety margins. It should be stressed that the cues used to identify such deviations, and more generally identify the situation they are faced with, are for the most part informal. It should also be noted that these informal cues are referred to mainly by experienced drivers.

4.3. Evaluation and management of safety margins in car-following situations

Observations of driver behaviour indicated that the margins adopted frequently varied during the experimental drive. Although these variations were very often due to the driver's behaviour, they were also the result of the behaviour of others drivers (cutting in on the lane of the subject, for instance). The following section will deal with the different variables likely to influence the safety margins adopted by drivers or their reactions to the variations introduced by others. The analysis is based primarily on the drivers' comments on a number of car-following situations encountered during the journey (39 comments for novices and 26 comments for experienced drivers, who were less involved in car-following than novices). These variables will be classified in two main categories, depending a) on whether they encourage drivers to increase their margins, or b) whether they encourage them to reduce margins or accept a temporary variation. We will then examine a number of incidents that occurred during the drive which will help us to identify some of the difficulties related to margin control.

First, mention should be made of a number of general rules relating to the control of safety margins, such as length of the journey, road skid-resistance, level of alertness and so on. Such rules probably determine the modal values and limits of acceptable variations of margins in the course of a journey. The more general rule is to increase distance with speed. Our analysis will, in fact, be focused on the conditions that, during a given journey, may account for margin variations.

4.3.1. Conditions that produce an increase of margins

- *Difficulty of anticipation* : any interaction with a vehicle that prevents the driver from anticipating traffic status, incites him to increase safety margins. This is particularly relevant when driving behind a HGV and, more generally, behind any "opaque" vehicle. This is also the case when the behaviour of one or several other road users in the immediate vicinity produces uncertainty as to their intentions and the manoeuvre they are about to perform.
- *Traffic instability within the lane*: in the unstable driving conditions described in the previous section, where variations in speed and headway are frequent, drivers state that they tend to increase their margin to avoid these variations and the subsequent readjustments to be carried out. We will see that this rule may be amended when this instability is only temporary, or when there is also instability between lanes. More generally, when traffic conditions ahead are such that it is likely that there will be a significant slow-down, drivers state they increase their margins. This applies when detecting a slow-down from a distance and when the driver assumes this will spread back to him (the cues being the number of vehicles with brake lights on as well as the braking time). This also applies when approaching

certain specific motorway points where variations are more likely to occur (e.g. zones of directional change, slip roads where traffic joins the motorway).

4.3.2. Conditions that encourage a reduction of margins or a temporary acceptance of their reduction

- *Intentionally reducing margins prior or subsequent to manoeuvres* : all drivers state that they accept lower margins before overtaking or when waiting for an opportunity to do so. The usual strategy for overtaking is to close up on the preceding vehicle before changing lane. This is aimed at maintaining sufficient acceleration to be able to quickly adapt to the speed of the new traffic flow. When traffic conditions are such that there are few opportunities to overtake, or when following the route imposes a time constraint on a lane change, drivers may be willing to join another lane by adopting a short distance and then re-establishing a greater margin.

- *Intentionally reducing margin to prevent other drivers cutting in* : in unstable traffic conditions or in high density traffic, where it is already difficult to adapt to the situation, experienced drivers tend to reduce their margin to prevent others drivers cutting in on their lane. In this case, they think it is preferable and "safer" to control a relatively limited margin rather than leave an opportunity for other drivers to cut in on their lanes, which would be more likely to increase the instability of the situation even further. They may also intentionally reduce the margin to force the preceding driver, who "is not obeying lane discipline", to change lanes.

- *Temporary acceptance of a reduction in margins* : drivers are willing to accept a temporary reduction of their margin when they anticipate that a preceding vehicle will pull back into another lane, or that a vehicle that has just joined their lane will quickly accelerate. It also applies when a slight variation in the traffic flow is thought to be only brief. In general, any variation that drivers consider to be only temporary does not seem to be critical and does not therefore require any immediate corrective action. The traffic condition upstream of the lane is used as a reference to assess the importance and possible progression of these slight variations.

- *Reducing the margin and pressure of traffic* : this is linked to extremely heavy traffic conditions and is referred to as being a very significant constraint for all the users. Drivers admit that in these conditions, the margins adopted are extremely critical but that it is difficult, or even dangerous not to comply with the speed and general behaviour of other drivers. Novices are particularly affected by this constraint because of their difficulties in monitoring and adjusting their speed in high density traffic. Moreover, the difficulties they encounter in performing overtaking manoeuvres prevent them from avoiding these constraints by changing lanes as often as they would like.

4.3.3. An analysis of incidents in car-following situations

The foregoing analyses indicated that margins are regulated from a dynamic and overall perspective and are based on the anticipation and prediction of how other drivers will behave together with variations in traffic. An analysis of a number of "incidents" that occurred during the experimental drive (and later commented upon by subjects when shown the video recording of their journey) helps to identify some of the difficulties of ensuring this control. In this paper, we will restrict ourselves to defining the main characteristics of these incidents

(6 for novice drivers and 3 for experienced drivers). They are all linked to a lane-change manoeuvre or the phase leading up to this change. They indicate the problems involved in distributing attention between the various environmental sectors (near and distant, in front, behind and parallel) and reveal difficulties linked to the dynamics of road situations and predicting changes in situations.

For novice drivers, this largely involved incidents that caused a conflict with another user or a significant change in the subject's speed (braking) and/or discontinuing the manoeuvre initially planned. Thus, as an example, a novice driver pulls back from the outer lane to the central lane without noticing that another user was changing from the inner to the central lane at the same time. He brakes sharply behind the other user who has pulled in just in front of him. On nearing an area that joins up with another stretch of motorway, a novice driver is getting ready to overtake and is late in realising that he is approaching this area. He decides not to overtake and has to brake sharply to re-establish a margin with the preceding vehicle. Such incidents raise the question of the relevance of attentional distribution to driving demands in general and the manoeuvre to be performed in particular. Neboit [15] stressed the limits of visual search strategies for novice drivers, in terms not only of selectivity but also of anticipated search for information. Incidents such as these may reflect these difficulties and, more generally, the fact that novices have not acquired the knowledge that could enable them to predict that variations will occur, and direct their attention to areas where they are likely to appear.

For experienced drivers, the problem arising in these incidents was to counteract, by a slight change in speed, an uncontrolled variation of the margin with the preceding vehicle. This, for example, is the case for a driver who, anticipating that he would join a stretch of motorway, scans the traffic on the section, and is late in detecting that the vehicle preceding him has slowed down. The same scenario was observed for another driver who, trying to find a gap to overtake, is late in detecting that the traffic in his lane has slowed down. The driver's attentional strategies are directed by the manoeuvre he intends to perform. He distributes his attention between the different sectors that are "useful" for carrying out this task. Distributing attention between these sectors depends on the categorisation of the on-going traffic situation and how it is likely to progress. In these incident-related situations, unexpected variations occurred between two attentional shifts.

Although the incidents noted in these situations were remedied, proving the effectiveness of information processing and/or remedial action taken by the drivers, they nevertheless revealed the fragility of these mechanisms, which could in more unfavourable circumstances lead to a collision. They illustrated the problems encountered when monitoring dynamic situations linked to the temporal dimension and the evolutionary nature of the events to be controlled [16].

5. CONCLUSION

The analysis of drivers comments on the margins they adopted during the experimental drive reveals the diversity of cues they considered in order to assess the critical nature of safety margins in car-following situations : overall speed, density and the stability of the traffic situation; type, vicinity, extent and duration of traffic variations; and the nature of the immediate interaction with other drivers. Thus, their assessment appears to depend, not only on the absolute value of the margin itself but also on the global context of the traffic situation in which it is adopted and on drivers' motives and priorities in this context. Furthermore, drivers are more likely to base their decisions on whether or not to undertake regulating action on their assessment of the possible development of the situation in hand, than on its momentary characterization. Temporal aspects and anticipation mechanisms seem to play an important role in the monitoring and regulation of these margins. This anticipation is dependent upon the cues available in the situation itself, but also on the driver's representation of the events likely to occur in certain situations, and on the behaviour generally adopted by the other users in these situations. It can indeed be supposed that driving in these conditions would be particularly difficult if the driver did not assume that other road users would adopt some form of behavioural norm such as complying with the "average" behaviour of the traffic flow, without stopping, braking suddenly or changing lane for no apparent reason. To analyse the way this "repertoire" of assumptions is built up and organised with experience and how they are activated when driving may be crucial to understanding the behaviour adopted in these situations. One of the main problems from a safety standpoint is identifying the information required by the driver if he is to realise that his assumptions, and more generally the situational model on which he is basing his behaviour, are no longer appropriate and must be modified. This aspect is illustrated by the incident analysis. The results of this analysis reveal the importance of an in-depth investigation of cognitive mechanisms to understanding the malfunctions observed in car-following situations and to identify ways of reducing their occurrence [6, 17].

A follow-up to this work will be to determine the range of the different variables identified in the overall and circumstantial orientation of behaviour. This will involve parameterizing the strategies indicated by the drivers during their interviews and suggesting a more structured model of behaviour in car-following situations. This work, based on an analysis of the observational data, should enable us to specify the circumstances in which different strategies are implemented, and quantify the margins adopted in the different situations that have been singled out and how long they were applied. A first global analysis of driver behaviour shows that novices are more involved in car-following than experienced drivers (76% of their journey compared to 58% for experienced drivers) and, in particular in close-following. It also indicated that these drivers are more likely to be subjected to variations linked to another user joining their lane (24) than experienced drivers (13), manoeuvre which is very often the origin of a car-following sequence. One may wonder if this result is not indicative of these drivers' difficulty in extracting themselves from car following situations rather than the result of their deliberate choice. More generally, one may assume that novice drivers are less able to anticipate the complex interaction involved in the management of car-following situations and/or take so long to make their decisions, that they stay longer in these critical situations. A more in-depth analysis of the observational data should enable us to obtain further information on this point.

ACKNOWLEDGEMENT

Part of the work involved in this research was supported by the USAP (Union des sociétés d'autoroute à péage) research-development programme under the control of ISIS.

REFERENCES

1. Leutzbach, W. (1974). Collisions par l'arrière. 12 ème semaine internationale d'étude technique de la circulation et de sa sécurité. Thème VI : collisions en chaîne. Belgrade 2 - 7 Septembre.
2. Carré, J.R., Lassarre, S. & Liger, M. (1984). Fluidité-sécurité : Faut-il choisir ? TEC, N°66, 14-19.
3. Sumner, R. & Baguley, C (1978). Close following behaviour at two sites on rural two lane motorways. TRRL LR 859, 7 p.
4. Evans, L. & Wasielewski, P. (1982). Do accident-involved drivers exhibit riskier everyday driving behavior ? Accident Analysis and Prevention, 14, 1, 57-64.
5. Postans, R.L. & Wilson, W.T. (1983). Close-following on the motorway. Ergonomics, 26, 4, 317-327.
6. Colbourn, C.J., Brown, I.D. & Copeman, A.K. (1978) - Drivers' judgments of safe distance in vehicle following. Human Factors, 20, 1, 1-11.
7. Fuller, R.G.C (1981). Determinants of time headway adopted by truck drivers. Ergonomics, 24, 6, 463-474.
8. Sperandio, J.C. (1984). L'ergonomie du travail mental. Masson.
9. Leplat, J. (1985). Erreur humaine, fiabilité humaine. Armand Colin - Collection U.
10. Hale, A.R. & Glendon, A.I. (1987). Individual behaviour in the control of danger. Industrial Safety Series, Volume 2. Elsevier, Amsterdam - Oxford - New York - Tokyo.
11. Saad, F. & Khoudour, L. (1991). In-Depth analysis of driver behaviour in car-following : Methodological aspects and global behaviour analysis. In PTRC, 19Th Summer Annual Meeting, Traffic management and road safety, Proceedings of seminar K.
12. Leplat, J. & Hoc, J.M. (1981). Subsequent verbalization in the study of cognitive processes. Ergonomics, 24, 10, 743-755.
13. Allen, T.H., Lunenfeld, H. & Alexander, G.J. (1971). Driver information needs. Highway Research Record 36, 102-115.
14. Näätänen, R. & Summala, H. (1974). A model for the role of motivational factors in drivers' decision-making. Accident analysis and prevention, 6, 243-261.
15. Neboit, M. (1982) - L'exploration visuelle du conducteur : rôle de l'apprentissage et de l'expérience. Cahier d'étude ONSER, N° 56.
16. Senach, B. (1984). La recherche de solution aux incidents en contrôle de processus. Psychologie Française, 29, 3-4, 279-283.
17. Brown, I.D. & Groeger, J. (1988). Risk perception and decision taking during the transition between novice and experienced driver status. Ergonomics, 31, 4, 585-597.

VISION IN VEHICLES - V
A.G. Gale et al. (Editors)

The Role Of Driving Expertise In The Visual Anticipation Of A Collision

Catherine Berthelon[a], Daniel Mestre[b] and Rémi Taramino[c]

[a]INRETS (Département Mécanismes d'Accidents), Chemin de la Croix-Blanche, 13330, Salon de Provence, France

[b]Cognition & Mouvement, CNRS & University Aix-Marseille II, Traverse Charles Susini, 13000 Marseille, France

[c]Université de Provence, Avenue Robert Schuman, 13000, Aix-en-Provence, France

1. INTRODUCTION

Visual motion perception plays a fundamental role in vehicle guidance. For example, the control of one's trajectory is mainly performed on the basis of visual information about the characteristics of the trajectory and about the spatial layout (1). In particular, the pattern of optical flow resulting from the observer's self-motion through a stable environment is used by the subject to obtain information about his direction or speed of self-motion (2 and 3).

However, little is known about the twofold task of a driver approaching an intersection, where he/she must control both his/her trajectory and detect the motion of other vehicles. Using visual simulations of car driving situations (such as an approach course to an intersection), we have previously shown that observers are quite able to detect the presence of a moving object during self-motion. Nevertheless, the global apparent motion of the environment resulting from their rectilinear or curvilinear self-motion affects their perceptual judgment about the spatio-temporal characteristics of the moving object. In addition to this effect of the global optical flow, there seem to exist more local determinants of perception. In particular, the presence of a road sign near the intersection (acting as a spatial reference cue) allowed for more accurate perception (4). In the case of curvilinear self-motion, the motion parallax between the road sign and the moving vehicle enabled the subjects to differentiate between the conditions where the moving vehicle arrived at the intersection after or before the subject. A second type of local information was the visual motion of the approaching vehicle itself. A reversal of its direction of visual motion indicated that it would reach the intersection before the observer. Inversely, no reversal indicated that it would reach the intersection after the observer (5, 6 and 7).

In the present experiment, we tried to evaluate precisely the perceptual ability of observers, in relation to their level of driving expertise. On the average, it is intuitively accepted that novice drivers experience difficulties selecting the relevant visual information in a complex environment and that it takes them longer time than expert drivers to evaluate the characteristics of a given situation. They tend to look closer to their vehicle than experienced drivers, irrespective of their forward speed, whereas experienced driver tend to look farther forward as their speed of self-motion increases (8 and 9). This adaptive behavior observed in experts might be defined as part of a perceptual expertise, defined as an ability to anticipate future events from the extraction of predictive visual information in the environment (10 and 11). In this sense drivers have to detect potential dangers farther away (in space an time) as their speed increases, so it is easily conceivable that they tend to fixate their direction of gaze farther away.

In this experiment, we also tried to study the relationships between abstract images and realistic images, a problem which has been extensively studied in the context of aerial navigation (12). In abstract images, only the visual information necessary to evaluate the motion of the aproaching vehicle was presented. In realistic images, a complex visual scene close to a real visual environment was presented. This manipulation enabled us to try to study two non exclusive hypotheses:

- Visual expertise resides in increased anticipatory capacities (in this case experts should be better with abstract images).
- Visual expertise resides in a more efficient ability to select the relevant information in a complex visual scene (in this case experts should be better with realistic images).

2. EXPERIMENTAL SECTION

2.1. General methods.

Visual sequences simulated curvilinear approach of a driver to an intersection. Another vehicle was approaching the intersection, on a radial path, from the outside of the curve. In some conditions, a road sign was placed near the intersection. Images could be realistic (figure 1A) or abstract (figure 1B). In these latter, the environment was not represented. Only the approaching vehicle and the road sign were represented as spheres of different colors.

Two sets of 8 experimental sessions were run. Each set lasted for 2 hours. In each set (abstract or realistic images), eight randomized sessions were run, corresponding to the combination of different experimental factors: two radii of curvature of the trajectory (120 or 425 meters), two temporal windows (the visual information could be presented either from 6 to 4 seconds before the driver reached the intersection or from 4 to 2 seconds before the driver reached the intersection), and finally the presence or absence of a road sign near the intersection. The approaching vehicle could reach the intersection 1 second, .5 second or .2 second before or after the observer. Each of these 6 conditions of arrival were presented 10 times in a given session, resulting in 60 visual sequences presented in a randomized order.

A

B

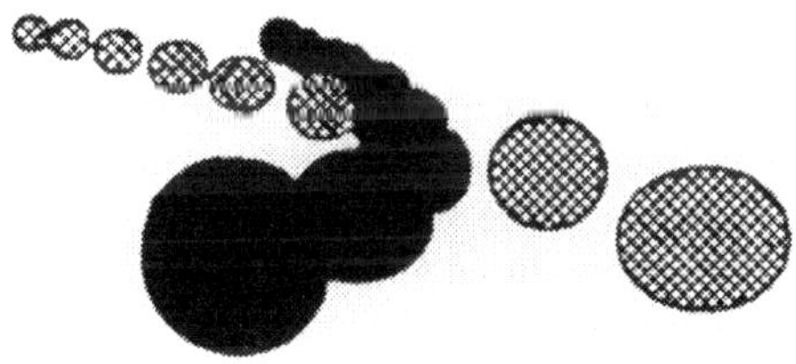

Figure 1. Examples of visual scenes used in the experiment. In this case the approaching vehicle will reach the intersection one second before the observer. A) realistic scene, B) abstract scene, in which the successive position in the visual scene of the vehicle (black sphere) and road sign (grey sphere) are depicted, as the observer approaches the intersection point.

28 subjects volunteered to participate in this experiment. They received 100 FF for their participation. They were aged between 18 and 25 years and were segregated in three groups, depending on their level of driving expertise.

- 8 were non drivers
- 11 were novice drivers (having less than 5 years of driving experience)
- 9 were experienced drivers (having more than 5 years of driving experience)

Subjects had to decide, on a forced-choice basis, whether the aproaching vehicle would reach the intersection before or after them.

2.2. Results

2.2.1 Overall effects

Subjects' answers were analysed in terms of perceptual thresholds (the minimum temporal interval for which the subjects were able to detect that the approaching vehicle would reach the intersection before or after them in more than 75 % of the cases) and perceptual bias (a systematic tendency to under- or overestimate the arrival time of the approaching vehicle at the intersection). These data were submitted to an analysis of variance.

In all subjects, thresholds were lower (.19 second) in the second temporal window (when the information was presented between 4 and 2 seconds before the intersection) than in the first window (.31 second, when the information was presented between 6 and 4 seconds before the intersection, $F[1,25] = 81.54$; $p<.001$).

Thresholds were also lower with than without a road sign (.22 vs .27 second, $F[1,25] = 22.43$; $p<.001$) and with large than small radii (.22 vs .28 second, $F[1,25] = 17.04$; $p<.001$). Notably, thresholds were lower with road sign than without when the radii were small in the first temporal window (.25 with road sign vs .46 s without, $F[1,25]=10.09$; $p<.005$).

Finally, thresholds were lower with abstract than with realistic images (.21 vs .28 second, $F[1,25] = 39.67$; $p<.001$).

Concerning perceptual biases, subjects had a systematic tendency to overestimate the arrival time of the approaching vehicle at the intersection (they perceived the vehicle as arriving after them in situations where it arrived in fact slightly before them) in the first temporal window. This bias was reduced and close to zero in the second temporal window (when the visual information was presented close to the intersection). Biases were equal to .23 second and to .03 second, in the first and second temporal window, respectively ($F[1,25] = 23.47$; $p<.001$).

The bias was higher for large radii than for small radii (.18 and .08 second, respectively, $F[1,25] = 6.46$; $p<.025$), in particular in the first temporal window.

The presence of a road sign reduced biases (.19 and .07 second, without and with a road sign respectively, $F[1,25] = 10.05$; $p<.005$). In the second temporal window, the road sign even changed the sign of the bias (.12 and -.05 second without and with a road sign, respectively, $F[1,25] = 20.36$; $p<.001$). In this last condition, the road sign induced a tendency to perceive the vehicle as passing before the observer in situations where it passed in fact after him. This effect might be related to a perceptual effect of the relative visual motion between the road sign and the approaching vehicle.

Finally, the bias was more important with abstract images than with realistic images (.20 and .06 second, respectively, $F[1,25] = 7.27$; $p<.025$).

2.2.2. The effect of level of expertise

The level of expertise did not induce a straightforward effect. However, interaction effects revealed differences between the three groups of subjects, only in the case of realistic images.

Thresholds were significantly elevated in non-drivers, when the information was presented far from the intersection, without a road sign, with a small radii and with realistic images. The average threshold values were equal to .79, .47 and .49 second, for non-drivers, novice and expert drivers, respectively. Partial comparisons revealed that the diference was significant when comparing non-drivers to expert and novice drivers ($F[1,25] = 13.81$; $p<.005$; figure 2).

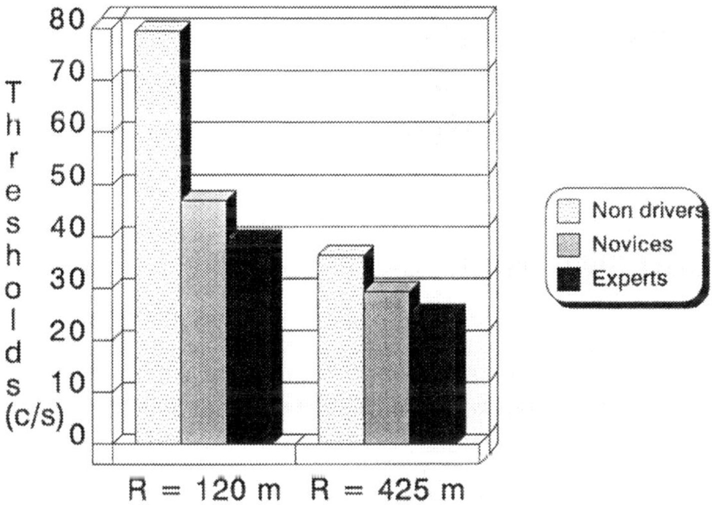

Figure 2. Average values of thresholds (expressed in 1/100 of second) as a function of the radius of curvature of the observer's trajectory, in the case when the information was presented far from the intersection, without a road sign and with realistic images.

Novice drivers revealed important biases when the information was presented in the first temporal window, for a small radius and notably with a road sign (bias was equal to -.48 second in novice drivers, to .02 second in the other two groups, $F[1,25] = 5.92$; $p<.025$; figure 3).

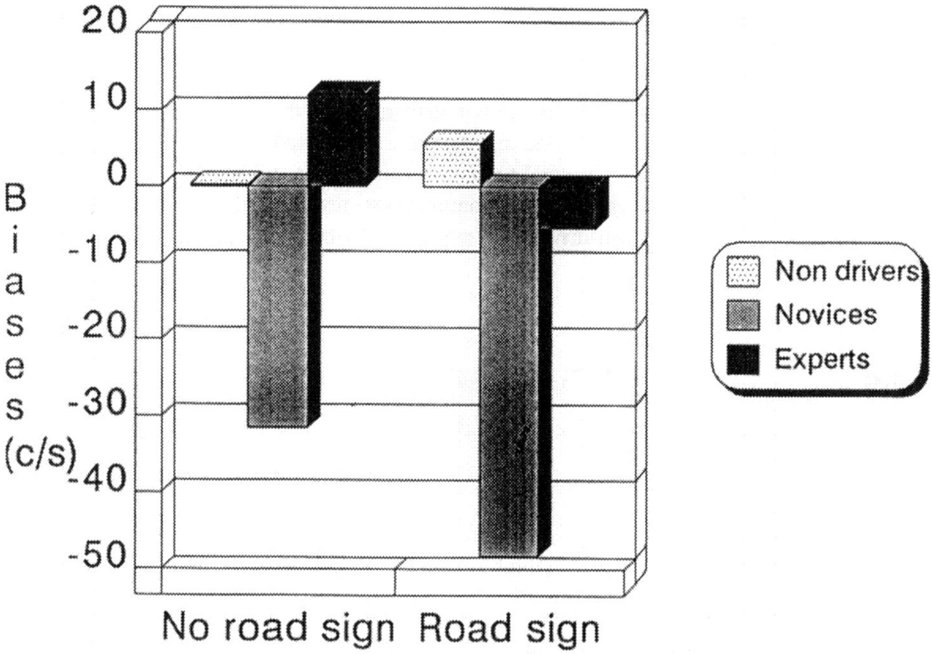

Figure 3. Average perceptual biases as a function of the group of subjects (expressed in 1/100 of second), when the information was presented far from the intersection, for a small radius of curvature of the observer's trajectory and with realistic images. A positive (negative) bias signifies that the subject tend to perceive the approaching vehicle as arriving after (before) her/him in situations where it in fact passes before (after) her/him at the intersection.

3. DISCUSSION

Overall, subjects' responses were relatively precise (average thresholds equal to .25 second). However, there was a systematic tendency to perceive the vehicle as arriving after them at the intersection in situations where it arrived in fact slightly before them (average bias equal to .13 second). Moreover, estimations were less precise and biases more important when the visual information was presented far from the intersection. These effects might be due to an induction effect of the global optic flow field on the vehicle's perceived motion and also to difficulties in perceiving future events from predictive visual information, especially when visual information is presented far ahead in time from the event of interest.

Furthermore, the presence of a road sign near the intersection reduced perceptual thresholds, notably for small radii of curvature when information was presented far from the intersection. A road sign also reduced perceptual bias when information was presented close to the intersection. These results suggest that the road sign acts as a spatial reference, which enables the observer to better analyse the visual motion of the vehicle.

With realistic images, biases were lower than with abstract images, suggesting that realistic images contain further useful cues. However, the level of precision of responses was lower with these realistic images, which poses the question of the equivalence of the total pattern of optical flow in the two images. It might be that, with abstract images, the higher level of precision is due to the fact that the visual motion of the vehicle is presented in isolation, whereas in realistic images, the global optical flow due to other elements in the environment disturbs the perceptual analysis.

Finally, level of expertise influenced performance only with realistic images. Non-drivers were "impaired" when the visual information was presented far in time form the intersection and when the radius of curvature of their trajectory was small. In this case, the optical flow resulting from the curved self-motion was more important. This result suggests that non-drivers might be highly sensitive to this optical flow. It might then be that the multiple elements of a realistic image have a dual effect on non-drivers performance. First, non-drivers would have difficulties in selecting the pertinent cues in a complex visual scene. Second, they would have difficulties in correctly anticipating the outcome of a situation from early predictive information.

Moreover, novice drivers appeared to base their judgment on "misleading" spatial cues. In particular, their tendency to perceive the vehicle as passing before them might be due to the fact that they used the side of the road as a decision criterion (the vehicle necessarily reaches the side of the road before it reaches the middle of the driver's lane, which was the correct intersection point). This suggests that novice drivers might select misleading cues in the environment and/or be sensitive to a local induction effect resulting from the relative visual motion between the vehicle and environmental elements such as the road sign or the side of the road. Expert drivers presented the lowest thresholds and biases. They evidently selected the correct cues and were able to correctly anticipate the evolution of the situation.

These results suggest that experience of driving is related to an increased ability to quickly select relevant cues in the environment and to an ability to perceive correctly the characteristics of the trajectory of a moving vehicle during self-motion, irrespective of global or local induction effects related to the global optical flow resulting from self-motion or to local relative optical motion between the vehicle and environmental elements, respectively.

4. CONCLUSION

In this experiment, we show that the optical motion resulting from a moving vehicle during self-motion contains predictive information concerning the trajectory of the vehicle, in relation with the trajectory of the observer, which is of major importance for collision avoidance in vehicle driving. The fact that observers are able to correctly perceive the evolution of such a situation with abstract as well as with realistic images, enables us to think that such visual analysis also occurs during real driving. However, the fact that the level of expertise of driving has an effect only on the visual analysis of realistic images suggests that the difference between non-drivers and drivers resides less in their "basic" visual capacities than in their ability to analyse complex visual scenes. In this sense, the analysis of the driver's environment might call on other internal processes, such as a functional representation of the driving situation itself (13). Obviously, further research is needed on this point, the results of which might help improve the teaching of those basic ability which are necessary to learning how to drive safely.

REFERENCES

1. Gibson, J.J. (1979). The ecological approach to visual perception. Boston: Houghton Mifflin.
2. Warren, W.H., Mestre, D., Blackwell, A.W., Morris, M.W. (1991). Perception of circular heading from optical flow. Journal of Experimental Psychology : Human Perception and Performance, 17, 28-43.
3. Mestre, D. (1992). Visual perception of self-motion. In L. Proteau and D.Elliott (Eds.). Vision and motor control. Amsterdam: North Holland, pp 421-440.
4. Berthelon, C., Mestre, D. (1990). Perception visuelle d'un mobile lors du déplacement: application à la conduite automobile. Le Travail Humain, 53, 17-32.
5. Mestre, D., Berthelon, C. (1991). Visual perception of a moving object during self-motion. In P.J. Beek, R.J. Bootsma and P.C.W. van Wieringen (Eds.), Studies in Perception and Action. Amsterdam Rodopi. pp. 126-130.
6. Berthelon, C., Mestre, D. (1993). Visual cues for the detection of impending collision at crossroads: The case of curvilinear self-motion. In A.G. Gale et al. (Eds), Vision in Vehicles IV. Amsterdam: North-Holland. pp101-108.
7. Berthelon, C., Mestre, D. (in press). Curvilinear approach to an intersection and visual detection of a collision. Human Factors.
8. Neboit, M. (1983). Evolution de l'exploration visuelle avec l'apprentissage et avec l'expérience professionnelle. Le travail humain, 46, 33-48.
9. Mourant, R.R., Rockwell, T.H. (1972). Strategies of visual search by novice and experienced drivers. Human Factors, 14, 325-335.
10. Albernethy, B. (1990). Expertise, visual search, and information pick-up in squash. Perception, 19, 63-77.
11. Deary, J., Mitchell, H. (1989). Inspection time and high-speed ball games. Perception, 18, 789-792.
12. Lintern, G., Sheppart, D.J., Parker, D.L., Yates, K.E., Nolan, M.D. (1989). Simulator design and instructional features for air-to-ground attack : a transfer study. Human Factors, 31, 87-99.
13. Ochanine, D.A. (1964). L'acte et l'image, problème d'ergonomie. XVII ème Congrés International de Psychologie, pp 81-88.

VISION IN VEHICLES - V
A.G. Gale et al. (Editors)

An Analysis of Driving Accident Narratives As A Means of Determining Problems Caused By In-Vehicle Visual Allocation and Visual Workload

Walter W. Wierwille[a] and Louis Tijerina[b]

[a]Vehicle Analysis and Simulation Laboratory, Virginia Polytechnic Institute and State University, Blacksburg, Blacksburg, Virginia, 24061-0118, USA

[b]Battelle Memorial Institute, 505 King Avenue, Columbus, Ohio, 43201, USA

An accident data base search was performed to determine the effects of driver visual allocation into the vehicle (interior visual workload) on accident rates. The study was carried out using the North Carolina (U.S.) accident data base, which has investigating-officer written narratives entered and which is accessible through keyword searches. The search was conducted on the entire 1989 data base and on the first four-month period of 1992. The results show clearly that numerous accidents are caused by visual allocation into the vehicle. Areas showing high rates are radio usage, mirror usage, attention to loose objects in vehicle, interaction with another person or animal in vehicle, and involuntary visual occlusion attributed to several sources. Numerous other sources also cause smaller numbers of accidents. Comparison of the 1989 and 1992 data bases indicates that cellular phone usage accidents are becoming more prevalent and that citizen's band radio usage accidents are becoming less prevalent, probably because of the relative change in numbers of these devices in vehicles.

1. INTRODUCTION

It is common practice for researchers to examine accident records or accident histories of individuals as a means of relating a psychological or physiological trait, or other aspect of performance to accident rate. Numerous examples of such procedures exist in the literature, many of which have been cited or discussed in previous Vision in Vehicles Conferences (Davison, 1986; de Velde Harnsenhorst and Lourens, 1991; Janke, 1983; Mihal and Barett, 1976; Tilley, Erwin, and Gianturco, 1973; and Treat, Tumbas, McDonald, Shinar, Hume, Mayer, Stansifer, and Castellan, 1977). The goal of performing such analyses is either the reduction or prevention of future accidents, or the reduction of severity if such accidents do occur (Brown, 1990).

The great majority of data bases contain only general information such as time of day, conditions, model and year of vehicles involved, severity information (including injury level, deaths, and estimated property damage), age and apparent condition of the drivers, assessed fault, and in some cases, likely cause. Another type of database involves accident "narratives." In many jurisdictions the investigating officer provides a narrative of about one paragraph, describing the accident occurrence and what each driver/vehicle did. Narratives of this type can provide greater insight into accident causes, if an appropriate subset of narratives can be retrieved and properly classified.

The State of North Carolina (U.S.) has had such a program in effect for many years. Virtually all police-reported accidents within the state contain narratives. The narratives are entered into a data base, along with other, standardized information such as that previously described. The data can then be accessed by keywords using computer programs developed at the Highway Safety Research Institute in Durham. Thus, all narratives containing the keyword can be accessed and printed.

Perel (1976, 1988) has used this narrative approach to examine driver/vehicle interaction problems in automobiles, particularly those caused by hand and foot controls. His work is summarized by Wierwille (1991) and shows that indeed a small percentage of automobile accidents is caused by control usage or misusage.

Recently the (U.S.) National Highway Traffic Safety Administration funded a program examining heavy-vehicle driver workload. As part of this program, an attempt was made to use the North Carolina data base to examine accidents caused by allocation of visual resources or by what might be termed visual workload. The search included all motor vehicles, not just trucks. The fundamental concept was to determine the "safety relevance" of in-vehicle visual allocation. In other words, is visual allocation into the vehicle a substantial cause of accidents? If so, is there anything that can be learned from the relative numbers of such accidents? Because of the highly specific nature of this topic, it was apparent that narrative search by appropriate keywords would be the only feasible approach.

2. METHOD

An initial keyword list was developed and checked by having it run on a small portion of the data base. The list was then revised and subsequently run on the entire data base for 1989 and the available data base for 1992. A partial listing of keywords is shown in Table 1. In the table, some words are truncated (as indicated by a comma) so that narratives containing stems with different endings could be retrieved. In addition, specific combinations of words were used as keywords in an attempt to target specific vision-related accidents as they might have been described in police reports.

The 1989 data base contained 189464 total narratives. The retrieval procedure resulted in 14372 "hits." These hit narratives were printed, carefully read, and classified. Hits not relevant to visual allocation and workload were deleted. The 1992 data base available at the time that the search was conducted contained 61707 total narratives. These were for accidents occurring in the first four months of 1992. In this case 3247 hits were obtained and classified separately, but in exactly the same way. It should be noted that the 1992 data base was almost exactly one-third the size of the 1989 data base. Thus, approximate comparisons could be made by multiplying the 1992 culled occurrences by a factor of three and then comparing the results with the 1989 results.

One of the major difficulties is dealing with relevant citations that may fit in more than one place. For example should a "dropped cassette tape" accident be classified under removing/inserting cassette or under "loose, specified object in vehicle"? This issue was resolved by considering that once the tape was dropped it simply became another loose object in the vehicle and was thus classified. The researcher or analyst must take care to find the most appropriate category for each citation. To some extent this process depends on objectives. For example, if it is desired to know how cassette-playing radios affect accident rates, then dropped-cassette accidents should be included with other cassette-related accidents. In any case, decisions must be made so that a given narrative appears only once in the classification scheme. To minimize difficulties, careful consideration must be given in selecting non-overlapping categories and subcategories.

The criteria for inclusion in the classification scheme were:

1) A driver's vision was directed away from the forward scene, and
2) This visual allocation process was the primary cause of the accident.

Additional criteria for inclusion were based on reportability. For inclusion in the accident data base, the accident had to involve estimated property damage in excess of $500 U.S., or injury or death.

3. RESULTS

The 1989 results appear in Tables 2 through 14. In all, 2816 relevant citations were found. Of these, visual allocation *into* the vehicle was clearly noted in 1562 cases, allocation outside the vehicle was clearly noted in 661 cases, and unspecified visual allocation was noted in 593 cases. Interpreted examples of each would be:

Interior: "The driver was adjusting the radio and not paying attention to the car in front."

Exterior: "The driver was searching for a house number when he collided with the parked car."

Unspecified: "The driver looked away for a moment and ran the red light, colliding with a car entering the intersection on green."

It should be understood that those citations in the "unspecified" category must have been interior or exterior, but could not be classified further because of lack of available information in the narratives.

By way of further explanation, if the driver was looking into the mirrors, this was initially classified as interior and then later subclassified in accordance with whether the driver was viewing something in the mirror that was inside or outside the vehicle. Thus, all mirror-related accidents were initially classified as interior, even though side mirrors are in fact just outside the vehicles.

The interior-source citations were then further classified as shown in Table 2. As can be seen, eleven subcategories were developed, based largely on interior vehicle areas or functions. This classification demonstrates clearly that accidents are caused by a variety of interior aspects. Tables 3 through 14 show further classifications, which are self-explanatory.

The available 1992 data base, as indicated earlier was approximately one-third the size of the 1989 data base. It was examined to determine trends that might be occurring as newer equipment is added to the vehicle and older equipment is phased out. Tables 15 through 17 show three of the subcategories of the 1992 classification. In each case the number of citations has been multiplied by 3 to make the results comparable to 1989. Table 15 shows that the results for "standard radio" are similar to those of 1989. However, the equivalent of six accidents caused by compact disk handling appears in the 1992 data base that are not present in the 1989 data base. Table 16 shows the results for two-way radio, in which fewer accidents were caused by them in 1992. This reduction can be attributed to the decline in popularity of citizen's band radios between 1989 and 1992. Finally, in Table 17, the number of accidents attributable to cellular phones shows a marked increase. This increase is probably a result of the increased number of such phones in vehicles.

It should be mentioned before leaving the topic of the 1992 citations that some unexplained discrepancies were noted. For example, there was a large drop in HVAC (heating, ventilating and air conditioning) related accidents between 1989 and 1992. It is difficult to pinpoint the cause of this reduction. However, North Carolina is in a moderate/subtropical climate zone, and it is possible that drivers did not need to pay much attention to their HVAC systems during the first several months of the year. In any case, because of truncation, the 1992 results should be considered as indicative and not conclusive.

4. CONCLUSIONS

The results of the analyses speak for themselves in that they indicate the relative prevalence of accidents. One need only examine the various tables to determine which interior sources are causing the most problems. Nevertheless it is probably worthwhile to state certain general conclusions:

1. Visual allocation into the vehicle causes numerous accidents. These accidents are caused by a wide variety of interior sources.

2. The introduction of any new item into the vehicle which requires vision while the vehicle is in motion can be expected to cause an increase in accident rate. Good examples are compact disk players and cellular telephones.

3. Categories of sources currently causing large numbers of accidents (more than 100 in the classification scheme) include standard radios, mirrors, loose objects in vehicles, interactions with other persons or animals, and involuntary visual occlusion.

4. Within the loose objects category, it may be surmised that a good portion of the problem is the perceived need for immediate attention. For example, spilling a drink, finding a dropped lit cigarette, or shooing an insect all appear to require immediate attention.

5. In the category of interactions with another person or animal, it may similarly be surmised that the perceived need for immediate attention is a contributor to the large number of accidents.

6. Conclusions 4 and 5 suggest that one effective way to reduce accident rates it to eliminate or modify those interior sources that appear to demand *immediate* attention. A good example would be using child and animal restraint systems that prevent them from getting loose and distracting the driver.

7. It is clear that radios do cause some difficulties and that efforts should be directed at reducing the visual demands they induce. Reducing the number and length of glances to perform various radio adjustment operations should result in a reduced accident rate.

8. Because loose objects cause so many accidents, efforts directed at educating drivers to this hazard should be made. They further should be advised in regard to how to handle problems with loose objects should they occur. It is obvious that many are not handling them correctly at present, in that they are giving such situations undeserved priority.

9. Any changes in mirror systems used in vehicles should be carefully checked. The safety advantage of reducing blind spots may increase the opportunity for visual distraction.

More generally, it can be concluded that performing a data-base search employing key-words applied to accident narratives serves as a useful adjunct to the conventional accident-record analysis technique. Of course, narrative analyses are subject to inaccuracies caused by such factors as misrepresentation of the true cause of an accident by interviewed drivers, or by incorrect interpretation or analysis on the part of the investigating officer. Furthermore, as in this particular case, one state may not be precisely representative of the entire country. (North Carolina does not include a major metropolitan area such as Chicago, Los Angeles, New York, or Washington, D.C. It can be expected that accidents typical of such major areas, say for example cellular phone accidents, would be underrepresented in the North Carolina data base.) There is also the limitation that many property-damage accidents do not get reported to the police, resulting in general underrepresentation of "true" accident rates. Despite such limitations, detailed information on problems occurring in the driver/vehicle/roadway system can be gained by such methodology.

ACKNOWLEDGMENTS

This research was sponsored by the National Highway Traffic Safety Administration (NHTSA) Office of Crash Avoidance Research. The authors wish to thank Robert Clarke, Michael Goodman and Michael Perel of NHTSA for helpful suggestions. The authors also wish to thank Eric Rodgman and Donald Reinfurt at the Highway Safety Research Center at the University of North Carolina for their careful execution of the computerized retrieval process.

REFERENCES

1. Brown, I. D. (1990). Accident reporting and analysis. In Wilson, J. R. and Corlett, E. N. (Eds.) *Evaluation of Human Work*, Taylor and Francis, London, 755-778.
2. Davison, P. A. (1986). Inter-relationships between British drivers' age, visual attributes, and road accident histories. In A. G. Gale, et al (Eds.) *Vision in Vehicles*, Elsevier Science Publishers (North Holland), Amsterdam, 25-32.
3. de Velde Harnsenhorst, J. J. and Lourens, P. F. (1991). Aspects of driving behavior in learner and inexperienced drivers. In A. G. Gale, et al (Eds.) *Vision in Vehicles III*, Elsevier Science Publishers (North Holland), Amsterdam, 63-70.
4. Janke, M. K. (1983). Accident rates of drivers with bioptic telescopic lenses. *Journal of Safety Research*, *14*(4), (Winter), 159-165.
5. Mihal, W. L. and Barett, G. V. (1976). Individual differences in perceptual information processing and their relation to automobile accident involvement. *Journal of Applied Psychology*, *61*(2), 229-233.
6. Perel, M. (1976). Analyzing the role of driver/vehicle incompatibilities in accident causation using police reports. DOT-HS-801-858. Washington, DC: National Highway Traffic Safety Administration.
7. Perel, M. (1988). An analysis of pedal-related accidents using police narratives. (Unpublished manuscript available from the author.) Office of Crash Avoidance Research, National Highway Traffic Safety Administration, Washington, DC.
8. Tilley, D. H., Erwin, C. W., and Gianturco, D. T. (1973). Drowsiness and driving: preliminary report of a population survey. Paper No. 730121. Warrendale, PA: Society of Automotive Engineers (SAE).

9. Treat, J. R., Tumbas, N. S., McDonald, S. T., Shinar, D., Hume, R. D., Mayer, R. E., Stansifer, R. L., Castellan, N. J. (1977). Tri-level study of the causes of traffic accidents. DOT-HS-034-535-77-TAC(1). Institute for Research in Public Safety. Bloomington, IN: Indiana University.
10. Wierwille, W. W. (1991). Driver error in using automotive pedals. In Peters, G. A. and Peters, B. J. (Eds.) *Automotive Engineering and Litigation, Volume 4*. Wiley Law Publications (John Wiley and Sons), New York, 359-394.

Table 1
Partial listing of keywords used in the visual allocation data base searches (A through D, only, shown).

ACTIVAT,	BEND	CHANG,	CONCENTRAT,	DISTRAC,
ADJUST	BENT,	CHANNEL	CONSOL,	DIVERT,
AIR CONDIT,	BUG	CIGAR,	DASH,	DRINK
ARTIC,	CASSETT,	CITI,*BAND	DEFOG,	DRINKS
ASHTRA,	CB	CLUST,	DEFROS,	DROP,
ATTEN,	CD	COFFE,	DETRAC,	
BEE	CELLUL,	COKE	DIAL,	

Table 2
Occurrences in the interior source category, 1989 data base

Interior source (1562)
Objects in vehicle (549); Table 3
Interaction with another person or animal in vehicle (210); Table 4
Dash/Console/Steering Col., Pedals (203); Table 5
Visual occlusion (172); Table 6
Mirrors (101); Table 7
Reading in vehicle (40); Table 8
Seat/Seat belt (23); Table 9
Locks/Side windows/Doors (10)
Adjust visor (5)
Unspecified interior source (249)

Table 3
Occurrences in the objects-in-vehicle group, 1989 data base

Objects in vehicle (549)
Food, drink (93)
Smoking, lighting (79)
Insect (62)
Specified miscellaneous item (208)
Unspecified object (107)

Table 4
Occurrences in the interaction group, 1989 data base

Interaction with another person or animal in vehicle (210)
Reaching, controlling, monitoring child, animal, or adult (118)
Talking, listening, arguing (80)
Fighting (8)
Unspecified (4)

Table 5
Occurrences in the dash/console/steering column/pedals, 1989 data base

Dash/console/steering col./pedals (203)
Standard radio (104); Table 10
Instrument cluster (25); Table 11
Gearshift (17)
HVAC (15); Table 12
Wiper/washer (12)
Cellular phone (11); Table 13
Two-way radio (8); Table 14
Pedals and floor (7)
Unspecified and miscellaneous (4)

Table 6
Occurrences in the visual occlusion group, 1989 data base

Visual occlusion (172)
Faulty defroster or wiper, sun or headlight glare, dirty windshield, hood opening, etc. (86)
Temporary incapacitation (excluding falling asleep) (43)
Object in or over eye(s) (17)
Sneezing (13)
Flying debris (13)

Table 7
Occurrences in the mirrors group, 1989 data base

Mirrors (101)
Observing external vehicle, pedestrian, object, animal, etc. (50)
Adjusting mirror(s) (7)
Observing internal object, person, animal, etc. (3)
Observing external/internal, source unspecified (41)

Table 8
Occurrences in the reading-in-vehicle group, 1989 data base

Reading in vehicle (40)
Map (21)
Other printed or written matter (18)
Personal timepiece (1)

Table 9
Occurrences in the seat/seat-belt group, 1989 data base

Seat/seat belt (23)
Buckling/unbuckling belt (11)
Adjusting seat (5)
Looking into seat (unspecified) (5)
Adjusting seat belt (1)
Searching for seat belt (1)

Table 10
Occurrences in the standard radio subgroup, 1989 data base

Standard radio (104)
Adjust, observe (otherwise unspecified) (65)
Tune, change station (24)
Insert, remove cassette (15)

Table 11
Occurrences in the instrument cluster subgroup, 1989 data base

Instrument cluster (25)
Speedometer (17)
High beam indicator, light switch (3)
Fuel gauge (2)
Clock (2)
Oil pressure gauge (1)

Table 12
Occurrences in the HVAC subgroup, 1989 data base

HVAC (15)
Adjust defrost/defog (5)
Adjust heater (4)
Adjust vent(s) (3)
Adjust A/C (2)
Adjust temperature (1)

Table 13
Occurrences in the cellular phone subgroup, 1989 data base

Cellular phone (11)
Talking, listening (6)
Reach for, replace handset (3)
Dialing number (1)
Beeping, ringing (1)

Table 14
Occurrences in the two-way radio subgroup, 1989 data base

Two-way radio (8)
Reach for, replace mike (4)
Change channels (1)
Talking, listening (1)
Adjust (1)
Unspecified (1)

Table 15
Occurrences in the standard radio subgroup, multiplied by 3; 1992 data base

Standard radio (111)
Adjust, observe (otherwise unspecified) (66)
Tune, change channel (27)
Insert, remove cassette (12)
Insert, remove CD (6)

Table 16
Occurrences in the two-way radio subgroup, multiplied by 3; 1992 data base

Two-way radio (3)
Unspecified (3)

Table 17
Occurrences in the cellular phone subgroup, multiplied by 3; 1992 data base

Cellular phone (27)
Reach for, replace handset (15)
Talking, listening (12)

VISION IN VEHICLES - V
A.G. Gale et al. (Editors)

Patterns of Perceptual Failures at Intersections of Arterial Roads and Local Streets

Peter Cairney and John Catchpole

Australian Road Research Board Ltd, PO Box 156, Nunawading Vic 3131, Australia

Abstract

About 30% of casualty accidents in the Melbourne metropolitan area occur at arterial/local intersections, which is more than occur at arterial mid-block locations, at arterial/arterial intersections, or on the entire local street system. Since little was known about these accidents, a screen-based procedure for interrogating police accident files containing records of interview and statements as well as accident report forms was developed. The procedure asked about very specific aspects of accident participants' behaviour, including the manner and speed with which they approached the accident situation, whether there were distractions, whether they saw the other vehicle, whether they had looked, whether they made wrong assumptions about what the other traffic unit would do, and what they did to avoid the collision. Files relating to seven accident types based on traffic movements were examined. Not seeing the other traffic unit in time to avoid a collision was the most frequent failure identified. The percentage of drivers not seeing the other traffic unit varied with accident type. At least one driver failed to see the other vehicle in 69-80% of vehicle-vehicle collisions, and 33% of drivers in single vehicle accidents failed to detect the hazard collided with. There was little attempt to attribute faulty behaviour such as speeding or failure to signal to the other driver. In many cases, the driver looked in the appropriate direction but failed to see the other vehicle. In other cases, the view of the approaching vehicle was obscured by other traffic. The implications of these findings for countermeasures are discussed, including kerb extensions and median treatments, daytime running lights, and driver education.

1. INTRODUCTION

Earlier research by the first author found that more casualty accidents occurred at intersections of local streets and arterial roads than at any other type of location on the road network in Metropolitan Melbourne (Cairney 1986), with 31% of accidents occurring at these locations compared to 19% at arterial/arterial intersections, 28% at arterial mid-block locations, and 22% on the local street system. This large proportion of accidents is particularly disturbing in view of the relatively small number of turning movements at arterial-local intersections.

2. METHOD

This study was only possible because of the very detailed accident files maintained by the Victoria Police. Accident report forms, records of interview with and statements from accident participants and witnesses, and details of court proceedings were all filed together. Changes in police procedure mean that this data source is now available for only a small proportion of accidents, rather than for most reported accidents as was the case at the time of the accidents included in the study.

Previous investigations of behaviour associated with accidents have required coders to make a global judgement about the type of behaviour principally responsible for the accident (e.g. Lohman et al. 1976, Treat et al. 1979). When the categories and definitions developed in these studies were applied to the records available from an earlier Australian in-depth study, they were found to require heavily subjective interpretations on the part of coders and to give rise to problems distinguishing overlapping categories (Charlesworth and Cairney 1988). A different approach, pioneered by Charlesworth and Cairney (1988), was further developed in the present study. Aspects of behaviour were broken down into discrete elements, and the coder was asked to judge, on the basis of the material in the file, whether each of these elements occurred, did not occur, or could not be determined. A program was written in dBASE III which presented the questions in their correct logical relation to the coder and stored the responses. Two coders worked through the accidents independently and their answers were later compared, and any discrepancies reconciled through joint discussion and reconsideration. A full account of the process and the flowcharts used may be found in Cairney and Catchpole (1991).

So far as the study of behaviour is concerned, this approach has both advantages and disadvantages compared to in-depth accident studies. The disadvantages are that the investigator cannot determine which questions are asked of participants, cannot talk to accident survivors, and cannot seek confirmation from physical traces of events. These are offset by the advantages of being able to select the type of accident studied and by having access to enough cases to build up a picture of what typically goes wrong in specific types of accident, rather than in accidents in general.

The seven accident types listed in Table 1 were selected for study, Cairney (1986) having shown that these accounted for 80% of casualty accidents at local/arterial intersections. The link between road classification and the accident data base was available only for the year 1981, so the study was confined to accident data for that year. One hundred accidents of the six most common accident types were randomly selected. These are shown in Table 1. At the time of sampling, it was proposed to treat pedestrian and cyclist accidents as a single category, but closer examination indicated it would be more appropriate to analyse them separately. A number of cases had to be rejected, usually because the locations or the accident types had been misclassified. Very few cases had to be rejected because of irreconcilable accounts from different participants.

3. RESULTS

The key results for each type of accident participant are given in Table 1.

Table 1. Numbers of road users in different accident roles to whom particular behaviours were attributed.
Figures in brackets are percentages of all cases.

Accident type	Road user movements	Role	N	Did not see other vehicle/ road user	Looked	Visual obstruction	Other comments
Cross traffic	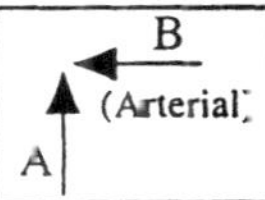	A	87	68(78)	34(39).	22(25)	62% of minor road drivers from left, 38% from right
		B	87	52(60)	35(40)	17(20)	
Right near		A	92	74(80)	48(52)	36(39)	
		B	92	53(58)	55(60)	30(33)	All but 1 were on arterial road
Right against	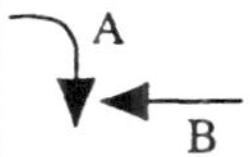	A	90	62(69)	49(54)	33(37)	91% of drivers with obstruction failed to see other vehicle; uninvolved vehicle gave way to turner in 21%
		B	90	36(40)	29(32)	28(31)	
Pedestrian		Driver	67	40(66)	13(19)	21(31)	16% had visual interference (poor contrast, glare)
		Pedestrian	67	43(64)	11(16)	19(28)	20% affected by alcohol; 27% subject to distraction
Cyclist		Driver	26	22(85)	15(58)	9(35)	
		Cyclist	26	10(38)	2(8)	5(19)	
Rear end	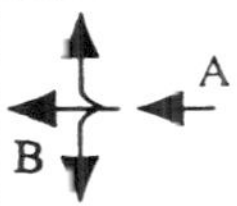	A	85	13(15)		4(5)	6% misjudged distance; 10% failed to anticipate stop; 23% noticed braking too late
		B	85	13(15)			46% turning; 13% behind turner; 2% braked or diverged suddenly
Single vehicle		Driver	91				33% failed to detect hazard; 19% lapses of attention 14% distraction; 15-22% speeding; 28% avoiding

JD: cairney table

3.1. Results for the seven accident types

1. Cross-traffic accidents

In 62% of cases, the vehicle on the minor road approached the vehicle on the arterial from the left. Sixty per cent of the arterial road drivers and 78% of the minor road drivers failed to see the other vehicle in time to avoid a collision. Visual obstructions, most usually manoeuvering vehicles, were present for 20% of drivers from the arterial road and 25% of drivers from the minor road.

2. Right-near accidents

In all cases but one, the driver proceeding straight through was on the arterial road and the turning driver approached along the minor road. Fifty eight per cent of the arterial road drivers and 80% of the minor road drivers did not see the other vehicle in time to avoid a collision. A visual obstruction was present for 33% and 39% of drivers respectively.

3. Right-against accidents

Both drivers were proceeding along the arterial road in 89% of cases, and along the minor road in 11% of cases. Forty per cent of the through drivers did not see the turning vehicles, whilst 69% of the turning drivers failed to see the through vehicle. Visual obstructions were present for 31% and 37% of drivers respectively.

4. Pedestrian accidents

Nineteen per cent of the pedestrian accidents in the sample were hit and run accidents. Sixty per cent of drivers did not see the pedestrian, and a further 22% assumed the pedestrian would stop. Only 15% of the pedestrians saw the vehicle which hit them. Ninety-four per cent of pedestrians were crossing the arterial road, the vast majority being struck by traffic proceeding straight along it. Thirty-seven per cent of pedestrians stepped onto the road in such a way as to give the driver no opportunity to take evasive action. Ten pedestrians were affected by alcohol.

5. Pedal cycle accidents

Although few cycle accidents were included in the sample, some clear patterns emerged. In 31% of cases, the driver was distracted from monitoring the cyclist (or the direction of the cyclist's approach) by some other aspect of the driving task itself, and a visual obstruction was present in 35% of cases. Eighty five per cent of drivers did not see the cyclist. Thirty-eight per cent of cyclists did not see the motor vehicle. In all of the thirty-eight per cent of cases where the cyclist had priority, the cyclist assumed that the motor vehicle would stop.

6. Rear-end accidents

Both drivers were proceeding along the arterial road in 94% of cases, and both were proceeding along the minor road in the remaining 6% of cases. Of the front drivers, 46% were turning, usually to the right, and 13% were queued behind a turning (usually right-turning) vehicle. Of the rear drivers, only 15% did not see the other vehicle, but 22% failed to notice braking by the front vehicle and 7% had been following too closely.

7. Single vehicle accidents

There was a very high proportion (19%) of single vehicle accidents due to involuntary lapses of attention, evenly spread amongst fatigue, alcohol and illness. There was also a high proportion of single vehicle accidents where distraction was a factor, often a distraction within the vehicle itself. Speed also appeared to be more of a factor in this class of accidents than in the other categories. Twenty-seven per cent of drivers claimed to have been avoiding something at the time of the accident, usually another vehicle. The pattern of casual factors differs greatly from the other accident types.

3.2. Day-time/night-time differences

For most accident types, between 18% and 33% of accidents happened at night, the exception being single vehicle accidents, 56% of which happened at night. For accidents involving more than one road user, the proportions of accidents where the other unit was not seen was similar among day-time and night-time accidents. There were, however, many more visual obstructions present in day-time accidents, the majority of them other vehicles.

3.3. Comparison of driving behaviours across accident types

Involuntary lapses of attention were rare except in the single vehicle accident category. Nine per cent of drivers were distracted, usually by other aspects of the driving task itself. Approximately 25% of drivers were affected by visual obstructions. Almost 70% of those obstructions were manoeuvering vehicles, and only 12% were parked vehicles. The proportion of visual obstructions which were caused by manoeuvering vehicles was particularly high amongst right-against and right-near accidents.

Fifty-four per cent of drivers did not see the other road user in time to avoid a collision, and in approximately 50~o of the cross-traffic and right-against accidents, neither driver saw the other vehicle.

Evasive action was taken by 37% of the road users. It was comparatively uncommon in the case of single vehicle and bicycle accidents. It was taken far more often by the driver than by the pedestrian in pedestrian accidents. In cross traffic and right-near accidents, it was taken more often by the driver on the arterial road than the driver on the minor road. In the case of right-against accidents, it was more often taken by the through driver than by the turning driver. In only 9% of cases where evasive action was taken was it judged inappropriate, and in only 2% of cases where evasive action was not taken was it judged that evasive action could usefully have been taken.

3.4. Factors which contributed to few accidents

Many of the behaviours about which questions were asked in the encoding procedure contributed to very few accidents. It is important to recognise behaviours which may be of general concern, but which in fact contribute little to accident causation.

Incorrect signalling was a factor in less than 1% of accidents and failure to use headlights when required was a factor in a further 1%. Visual obstruction caused by roadside furniture, and visual interference caused by headlight glare and fogged windows each occurred in less than 1% of accidents.

Although 63% of drivers in single vehicle accidents lost control of their vehicle, this was rare in other accident types. Eight per cent of the rear drivers in rearend accidents lost control, but less than 1% of drivers in all other accident types did so. This emphasises the point that single and multiple road user accidents result from verv different sequences of events and behaviours.

3.5. Validity and limitations of the study

Although the data used in the studv were encoded from descriptions of events given to the police, in which the individual would be likely to minimise his or her responsibility for the accident, there were few instances of irreconcilable differences in different participants' versions of events. There were also few claims of illegal or aberrant behaviours on the part of other drivers. These two features of the data encourage the view that the material analysed was a reasonable if imperfect portrayal of events.

It is important to recognise that only rarely is there evidence of excess speed available in the files, and that only accounts of uninvolved witnesses or tangible evidence such as skid marks, when reported, could be so regarded. The study can therefore provide very little in the way of understanding the contributory role of speed in accident causation. It should not be interpreted as showing that speed makes little contribution.

4. DISCUSSION

The most striking finding was the high proportion of drivers who did not see the vehicle or road user they struck. Several other investigators have drawn attention to the importance of visual factors in accident causation. For example, Sabey and Staughton (1975) concluded, on the basis of interviews with accident participants and on-scene investigations, that 10% of drivers had looked in the appropriate direction but had not seen the traffic unit collided with, while a further 6% had failed to look. Sixteen percent of pedestrians were judged to have looked but failed to see, and a further 46% not to have looked at all. A slightly later Australian study using generally similar methods but a different scheme for coding behaviour estimated that 17% did not adequately monitor either the approach of other traffic or the path they themselves were following (McLean 1979). Although not explicit about how error types were assigned to accidents Nagayama (1978) found that just over 50% of accidents involved perceptual factors, including 21.6% where the driver was preoccupied or did not notice, 16.3% where the driver believed he was attending fully, 8.1% where visibility was obstructed, and 7.8% where the hazard was seen late for other reasons.

The value of the present study lies in being able to demonstrate the extent of the problem according to the type of accident and the role played in it, and in highlighting the role of other traffic in obscuring views. The present study was designed with a view to assessing a wide rage of behavioural factors which might contribute to accident causation. The large proportion of accidents in which failure to see the other vehicle or road user is implicated is striking, as is the small proportion with factors such as misjudging speed or distance or assuming the other driver would do something else. This suggests that increased attention to measures designed to increase visibility would be worthwhile.

Pedestrians would be greatly helped by physical engineering measures which enable them to see and be seen, while still offering protection, such as kerb extensions, raised medians and pedestrian islands.

Some form of daytime running lights would also appear to have considerable potential. Swedish experience has demonstrated that the biggest resulting reductions appear to be in pedestrian and cyclist accidents, and to a lesser extent, in cross traffic accidents (Andersson and Nilsson 1981). The main benefits are therefore likely to be experienced in urban areas. As daytime running lights appear to be of little benefit in improving conspicuity at daylight levels exceeding 1200 lux (Horberg and Rumar 1979), it may be worth developing a lighting system which switches on daytime running lights when daylight falls below this critical level. Regions of the world with good natural daylight for much of the year are likely to benefit most from such technology. Possibly, much of the benefits of daytime running lights could be achieved simply and cheaply by bringing forward lighting up times. The case for earlier lighting up times in Australia has been persuasively argued by Williams (1989, 1991).

While daytime running lights may be an effective countermeasure for the 'looked but failed to see' accident, they are not likely to be much help in enabling drivers to see vehicles hidden by other traffic. While it is difficult to establish tangible benefits for countermeasures based on publicity and education alone, the issue of vehicles hidden by traffic has some characteristics which may enable it to be effectively tackled by these measures. It ought to be possible to produce video footage which shows vehicles emerging in unexpected ways which will prove memorable and make an impact, and the behavioural change sought is clear and simple.

REFERENCES

Andersson, K. and Nilsson, G. (1981). The effects of accidents on compulsory use of running lights during daylight in Sweden. VTI (Swedish Road and Traffic Research Institute), Rapport 208A.

Cairney, P.T. (1986). Major/minor intersections and junctions - a greater problem than we think? Proceedings of the 13th Australian Road Research Board Conference, Part 9, pp. 78-89.

Cairney, P.T. And Catchpole, J.E. (1991). Road users behaviours which contribute to accidents at urban arterial/local intersections. Australian Road Research Board, Research Report ARR 197. Charlesworth, K.D. and Cairney, P.T. (1988). Development of techniques for studying unsafe driving actions. Australian Road Research Board, Special Report SR 39.

Horberg, U. and Rumar, K. (1979). The effects of running lights on vehicle conspicuity. Ergonomics, 22, pp. 165-173.

Lohman, L.S., Leggett, E.C., Stewart, J.R. and Campbell, B.J. (1976). Identification of unsafe driving actions and related countermeasures. Chapel Hill, University of North Carolina, Report No. DOT-H-5-01259. Mclean, A.J. (1979). Adelaide in-depth accident study 1975-1979, part 8: summary and recommendations. University of Adelaide, Road Accident Research Unit, Adelaide, South Australia.

Nagayama, Y. (1978). Role of visual perception in driving. IATSS Research, 2, pp. 64-73.

Sabey, B.E. and Staughton, G.C. (1975). Interacting roles of road environment, vehicle and road user. Proceedings of the 5th Conference of the International Association for Accident and Traffic Medicine, London, 1-5 September 1975.

Treat, J.R., Tumbas, N.S., Mcdonald, S.T., Shinar, D., Hume, R.D., Mayer, R.E., Stansifer, R.L. and Castellan, N.J. (1979). Tri-level study of the causes of traffic accidents: final report, Volume 1: Causal factor tabulations and assessments. U.S. Dept Transport, National Highway Traffic Safety Admin, Washington DC, Report DOT-HS-805-085.

William, P.R. (1989). Driving at dusk and the conspicuity role of vehicle lights: a review. Awtralian Road Research, 19(4), pp. 277-287.
Williams, P.R. (1991). Use of vehicle parking lights during dusk. Australian Road Research, 21(4),pp.70-77.

3: COGNITIVE ASPECTS OF VISUAL INFORMATION PROCESSING

VISION IN VEHICLES - V
A.G. Gale et al. (Editors)

Beyond the Eye: Cognitive Factors in Drivers' Visual Perception

M. Wierda

Traffic Research Centre, University of Groningen, P.O. Box 69, 9750 AB Haren, The Netherlands

Summary

Moving around in traffic with a vehicle or as a pedestrian requires an enormous amount of visual information to be processed. Accident analyses stipulate the role of human perceptual errors. The qualitative aspects of this type of error besides a normative analysis of 'vision in driving' are used to formulate the requirements for a comprehensive theory of seeing during driving. The theory concentrates on the internal, mental representation of the driving environment while an attempt is made to formalize the process of learning by experience. Finally the theory is applied to practical traffic research issues in which the faculty of seeing is dominant.

1. INTRODUCTION

"The eye seems to have a mind of its own, while the mind appears to peek in the eye's mind". This poetic claim may have, even if only partly true, great consequences for those who try to understand the performance and perceptual strategies of road users. This conclusion is enforced by another almost poetic yet undocumented claim: "Driving is Seeing".

Frequently poetry gives the reader implicit answers to unraised questions but, moreover, it mainly yields explicit questions. For the assertions above we may wonder what 'seeing', 'an eye's mind' and 'peeking' is.

In the next sections a summary of a theory is given that is intended to capture the notion of seeing in the context of driving. In doing so some arguments are raised against the suggested independency of the eye and mind. The starting point of the theory is the assumption that the human being uses highly structured internal representations of his environment and that he uses these structures to organize, filter or block perceptual input from the diverse sensory systems.

Before starting the tour along a shorthand normative analysis and theoretical model of seeing while driving (sections 3 and 4 respectively) and the evaluation of some empirical phenomena (section 5) two observations concerning visual perception and accident involvement will be discussed.

The reported research is supported by the Division of Transportation and Traffic Engineering of the Dutch Ministry of Transport and Public Works.

2. A MAIN CAUSE OF ACCIDENT INVOLVEMENT: PERCEPTUAL ERROR

An in-depth analysis of 2,036 traffic accident (Staughton and Story, 1977) revealed that 95% of accidents were due to human error. Dominant types of error were characterized as 'perceptual' and listed as 'Distraction' and 'Looked, but failed to see' (causing 16% and 17% of the total number of accidents reported respectively). The study used post-accident, structured interviews, perhaps an appropriate method to extract simple 'single factor' causes but prone to subjectivity since the driver has had ample time to reconstruct the accident and rationalize about what happened . Above that, complex accident causations are unlikely to be found. Firstly because the driver might not be able to remember what happened since he/she could be 'confused' (a typical perceptual error) and secondly because the complex, dynamic perceptual information is not at all easily introspectively accessible.

In a recent study into the causes of urban accidents, Carsten et. al. (1989) conclude that 70% of the 1,254 reported accidents occurred at junctions. Strikingly only 12% were 'uncontrolled: 12% had traffic lights and 72% (!) had Give Way signs. Perhaps surprisingly, in 93% of accidents the involved road users knew the road 'well' or 'quite well'. Urban accidents are most frequent. In the Netherlands 60% of all accidents happen in built up areas (CBS, 1992). If we may assume that the findings of Carsten et. al. can be generalized we must conclude that most accidents occur in built up areas on regulated junctions that are known 'well' to 'quite well'.

From these two sets of data two requirements for a theory on vision while driving are formulated. Firstly the theory should account for the type of error indicated above. Secondly it must explain, and better predict, the fact that a major part of accidents happens on regulated intersections that are known or quite well known. In the next section a number of visual tasks are discussed that should be accounted for as well.

3. NORMATIVE VISUAL TASKS IN DRIVING

Breaking down 'vision in driving' pragmatically results in a long list of both elementary and complex perceptual tasks (see Wierda and Aasman, 1991). An excerpt of the taxonomy is given below.

1. Determination of lateral and longitudinal position, changes in these positions and alternations in the changes (lateral and longitudinal speed and acceleration respectively)
2. Same as 1 but for heading angle
3. Detection of obstacles
4. Localization and reading of route indications
5. Localization, recognition and classification of road users
6. Recognition of prototypical, actual traffic situation
7. Control over the orientation of the selective visual perceptual system (via body, head, and eye-movements and shifts of attention)

The taxonomy has been shortened significantly but it allows the following observation: the subtasks can be grouped into three qualitatively different sets.

- Tasks 1 and 2 are 'continuous' in character and might be conceived of as first order (position), second order (speed) and third order (acceleration) error minimalization routines or control loops. This type of compensatory mechanism requires frequent input. As such the visual perceptual channel must be allocated to these tasks most of the time. The resulting scanning behaviour with respect to these tasks may be modelled mathematically. For instance Riemersma (1987) found that drivers permit themselves NOT to look for a period at the straight road they are driving on that is dependent on the moment the drivers expect to come close to the side or middle road striping. The Time to Line Crossing (TLC) theory predicted that the period of time drivers allow themselves not to look at the road becomes shorter if the driving speed increases. The prediction was quite accurate.
- Obstacles as mentioned in Task 3 are, by definition, unexpected and have therefore an exogenous perceptual character: they are to be detected 'bottom up'. The phylogenetic 'old' orientation reflex (see Solokov, 1976) is considered a major mechanism in the smooth but quick change of attentional orientation. For instance a moving object, a potential obstacle, may 'attract' attention while 90 degrees out of the line of sight, resulting in a body- and/or head- and/or eye movement. Besides the change of the attentional orientation the reflex also prepares the subject for quick action by, amongst others, changes in the muscle tone and heart rate.
- Tasks 1 through 3 are distinguishable from the remainder of the list by the fact that the driver may perform these tasks 'empty-minded': to drive (more or less) straight and to respond to a potential dangerous object/obstacle it is not required for the subject to bring any conceptual knowledge or 'meaning' to bear. Visual perception in these situations is 'data driven' or 'Bottom Up'. In contrast, tasks 4 to 7 do require a priori knowledge about the task-environment: recognition of a prototypical, actual traffic situation presumes an instant matching of a perceived element against an internal representation. Therefore visual perception is thought to be 'conceptually driven' or 'Top Down'. It is claimed that the Top Down capability is a major factor in 'adequate driving' and as such the form and qualities of the internal representation (and its development during practice) play a crucial role in our understanding of 'seeing in driving'.

4. A FUNCTIONAL MODEL OF VISION AND SPATIAL RECOGNITION IN DRIVING

In the first part of this section four psychological phenomena will be discussed as arguments for the claim that a clear functional distinction exists between the lower visual representations and abstract, high order representations. It will be claimed furthermore that our capability to be aware of a dynamic, spatial environment resides in the abstract representation. In the second part of this section a proposal for a theory of 'spatial awareness' is outlined.

The first observation is that we are aware of and act in a highly stable spatial environment while retinal input is rather *un*stable due to motion in the perceived scenery, for example moving road users and waving trees, and due to motion of body, head and eye, inclusive of micro saccades.

The second observation concerns recognition. If an object was to be recognized by its physical surface structure, comparable to a 'bitmap', the brain would have to store an endless number of appearances of the object since we are able to recognize, for example, a tree that was never seen before, from an infinite number of viewing angles. Above that, recognition by matching would require an infinite number of memory traces to be tested against an infinite number of retinal impressions, an implausible solution indeed. Furthermore, recognition by partial stimulus information is hardly feasible by matching 'bitmaps', while humans are extremely good at overcoming stimulus degradation.

The third argument is based on the fact that we make many mistakes in our daily life. It is called 'stupid' to run into a closed door and 'miss' a red traffic light, yet it may happen any time. Above that, we quite easily accept our mistakes and change our ideas about the actual environment. The question is: what is changed and how. It is unlikely that a 'bit-map' like representation is 'repainted'. A major argument for this claim will be given at the end of the section.

A last argument concerns the human capability to 'reason' over spatial relations among objects. Irrespective of viewing position we are capable of indicating relative position and motion, height in the plain and distance among objects: "that car is farther away than that one, but the first is closing in rapidly". According to Piaget this capability develops during the 'concrete operational' phase of cognitive development (see Phillips, 1975, for an overview). A crucial process required for this capability is an internal representation of the environment that allows a shift from the viewer centred perspective to an object centred perspective.

A full description of the model of vision during motion can be found in Wierda and Aasman (1991) here the text will concentrate on the 'higher' internal representations and processes that allow spatial reasoning. A series of elementary visual routines are assumed that are considered capable of deriving 'data driven' an internal representation from the retinal impression. Examples are contour detection based on motion of a 'blob' against a background, detection of closed contours by boundary tracing and the detection of separated fields by distinguishable 'features'. Results of these elementary routines add to a representation that captures the visual environment in separated blobs while the orientation of the surface of the blob is roughly known.

A qualitatively important step is the transformation from this low level 'blob' representation (no objects and backgrounds are identified yet) to an object centred spatial representation. Marr's 'skeleton' model (1982) and implicitly Minsky's 'visual frames' (1975) are capable of explaining the transformation. The former will be discussed shortly.

The skeleton theory assumes that a blob is analyzed in terms of a main and auxiliary axis. The first roughly indicates the orientation, for example a vector running from the feet to the head in the case where we perceive a human torso, while the auxiliary axis indicates the 'volume' of the object. These internal representations are called generalized cones. Complex objects, for example a human figure inclusive of legs, arms, head, hands and feet, are composed of series of generalized cones. The main axis of the constituents are connected to the prime main axis hierarchically via slots. The latter specify the allowed movements of the elements with respect to the main axis. The number of formal variables (axis, degrees of freedom) is surprisingly low with the consequence that vast numbers of hierarchical constructed objects may be remembered with a minimum of storage capacity. Moreover recognition is simplified tremendously: a single remembered skeleton may be compared with a perceived object, from *any* viewing angle by internally manipulating the remembered skeleton. Examples are rotation of the main axis to compensate for the viewing angle and enlargement to compensate for viewing distance.

Recognition of stationary objects against a background is one thing, perception while moving through a scene with moving objects is another. During straight driving only a fraction of the retinal input is unchanged, yet we are capable of recognizing an entire scene in a flash. Can a skeleton-like theory, as outlined above, account for this remarkable capability? We would claim that it can, but need to assume that motion must be represented explicitly and, as such, be 'remembered' as an integral part of a three dimensional (3D) object. Wierda and Aasman (1991) proposed to add to the skeleton representation a single vector that indicates the direction and pace of movement along the main axis. It allows the recognition of objects, for example a nearly 'invisible' car (sic), by degredated contours *and* its typical speed. It is an ongoing debate, started by Kosslyn & Pomerantz (1977) whether or not people 'reason' in space and time in an analogue fashion. The current theory has been called the 3 1/2D model, indicating the 3 dimensions of space and the implicit, hence 1/2D, capability to represent the temporal, dynamic aspects.

Long Term Memory storage of 3 1/2D skeletons for moving objects consists of a main axis, indicating a length, an auxiliary axis, indicating volume, and a speed vector, indicating a direction and amount of displacement in time. The long term memorized skeleton may be adapted constantly with values for the axis and vectors that are encountered most frequently, as such *prototypes* for dynamic, 3 1/2D objects are *learned.* This flexible internal representation may explain why people adapt so easily to driving on the 'wrong' side of the road going from the continent to the UK or vice versa.

If values for the axis and speed vectors are not immediately available from bottom up perception, the values of the long term memory structure are activated, acting as default terminal values. The activation of default values may explain why we are capable of *generating* a vivid and detailed awareness of our spatial environment while visual input may be seriously hampered.

It is an intriguing issue where our awareness resides of a once recognized car, infrastructure or, more complicated, a specific traffic situation. Once a car on a road is detected and recognized, is it copled into some 'working memory' or written on a mental blackboard? Dennet (1992) takes a strong position by claiming that there is not such an isolated neurological locus, whether a 'blackboard' or isolated memory structure. To be more concrete consider the following example.

Imagine yourself riding a bicycle on a familiar, brick cyclepath. Tired as you are, you look down just in front of the cycle. You *realize* that the pattern in the bricks goes on for at least a kilometre, it is easy to imagine how the brick pattern looks like the next 10 meters without lifting your eyes.

It is conceivable that the basis for this 'brick cyclepath' mental image is a contoured blob filled with a pattern. This would imply that a mental 'blackboard' is required. However, the claim is made, following Dennet, that there is no such gadget, the argument for this conclusion is a question: If a blob is projected 'somewhere' and it is filled with the structure of the bricks, 'who' or 'what' is going to look at this projection?! A subsequent visual system that, in its turn, will project the perceived image 'somewhere'?! It would be a Homunculus theory pur sang.

It is concluded that the activation of a blob and the attribute that the blob has a certain surface brick pattern *is* the content of awareness. Nothing needs to be added or projected. The same line of reasoning may account for 3D object recognition: once a car is detected and recognized (it is 'seen') via a matching 3 1/2D skeleton prototype the activation of the prototype and adaption to the actual vehicle are the only required elements to make the driver 'aware' of the car.

In attempting to apply the 3 1/3D theory in traffic safety research (see for example Wierda & Maring, 1993) it became unpleasantly clear that the model is far from complete. It could not deal with several aspects of driving behaviour. Three important aspects are discussed shortly as an introduction to the extension of the theory given below.

Firstly, both novice and experienced drivers are able to take hints from an instructor such as 'look for *road users* on the left on *this type* of intersection' and on '*these roundabouts* merging *traffic* has priority', while for novice drivers it is a difficult task indeed. The questions are how conceptual/verbal instructions are transformed such that they are applicable in our spatial/visual reasoning and why novice drivers have to spend much effort. A closely related issue is our capability to 'reason spatially' in terms of centimetres and milliseconds, while we are mostly only able *to say* the car 'passed close' and 'drove fast'. Apparently we have no direct verbal access to the internal spatial representation. For this reason outcomes of accident studies in which post hoc interviews are used to find the cause of an accident are seriously doubted. However, quite often no other methods are available, though asking subjects to draw what happened might be a good suggestion: one drawing may say more than a thousand words.

Secondly it is yet an open question how recognized situations result in actions: when a car on a collision course is detected, how is the complex pattern of shifting back, releasing the gas pedal and braking, triggered and executed?

Thirdly, it is also an open question how one 'knows *where* to look'. Somehow, a traffic light is expected on the right side of the road, near an intersection. The issue is what this expectation is based upon.

All issues can be summarized by asking how conceptual, verbal, spatial/visual information and motoric output are functionally interrelated. For completeness we may add to this list olfactoric, haptic, auditive and rhythmical information. It is proposed that different types and pieces of knowledge are linked by spider like structures. Each leg of a 'spider' holds a slot for a piece of information of a specific type or it is connected to another spider's leg. Perceived and 'generated' information flows through the network of more or less sleeping or inactive spiders: if the number of active legs of the spider come above a critical minimum, the body of the spider awakes and arouses all its legs by which a spreading of activation is caused to (functionally related) neighbour spiders. The idea of spider information structures is partly comparable to Minsky's visual frames (see Minsky, 1986). It has been found that a network of spiders may act as a production rule system, which allows simulation of the network in a digital computer (see Anderson 1983).

For a spider to become active it is not necessary that all its terminals (legs) are activated. However, once awakened all terminals are aroused causing the 'transmission' through the network of type and form of information the leg initially expected. As such *default* values are added to the representation and we may become aware of them. It allows recognition of objects by partial stimulus information: while cycling on the right side of the road with the intention to turn left, it is enough to *hear* a car closing in from behind to 'know' that it will have a certain size, speed and that it follows a certain trajectory. A 'higher order spider' with one terminal triggered by 'the car from behind' spider and another by an intended manoeuvre to turn left, will awake hastily and inhibit any spider but a 'look over the left shoulder and hold' one.

Returning to the issues raised it is claimed that verbal instructions, and written signs and messages, must be converted from linguistic elements to conceptual representations. Only the latter are used directly in the spider-like structures. An answer to the last question, how does one know where to look, is given by assuming that it is learned. It is learned via changing the terminal defaults, while complex sequences are learned by compositions of specific spiders. A spider that 'recognizes' a specific traffic situation (its terminals match the current short term activity pattern) will directly activate a sequence of eye-, head- and body-movements.

It is conceivable that repeatedly concurrent active spiders are structurally connected: the defaults on the connecting terminals are omitted and a functional new spider is created that is more specific and faster in matching. It is, however, also more rigid: the connecting terminals cannot be adapted any more. See Anderson (1983) for a discussion of composition of data-structures.

5. SOME DRIVING BEHAVIOUR PHENOMENA RELATED TO THE THEORY

Realizing that the outline of the theory is truly concise (see Wierda & Aasman (1991) for an elaborated version) we turn to some phenomena that may be explained by the theory. The goal of doing so is twofold. Firstly from the examples it may become clear that the theory is highly flexible due to its capacity to explain learning and behavioral adaptation. Secondly, the virtue of flexibility may also be a curse: it may prohibit concrete behavioral predictions which prevents empirical verification. This major issue will be addressed in the discussion.

The conclusion of section 2 that most accidents occur on regulated junctions that are known 'well' to 'quite well' may be explained by indicating that the experienced driver will use specific, highly detailed visual/spatial prototypes activated in long term memory. As such the perception of the environment is for a large part Top Down: much of the spatial lay out of the infrastructure and presence and intended manoeuvres of other road users will be derived from memory. Given the complexity and number of objects to attend to, visual perception will mainly serve the verification of the internal representation. In this case, a single unexpected *and* undetected object may cause an error and, as such, an accident since the driver is completely unprepared.

In a study on the behaviour of cyclists on intersections (see Top and Timmermans, 1988) it was repeatedly observed that cyclists could not remember whether the intersection they just passed had traffic signs or triangular road markings. Above that, they had great difficulty in describing the situation encountered in terms of the presence and actions of other road users. Again, this phenomenon may be explained by pointing to the internal representation. For example the behavioral relevant information that an intersection is regulated will not be 'stored' via explicit entities for the signs but via a specific spider like structure that captures the spatial lay-out and that triggers the desired behaviour. When asked, the road user has to *reconstruct* the entire situation and 'peek' into the mental image. Above that, he has to transform the elements of the abstract representation into lexical entities and make a verbal 'story' out of the mental image: answering questions about experienced traffic situations is a complex process indeed and prone to error.

Currently in many European countries drivers are advised to use headlights during the day. The 3 1/2D model predicts that in the long term the default terminals of the driver's 3 1/2D prototypes of cars will be changed, it will have running lights. For immediate recognition, then, a car must have running lights and one may wonder how much the recognition of a single car without lights, in particular in a less optimal ambient light condition, is slowed down and to what accident involvement this may lead. It should be stressed that the cause of the delay is *not only* the difference in conspicuity but mainly the explicit expectation that [cars] have [lights].

6. CONCLUSION AND DISCUSSION

The 3 1/2D theory's competence to explain complex visual/perceptual phenomena during driving by pointing to internal processes such as prototype adaptation and composition of spider like information structures may be considered as a virtue but at the same time the model's generative character prevents explicit behavioral predictions: it may explain and predict anything. This would leave the theory un-testable and thus scientifically of no value if recent developments in cognitive science and Artificial Intelligence had not facilitated testing the theory via simulation. The 31/2D theory has partly been implemented in a production rule system called SOAR (Newell 1990), the results are highly encouraging. The implementation generates head and eye movements and is capable of shifting the locus of attention (Wierda & Aasman, 1991). Via the model empirically observed global and local eye movement scanpaths can be interpreted in terms of the perceptual goals that generate them, whether bottom up or top down. Above that, testing the implementation with empirical data allows continuous refinement of the 3 1/2D model.

The most important conclusion of this line of research is that the strategy of postulating and implementing internal representations and processes that are considered necessary and sufficient for the perceptual/cognitive task of driving, in short building a computational model, will be more fruitful than trying to give post hoc explanations of an ever growing pool of data.

REFERENCES

1. Anderson, J.R. (1983) The architecture of cognition. London: Harvard University Press. Carsten, O.M.J., Tight, M.R., Southwell, M.T. (1989). Urban Accidents: why do they happen. Leeds: Institute for Transport Studies.
2. CBS, Central Bureau for Statistics (1992). Statistic of accidents on public roads. The Hague: SDU/Publishers
3. Dennet, D.C. (1992) "Filling In" versus Finding Out; a ubiquitous confusion in cognitive science. In H.L. Pick jr., P van den Broek & D.C. Knill (eds.): Cognition, conceptual and methodological issues. Washington: American Psychological Association.
4. Kosslyn, S.M., & Pomerantz, J.R. (1977) Imagery, propositions, and the form of internal representations. Cognitive Psychology: 9, 52-76.
5. Marr, D. (1982) Vision. San Francisco: Freeman.
6. Minsky, M. (1975) A framework for representing knowledge. In P.H. Winston (ed.), The psychology of computer vision. New York: Prentice Hall.

7. Minsky, M. (1986) The Society of Mind. New York: Simon & Schuster.
8. Newell, A.N. (1990) Unified theories of cognition. London: Harvard University Press.
9. Phillips, J.L. (1975) The Origins of Intellect: Piaget's theory. San Francisco: Freeman.
10. Riemersma, J.B.J. (1987) Visual cues in straight road driving. Soest: Neo Print.
11. Solokov,E.N. (1976) Leaning and memory: habituation as negative learning. In M.R.
12. Rosenzweig & E.L. Bennet (eds.): Neural mechanisms of learning and memory. Cambridge, Mass.: MIT Press.
13. Staughton, G.C. & Storie, V.J. (1977) Methodology of an in-depth accident investigation survey. Report LR 762. Crowthorne: Transportation and Road Research Laboratory.
14. Top, T. & Timmermans, D. (1988) Behaviour of cyclists at intersections. In J.A.
15. Rothengatter en R.A. de Bruin (eds.): Road user behaviour. Assen: van Gorcum.
16. Wierda, M., & Aasman, J. (1991) Seeing and driving, computation, algorithms and implementation. VK 91-06. Haren: Traffic Research Centre.
17. Wierda, M., & Maring, W. (1993) Interpreting eye movements of traffic participants. In D. Brogan (ed.) Proceedings of the second international conference on eye movements. London: Taylor and Francis.

VISION IN VEHICLES - V
A.G. Gale et al. (Editors)

Iconic Information Presentation : Pictograms Understanding, Study about Ambiguity

M.P. Bruyas[a&b], B. Le Breton[a] and A. Pauzie[a]

[a] Laboratory Health COmfort, INRETS / LESCO,
109 avenue Salvador Allende, 69675 - Bron, France

[b] LEACM, University of Human Sciences, Lyon II, 69500 - Bron, France

1. INTRODUCTION

To answer the increasing mobility, it is necessary to use more and more symbolic information. To respond to the safety necessity, this information also needs to be as clear and as quickly understood as possible by the whole population, especially on the road where the time constraint is more important. Then, as an immediate source of information, pictograms are increasingly important in our environment. There are numerous advantages in using symbolic messages compared to written ones, as they are understood without involving language. The legibility distance is also higher than for written messages (Jacobs, 1975).

Nevertheless, even if, in some cases, the pictogram design has to fit into normalisation constraints, not all of them are equally recognised by the population (Bruyas & al., 1992). The understanding of a pictogram is not always given by the symbolic representation itself. To convey complex information, it is sometimes necessary to combine several elements or codes in the same pictogram. In some cases, these associations might lead to misunderstanding or ambiguity. Some of those combinations have been tested in the two following experiments, in order to elaborate some guidelines, and a comparison of pictogram understanding has been made between young and older people.

2. GRAPHIC CONTENTS AND GUIDANCE SIGNS

2.1 Method and design

The experiment was programmed by J.F. Laurens using an object oriented language. It was run on a compatible computer IBM/PC AT with DOS and Windows. The statistics were obtained under UNIX with the software SAS. In order to smooth the subject effect, the statistics were performed with standardised data.

32 subjects were tested :

- 16 young adults (26-35 years old, mean age = 30.5),
- 16 older adults (more than 61 years old, mean age = 66.5).

The majority were right-handed (except 2 subjects). None of them declared having any problem in using the computer. All the young subjects had good vision acuity, corrected or not, but 5 of the older ones had some deficiencies (as measured by the Ergovision test of acuity). Information pictograms with right or left orientation or composed of arrows were tested, paired with directional information. Each combination automatically appeared once in the centre of the screen of a computer until the subject answered. The subjects had to show in which direction they were supposed to go after the pictogram display, by manipulating the directional arrows of the computer keyboard : right, left, straight on or no direction. 84 different combinations were tested (sizes of the stimuli : 5*6,5cm and 5,5*5,5cm). The level of complexity was evaluated in term of response time.

To avoid a rank order, the pictograms followed one another in 4 different orders. A training session was run equally to prevent a training effect, the subjects began by learning the keys, answering other pictograms in the same conditions. Lastly, to understand the difficulties they met, a short interview was conducted during which the subjects explained how they reacted to the different combinations.

Three factors were studied :

- *The graphical content effect* (7 modalities), 4 icons with a specific orientation, and 3 others including arrow(s).

(1) Stairs down, (2) Stairs up, (3) Car, (4) Runner, (5) Entry, (6) Meeting Point, (7) Lift

The meaning of each symbol was given to the subjects before the beginning of the experiment. The 5 first ones were presented once left and once right in all of the following conditions.

- *The pictogram frames effect* (3 modalities) the icons could be inside or linked with an arrow or without a directional sign :

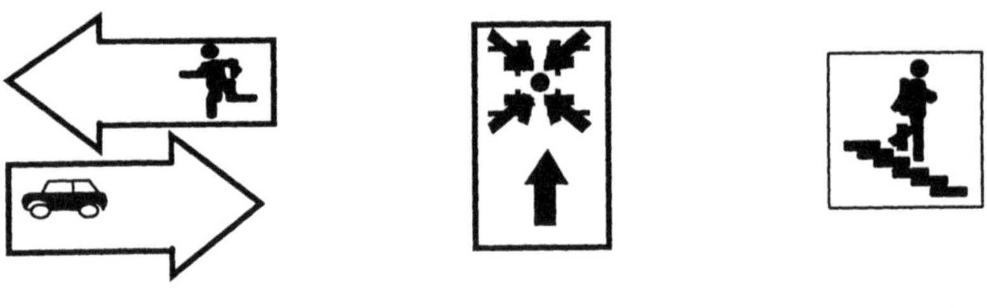

- *The concordance or discordance effect* between the orientation of the graphical content and orientation of the arrow (4 modalities), concordance, conflict, orthogonality (when the direction was straight on) and no direction.

2.2. Results

When a subject cannot ignore the direction given by a graphic content, a Stroop-like interference effect increases the response time needed to perceive the information conveyed by the additional arrowing. As a matter of fact, it seems to be interesting to define what produces the biggest ambiguity in the pictograms.

2.2.1. Informative value of the frame

The results showed that the type of arrowing could be more or less disturbing. The presentation of an icon inside an arrow shape frame was less confusing than when the icon and the arrow were combined in a rectangular frame (the response time was significantly higher, Mann-Whitney, $p<.01$). It seems to indicate different level of complexity. Besides, the interview which followed this part of the experiment showed that the presentation inside an arrow was preferred by most of the subjects.

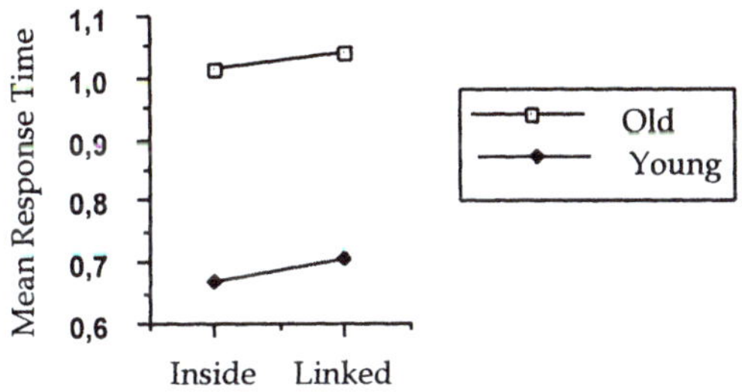

Figure 1. Response Time differences between the 2 types of frame (Unstandardised data).

The fact that the frame shape was obviously meaningful made the combination easier to understand because the two different types of information (arrowing and graphical content), were given in two different ways (graphic and frame), especially when these two types of information were very similar like "Entry" composed of an arrow.

The highest differences between the 2 information frames were obtained by :

- "Entry", "Stairs up" and "Car" (Mann-Whitney, $p<.01$), youngest subjects.
- "Stairs up" (Mann-Whitney, $p<.05$), oldest subjects.

2.2.2. Graphical content

An icon effect was registered showing that the arrowing was more or less disturbing (the response time increases) in combination with the icons (Kruskal-Wallis, $p<.01$).

Table 1.
General Mean Response Time (Unstandardised data)

Young			Old		
graphic contents	Mean	Std.Dev.	graphic contents	Mean	Std.Dev.
Car	.684	.211	Car	1.010	.387
Runner	.688	.200	Stairs down	1.025	.453
Stairs down	.700	.204	Runner	1.030	.398
Stairs up	.705	.195	Stairs up	1.074	.452
Lift	.742	.261	Lift	1.119	.493
Meeting point	.761	.223	Entry	1.141	.524
Entry	.777	.261	Meeting point	1.154	.476

When the graphic content is already composed of an arrow, the addition of an arrowing makes it harder to read (Table 1). The response time was significantly longer than for the other graphical contents (Mann-Whitney, $p<.01$). However, the fact that an icon could be read more or less as a whole moderates this effect.

Surprisingly, the "Meeting point", which contained 4 arrows disturbed some subjects less, especially young ones, because they considered the 4 arrows as a single piece of information (this result appeared through subject interviews). But it seemed to be totally disturbing for other subjects who could not consider it as a whole. The old subjects, who have more difficulties to extract some information out of a complex environment, were generally very disturbed.

2.2.3. Concordance and discordance

The response time increased significantly, for the 2 populations, when icons and arrowing were orthogonal, indicating to go straight on (Mann-Whitney, $p<.01$).

The discordance conditions had different effects in relation with the 2 populations. The response time was not significantly different for the young subjects, but it was for the old ones (Mann-Whitney, $p<.01$). For the latter ones, the pictograms which obtained the highest differences of response time (between concordance and discordance) were "Entry" ($p<.01$) and "Car" ($p<.05$). Whitaker & al. (1986), who had evaluated the matching of icons and arrowing with young subjects, showed that some of the combinations ("Amstrak", composed with an arrow and "Airport") were more conflicting than other ones. The plane of their "Airport" was oriented up and down, which is a common condition with regard to the "Stairs" in our protocol. These pictograms obtained longer response time in conflicting conditions, which could then suggest that, when an arrowing is associated with an oblique graphical content, it becomes harder to be understood.

2.2.4. Age effect

The response time obtained by the old subjects were less homogeneous than those of the young ones. Generally the young subjects answered more quickly, but sometimes the mean response time was quite similar. Different studies have shown an increase in the response time probably due to a longer decision time in relation to the age (Welford (1981) Mishara

(1984)...). With time constraints the older persons are also more penalised than the younger, and the individual variations increase over 70 years old. A great difference was established depending on the graphical contents. All the old subjects were disturbed by the icons which contained an arrow, but some were also disturbed by "Car", or "Man", saying it is dangerous to walk or drive backward (when icon and arrowing were conflicting), showing again more heterogeneity in the older persons. It seems as though they sometimes read the information at first sight, and need some more time to switch to the symbolic meaning.

3. REPRESENTATION OF INTERDICT

3.1. Method

The method used in this part was very similar that in the first experiment. It was run using the same material, with the same subjects. Five graphical contents have been presented, associated with 3 different frame shapes and various colours : red, blue, green, yellow and black (size of the stimuli : 4,5*4,5cm). At least 126 different configurations were obtained (one configuration was made of the combination of 1 shape, 1 or 2 colours for the background and outlines, 1 black or red graphical content). The subjects had to decide, as quickly as possible if the pictogram was showing something permitted or forbidden. Each pictogram stayed on the screen until the subject answered with one of the 2 keys of a mouse :

- Yes for authorised
- No for forbidden.

3.2. Results

Everybody has his own mental representation of interdiction symbols. For this experiment, the subjects generally adopted a rule to make their choice. Some of them carried out all the experiment using the same rule, others changed during the test. However, in spite of a chaotic aspect of the answers, each subject could at least explain how he decided to answer, faced to the unexpected aspect of the pictograms.

3.2.1. Effect of colour

The analysis of the interviews which followed the experiment showed that the subjects encountered great difficulties to encode the icon with *red*. Spontaneously, they decided that red indicated something forbidden, but, after seeing some pictograms, most of the subjects began to hesitate. They proposed different possibilities for the significance of the red colour :

- Red, especially paired with another colour, only conveys the warning of a danger. You can do it, but with some attention. Surprisingly, some of the subjects who have given this interpretation answered "authorised", and others "forbidden".

- Red determines the use of an object (for example, a red telephone is reserved for emergency), it is just an additional information. It means that the object has to be used by a certain category of persons and then it is forbidden and authorised at the same time.

- Red gives a constraint to the using of an object. A red camera means we must use a flash for example.

- Red enhances the object : it is not forbidden but nicer to see.

Even though most of the subjects considered red as indicating something forbidden (they mainly referred to the car driver conditioning), red associated with an icon seems to be an insufficient condition to forbid something or an action : red can reinforce when it is forbidden but is not sufficient to indicate it by itself. Nevertheless, the quantity of red in an icon modulates the responses, and the strategies of coding. A lot of red increased the response time, because the subjects who decided to code "Yes" were more disturbed. More "No" responses were equally obtained when the background was red (young subjects 73.9%, old ones 43.7%), than when the outlines were red (young subjects 43.5%, old ones 35.4%) or when just the graphical content was red (young subjects 32.2%, old ones 34.8%). The results were very similar when red was combined with another colour.

We can also notice that the old subjects were less sensitive to the red colour as an interdict (they answered "Yes" more often). This could be seen as a generation effect, refer to Mackie (1967) who noted that they often know less about the use of symbolic codes. Besides, the results showed that when red is associated with a *slash* across the pictogram, nearly all the subjects have considered that the action was forbidden.

As well, a slashed sign coloured in blue (which symbolises the end of something forbidden on the road), was considered forbidden by nearly all the subjects. But, for this colour, only one referred to the road signs, and answered "Yes". These results have been confirmed by the registered variations of response time. Young and old subjects answered significantly more slowly for the red pictograms without slash compared to the other ones (Mann-Whitney, $p<.01$), and quicker to the slashed pictograms compared to those without slash (Mann-Whitney, $p<.01$).

Table 2.
Mean Response Time for young subjects (Unstandardised data)

	Young						
Responses	"YES"			"NO"			
Pictograms	Red	Other colours	Total	Red	Other colours	Total	
Slashed	2	2	4	237	139	376	(Frequencies)
	1.076	.525	.801	.711	.787	.739	(Mean RT)
1 colour	184	510	694	131	16	147	
	.928	.743	.792	1.112	.964	1.096	
2 colours	201	363	564	168	15	183	
	.937	.812	.857	1.137	1.125	1.136	
Total	387	875	1262	536	170	706	
	.933	.771	.821	.943	.834	.916	

Table 3.
Mean Response Time for old subjects (Unstandardised data)

Old							
Responses	"YES"			"NO"			
Pictograms	Red	Other colours	Total	Red	Other colours	Total	
Slashed	6	10	16	234	131	365	(Frequencies)
	1.274	1.175	1.212	.878	1.086	.953	(Mean RT)
1 colour	205	483	688	123	30	153	
	1.045	.973	.995	1.269	1.472	1.308	
2 colours	225	322	547	150	44	194	
	.991	1.085	1.047	1.325	1.402	1.342	
Total	436	815	1251	507	205	712	
	1.021	1.020	1.02	1.105	1.210	1.135	

Among the other colours, *blue* obtained a particular status and increased the response time. The black contrast colour associated with which is considered as less legible (Cole, 1972), seems to interfere with the responses. Several subjects noticed they had some difficulties in perceiving the icons in this case. This could, partly, explain the increase of the response time. But, what is more surprising, is the number of "No" responses obtained when the background was blue. These responses have only been given by a few subjects who said that the "doom" aspect of the black and blue contrast influenced their choice. The connotation of blue was then more affective than in relation to the road sign symbols.

When the subjects talked about the *green* colour, they never associated it with road sign lights. Nature and environment were generally quoted (green and "Dog" means a field for dog, green and "Camera" means that the picture has to be taken outside).

Yellow was considered the most neutral colour for almost all the subjects. They generally assimilate it with "White" in terms of connotation.

In this type of experiment, the interview turned out to be very important in order to graduate the impact of the different colours.

3.2.2. Frame shape effect

There were no significant response time variations registered in relation to the different frame shapes (for the young and the old subjects), except when the pictograms were slashed. In this case, a frame shape effect was noticed for the old subjects but not for the young ones : the triangle was significantly more disturbing, than the round and the square (Kruskal-Wallis, $p<.01$).

Very few differences, between the shape frames, were obtained in term of "Yes" and "No" responses. The young subjects chose "No" for 40.5% of the squares, 41% of the rounds and 41.9% of the triangles. The old subjects modulated their responses a bit more : 39% of the squares, 40.3% of the round and 44.9% of the triangles were considered forbidden.

In this way, these results show that the frame shape was not a factor which really influenced the choice of the responses, which were more determined by the colours and mostly by the presence of a slash.

3. 3. Representation

The mental representations of the subjects were studied more precisely in asking them to make a pictogram indicating something forbidden. Each person received the drawing of a "Diver" before the beginning of the experiment. The instruction was to convey the message : "it is forbidden to dive". Different coloured pencils (light blue, dark blue, yellow, red) were given. A similar task was asked at the end of the experiment to indicate : "it is forbidden to wash your hands", to test a possible training effect.

3.3.1. First realisation

The most used colour was red (30/32 subjects), then black. Generally the persons preferred the square or the round for the frame shape. Only 2 triangles and 3 rectangles were drawn.

All the young adults and more than half of the old ones used different kinds of slash across the icon (15 crosses over all the icon, 7 slashes, 4 small crosses over a part of the icon were obtained). One quarter of the old adults chose unusual ways (reproducing the sign for "No entry for vehicular traffic" or justifying the interdiction by drawing a danger).

As they said during the interview, most of the subjects explained that those signs (slash, cross, etc.) were the best ways to indicate that it was forbidden.

Nearly all the subjects used the red colour, only 3 old subjects considered it sufficient in itself.

3.3.2. Second realisation

Few differences were noted between the 2 realisations, especially for the young subjects. Again, nearly all of them used some kind of slash. Only 1 old subject drew a sign for "No entry for vehicular traffic".

The old subjects changed their mind more often in the way of coding (2nd realisation). It may indicate less confidence in the representations they have of the different codes, and more difficulties to establish some confident guide marks through the signalling. Furthermore the unusual realisations (1st realisation) obtained showed again that for some old subjects, the representations to code an interdict were quite blurred.

4. CONCLUSION

These results showed that different informative values can be attributed to the different elements which composed a pictogram. Their impact is related to the other elements of the pictogram.

This may show that, in spite of a great inter-individual variability concerning mental representations of symbolic information, some common criteria can be found, such as :

- the use of an obviously meaningful frame to indicate a direction when the graphical content can be ambiguously associated with an arrow,
- the use of slash reinforced with red colour to indicate when it is forbidden.

A generation effect was verified with these 2 experiments. It seems as if the difficulties encountered by the older persons to establish some guide marks through the means of signalling correspond with less structured knowledge concerning the different codes generally used in the set of signals to convey symbolic information. The fact that they sometimes found it useless in daily life (they said they preferred to ask), may account for a lower level of confidence with their opinions, and a longer response time.

REFERENCES

1. Jacobs, R.J., Johnston, A.W., & Cole, B.L, (1975), The visibility of alphabetic and symbolic traffic sign, Australian Road Research Board, vol 5, n°7, 68-86.
2. Bruyas, M.P., Laurens, J.F., Pauzie, A.,(1992), Compréhension de pictogrammes selon l'âge, Séminaire Vieillissement et Transport, INRETS/LESCO, déc 1993.
3. Whitaker, L.A., & Sommer, R., (1986), Perception of traffic guidance signs containing conflicting symbol and direction information, Ergonomics, vol 29, N°5, 699-711.
4. Welford, (1981), Vieillissement et aptitudes humaines, Paris, P.U.F.
5. Mishara, B.L., Riedel, R.G., (1984), Le vieillissement, Presses Universitaires de France, Psychologie d'Aujourd'hui, Paris.
6. Mackie A.M. (1967), Progress in Learning the Meaning of Symbolic Traffic Signs, Road Research Lab., Crowthorne, Engl., Rept. LR 91.
7. Cole, B.L., (1972), Visual Aspects of Road Engineering, Australian Road Research Board, vol 6, n°1, 102-148.

VISION IN VEHICLES - V
A.G. Gale et al. (Editors)

Memory Codes for Traffic Sign Information: Visual vs Meaning Codes

Lloyd L. Avant, Alice A. Thieman, Amy L. Zang, & Shin-Ying Hsu

Iowa State University, Ames, Iowa 50011-3180, U.S.A.

Abstract

Fifty three subjects were asked to judge sign pairs as being visually identical or as having the same meaning. Signs pairs were identical signs, a symbol and a word sign of the same meaning, or signs of different meanings. Response latencies and accuracies were recorded. Latencies were faster, and accuracies generally lower, when the second sign followed the first by 500 msec than when signs were presented simultaneously. For identical signs, accuracies for both physical and meaning match judgments were high. Accuracies were lower for pairs of symbol and word signs of the same meaning. Merge and Keep signs with Left and Right directions produced high latencies and low accuracies for both physical and meaning match judgements.

1. INTRODUCTION

Our research interest has focused on the perceptual- cognitive operations that process traffic sign information once the sign image has reached the retina. With exclusion of "real world" constraints and with strict control over the visual input, our intent has been to identify particular mental operations that are critical in accurate and speedy responses to traffic signs. Thus, our studies contrast with those conducted in real or simulated situations which provide performance measures that incorporate both access to memory representations of traffic signs and effects unique to the driving situation tested [e.g.,1]. Briefly summarized, our previous data have shown that (a) meanings of signs are activated unconsciously well before the driver has any awareness of the sign's presence, (b) driver interpretation of sign meaning frequently mismatches the intent of the sign designer, and (c) alcohol influences the processing of sign information, more for females than for males, as early in the visual system as rods and cones [2-5]. The intent of the present study was to investigate the use of two formats for memory coding of traffic signs information.

Posner [6,7] designed a procedure to distinguish between physical (visual) and semantic (meaning) memory codes. Subjects were asked to report whether two letters (e.g., AA orAa) were physically or semantically identical. Response speed and accuracy showed that visual and semantic codes for letters are separable memory coding formats. For the present study, we borrowed Posner's procedure to investigate the use of visual and meaning codes for symbol and word versions of common United States traffic signs.

2. METHOD

The experimental procedure presented pairs of traffic signs in a same-different judgment task. On half of the trials, subjects were asked to decide whether the two signs were physically identical; for the remaining trials, subjects were asked to decide whether the two signs had the same meaning. For one group of subjects, the paired signs were presented simultaneously side-by-side on each trial; for the other group, the first centered sign was presented for 500 msec followed, after 500 msec, by the second sign.

2.1. Subjects

Subjects were 53 volunteers from undergraduate psychology courses. Twenty-six received simultaneous presentations, and 27 received sequential presentations. Subjects received course credit for participation. All had normal or corrected-to- normal vision.

2.2. Stimuli

Signs presenting four driver action messages (Stop, move Right, move Left, and Slow down), each in symbol and word versions, were used. The four Stop message signs were the regulation Stop octagon, a nonregulation diamond-shaped Stop sign, Do Not Enter symbol, and Do Not Enter word. The four move Right signs were the symbol and word versions of Merge Right and Keep Right. The move Left signs were the symbol and word versions of Merge Left and Keep Left. The Slow down signs were the symbol and word versions of Stop Ahead and Signals Ahead. Pairs of signs were arranged to form the following categories: Physically Same (each sign paired with itself); Meaning Same (the same action message presented in a symbol and a word sign); and Different (two signs that differed in both visual format and meaning). These pairs were presented in block randomized series in which Physically Same, Meaning Same, and Different pairs were balanced. The Different pairs varied across blocks. Each subject was presented a total of 352 trials.

2.3. Design

The manipulated variables were (1) Groups (simultaneous versus sequential presentation), (2) Task Instructions (Physical Match or Meaning Match instructions), (3) Stimulus Pair (Same or Different), (4) Sign Message (Stop, Right, Left, Slow), (5) Message Format (Stop/Do Not Enter; Keep/Merge Right; Keep/Merge Left; Stop Ahead/Signals Ahead), and (6) Sign Type (symbol or word). Response latency and accuracy were recorded.

2.4. Apparatus and Procedure

The MEL program (Micro Experimental Laboratory, Psychology Software Tool, Inc.) was used on an Apex 386 computer with a Zenith VGA color monitor to present sign pairs, control timing, and collect response latency and accuracy data. Subjects were tested individually, seated comfortably in front of the computer. They were presented instructions for each trial on the monitor; each trial was preceded by the words Physical Match (PM) or Meaning Match (MM) centered on the monitor to indicate the task for that trial. When the subject was ready, s/he pressed the computer space bar and two signs were presented, side by side for the simultaneous condition and successively centered on the monitor for the sequential condition. For simultaneous presentations, the sign pair remained on the monitor until the subject responded; for the sequential condition, the first sign appeared for 500 msec followed, after a 500 msec interval, by the second sign which remained on the screen until the subject responded. The F and J keys on the keyboard were relabeled to record Same and Different response accuracy and latency. The entire session required about 30 minutes for the simultaneous condition and about 60 minutes for the sequential condition.

3. RESULTS

3.1. Physical and Meaning Match judgments for identical signs

Three questions are particularly pertinent to our present purpose. The first addresses accuracies and latencies for correct Same judgments when each sign was paired with itself for both PM and MM response criteria. The second asks about correct Same responses when a word and symbol version of the same action message were presented and subjects were asked to detect message sameness when the two signs were physically different. The third question addresses particular confusions among directional signs. The mean response latencies and accuracies presented in Table 1 respond to the first question.

Table 1
Physically identical signs; Mean response latencies (msec) and probabilities for correct Same responses.

	Physical Match		Meaning Match	
Presentation	Latency	Accuracy	Latency	Accuracy
Simultaneous	981	.96	1053	.98
Sequential	744	.94	833	.95

These data make three points. First, as might be expected, PM judgments were faster than MM judgments for both simultaneous and sequential presentations, and the magnitude of the PM-MM difference was approximately the same for the two types of presentation (72 and 89 msec respectively). Assuming that the Same-Different decision makes the same processing requirement for PM and MM tasks, this suggests that subjects can activate and use a visual code format for matching the physical features of traffic signs faster than they can activate and use the meaning code format.

Second, both PM and MM judgments were faster for sequential than for simultaneous presentation and, again, the magnitude of the difference was about the same (239 and 221 msec respectively). Of course, sequential presentations permitted subjects to activate memory formats for the first sign before the second sign was presented, and Posner's work [1,2] suggests that the 1000 msec between onsets for the first and second sign is sufficient time to activate meaning as well as visual codes. With both codes activated when the second sign appeared, it is not surprising that both PM and MM judgments shortened the decision latency over that of simultaneous presentations by about the same time.

Third, probabilities of correct response were respectably high and did not differ for PM and MM judgments with both simultaneous and sequential presentations. Of course, such high accuracies indicate that subjects did, in fact, attend to the task such that the latencies can be trusted to reflect mental operations unique to traffic sign processing.

3.2. Response to symbol and word signs of the same meaning.

Table 2 presents mean latencies and probabilities of correct response when subjects were asked to make PM (i.e., Different) or MM (i.e., Same) judgments for word and symbol signs with the same meaning. Again, sequential presentations produced shorter latencies than simultaneous presentations. However, the advantage of sequential over simultaneous presentations was much greater for MM (i.e., Same) judgments (744 msec) than for PM (i.e., Different) judgments (206 msec). Independent activation of visual and meaning codes is indicated in the fact that, with simultaneous presentations, latencies were 586 msec faster for PM than for MM judgements; for simultaneous presentations, subjects seemed able to detect and use the physical dissimilarity between signs without any uncertainty that might be generated by activation

Table 2
Meaning identical word and symbol signs: Mean response latencies (msec) and probabilities for correct responses.

	Physical Match (Different)		Meaning Match (Same)	
Presentation	Latency	Accuracy	Latency	Accuracy
Simultaneous	1175	.73	1761	.85
Sequential	969	.69	1017	.87

of the meaning common to both signs. That sequential presentations activated meaning as well as visual codes is indicated by the observation that the relative advantage for PM over MM judgments was reduced from the 586 msec with simultaneous presentations to 48 msec.

Perhaps the most notable effect of presenting both word and symbol versions of each sign is the considerable cost in response accuracy. Compared to the mean probability of correct response with identical sign pairs (.96) the mean (.79) for word and symbol presentations produced a 21%, rather than a 4%, error rate. This difference seriously questions the wisdom of attempting to assure driver understanding of sign meaning by placing both versions of the same message at the same place.

3.3. The problem with Merge and Keep directional signs

The most informative results of the present study are summarized in Tables 3 and 4; this was the evidence on confusions among signs when subjects were required to detect differences between signs. These confusions occurred most notably with directional signs and caution signs. Table 3 presents mean latencies and probabilities of correct report when the common feature across pairs was the Merge message for both word and symbol signs, but one sign indicated Left and the other indicated Right. The correct response was Different.

Table 3
Left versus Right for Merge message: Mean response latencies (msec) and probabilities for correct responses

Simultaneous Presentations: Merge Left								
	Physical Match				Meaning Match			
	Symbol		Word		Symbol		Word	
Merge Right	Lat.	Acc.	Lat.	Acc.	Lat.	Acc.	Lat.	Acc.
Symbol	1520	.82	142	7.74	1867	.89	3129	.48
Word	1255	.80	2258	.54	2197	.54	1832	.71
Sequential Presentations: Merge Left								
	Physical Match				Meaning Match			
	Symbol		Word		Symbol		Word	
Merge Right	Lat.	Acc.	Lat.	Acc.	Lat.	Acc.	Lat.	Acc.
Symbol	1090	.75	1240	.78	1235	.89	1964	.73
Word	1154	.75	1436	.55	1412	.78	1081	.89

Clearly, the important message in these signs is that the driver should move the vehicle either left or right. However, a cursory review of Table 3 shows that, on average, subjects took 3129 msec to decide that a Merge Right symbol differs from a Merge Left word sign, and only 48% of those decisions were correct. Similarly, subjects took 2258 msec to decide that a Merge Right word sign differs from a Merge Left word sign, and only 54% of those decisions were correct. There are, of course, two messages in these signs (Merge vs Keep and Left vs Right) and, apparently, activation tof the meaning code for the more important directional message is being delayed and seriously interfered with by the apparently prior activation of the Merge vs Keep meaning code. And even the visual difference between symbol and word signs is not alleviating the confusion.

Table 4 presents mean latencies and probabilities of correct report when the common feature across pairs was the Left message for both word and symbol signs, but one sign indicated Merge and the other indicated Keep. The correct response was Different. Here the problem is not the directional message, but the difficulty of deciding whether to Merge or

Keep. Clearly, Merge and Keep have meaning codes that are not clearly distinguished from each other, and this uncertainty can produce delayed and incorrect decisions.

Table 4
Merge versus Keep for Left message: Mean response latencies (msec) and probabilities for correct responses.

Simultaneous Presentations: Merge Left								
	Physical Match				Meaning Match			
	Symbol		Word		Symbol		Word	
Keep Left	Lat.	Acc.	Lat.	Acc.	Lat.	Acc.	Lat.	Acc.
Symbol	1303	.89	1210	.82	2315	.57	2226	.43
Word	1424	.82	1433	.82	1866	.44	2127	.46
Sequential Presentations: Merge Left								
	Physical Match				Meaning Match			
	Symbol		Word		Symbol		Word	
Keep Left	Lat.	Acc.	Lat.	Acc.	Lat.	Acc.	Lat.	Acc.
Symbol	896	.80	849	.93	1083	.27	1288	.36
Word	989	.88	1128	.83	1301	.83	1131	.37

Table 4 shows that pairing the Merge Left symbol sign and the Keep Left symbol sign caused 73% errors in deciding that Merge and Keep do not have the same meaning. Obviously, for the typical driver, Merge and Keep do not have the clearly distinguished meaning codes that they appear to have in the memory of the sign designer.

4. CONCLUSIONS

Our conclusions are simple and straightforward. When signs activate a single visual code in the process of accessing the meaning code for that sign, decision latencies are typically 1 sec or less, and accuracies are respectably high. When, however, two visual codes (symbol and word) are used to activate a single meaning code, decision latencies lengthen and accuracies decrease. This result questions the wisdom of having more than one visual code by which to access a single meaning code.

For signs such as Merge Left and Keep Right which require the processing of two meaning codes (Merge vs Keep, and Left vs Right), and these meanings are represented in both symbol and word formats, decision latencies lengthen noticeably, and accuracies decrease dramatically. These results suggest research to determine whether some signs, particularly directional signs, should be redesigned so as to present clearly different visual formats for (a) the required direction of movement (Left vs Right) and (b) each of the auxiliary meanings (Merge vs Keep). Surely, the Merge and Keep versions of Left vs Right directional signs are intended to inform a driver of different needs for maneuvering a vehicle to meet unique highway conditions, but the drivers in the present study appear not to know how differences in those highway conditions are indicated by the difference between Merge and Keep signs.

REFERENCES

1. W.A.MacDonald and E.R.Hoffman, Ergonomics, 34 (1991) 585.
2. L.L.Avant, A.A.Thieman, K.A.Brewer, and W.F.Woodman. In A.G.Gale, M.H.Freeman, C.M.Haslegrave, P.Smith, and S.P. Taylor (eds.) Vision in vehicles, North-Holland, Amsterdam, (1986).
3. L.L.Avant, J.N.Nelson, N.Short, M.Connerley, M.Bowes and A.A.Thieman. In A.G.Gale, M.H.Freeman, C.M.Haslegrave, P.Smith and S.P.Taylor (eds.), Vision in vehicles II, North-Holland, Amsterdam, (1988).
4. L.L.Avant, M.Bowes, M.Tepin, and K.Kerwin. In A. G.Gale, M.H.Freeman, C.M. Haslegrave, P.Smith, and S.P.Taylor (eds.), Vision in vehicles III, Amsterdam, North-Holland (1990).
5. A.A.Thieman and L.L.Avant. In A.G.Gale, I.D.Brown, C.M. Haslegrave, H.W.Kruysse and S.P.Taylor (eds.), Vision in vehicles IV, North-Holland, Amsterdam, (1993).
6. M.I.Posner. In G.H.Bower and J.T Spence (eds.), The psychology of learning and motivation, Vol. 3, (1969) 44.
7. M.I.Posner, and R.F.Mitchell, Psych. Rev., 74 (1967) 392.

VISION IN VEHICLES - V
A.G. Gale et al. (Editors)

Visual search at intersections: An eye-movement analysis

Jan Theeuwes

TNO Human Factors Research Institute
P.O. Box 23, 3769 ZG Soesterberg, The Netherlands

The present study examines the balance between top-down search induced by the expectations of the road user and data-driven search induced by the properties of the visual scene. While viewing video recordings of intersection approaches, subjects searched for a blue traffic sign which was embedded in the intersection scene. Given the lay-out of the particular scene, the target sign could be located at an expected or an unexpected location within this scene. Dependent on the condition, another traffic sign or another traffic sign and crossing pedestrian were present in the scene. The results reveal the importance of top-down induced search in natural traffic scenes: eye movements were first directed to those locations where target objects were likely to be found. The importance of the role of expectations inducing strategic search was strengthened by the finding that the presence of a distracting sign and a pedestrian hardly altered this search pattern.

1. INTRODUCTION

In a road environment there is an enormous influx of visual information and the appropriate sampling and integration of information is critical for the driving task. In order to achieve an appropriate intake of information in a road environment, traditionally, driving relevant objects have been made conspicuous (Theeuwes, 1991). Typically, it is conceptualized that a conspicuous object exerts control over the visual system in such a way that attention is automatically attracted to the object (Engel, 1977).

The view that visual selection is a completely bottom-up process has been challenged by various studies. For example, in a study of Cole & Hughes (1988) in which eye movements were recorded of subjects watching a movie of the drivers' view of the road, different informational needs induced by instructions, gave different eye-movements patterns. In a series of laboratory studies, Theeuwes (1990, 1991, 1992) explicitly challenged the view that conspicuous objects attract attention automatically: subjects completely ignored very salient objects when these objects were irrelevant to the search task. Yet, when the objects were relevant, subjects could find these objects within a single glance of the display.

The traditional view that for optimal sampling, all relevant objects should be as conspicuous as possible can be contrasted with the view that assumes that drivers

The traditional view that for optimal sampling, all relevant objects should be as conspicuous as possible can be contrasted with the view that assumes that drivers actively interrogate the visual world during which they systematically detect and use meaningful patterns of relationship to decide where to look first and in what sequence to seek for further information. Especially in driving, these top-down effects might be important because driving --as an over-learned task-- might rely on many sampling typicalities. In addition, because drivers are confronted with an enormous influx of visual information which requires accurate and fast sampling, they will rely on this rapid resource-inexpensive and conceptually-driven search. Such a type of processing will especially occur under conditions of high visual and cognitive load and time pressure. The nature of top-down effects on the processing of traffic scenes is thought to be the result of an interaction between incoming perceptual information and higher level memory representations (i.e., schemata and scripts).

Recently, Theeuwes and Hagenzieker (1993) demonstrated the effect of contextual information on visual search in every-day life traffic scenes. More specifically, the study explored the effect of the object-context relation "position" as defined by Biederman et al. (1982). This property refers to the fact that objects which are likely to appear in a given scene often occupy specific positions in that scene. This effect on "position" information is particularly important because this relation might be violated in every-day life traffic situations. Theeuwes and Hagenzieker (1993) showed that errors evolved when road users had wrong expectations regarding the location of particular target objects. For example, when a traffic sign was located at an unlikely position within the traffic scene (on the left rather than on the right side of the road), in many cases, subjects thought that the traffic sign was not present.

The present study examined the balance between top-down search induced by the expectations of the road user and data-driven search induced by the properties of the visual scene. Subjects viewed video recordings consisting of trials made up from pieces of film depicting intersection approaches. Subjects had to search for a particular blue traffic sign indicating that a turn to the right or to the left was permitted. The target sign was either located at an expected or an unexpected location given the lay-out of the intersection. Dependent on the condition, one or two distracting elements were present: a sign (red and blue sign indicating that parking was not allowed) or a red and blue sign as well as a crossing pedestrian wearing an orange jacket.

In order to obtain an in-depth analysis of search behavior, both manual reaction time and eye-movement patterns were recorded. It is expected reaction time (RT) will be faster when the target is located at an expected than at an unexpected location. In conditions in which a distractor is present it is expected that RT will be larger than in conditions in which no distractor is present. The present study was designed to evaluate the relevance of eye-movement recording in relation to visual search in natural (traffic) scenes. Dependent measures of eye-movements which were a priori considered as viable were the latency of the first fixation of the target object, the fixation duration of the target object, the latency of first fixation of the distractors, and the particular scan path for each scene. Manual reaction time data were compared to the eye-movement data in order to evaluate the rationale for measuring eye movements.

2. METHOD

2.1 Subjects

Sixteen subjects ranging in age from 19 to 45 years participated as paid volunteers. Because it was anticipated that glasses and contact lenses might give problematic eye movement recordings only subjects without eye corrections were used. All subjects had their driving license for at least 1 year.

2.2 Apparatus

The video pictures were projected by means of a video projector (Barco data 400) on a white screen (170 x 205 cm). Subjects were seated 370 cm from the screen, with their chin resting in a chin rest. Stimuli subtended a visual angle of about 30° in the horizontal and about 25° in the vertical direction. The room was dimly illuminated.

A corneal-pupil reflection measurement device (Inducom Inc.) was built into a experimental configuration suited for measuring eye movements, recording of manual reaction times and on screen projection of video film (see Theeuwes (1992) for a full description of the measurement device). Figure 1 gives an overview.

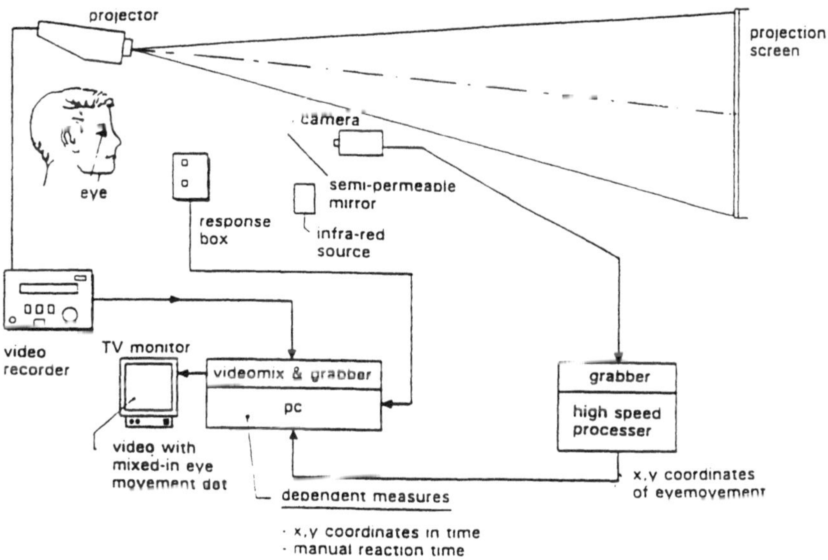

Fig 1: Experimental set-up for measuring eye movements and manual reaction times.

The infra-red light source and eye camera were situated slightly below eye level approximately 75 cm from the subject's eye. The infra red light was projected into the eye by means of a semi-permeable mirror. The eye camera was positioned behind the semi-permeable mirror so that the camera could be positioned exactly in the center of the reflected light containing the corneal and pupil reflection. Both reflections were fed into a high speed processor (Scanbeam Inc.), which computed the center of both cornea and pupil reflection, and calculated the difference vector. The output of the high speed processor consisting of x,y coordinates of the eye position was fed into a PC (IBM AT-3 with a video-digitizer Matrox Inc.). The coordinates were stored for later data analysis and were mixed on-line with the same video picture as was watched by the subjects. The output of the video picture with the mixed in x,y, coordinates was displayed on a tv monitor for on-line inspection. An S-R interface connected the response box to the PC.

2.3 Stimuli

The stimulus material used in the experiment consisted of video showing an approach of selected intersections. Subjects always had to search for a blue sign indicating that a turn to the left or to the right was allowed (new RVV sign D5 for 3-way crossings and D6 for 4-way crossings). There were two distractor conditions: one condition in which only a sign distractor was present (RVV sign D7 indicating that parking is not allowed) and one condition in which both the distractor sign and a pedestrian were present. The blue target sign could be located at an expected location (right side of the road, 2 meter above ground level) or at an unexpected location (anywhere on the left side of the road).

The conditions were enacted in real life on the selected sites. An experimental car (Chrysler Voyager) in which a camera was mounted at eye level (approximately 1.60 meter) approached the intersection with an average speed of about 50 km/h (13.9 m/s). A camera with a visual angle of about 45° recorded this approach. In order to ensure that only the experimental signs were visible on video, signs which were already present at the intersection were covered by means of grey plastic. Also, while recording the approach it was ensured that no other traffic (cars, bikes, pedestrians) was present at the intersection. Dependent on the condition, the experimental and distractor signs were mounted on wooden poles, 2 meters or 0.5 meter above ground level. Target sign and distractor sign were always located at the same side approximately 1.5 meter form each other. In the sign + pedestrian distractor condition, just before the car arrived at the intersection, a pedestrian wearing an orange fluorescent jacket coming from the opposite side to where the target sign was located, crossed the street.

For each intersection, 7 recordings were made. One recording consisted of an intersection in which neither signs nor distractors were present (empty scene). Three recordings comprised the target-at-an-expected-location condition consisting of a recording with no distractor, a sign distractor and a sign + pedestrian distractor. The same three distractor conditions (no distractor, sign distractor and sign + pedestrian distractor) were enacted for the target-at-an-unexpected location condition. The direction which the target sign indicated (a turn to the left or a turn to the right) was varied randomly from trial to trial.

In order to create trials consisting of pieces of video, the original video recordings were edited. The sequence of events during a trial was as follows: one second before a piece of video was presented, a fixation dot was displayed at the center of the visual field. This was followed by a piece of video showing the intersection without the target sign and distractors ("empty intersection"). This piece of video was displayed for 2 sec and showed the intersection from a distance, that is, at the beginning of this piece of video the intersection was exactly 7 sec away (97.3 meter), and at the offset of the piece of video the intersection was exactly 5 sec away (69.6 meter). This scene was presented in order to prepare the subjects for the upcoming type of scene. The "precue" scene was followed by a black time for 3 sec consisting of a blue field with a fixation dot in the center. Finally, the search scene which possibly contained the target sign was presented for 2 sec. The search scene started exactly 2 sec (27.8 meter) before the intersection, that is 2 sec before the target sign disappeared from the video screen. This implied that subjects only had 2 sec to locate and identify the target sign. Dependent on the condition, this search scene also could contain one or two distractors. The end of the trial was marked by 15 sec of black time.

The total time between the beginning of the precue scene and the end of the search scene was 7 sec (2 sec preparation time, 3 sec black time, 2 sec search time). Because the precue scene showed the intersection from a distance from 7 to 5 sec before the end of the intersection, it appeared as if the video tape showed a continuous 50 km/h approach to the intersection which was occluded for about 3 sec. It should be noted that in reality this was not the case because the precue video piece never contained a target or a distractor. This was done on purpose so that subjects could not start searching during the presentation of the precue video section. Figure 2 shows the sequence of events.

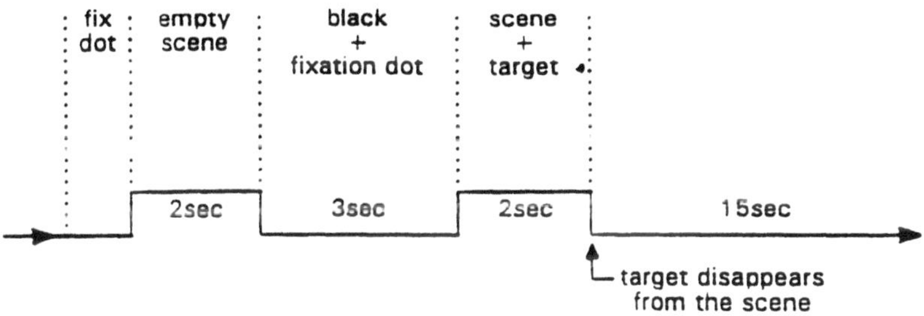

Fig. 2: Sequence of events during a trial. A trial involved the presentation of a moving video consisting of "precue" video piece (an overview of the scene from a distance) followed, after a black time, by the search video piece in which the target sign was inserted at an expected or unexpected location.

2.4 Experimental Design and Procedure

The experiment involved a within subject design with 4 factors: expectancy (target sign at an expected or at an unexpected location), distractor (no distractor, a sign distractor, sign + pedestrian distractor), and repetition (first or second time of presentation). Three different types of visually simple intersection approaches were used.

There was one, randomly chosen, sequence of order of trial presentation. Subjects were asked to search for the blue target sign as fast as possible while minimizing errors. As soon as they detected the blue target sign, they had to press a right button when the sign indicated that a right turn was allowed and a left button when a left turn was allowed. If no target sign was present they had to refrain from responding. It was explained that the precue scene was similar to the search scene and that they should make use of this information to prepare for the upcoming search scene. Before the experiment, subjects received 5 practice trials.

Subjects were seated with their heads resting on a chin rest. The eye camera was adjusted so that the eye was clearly in focus. Before the experiment started, the eye movement apparatus was calibrated. Subjects were asked to fixate the left side, top, right side and bottom of the white screen on which the video would be projected. For each fixation, the vector describing the difference between the pupil and corneal reflection center was stored in memory. The calibration procedure took about 3 minutes remained accurate throughout the whole experiment.

3. RESULTS AND DISCUSSION

3.1 Reaction time analysis

Due to apparatus malfunctioning and problems with the eye-movement recordings the data of five subjects were not included in the analysis. For the remaining 11 subjects, mean RTs were computed for each subject in each condition. Response times longer than 1.5 sec were excluded from the analysis which led to a loss of well under 1% of the trials. This measure was subjected to separate ANOVAs, with expectancy (expected vs unexpected), distractor (no distractor, sign distractor, sign + pedestrian distractor), type of intersection and repetition (first vs second time presented) as main factors. Figure 3 presents the subjects' mean RT.

There was a main effect on RT for expectancy ($F(1,10) = 80.5$; $p < .01$), distractor ($F(2,20) = 11.3$; $p < .01$) and run ($F(1,10) = 10.7$; $p < .01$). Also the interactions between expectancy and distractor, expectancy and intersection type, expectancy and run, and distractor and intersection type were significant (all $p < .05$). As clear from Figure 3, it takes about 130 ms longer to find the target when it is located at an unexpected location than when it is located at an expected location, a result which confirms earlier findings (Theeuwes & Hagenzieker, 1993). When the target is located at an expected location, planned comparisons show that relatively to the no distractor condition search is somewhat --yet reliably-- slowed down (about 35 ms) when a distractor is present (both comparisons ps < 0.05). There is no difference between the two distractors conditions. The distracting effect is small; yet, this effect cannot be attributed to particularly long RTs of a few subjects. Relative to the no distraction condition, eight of the eleven subjects had longer RTs in both the sign and the sign and the sign + pedestrian distracting conditions.

For the condition in which the target was located at an unexpected location, relative to the no distractor condition search is faster when there is only a sign as a distractor, and search is slower when there is both a sign and a sign +

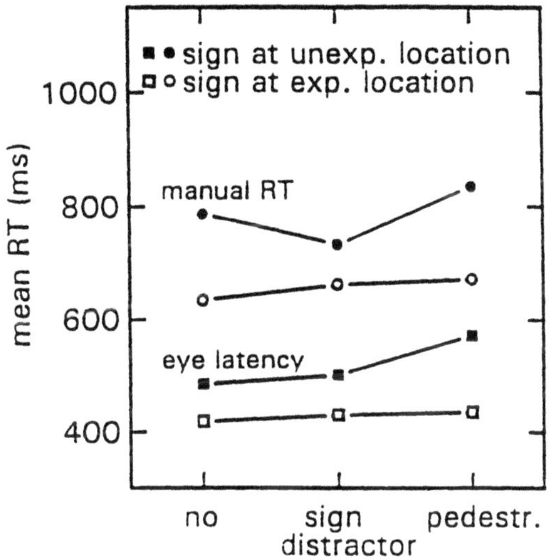

Fig. 3: Mean time to fixate the target sign and mean time to press one of the response buttons (RT) for the expected and unexpected location condition.

pedestrian as a distractor (both ps < .05). The finding that search is faster when there was a sign distractor was not expected; yet, there is a possible explanation: because the distractor sign was always located near the target sign, the distractor sign might have been used as a cue for where in the visual field the target sign was located. This strategy is apparently effective in conditions in which the target sign is located at an unexpected location.

3.2 Eye-movement data

As soon as an eye fixation falls within a predefined target area, the target sign can be considered as being detected. The time it takes for the eye to enter the target area can be considered as a true estimate for actual search time. The eye-movement pattern consisting of location coordinates of the eye in time were compared to the location coordinates of the target traffic sign in time. This analysis was performed for the time interval between the beginning of the search video piece and the depression of one of the buttons of the response box. The latency between the beginning of the search piece and the instant that the eye coordinates fell within the target area defining the target traffic sign, was recorded. The target area defining the traffic sign consisted of the actual outlines of the traffic sign on video extrapolated relatively with a factor 1.5 in order to incorporate a somewhat larger target area. A somewhat larger delineation of the target area is required because it is possible to identify the target sign without a clear fixation of the sign.

Mean eye-movement latencies were recorded for each subject in each condition. This measure was subjected to the same ANOVAs as used for the RT data. Figure 3 presents the subjects' mean eye-movement latencies and the reaction time data (time to press one of the response buttons). There was a main effect on eye-movement latency for expectancy ($\underline{F}(1,10)= 68.0$; $\underline{p} < .01$), and for distractor ($\underline{F}(2,20)= 13.5$; $\underline{p} < .01$). Also the interactions between expectancy and distractor, expectancy and intersection type, and distractor and intersection type were significant (all $\underline{p}$s < .05). As for the RT data, the analysis suggests that search time is longer when the target is located at an unexpected location than when it is located at an expected location (about 90 ms longer). Overall, the presence of the sign + pedestrian distractor reliably slows down search for the target sign (about 50 ms). Additional planned comparisons show that, contrary to the RT data, in the expected location condition, there is no reliable difference between the different levels of distractors. In the unexpected condition, the sign + pedestrian distractor condition was significantly slower than the no and sign distractor condition (all comparisons $\underline{p}$s < .05).

An additional ANOVA was carried out in order to test whether the effects on reaction time and eye-movement latency were additive, that is, to test whether the variables manipulated had the same effect on reaction time as they have on eye movement latency. This additivity can be expected when it is assumed that the reaction time reflects the search time plus some constant additional time to identify the target sign and press the appropriate response button. The factor reaction time vs eye movement latency interacted with expectancy ($\underline{F}(1,10)= 10.1$; $\underline{p} < .01$), and repetition ($\underline{F}(1,10)= 7.8$; $\underline{p} < .05$). The interaction with expectancy showed an overadditivity indicating that the reaction time increase from the expected to unexpected location condition was larger (an increase of about 130 ms) than the increase in eye-movement latency going from expected to unexpected condition (an increase of about 94 ms). This finding is important because it suggests that the expectancy manipulation not only affects time to find the target but also time to <u>identify</u> the target. This suggests that after the object has been detected, identification of the target is somewhat slowed down because the object is located at an odd location. The interaction with repetition indicates that the advantage of presenting the stimulus the second time is greater for reaction time than for eye movement latency, which simply might reflect that in case of reaction time there is more room for improvement.

4. GENERAL DISCUSSION

The present study demonstrates that search for target signs in moving video is biased towards certain portions of the visual field. Both manual reaction time and eye-movement latency show that subjects first search those locations where targets are likely to be found and then search the less likely locations. These results are comparable to earlier studies in which subjects searched for targets in black-and-white stationary pictures (Theeuwes & Hagenzieker, 1993).

After detecting the target object, it has to be identified in order to determine the appropriate response. The comparison between manual RT and eye-movement latency indicates that the time to identify the target object is also affected by the location expectancy manipulation. Obviously, the extent to which an object fits into the environment has an effect on the time to identify that object. The present study shows that when the object was located at an unexpected location, identification of the object was slower than when it was located at an expected location.

The method used to measure eye movements turned out to be adequate. Calibration was easy and the accuracy of the measurement remained high. The only eye movement measure that gave problems was the determination of the fixation duration of the target object. Because to some extent identification was possible by means of peripheral vision, precise fixation of the target sign was not required.

The present study shows the importance of top-down induced search in natural traffic scenes. It demonstrates scene dependent scanning behavior denoting that eye movements are first directed to those locations where target objects are likely to be found. The importance of the role of expectations inducing strategic search through the traffic scene is strengthened by the finding that -- especially in visually complex circumstances-- the presence of conspicuous objects hardly alters this search pattern. The results pinpoint the importance of designing so called "Self-Explaining Roads", roads which are designed in line with the expectations of the road users (Theeuwes & Godthelp, 1993).

5. ACKNOWLEDGEMENT

This research was funded by the Institute for Road Safety Research SWOV.

REFERENCES

Biederman, I., Mezzanotte, R.J., & Rabinowitz, J.C. (1982). Scene perception: Detecting and judging objects undergoing relational violations. Cognitive Psychology 14, 143-177.

Cole, B.L. & Hughes, P.K. (1988). Drivers don't search: they just notice. In D. Brogan: Visual Search. London: Taylor & Francis.

Engel, F.L. (1977). Visual conspicuity, visual search and fixation tendencies of the eye. Vision Research 17, 95-108.

Theeuwes, J. (1990). Perceptual selectivity is task dependent: evidence from selective search. Acta Psychologica, 74, 81-99.

Theeuwes, J. (1991). Cross-dimensional perceptual selectivity. Perception & Psychophysics 50, 184-193.

Theeuwes, J. (1991). Visual selection: Exogenous and endogenous control. In Gale et al. (eds.): Vision in Vehicle III, North Holland, Amsterdam.

Theeuwes, J. (1992) Visual search of at intersections: an eye-movement analysis. Report IZF 1992 C-43. TNO Institute for Perception.

Theeuwes, J. (1992). Perceptual selectivity for color and form. Perception & Psychophysics 51, 599-606.

Theeuwes, J. & Godthelp, J. (1993). Self-Explaining Roads. In de Kroes & Stoop (eds.): First World Congress on Safety of Transportation. Delft University Press.

Theeuwes, J. & Hagenzieker, M.P. (1993). Visual search of traffic scenes: on the effect of locations expectations. In Gale et al. (eds.): Vision in Vehicle IV. North Holland Amsterdam.

VISION IN VEHICLES - V
A.G. Gale et al. (Editors)
1996 Elsevier Science B.V.

Estimation Of Time To Arrival In A Real Vehicle And In A Simulation Task: Effects Of Sex, Driving Experience, Speed And Distance

M. A. Recarte*, L. M. Nunes** and J. Lillo*

* Department of Basic Processes. Faculty of Psychology. U. Complutense. Madrid.
** Driver Research and Training Department. Dirección General de Tráfico. Madrid.

Abstract

Sixty subjects of both sexes and three levels of driving experience participated in an experiment of time to arrival in a real vehicle in which they were passengers in a straight stretch of 400 m long in a circuit. Subjects had to press a button when they estimated the car was passing between two targets placed on both sides of the lane during a period of visual occlusion, after a previous time where vision was allowed while approaching the targets at constant speed. In the simulation task, the same subjects had to estimate the time in which one mobile target shown in a computer display should appear after being occluded in its horizontal trajectory by a rectangle. While some results are consistent with the more general trends observed in other works, such as the general tendency to underestimation and sex differences, other results reveal remarkable deviations from the findings of other authors, such as the effect of driving experience, that was the reverse than expected, or the general assumption concerning the constant proportion between real time and estimated time. The comparison of both tasks revealed two different processes.

1. INTRODUCTION

The concepts of time to collision, contact time or time to arrival have been used as a general paradigm in the context of driving research in very different experimental settings. The different versions include transverse movement of one point in a computer display (Peterken et al., 1991), ordinary straight movement in real vehicle, (Cavallo & Laurent, 1988; Cavallo, Laya & Laurent, 1986) or in curves, (Cavallo et al., 1988), films of vehicles approaching a target (Groeger & Cavallo, 1991; Groeger & Brown, 1988; Mc Leod & Ross, 1983) or vehicles approaching the observer, (Schiff & Detwiler, 1979; Schiff & Oldak, 1990). Such different experimental conditions lead us to ask about the equivalence of the implied processes in different tasks included in the same general paradigm. Considering that some of the effects have been observed in a limited range of conditions (the effect of sex has not been tested in real vehicle conditions, and there is a lack of research with high speed values), we established as main objectives for this work :

This research was supported by D.G.T. (Dirección General de Tráfico), who provided human, economic, and material resources that made possible it's achievement.

a) To replicate and test the *time to arrival paradigm* in a real vehicle setting and describe the magnitudes of these effects for a wide range of values of variables.
b) To compare the results obtained in a real vehicle setting with the results obtained in a simulated task, considering the possible differences in the aptitudes required to achieve each task.

2. METHOD

2.1. Subjects

Subjects were selected from different sources, and all of them participated in both real vehicle and simulation experiments. There were 30 of each sex, and they were assigned to six groups of 10 subjects considering three levels of driving experience for each gender: no driving experience at all, less than 2 years, and more than 5 years. The range of ages varied from 25 to 45 years. Visual acuity was controlled and the subjects were paid for participating in the experiment. Because of some significant differences in the age of the different groups the variance analysis was made with age as covariate, and it revealed that there was no age effect within the range that was considered.

2.2. Experimental Design

2.2.1. THE REAL VEHICLE EXPERIMENT

Four values of *speed* (60, 80, 100 and 120 Km/h) were orthogonally varied with four values of *distance* for the stretch of visual occlusion before the targets (150, 125, 100, and 75 meters). The 16 combinations of speed and distance led to 13 different times that vary from 2.25 s to 9.00 s. The same time (4.5 s) corresponds to the four conditions of the diagonal of the matrix of the 16 experimental conditions to which each subject is submitted. The sequences of the 16 trials were systematically varied among subjects.

2.2.2. THE SIMULATION EXPERIMENT

The simulation task is a standard test of speed perception, the LND 101, that is used for driver selection. There are two values of speed (2.85 cm/s and 4.27 cm/s) with one single distance value. Consequently, there are two values for the time (2.46 s and 1.65 s). The magnitude of these time values is comparable with the lower values of the vehicle experiment. Each subject made 6 estimations, 3 for each speed.

2. 3. Apparatus

2.3.1. THE REAL VEHICLE EXPERIMENT

One experimental car is used in a circuit provided with a straight lane of 400 m long, in which one stretch of 225 m long and 10 metres wide was defined for the experimental purpose. Visual occlusion was controlled by a device based on a pair of liquid crystal spectacles (Milgram, 1987). A system of infrared barriers was installed along the experimental lane and a system was developed to control automatically the operation of the liquid crystal spectacles by means of a microprocessor.

The targets were two square yellow drapes of 1.50 x 1.50 metres, mounted on two structures placed on both sides of the lane, at 0.50 m high from the floor. From the distance of

225 m, and an approaching speed of 60 Km/h, the expansion of the retinal image of the targets is 0.294°/s, which is clearly over the threshold of 0.08°/s pointed out by Lee (1976).

The experimental car is provided with a special Data Acquisition System where the significant parameters are continuously recorded (at a 50 Hz rate), including the operation of the visual occlusion system and the operation of the button that subjects used to make their estimations. The car was driven by a trained driver and the constancy of the speed was controlled by checking for each of the 960 trials (16 trials x 60 subjects) the continuous recording of the speed provided by the Data Acquisition System.

2.3.2. THE SIMULATION EXPERIMENT

The speed perception test LND 101 is a computerized test in which one small red circle of 0.5 cm diameter runs from left to right of the display along a straight horizontal line. One rectangle of 7 cm wide occludes the trajectory in the right side of the display. There are two speed values for the mobile target, and subjects are not given any feed-back about their performance. One button is installed in a response box.

2.4. Procedure

2.4.1. THE REAL VEHICLE EXPERIMENT

Subjects are seated in the front right seat of the car, provided with the spectacles in the transparent mode and the push-button in one hand. A demonstration trial is made to be sure the instructions have been correctly understood. A ring of 2.8 Km long is used to go back to the beginning of the experimental lane. On the last meters before entering the straight lane subject's vision is occluded until the vehicle reaches the beginning of the experimental lane, 225 meters before the targets, where the spectacles change automatically to the transparent mode, allowing subject's vision during a preprogrammed distance before reaching the targets. At the end of this distance subject's vision is occluded and they make their estimations by pressing a button. Two experimenters are required: the first one drives the car according to one of the established sequences of speeds, and the second one, seated in the back seat, controls the Data Acquisition System, and the microprocessor that controls the operation of the liquid crystal spectacles according to the set distances. The speedometer was made invisible for the subjects.

2.4.2. THE SIMULATION EXPERIMENT

Subjects are placed 1m from the screen, and have to press a button when they estimate the red circle shall appear on the other side of the rectangle. There is one demonstration trial, and a sequence of the 6 trials where the speeds are presented alternatively.

3. RESULTS

3.1. The Real Vehicle Experiment

A previous analysis of the actual speed of the car revealed that the driving conditions were highly satisfactory. The actual speed was measured and analized for each of the 960 turns, and each estimation was compared individually with the real time measured. The real times of the following tables and figures are really measured data, and the values 60, 80, 100 and 120 Km/h shall be interpreted as categories of speeds defined for variance analysis purpose. The actual mean speeds were 61.1, 81.6, 101.1 and 121.8 Km/h.

3.1.1. ANALYSIS OF ESTIMATED TIMES

The relation between *estimated time (Et)*, *proportional time (10Et/Rt)* and *real time (Rt)* in vehicle and simulation experiments is shown in figure 1.

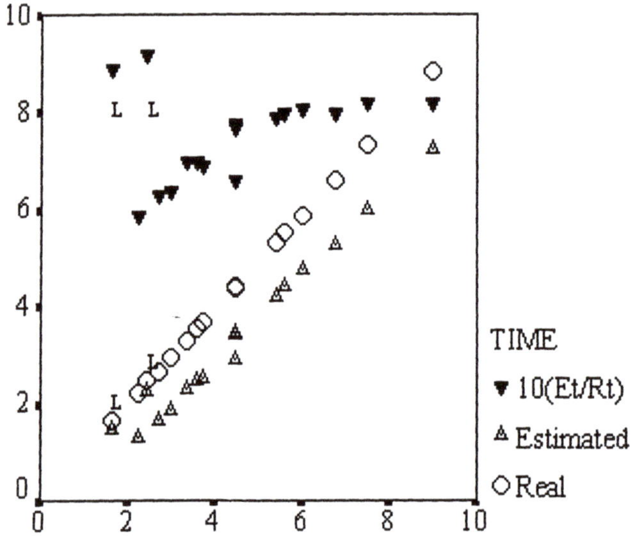

The correlation Et-Rt is R=0.796 and the general regression equation is:

Et = 0.918 Rt - 0.75

In the figure can be seen:

a) the lack of alignment of the LND simulation task times.

b) The no-linearity of de proportional (Et/Rt) estimates.

c) The exceptional value in the 4.5 s condition.

Fig. 1: Real, estimated and proportional times (L = LND).

In order to determinate the contribution of experimental and subject variables an analysis of variance was performed considering 2 sexes x 3 levels of experience x 4 speeds x 4 distances, with repeated measures for these speed and distance, using age as a covariate.

The main effects are all significant. The general underestimation is confirmed (Fig. 1).

With respect to *subject variables*, this underestimation is higher for female than male subjects ($F=4.70$; $p= 0.35$). Subjects without driving experience make better estimations than the groups with some experience ($F = 3.55$; $p = 0.036$). Table 1 shows the main effects of sex and experience in six dependent variables

Regarding the interactions we observe a significant interaction of sex x distance, ($F = 4.23$; $p = 0.007$), and also sex x distance x speed, ($F = 2.14$; $p = 0.025$), not included in the tables. Both interactions, together with the no significant sex x speed, indicate that the sex differences increases as the occlusion time also increases. Driving experience does not interact with any variable.

Table 1: Estimated time, proportional time, and errors, by sex and experience.

	SEX				EXPERIENCE					
	Male		Female		None		0 - 2 year		5 - more	
	mean	sd	mean	sd	mean	sd	mean	sd	mean	sd
Real time	4.73	1.74	4.73	1.75	4.73	1.74	4.72	1.74	4.73	1.76
E	3.83	2.14	3.35	1.83	4.00	2.15	3.31	1.87	3.45	1.91
Et/Rt	0.81	0.25	0.71	0.23	0.83	0.25	0.68	0.24	0.70	0.22
Error	0.89	1.27	1.38	1.15	0.72	1.27	1.41	1.23	1.27	1.08
Abs. error	1.23	0.94	1.51	0.99	1.16	0.90	1.52	1.10	1.43	0.87
Overest. er.	0.16	0.36	0.08	0.27	0.22	0.41	0.07	0.23	0.08	0.27

The effects of the *experimental variables* are shown in the fig. 2. Table 2 shows the general results of the 16 experimental conditions in six dependent variables.

As seems natural, the effect of both variables that produce different real times is significant: the effect of distance: ($F= 346.07$; $p < 0.000$) and the effect of speed: ($F = 505.83$; $p < 0.000$), the latter stronger than the former.

The interaction between speed and distance is also significant and it can be observed in Table 2 and Fig. 2 ($F = 17.98$; $p < 0.000$). There is a good fit between the estimated times and the linear pattern of real times, accepting the general underestimation pattern.

The main exception to this regularity is the estimated time at 120 Km/h with a distance of 150 m. This deviation is consistent in all dependent measures, but it becomes more evident observing the diagonal values. In this four conditions the real time is practically the same, and the estimated time for 120 Km/h shows a clear deviation from linearity. The variance analysis for these four conditions shows significant effects ($F = 3.81$; $p = 0.011$) and Duncan's range test confirms that the significant difference takes place between the first condition and the other troo. The same results are obtained from the analysis of *errors* ($F = 3.93$; $p = 0.009$) or the analysis of proportional times ($F = 3.93$; $p = 0.009$).

When the proportional time (Et / Rt) is analized it can be seen the effects of sex and experience remain unaltered. The same happens for the effects of distance ($F = 18.28$; $p = 0.000$), and speed ($F = 59.59$; $p < 0.000$) and the interaction ($F = 2.07$; $p = 0.031$). However, these last effects lose the regularity and linearity observed in estimated times. These, remain relatively stable with time values over 4.5 s and the linearity is broken below this limit. This effect is particularly evident in the condition 120 Km/h and 150 m. (Fig. 1)

3.1.2. ANALYSIS OF ERRORS

When the *errors* are analized there is found to be a significant effect that shows the increase in errors as the distance increases ($F = 8.43$; $p < 0.0000$). There is no effect of speed, possibly as a consequence of the increasing errors in the 120 Km/h condition. No interaction effect for speed x distance was found.

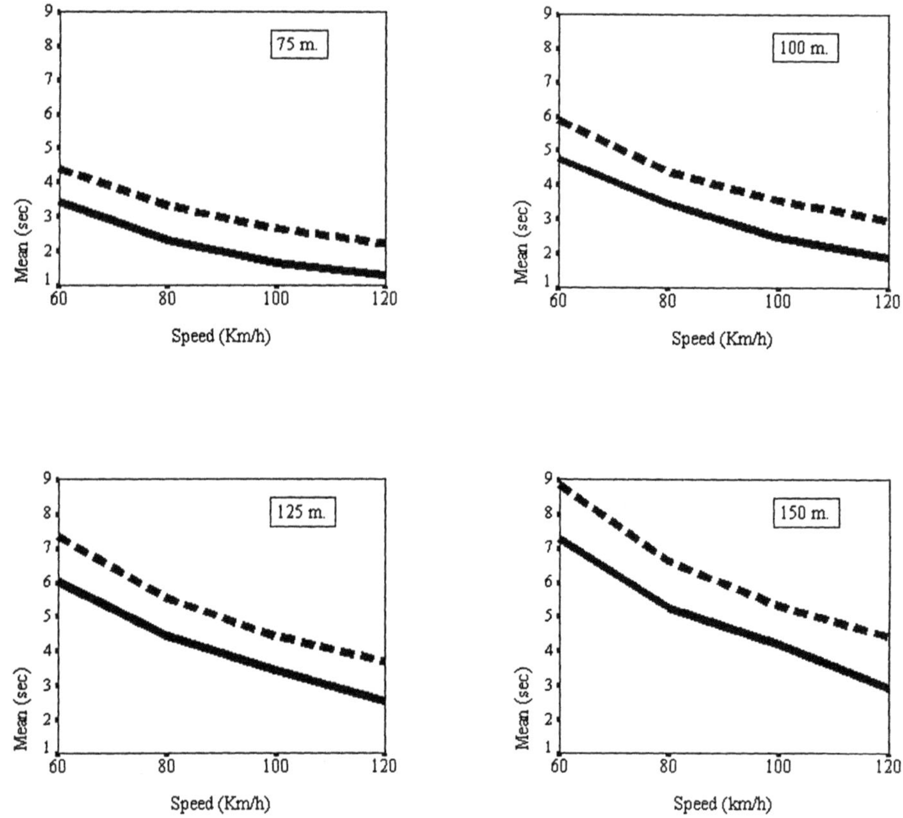

Fig. 2: Real (----) and estimated (——) time as a function of distance (m) and speed (Km/h)

Considering the *absolute value errors*, where an overestimation is not compensated by an underestimation, the effects of sex and experience are attenuated and the differences are not significant. The better estimations of male or non experienced drivers are partially due to a larger proportion of overestimation. There are significant effects of distance, ($F = 59.35$; $p < 0.000$), speed, ($F = 373.27$; $p < 0.000$), and the interaction of both ($F = 2.49$; $p = 0.009$). The difference between *absolute errors* and simple *error* in the condition of the lower speed and higher distance (60 Km/h; 150 m) is apparent and shows that in this condition the likelihood of overestimation is higher.

3.1.3. RELIABILITY OF ESTIMATIONS

The mean of the 120 correlations resulting from the comparison of the 16 experimental conditions is 0.63, all of them being significant $p < 0.01$, and in the range of 0.40 to 0.80. Considering that each condition differs from others either in speed or in distance, we can refer to the ability to estimate the time to arrival as a consistent trait among individuals.

Table 2: Mean values and standard deviations for each of the 16 experimental conditions.

	Km/h	60		80		100		120		TOTAL	
DIST		mean	sd	mean	sd	mean	sd	mean	sd	mean	sd
150	Rt	8.86	0.24	6.62	0.12	5.32	0.07	4.42	0.06	6.31	1.68
	Et	7.28	2.26	5.26	1.72	4.21	1.29	2.93	0.91	4.92	2.27
	Et/Rt	0.82	0.25	0.80	0.26	0.79	0.24	0.66	0.20	0.77	0.24
	Error	1.58	2.23	1.36	1.74	1.11	1.29	1.49	0.91	1.39	1.60
	Ab.Er.	2.27	1.51	1.82	1.23	1.40	0.96	1.54	0.81	1.76	1.22
	Over.	0.20	0.40	0.15	0.36	0.17	0.38	0.03	0.18	0.15	0.34
125	Rt	7.35	0.17	5.53	0.09	4.43	0.07	3.69	0.05	5.25	1.38
	Et	6.03	1.70	4.43	1.27	3.43	1.08	2.53	0.87	4.10	1.82
	Et/Rt	0.82	0.23	0.80	0.22	0.77	0.24	0.69	0.24	0.77	0.24
	Error	1.32	1.68	1.10	1.24	1.01	1.08	1.16	0.87	1.15	1.28
	Ab.Er.	1.71	1.28	1.37	0.93	1.24	0.81	1.27	0.69	1.40	0.98
	Over.	0.17	0.38	0.13	0.34	0.13	0.34	0.08	0.28	0.13	0.34
100	Rt	5.89	0.11	4.40	0.08	3.55	0.05	2.96	0.03	4.20	1.11
	Et	4.77	1.54	3.45	1.01	2.48	0.89	1.89	0.67	3.15	1.53
	Et/Rt	0.81	0.26	0.78	0.23	0.70	0.25	0.64	0.23	0.73	0.25
	Error	1.13	1.55	0.96	1.02	1.08	0.89	1.06	0.67	1.06	1.08
	Ab.Er.	1.58	1.07	1.16	0.77	1.19	0.73	1.09	0.63	1.26	0.85
	Over.	0.13	1.34	0.13	0.34	0.08	0.28	0.05	0.22	0.10	0.30
75	Rt	4.39	0.09	3.31	0.05	2.65	0.03	2.22	0.03	3.14	0.82
	Et	3.44	1.03	2.32	0.83	1.67	0.63	1.30	0.47	2.18	1.09
	Et/Rt	0.78	0.24	0.70	0.25	0.63	0.24	0.59	0.21	0.68	0.24
	Error	0.95	1.05	0.99	0.82	0.98	0.64	0.92	0.47	0.96	0.77
	Ab.Er.	1.25	0.67	1.11	0.64	1.02	0.57	0.94	0.44	1.08	0.62
	Over.	0.15	0.36	0.13	0.34	0.07	0.23	0.03	0.18	0.10	0.30
T	Rt	6.63	1.67	4.96	1.24	3.99	1.00	3.32	0.82	4.73	1.74
O	Et	5.38	2.25	3.86	1.65	2.95	1.35	2.16	0.95	3.59	2.00
T	Et/Rt	0.81	0.25	0.77	0.24	0.72	0.25	0.64	0.22	0.76	0.25
A	Error	1.25	1.71	1.10	1.24	1.04	1.00	1.16	0.77	1.14	1.23
L	Ab.Er.	1.70	1.26	1.37	0.96	1.21	0.80	1.21	0.69	1.37	0.97
	Over.	0.17	0.36	0.14	0.35	0.12	0.32	0.05	0.22	0.12	0.32

3.2. The Simulation Experiment

A variance analysis was made for 2 times x 3 trials x 2 sexes x 3 levels of experience, with repeated measures in the two first variables. The effect of time (or speed in this case) is the only significant effect that was found ($F = 272.3$; $p < 0.000$). The data are shown on the margin. Considering the proportional times, there are no significant differences.

REAL TIME	EST. TIME	Et / Rt
2.46	2.25	0.915
1.56	1.44	0.925

The mean correlation resulting from considering each of the 6 trials is 0.62, and the range of the values is from 0.50 to 0.80. These values are very similar to those obtained in the real vehicle experiment. If we consider the tree trials for each speed, the correlation between the estimations of both speeds is 0.75. Consequently, we can also consider the existence of one consistent individual aptitude.

3. 3. Comparison between both experiments

The results show important differences between both tasks. As it can be seen in Fig.1, the estimated times of the simulation task do not follow the tendency of the same variable in the vehicle task. Additionally, in the simulation task significant differences in sex, experience, or in the proportion of Et / Rt, (whose magnitude, 0.92, is much higher than the vehicle experiment value, 0.76) were not found .

However the clearest evidence that suggest the existence of two different processes is given from the correlation analysis. The correlation between the different trials of each task is high enough to consider, in both cases, the existence of one consistent aptitude. But considering the 32 correlations resulting from comparing the 2 speeds of the simulation task with the 16 conditions of the vehicle task, we observe that none is significant. The mean correlation is 0.03, and the values oscillate between 0.28 and -0.20.

4. DISCUSSION AND CONCLUSIONS

As it has been previously pointed out, these experiments confirm, in a real vehicle, some of the results verified in other versions of the paradigm. Otherwise, there were found remarkable deviations from the literature, some of them surprising in some aspects.

4. 1. The general underestimation

This phenomena is confirmed as a general tendency, but the proportional time with a real vehicle (Et / Rt = 0.76) is higher than the values found by other authors (0.63 was found by Cavallo & Laurent, 1988). For the simulation task the proportion is higher (0.92).

4. 2. Sex differences

The same differences found by other researchers with vehicle films (Mc Leod & Ross, 1983; Schiff & Oldak, 1990) were replicated in the real vehicle experiment. However, this difference was not found in the simulation task. Because of the characteristics of the sample, this effect is clearly separated form the effect of experience, although the experimental design does not allow us to attribute this differences to different risk acceptance or decision criteria, according to the prevailing interpretation.

4. 3. Experience effects

In the real vehicle experiment, the group with *no driving experience* shows the best estimations, partially due to a higher percentage of overestimation trials (20%). These results seem apparently contradictory with other experimental results, although a deeper analysis indicates that these data can be understood consistently with other empirical results or their theoretical interpretations. Empirically, the usual effect of experience (expert drivers make better estimations than novice drivers, - Cavallo & Laurent, 1988), has not been tested with subjects with no experience at all; sometimes there was found to be no effect of this variable (Horst, 1991). Theoretically these data have been considered as an argument against the optical flow hypothesis and the retinal image expansion as an exclusive underlying mechanism to the time to arrival estimation (Cavallo & Laurent, 1988; Tresilian, 1991). The data of the real vehicle experiment can also be interpreted in the same sense: In the subjects with no experience should operate the basic perceptive processes, with little influence of other cognitive aspects. Cognitive processes, such as mental representations of motor response patterns associated with the driving task could be affecting the processing of basic perceptual cues in experienced drivers. In the simulation task, there should mainly operate optical information, and neither the type of movement, nor the task itself gives any advantage to any group.

4. 4. The linearity of the estimations

The wide range of values of speed and distance combinations for the vehicle experiment makes it possible to test the estimation's linearity. The data suggest the existence of some limit condition in which the ordinary perceptual or cognitive processes are disorganized. The general use of proportional time as a dependent measure may be misleading to evaluate the effect of some variables, considering that the variation of this measure with time is non linear. The assumption of the constant proportion of Et / Rt has been verified in the simulation task and in a certain range of time values for the vehicle experiment. Below the diagonal of 4.5 s, there is an observable deviation, particularly salient in the 120Km/h x 150 m condition.

4. 5. The two concepts of error

The consideration of error as the *algebraic sum of deviations from real time* or in *absolute value* can lead to quite different results. In fact, both measures refer to different concepts, especially when the number of overestimations increase. We considered more adequate to inform about both types of error, and we should point out that while the condition of 150 m leads to an abrupt reduction of estimated time at 120 Km/h, the same distance produces a notable increase in overestimations when combined with the speed of 60 Km/h.

Again, the results seem to suggest the existence of some limit condition associated with an extreme condition (low speed, maximum distance). A sudden increase in uncertainty of estimations with estimation times near 9 s has been pointed in the literature (Thomson, 1983), although such a limit condition has been debated by Reiser et al. (1990). Because of the limited range of values in the simulation task, this effect could not be observed.

4. 6. The comparison between both experiments

It has been demonstrated that the results of both tasks imply different psychological processes unconnected, while each task represents a consistent aptitude. This result alerts us to the risk of generalizing to real situations the results obtained with simulation tasks before verifying the equivalence of procedures. Although it must be pointed that in this case there were chosen the two versions that could be considered extreme versions of the same paradigm to estimate the time to arrival.

REFERENCES

Cavallo, V., Brun-Dei M., Laya O. & Nebiot, M. (1988) Perception and anticipation in negotiating curves: The role of driving experience. A.G. Gale et al. (Eds.) Vision in Vehicles II. Amsterdam: Elsevier.

Cavallo, V. & Laurent, M. (1988): Visual information and skill level in time-to-collision estimation. Perception, 17, 623-632.

Cavallo, V., Laya, O. & Laurent, M. (1986): The estimation of time-to collision as a function of visual stimulation. A.G. Gale et al. (Eds.): Vision in Vehicles. Amsterdam: Elsevier.

Groeger, J. A. & Brown, I.D. (1988): Motion perception is not direct with indirect viewing systems. Vision in Vehicles II. A. G. Gale et al. (Eds.). Amsterdam: Elsevier.

Groeger, J.A. & Cavallo, V. (1991): Judgements of time-to-collision and time-to-coincidence. A.G. Gale et al. (Eds.): Vision in Vehicles III. Amsterdam: Elsevier.

Groeger, J.A., Grande, G. & Brown, I.D. (1991): Accuracy and safety: effects of different training procedures on a time-to-coincidence task. A.G. Gale et al. (Eds.): Vision in Vehicles III. Amsterdam: Elsevier.

Horst, R. (1991): Time-to-collision as a cue for decision-making in braking. A.G. Gale et al.(Eds.): Vision in Vehicles III. Amsterdam: Elsevier.

Lee, D.N. (1976): A theory of visual control of braking based on information about time-to-collision. Perception, 5, 437-459.

Mcleod, R.W. & Ross, H.E. (1983): Optic-flow and cognitive factors in time-to-collision estimates. Perception, 12, 417-423.

Milgram, P. (1987): A spectacle-mounted liquid-crystal tachistoscope. Behavior Research Methods, Instruments & Computers, 19, 449-456.

Peterken, C., Brown, B. & Bowman, K. (1991): Predicting the future position of a moving target. Perception, 20, 5-16.

Reiser, J.J., Ashmead, D.H., Talor, C.R. & Youngquist, G.A. (1990): Visual perception and the guidance of locomotion without vision to previously seen targets. Perception, 19, 675-689

Schiff, W. & Detwiler, M.L. (1979): Information used in judging impending collision. Perception, 8, 647-658.

Schiff, W. & Oldak, R. (1990): Accuracy of judging time to arrival: effects of modality, trajectory, and gender. J. of Experimental Psychology: Human Perception and Performance, 16, 303-316.

Thomson, J.A. (1983): Is continuous visual monitoring necessary in visual guided locomotion? J. of Experimental Psychology: Human Perception and Performance, 9, 427-443.

Tresilian, J.R. (1991): Empirical and theoretical issues in the perception of time to contact. J. of Experimental Psychology: human perception and performance, 17, 865-876.

VISION IN VEHICLES - V
A.G. Gale et al. (Editors)

Possible Penalties Of Motorcyclists' Daytime Headlight Use: An Experimental Investigation

G. J. Hole and L. Tyrrell

School of Cognitive and Computing Sciences, University of Sussex, Falmer, Brighton, BN1 9QH.

1. INTRODUCTION

The most common form of multi-vehicle accident involving motorcyclists is for another road-user to manoeuvre directly into the motorcyclist's path (Fulton, Kirkby and Stroud, 1980). Following such accidents, drivers frequently claim that they "failed to see" the motorcyclist. This has led to numerous studies of how motorcyclists' conspicuity can be enhanced by aids such as fluorescent clothing and daytime headlight use (reviews in Thomson 1980, 1982).

Successful detection of another road-user's presence involves more than low-level perceptual processing, however; one must also correctly interpret what one sees, and this may be affected by attention and expectation. Rumar (1990) distinguished two basic types of driving error: failures of "perceptual detection" and failures of "cognitive expectation". While there is little doubt that motorcycles are harder to detect than other vehicles, probably as important in causing accidents is the driver's interpretation of what he is seeing.

Thomson (1980) suggested that voluntary daytime headlight-use by motorcyclists might increase their conspicuity at the expense of *reducing* the conspicuity of non-users. Due to repeated encounters with headlight-users, other motorists might develop a perceptual "set" for detecting point sources of illumination (headlights) rather than moving objects (motorcycles). The consequence might be to make headlight non-users effectively less visible than they would otherwise have been, and so put them at greater risk of accident. The present experiment investigated this issue experimentally, by encouraging subjects to use either shape or illumination as a cue to the presence of a motorcyclist.

2. METHOD

2.1. Design

Each subject saw 56 colour slides of traffic. The first 55 of these consisted of a random mixture (different for each subject) of 23 slides in which a motorcyclist was present somewhere in the scene, and 32 slides in which no motorcyclist was present. The last, "test", slide always contained a motorcyclist. The subject's task was to decide as quickly as they could, whether or not a motorcyclist was present or absent in each of the slides shown, and press one of two buttons accordingly.

In the final slide, the motorcyclist's headlight was either on or off. For those preceding slides in which a motorcyclist was present, headlight use was either consistent or inconsistent with that of the motorcyclist in the last slide (i.e., either on or off). There were thus four conditions:

ON/ON: exposure to slides of motorcyclists with their headlights on, followed by a final slide of a motorcyclist with his headlight on.

ON/OFF: exposure to slides of motorcyclists with their headlights on, followed by a slide of a motorcyclist with his headlight off.

OFF/OFF: exposure to slides of motorcyclists with their headlights off, followed by a slide of a motorcyclist with his headlight off.

OFF/ON: exposure to slides of motorcyclists with their headlights off, followed by a slide of a motorcyclist with his headlight on ("OFF/ON").

2.2. Subjects

Subjects were 112 students, mostly recruited from Open University summer-schools held at the University of Sussex. All were naive volunteers. Mean age was 33, with a range from 17 to 65. 82 subjects had held full car driving licences, for a mean 16 years (ranging from 2 to 48 years). The remaining 30 subjects were either non-drivers or had held a provisional licence for a year or less. There were 73 women and 39 men. All had normal or corrected-to normal vision.

2.3. Apparatus and materials

Each colour slide showed a view of either an "urban" location (Marlborough Place, a one-way street in Brighton, East Sussex) or a "rural" location (the north-bound carriageway of the A270 on the outskirts of Brighton). All slides of a given scene were taken from the same position, and showed the view which would be obtained by a driver who was emerging from a side-turning into the street in question.

All slides were taken at approximately the same time (15.00-16.00 hours, during July), but on two separate occasions. The first of these was a bright sunny day; the second, a bright but overcast day.

The slides containing a motorcyclist were taken with the aid of an assistant, who rode an unfaired Kawasaki GT550 motorcycle. Photographs were taken with the motorcycle at various positions in the road (i.e., left lane or right lane) and at three different distances from the camera. These distances varied according to the location. For the "urban" site, the motorcyclist was approximately 87 m, 28 m and 7 m away from the photographer. For the "rural" site, the three distances were 225 m, 113 m, and 29 m.

The two final slides showed a motorcyclist in the "urban" setting, either with his headlight on or off: in both of these slides, the motorcyclist was positioned 7 m from the photographer, and in the leftmost lane of the carriageway (leftmost from the subject's viewpoint). A pre-test confirmed that the motorcyclist was equally detectable in both slides.

Slides were presented by a Kodak S-AV 1010 slide-projector, fitted with a Compur Ltd. electronic shutter which enabled precise control of exposure onset and offset. Opening of the shutter started an electronic timer, which was stopped by the subject pressing one of two buttons on a hand-held button-box.

2.4. Procedure

Each subject was randomly allocated to one of the four experimental conditions, and tested individually. They were seated in a darkened room. Each slide subtended approximately 30 degrees of visual angle. The slides were presented sequentially, under computer control. A slide was presented for four seconds, or until the subject pressed one of the buttons, whichever was quicker.

3. RESULTS

3.1. Effects of headlight use on motorcyclists' visibility

The **ON/OFF** and **ON/ON** subjects received exactly the same set of slides, except for the final slide. The same was true for the **OFF/OFF** and **OFF/ON** groups. If the responses to the final slide for each condition are excluded, the data for the first two groups can be combined to produce an overall **headlight-ON** condition, and the data for the second two groups can be combined to obtain an overall **headlight-OFF** condition. The reaction times for these two conditions can then be compared, to determine whether headlight use *per se* affected the motorcyclist's detectability. This was done separately for the "rural" and "urban" locations.

Figure 1 shows the mean reaction times for the **headlight ON** and **headlight OFF** conditions in the two locations, and at each of the three distances used.

In both locations, headlight use enhanced conspicuity. This enhancement was greatest when the motorcyclist was farthest from the viewer: at close range, headlight use made no apparent difference to conspicuity. For the "urban" location, a two-way ANOVA on the reaction times revealed no significant main effect of headlight use (F 1, 110 = 2.57, $p>0.11$), but a highly significant effect of distance (F 2, 220 = 68.06, $p<0.0001$), and a highly significant headlight by distance interaction (F 2, 220 = 16.28, $p<0.001$). For the "rural" location, a two way ANOVA on the reaction times revealed highly significant main effects (for headlight use, F 1, 110 = 30.06, $p<0.0001$; for distance, F 2, 220 = 91.37, $p<0.0001$), and a highly significant headlight by distance interaction (F 2, 220 = 32.83, $p<0.001$). Taken together, these results suggest that headlights improve conspicuity most when the motorcycle is at some distance from the observer (at distances greater than approximately 30 m in the case of the present study).

3.2. Effect of prior slides on reaction times to the final slide

For each subject, the overall mean reaction time for "correct positive" decisions was calculated - i.e., the mean reaction time for the 23 slides in which a motorcyclist was present, and to which the subject responded correctly. This mean was subtracted from the subject's reaction time for the final slide, to give a difference score for each subject. A positive difference score indicates that a subject was faster to detect the motorcyclist in the final slide than to detect the motorcyclists in the previous slides; a negative score indicates the opposite.

Fig. 1: mean reaction times to detect a motorcyclist's presence

(a) "Urban" location:

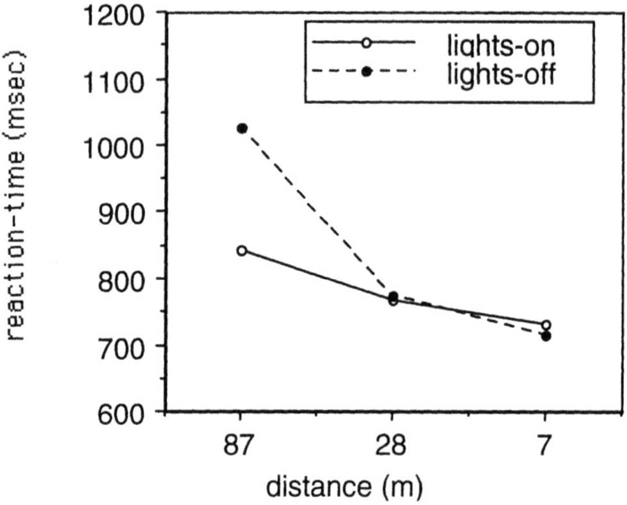

(b) "Rural" location:

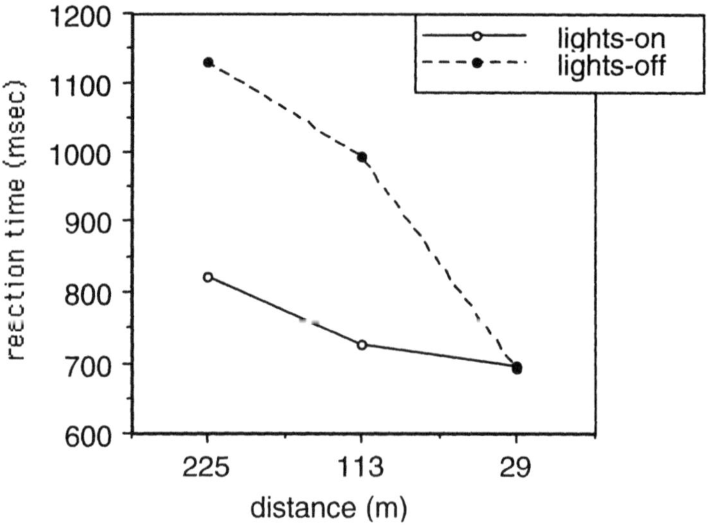

Table 1 shows the mean difference scores for subjects in each of the four conditions (**ON/ON, ON/OFF, OFF/ON, OFF/OFF**). Only the **ON/OFF** group showed a negative mean difference-score (reflecting the fact that subjects were slower to respond to the test slide than they were to the preceding slides containing a motorcyclist).

Table 1
Effects of perceptual "set" on reaction times.

experimental condition (n=28 per group)	mean difference score (standard deviation in brackets)	no. subjects slower on test slide (as % of total no. subjects in each group)
ON/ON:	69.1 (236.8)	8 (29%)
OFF/ON:	128.2 (157.7)	2 (7%)
ON/OFF:	-106.8 (199.7)	19 (68%)
OFF/OFF:	111.3 (285.5)	7 (25%)

The other three groups were faster on the last slide than they were on their previous slides (presumably due to practice on the task). A one-way ANOVA performed on these data showed that there was a significant difference between the four groups (F 3, 108 = 6.42, $p<0.001$). Neumann-Keuls post-hoc comparisons showed that the **ON/OFF** condition was significantly different from the other three conditions (**ON/OFF** versus **ON/ON**: $p<0.05$; **ON/OFF** versus **OFF/OFF** and **ON/OFF** versus **OFF/ON**: both $p<0.01$). There were no significant differences between the **ON/ON**, **OFF/OFF** and **OFF/ON** groups.

An alternative approach is to consider how many subjects in each condition were slower on the final slide than on the previous slides, disregarding the magnitude of the difference. Table 1 shows that for the two conditions in which the test slides were similar in nature to the inducing slides (the **ON/ON** and **OFF/OFF** conditions), approximately a quarter of subjects were slower on the test slide than on the inducing slides For the **ON/OFF** condition, the majority (68%) of subjects were slower on the test slide; and for the **OFF/ON** condition, the majority (93%) were faster on the test slide. A Chi-Square test on the raw frequencies showed that they were significantly different from what would be expected by chance (Chi-Square = 18.14, with 3 df; $p<0.001$).

In summary, exposure to slides in which motorcyclists consistently used their lights, appears to have led to the establishment of a perceptual "set" in the **ON/OFF** subjects.

Because subjects in this group adopted a strategy of looking for "lights" rather than motorcyclists, they were slower to detect the motorcyclist in the final slide - despite the fact that he was in full and clear view.

4. DISCUSSION

The principal findings of this study are: (a) that headlight use improved motorcyclist conspicuity, and that this enhancement was greatest for motorcycles that were furthest from the viewer; and (b) that repeated exposure to motorcyclists with their headlights on resulted in delayed detection of a motorcyclist with his headlight off - despite the latter being readily detectable in other circumstances.

The finding that headlight use improved conspicuity is consistent with the results of previous studies, both in the laboratory and in the field (reviews in Thomson 1980, 1982).

The fact that subjects in the **ON/OFF** condition were slower to detect the presence of a motorcyclist in their final test slide, *despite the motorcyclist being in full and clear view,* appears to offer some experimental support for Thomson's (1980) speculation that if the majority of motorcyclists used their headlights in daytime, the minority who did not use lights might be placed at greater risk of not being seen. Other motorists might develop a strategy of looking for lights rather than for motorcycles *per se*. The **ON/OFF** subjects may have been suffering from the type of detection error described by Rumar (1990) as a "lapse of cognitive expectation", engendered by repeated exposure to slides of motorcyclists with lights on. This agrees with Hills (1980) who, in a review of visual factors influencing driving, concluded that cognitive factors (driver expectancy, and failures thereof -e.g., failure to expect motorcyclists or cyclists to be present) were probably far more potent in causing accidents than were sensory limitations (e.g., reduced acuity, poor contrast sensitivity, etc.).

One should obviously be wary of extrapolating incautiously from laboratory to field conditions. It is impossible to be certain that one is simulating the crucial aspects of the driver's environment and task demands. However, if the present findings have any ecological validity, they suggest that policies of recommending motorcyclists to use their headlights may not have the desired effects in terms of reducing overall accident levels, unless such recommendations are accompanied by clear warnings to two other groups of road-user: to those motorcyclists who elect not to use their headlight, pointing out that they may need to ride more defensively to maintain their safety; and to four-wheeled motorists, instructing them not to rely on lit headlights as a cue to the presence or absence of motorcyclists in traffic.

REFERENCES

Fulton, E.J., Kirkby, C. and Stroud, P.G. 1980, Daytime motorcycle conspicuity. Transport and Road Research Laboratory Supplementary Report, 625.

Hills, B.L. 1980, Vision, visibility, and perception in driving. Perception, 9, 183-216.

Rumar, K. 1990, The basic driver error: late detection. Ergonomics, 33 (10/11), 1281-1290.

Thomson, G.A. 1980, The role frontal motorcycle conspicuity has in road accidents. Accident Analysis and Prevention, 12, 165-178.

Thomson, G.A. 1982, Do measurements of motorcycle conspicuity really measure conspicuity effects? Ergonomics 25 (9), 771-782.

VISION IN VEHICLES - V
A.G. Gale et al. (Editors)

The Relations Between Head and Eye Movements During Driving

Michael Land and Julia Horwood

Sussex Centre for Neuroscience,
School of Biological Sciences,
University of Sussex, Brighton BN1 9QG, UK

Abstract

Eye, head and gaze movements were measured during driving using a new, portable eye-movement camera. The coupling between head and eye movements was studied. In general the two are closely related, and both are accurately predicted from the size and timing of each saccadic gaze change. When driving round bends three different phases of gaze behaviour were apparent. During the approach the eyes seek out clues to the bend's curvature from the changes in the appearance of the road's edge. When rounding the bend the eyes look into the curve, and thus away from the car's heading. During the exit gaze is held on targets beyond the bend, and the car and body counter-rotate beneath the head.

1. INTRODUCTION

As we drive we obtain information from many parts of the visual surroundings, which means that we must frequently change the direction of gaze. This, in general, requires a coordinated movement of the head (relative to the body) and eye (relative to the head) so that their sum (gaze direction) gives a clean, rapid change. In typical traffic conditions we make these "saccadic" gaze changes as often as three times per second, and in spite of the subjective feeling that our gaze moves freely across the scene, this is never what actually happens. The movements are always fast and jerky, with brief but stable fixations in between. One reason for studying head-eye coordination during driving is that we are so busy with the task itself that the behaviour we see is likely to be "natural" - not affected by conscious control. In that sense it should represent the "default" pattern of coordination that the brain adopts automatically.

To make a gaze saccade the eye and head must move together, but their proper coordination is not simple because the low inertia eye moves fast for tens of milliseconds, while the heavier head takes about half a second to complete its part of the manoeuvre. Laboratory studies of primates in the early 1970's (Bizzi et al., 1971, Morasso et al.,1973) suggested how this might be done. Eye and head both receive a command to turn; the eye leads the way and the head follows more slowly. If the head is prevented from moving, the eye completes the gaze shift on its own.

This study was supported by grants from the SERC and the MRC, UK.

With the head free, however, the combined manoeuvre reaches the same end point, because a signal exactly equal and opposite to the rotation of the head is added to the eye movement, so that as far as the gaze change is concerned the head movement has no effect. The mechanism that supplies the head movement signal is the vestibulo-ocular reflex (VOR), mediated by the angular velocity receptors of the semi-circular canals of the inner ear. The head movement is not irrelevant, however, because as the head rotates the eye counter-rotates back towards its resting forward-pointing position, ready for another manoeuvre, and the head movement has in effect taken up the slack (Guitton, 1992).

In this paper we consider whether this Bizzi-Morasso model of the way gaze changes are made provides an adequate account of what we do during the continuous sequences of movements that occur during driving. Two different situations are examined. The first is a road intersection where the driver is nearly stationary, making large gaze saccades to check both directions before proceeding; this study has been presented briefly elsewhere (Land, 1992). The second is the more complex situation of negotiating a bend in the road. This also involves gaze saccades, but also requires the eye and head to make tracking movements, particularly as the vehicle emerges from the bend. We have hints, too, of the strategy the brain adopts in preparation for the bend; the eyes seem to be making subtle surveying measurements in order to estimate the bend's curvature.

2. METHODS

Eye and head movements were monitored by means of a small video camera (ELMO) mounted on a band from a construction helmet clamped firmly to the head. The camera's field of view was split optically so the upper two-thirds imaged the view ahead via a partly silvered mirror in front of the left eye. The lower third imaged the eye itself via a concave mirror in front of and slightly below the eye. In this way the scene ahead, and the eye with its various movements, were recorded together onto a SONY portable video recorder. Later, the tape was played back frame by frame, via a mixer that added a computer-generated model of the eye in which the outline of the modelled iris was marked with a bright ring. This model could be manipulated with a trackerball, so that the model iris fitted the real one. With proper calibration this fit meant that the angular coordinates of the model corresponded to the direction of view of the eye itself, relative to the head. These were stored, and also used to generate a spot that was superimposed onto the "head's eye" view. This spot showed the direction of gaze on the scene, to an accuracy of about 1°. The matching process takes less than 1s, and each frame was dumped to a second recorder (Panasonic AG-6720). This process provided the eye-in-head movements. The head-in-world movements were generated from the same videotape by tracking a distant object in the image, again with a computer-generated cursor. In some cases a point on the car body was tracked instead (e.g. Fig 6). Since movements of the image are caused by head movements, this allows the head movements to be measured, and these can then be added to the previously stored eye movements, to generate the gaze movements themselves. The method is described in more detail elsewhere (Land, 1992, 1993). The car drivers in this study were the author, Julia Horwood and Jay Butler.

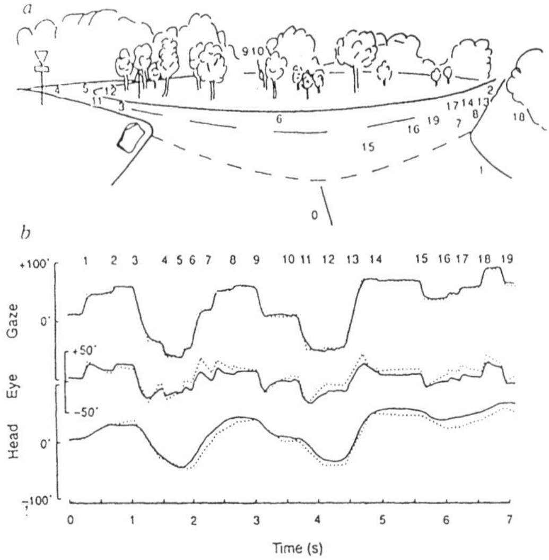

Figure 1. a) Sketch of a road intersection where the driver is about to turn right. Numbers mark the destinations of the gaze saccades shown below. b) Solid lines: Records of head, eye and gaze movements made while checking the intersection. The dotted lines show the output of the model presented in Fig 2, in which the head and eye movements are generated entirely on the basis of the amplitude and timing of the gaze saccades. From Land (1992).

3. EYE-HEAD COORDINATION AT A ROAD INTERSECTION

Fig 1a shows a sketch of a "T" intersection where the driver is about to turn right. The record shows two complete right-left-right gaze saccade sequences (as prescribed by the UK highway code!) before the car moves off at about saccade 16. An inspection of the eye and head records shows that each saccade has three components: a fast movement by the eye, a slower but larger movement by the head, and a counter-rotation by the eye at the completion of each saccade (Fig 1b). This is precisely the pattern described by the Bizzi-Morasso model, outlined earlier.

This qualitative account is not sufficient, however, to predict the eye and head movements in detail. To do that we need to know: 1) Whether head and eye movement systems get the same (gaze-change) command at the same time; and 2) if so, how does each system execute it? Assuming for the moment that the answer to 1) is "yes", we can examine the rules that specify the size and time-course of the eye and head movements. Basically, the eye moves at an almost constant velocity of about $500°.s^{-1}$ for large saccades, and the size of the eye movement is specified by its duration (Fig 2). The head, however, moves for a constant duration of about 0.4s, independent of the size of the movement, and the angle through which it moves is set by the velocity it attains. Thus eye and head are programmed in quite different ways; via duration in one and speed in the other. For details see Land (1992). The remaining component of the model is the vestibulo-ocular reflex, which reduces the eye velocity by the amount of the head velocity. Here we assume that VOR operates all the time, both during and between saccades. (There is still some confusion as to what really happens during saccades (see Becker, 1991), but the simple additive model predicts the outcome well enough). The result of a simulation employing the mechanisms just described (Fig 2) is shown by the dotted line in Fig 1b.

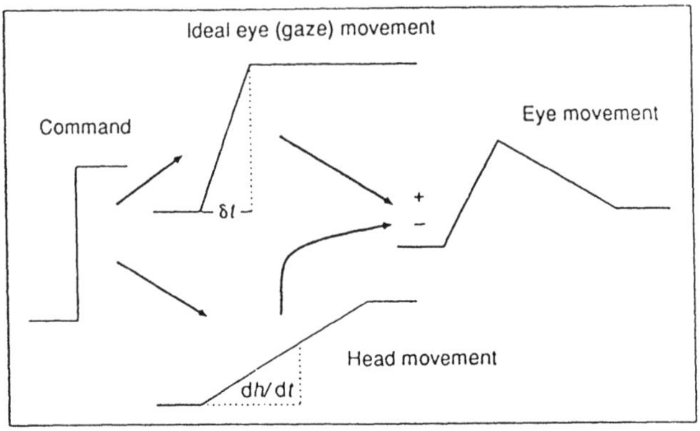

Figure 2. Method of calculating head and eye movements from gaze change commands, employed to generate the dotted lines in Fig 1b. The command specifies the duration of the eye movement (dt) made at constant velocity, and the velocity of the head movement (dh/dt) made for a constant duration. The head movement is subtracted from the "ideal" eye movement by the VOR, and the final gaze change is the sum of the eye and head movements - which will re-constitute the ideal gaze movement. Compare with Fig 1b. Further details in the text and in Land (1992).

The most important feature of the model is that it works. Given only the size and timing of the gaze commands (which we assume are the real instructions from the brain) it predicts surprisingly accurately the form of the head movements, and quite well the time course of the eye movements (Fig 1b). Where problems occur with the model, they seem to have two causes. Sometimes the eye and head do not move together - just before Second 2 the head "jumped the gun" by about 50ms. This asynchrony seems to be uncommon, however. Usually eye and head receive the same command at the same time. The other cause is also rare. When the eye is already near the limit of its travel when a new instruction arrives it may be physically unable to move far enough to execute the command, and then the head has to carry the gaze to its conclusion alone. To account for this does require modifications to the model of Fig 2, but these will not be considered here.

Given that the magnitude and timing of the gaze changes are already specified, the model gives us a reasonably accurate account of the way they are executed. In many ways the more interesting questions concern the commands themselves: why do we change gaze when we do? So far the rules of this "strategic" process seem to have eluded everybody, and this study does not add anything. Knowing about gaze saccade execution helps, however, because it shows that there is less going on than one might have feared; the eye and head movement systems at least seem to share the same "command" agenda.

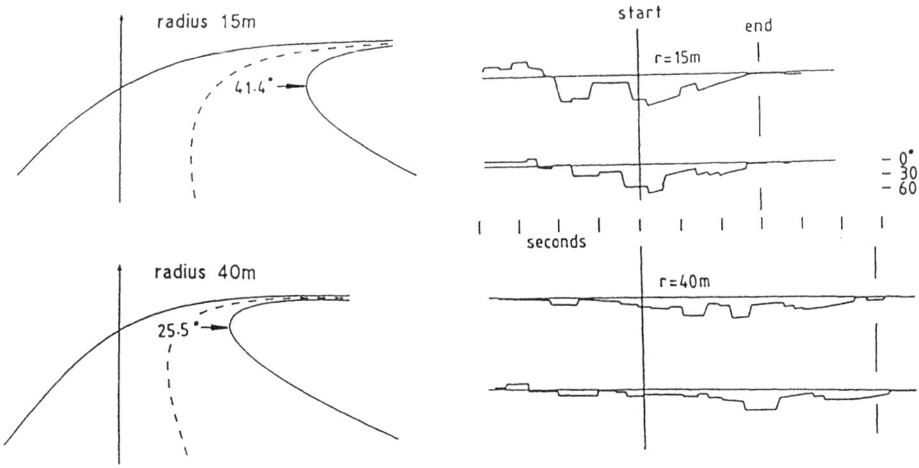

Fig. 3. Left: Appearance of two 90° bends with different central radii of curvature, as seen by a driver 1.1m above the road, which was 6m wide. The car's instantaneous heading is shown by the long arrow. The short arrows show the large difference in the position of the tangent to the far-side kerb in the driver's field of view, if he were looking in the direction of the car's heading. Right: Records of gaze movements of a driver (ML) negotiating 2 curves of similar radii to those on the left. Notice ranging movements to the right before the start of each bend, and the ramp-like rotation of gaze (relative to the car) during the exit from the bend.

4. DRIVING ROUND BENDS

In negotiating a bend the main job of the driver is to keep the steering adjusted to the curvature of the road. There are clearly three phases to this process. Entering a bend the curvature has to be estimated and the wheel set; during the bend the wheel position is maintained and perhaps corrected; and leaving the bend the steering is returned to the central position. The eye, head and gaze movements associated with each phase have proved to be different, and fairly consistent for three drivers and some preliminary conclusions are presented here. Fig 3 shows the appearance of two 90° bends to a driver about to enter them (driving on the left in the UK); one is tight (radius 15m) and one gentle (radius 40m), and both represent a two-lane road. The figure also shows pairs of gaze records of a driver negotiating similar bends.

4.1 Approach

About 2 seconds before the beginning of the turn the gaze is directed to the right, towards the far-side kerb. In tight radius bends the kerb appears to move right from the line of the car's heading quite fast at this time, and this is reflected in the large gaze movements. For the gentler curve the apparent kerb movement is smaller. At the beginning of the bend itself the position of the tangent to the kerb (reversal point), relative to the direction of travel of the vehicle, is characteristic of the curvature of the bend (Figs 3 & 4), and this is perhaps the most reliable of the clues to bend radius listed by Riemersma (1991). In both tight and gentle curves the gaze changes are similar: the eyes look right for about a second, back to the car's heading, and back right to the kerb at the start of the bend. It is tempting to think that these are "ranging" movements that the visual system uses to form an estimate of the curvature of the bend. This is not unlikely: the steering wheel must be turned by roughly the correct amount at the beginning of bend.

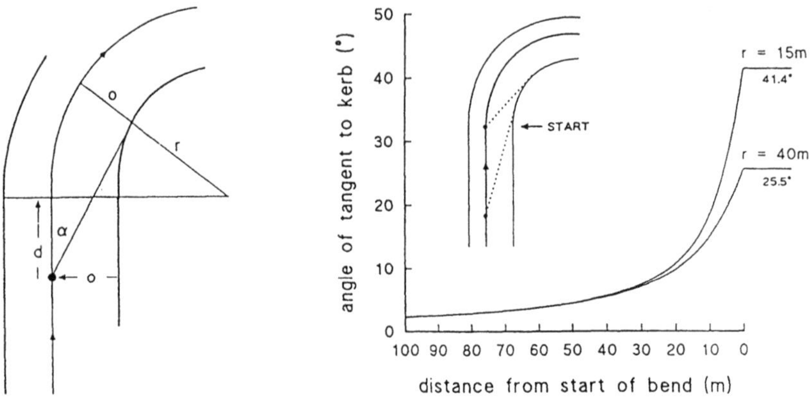

Figure 4. The change in apparent angular position of the tangent to the kerb (reversal point) as the bend approaches. Note that bends of different radii become distinguishable about 30m from the beginning of the start of the bend, but not earlier. The curves were calculated from the following expression derived from the geometry shown on the left.

$$\text{angle from line of travel to the tangent to the kerb} = \arctan (r+o)/d \; - \; \arcsin r/Ö(d^2+(r+o)^2)$$

where r is the radius of the inner kerb, o is the distance of the line of travel out from the inner kerb, and d is the driver's distance from the start of the bend. (In the figure itself the radii referred to are to the centre line of the road, not the kerb).

In fact the timing of these eye movements corresponds rather well to the availability of information about the curvature of the bend. Fig 4 shows that as the vehicle approaches the corner the far side kerb begins to move laterally about 30m from the beginning of the bend. Furthermore it is about this point that differences in bend curvature begin to show up as differences in the rate at which the tangent to the kerb appears to move away from the line of travel. At 10m.s^{-1} (22mph), 30m corresponds to 3 seconds, which is approximately the time before the bend that the "ranging" eye movements are seen in Fig 3.

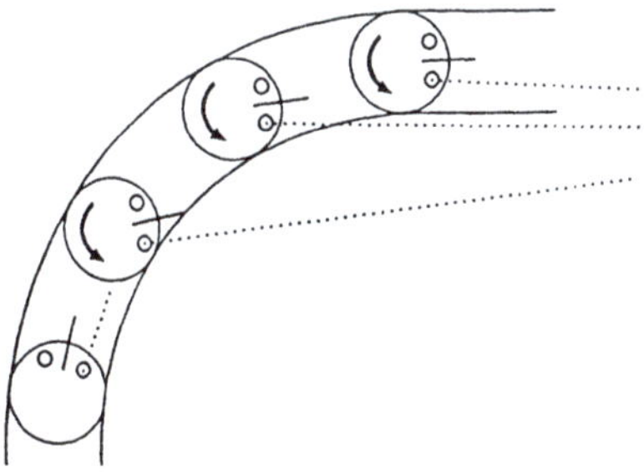

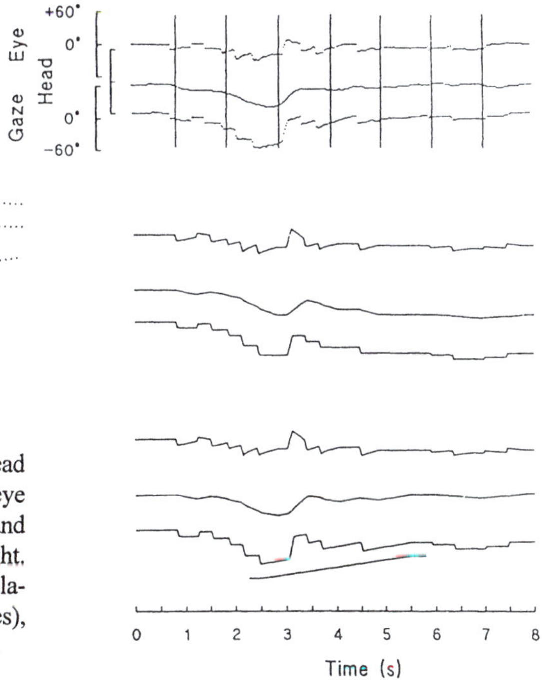

Figure 5. Behaviour of eye and head during the exit from a bend. The eye fixates objects beyond the bend, and gaze continues to move slightly right. The head, however, rotates left relative to the body and car (solid curves), allowing the car to rotate beneath it.

Figure 6. An attempt to model the eye-head coordination pattern through a 90° bend. Top traces: record of eye, head (relative to car) and gaze. The turn is entered with a series of saccades (0 - 2.5 seconds), but the exit involves a slow gaze rotation (see Fig 5) with some saccades superimposed (2.5 - 5 seconds). Middle traces: simulation using the model in Fig 2. This accurately predicts the behaviour of head and eye from the gaze saccades during the entry to the bend, but does not predict the ramp rotation during the exit. Lower traces: the same, but with the addition of a ramp rotation to the head, and hence the gaze trace (indicated below). The result gives a near perfect simulation of the actual records, and means that the neck muscles receive a tracking command, in addition to the commands that accompany the gaze saccades.

4.2 Rounding the Bend

In the bend itself the gaze maintains a direction to the right of the car's heading, represented by the straight line on the figures. The driver is looking into the turn rather than in the direction of travel, as noted previously by Shinar et al (1977). In the 15m bend this phase is almost non-existent, because the driver has already begun to fixate on targets beyond the bend. In the 40m bend, however, it lasts for 2-3 seconds, with gaze ranging from 20 - 40° to the right of the car's heading, before the "pull-out" stage begins.

4.3 Leaving the Bend

Coming out of the bend, the gaze appears to shift continuously and smoothly, resulting in a very obvious "ramp" in the case of the tighter 15m bend. Gaze direction in these records was measured relative to the car rather than the distant horizon, and the gaze changes reflect the rotation of the car, not the head. Gaze, during this phase, was actually fixated on distant objects beyond the bend. Thus the meaning of the ramp is that the car is actually rotating beneath the eye (Fig 5). This is in contrast to phase (4.2) where the eye and car rotate together, with the gaze following the road round. As in other phases, the eye may make saccades from one target to another, and these are accurately accounted for by the model described earlier (Fig 2). In addition, however, the head receives a command generated by the task of tracking distant objects. As Fig 6 shows, this command is unrelated to the saccadic gaze changes, and is added mainly to the head movement system. It is this tracking command that shows up as the ramp movements in the gaze records of Figs 3 & 6.

To summarize, the approach to a bend is characterised by "ranging" saccades that probably help to estimate the size of the turn required. These leave the eye pointing into the turn, where gaze remains until the exit is visible. The visual system then finds objects beyond the turn and fixates them, providing a signal that rotates the head relative to the trunk as the car completes the bend.

REFERENCES

1. Becker, W., Saccades. In: Vision and Visual Dysfunction. Vol.8. Ed. Carpenter R.H.S. pp 95-137, Macmillan, Basingstoke, 1991
2. Bizzi, E., Kalil, R.E. and Tagliasco, V., Eye-head coordination in monkeys: evidence for centrally patterned organization. Science, 173, 452-454, 1971
3. Guitton, D., Control of eye-head coordination during orienting gaze shifts. T.I.N.S., 15, 174-179, 1992
4. Land, M.F., Predictable eye-head coordination during driving. Nature, 359, 318-320, 1992
5. Land, M.F., Eye-head coordination during driving. IEEE Systems, Man and Cybernetics Conf Proc, Le Touquet, Vol 3, 490-494, 1993
6. Morasso, P., Bizzi, E. and Dichgans, J., Adjustment of saccade characteristics during head movements. Exptl Brain Res, 16, 492-500, 1973
7. Riemersma, J.B.J., Perception of curve characteristics. In: Vision in Vehicles III. Eds. Gale, A.G., Brown, I.D., Haslegrave, C.M., Moorhead, I., Taylor, S. pp 163-170. Elsevier, North Holland, 1991
8. Shinar, D., McDowell, E.D. and T.H.Rockwell, T.H., Eye movements in curve negotiation. Human Factors, 19, 63-77, 1977

4: VISUAL REQUIREMENTS OF IN-VEHICLE GUIDANCE SYSTEMS

VISION IN VEHICLES - V
A.G. Gale et al. (Editors)

Visual Requirements Of Vehicle Guidance Systems: Central Versus Peripheral Preparatory Information Display

A. Pauzié[a] and S. Anadon[b]
with the collaboration of R. Trauchessec[a]

[a] Laboratory Ergonomics Health COmfort, INRETS / LESCO,
109 avenue Salvador Allende, 69675 - Bron, France*

[b] LEACM, University of Human Sciences, Lyon II, 69500 - Bron, France

1. INTRODUCTION

1.1. Visual search for landmarks and guidance systems

While driving, the operator is in *perpetual* search for spatial landmarks, in order to set up orientation processes, in parallel with the operational and tactic vehicle control processes. All these activities are conducted under temporal constraint, the aim being to avoid any dysfunctioning with potential consequences in terms of road safety.
If the driver's attentional demands involved in the skill-based and rule-based behaviour stage processing are quite low (experienced driver, easy traffic and simple network structure), the driver's attention focuses easily on navigation and guidance tasks. But when the external situation induces an heavy mental workload for the driver, the strategic level is considered less in order to concentrate on the other levels.

Navigation and guidance systems will support the driver, by giving directional information on the route to follow, at the right time, during the trip, making this orientation process level easier to handle. On the other hand, this supplementary source of information displayed on a screen might create a new situation of attention sharing.

1.2. Efficiency of preparatory processes for guidance activity

Preparatory adjustment aim at an increased efficiency in detecting a specific event happening at a given time. The preparatory processes might concern the timing of the event happening -*non specific preparation*- or the event type -*specific preparation*-. Both aspects will be considered in this paper. Furthermore, the visual and/or auditory modality of the preparatory signal presents advantages and disadvantages that must be defined precisely in the driving context.

* This research was supported by a grant from the convention between the National Centre of Scientific Research (Pirville) / INRETS, project in collaboration with B. Thon, Research Centre of Behavioural Biology, ERS65 du CNRS, University Paul Sabatier, 31000, Toulouse, France. We wish to thank all the following participants for their collaboration in the project: B. LeBreton, H. Moussavi (statistics), Ph. Deleurence (electronic) and B. Piechnik (mechanic). This paper was presented by M-P. Bruyas, INRETS/LESCO.

2. OBJECTIVE

The purpose of the study was to evaluate the efficiency of preparatory processes, according to various information presentation modalities, in a guidance driving task controlled by visual directional messages. These messages were displayed on a screen located in the middle of the dashboard. Correct detection, at the right time, of these messages by the driver is fundamental, knowing that this information has direct consequences on further decisions concerning the route to follow.

The various preparatory modalities were visual, well centred in the driver's field of view or off-centre, and auditory, non-specific such as a "beep" or specific such as a "verbal message".

Ageing has important consequences in terms of functional capacities, concerning perceptual and cognitive levels, in the context of the driving activity [1]. The concept of age raises many questions. In this specific situation, the word "age" is used for "still young" people presenting well established presbyopia, with the well-known consequences on intermediate distance legibility difficulties, taking into account that this distance is critical for the dashboard screen legibility. Improvement of driving aid systems used as compensatory support for "elderly" drivers, must take this fact into consideration. Furthermore, it has been shown in previous studies that "elderly" drivers have a tendency to check the screen visually, on a regular basis, whether the information is displayed or not [2]. The question raised in this paper was to identify whether this behaviour is maintained even in the situation where the driver is systematically informed by pre-cue information about display happenings.

3. METHOD

3.1. Experimental procedure

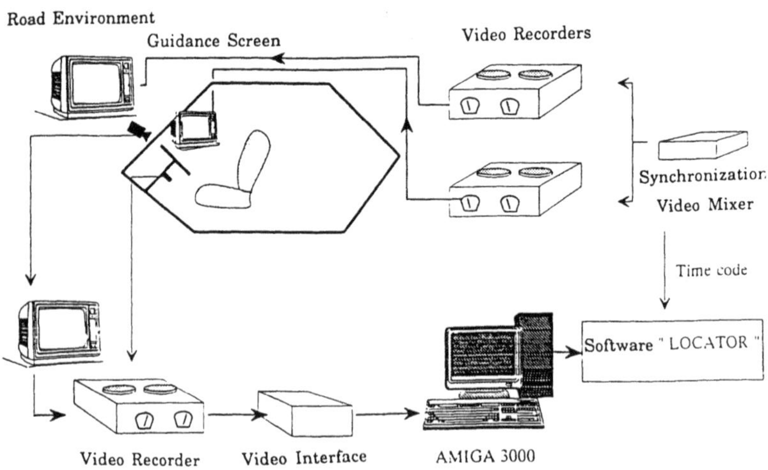

Figure 1 : Schematic representation of the driving simulator.

Driving task: The subject sat in a static driving simulator (figure 1), and could manipulate the steering wheel and the flashing light. In central vision, a video recording on a big screen showed the road environment. This route was characterized by a series of identified turns and intersections. Recording of the engine and tyre/road noise in parallel with the video recording constituted the noisy background.

Guidance task: The driver task was to follow the route according to the directional arrows displayed on the small screen of the dashboard. The guidance messages were similar to those displayed by existing systems. This mode of symbolic information had already been tested in relation to modality of information presentation such as size and contrast [3] and in terms of efficiency in comparison with the paper map in real road situations [4]. Results from this second study indicated firstly that elderly drivers spent 6.3 % of their time glancing at the screen, as compared with 3.5% of the time for the young sample, and secondly that guidance systems induced fewer navigational errors than paper maps whatever the driver's age.

In the present study, arrows were divided into two categories according to the complexity of their design.

Category n°1 Category n° 2

Figure 2 : Directional arrows presenting various complexity of information.

In order to characterize the arrow legibility according to its size for this experiment, the angular size had been computed by combining the actual arrow size and the driver's visual distance. The angular size was 6.84°, quite a high value intentionally chosen to make the perceptual processes easy for the driver, whatever his age and his visual abilities.

Preparatory signals:

- visual modality: the visual preparatory signal allowed non specific preparation, giving information on the arrow display timing, and so, reducing temporal uncertainty. This preparatory information was given according to two locations: in *central vision* - simulating the HeadUp Display principle where driving aid information is displayed on the windshield - and in *peripheral vision* - on the same screen which displays navigational arrows-. Whatever the location, the signal was the same, that is to say a flashing red spot display. In the first case, there was less constraint on visual accommodation and immediate detection; on the other hand, some previous studies had shown that this type of display might induce potential unease because it is unusual for the driver.

- auditory modality: the auditory preparatory signals allowed *specific* and *non specific preparation*, by giving (or not giving) preliminary information on the driver's future action. In the first case, the auditory information was given by a spoken message, recorded in synchronization with the video tape, preparing the driver for a precise navigational manoeuvre before the display. In the second case, a sound such as a "beep" came before the arrow, a few seconds before the directional information.

The experimental session lasted 20 minutes with a succession of 40 turns, 20 on the left, 20 on the right.

3.2. Sample

Drivers tested (males and females) belonged to two age categories; the young group with a minimum of 23 years old, a maximum of 30 years (mean = 25.5; n = 10 subjects) and the "older" one with a minimum of 55 years old, a maximum of 64 years (mean = 59.8; n = 10 subjects).

3.3. Visual tests

Individuals present heterogeneity in terms of visual abilities; this trend is even stronger for the "more than 55 years old" persons where a chronological age does not give much information about the real functional age, especially in terms of visual abilities. In order to have more knowledge on this point, a series of visual tests had been conducted on the subjects :

- Binocular intermediate vision (visual acuity at 66 cm)
- Long distance binocular vision (visual acuity at long distance) - Visual fatigue (alternative reading to far and short distance vision, with a timing sequence of 3 seconds)

Subjects were asked to wear their glasses during the tests as well as during the experiment if they normally did so when they drove their cars.

3.4. Questionnaire

A questionnaire was filled in by the drivers at the end of the experimentation. It took 10 to 15 minutes to answer all the questions. It was divided into 6 parts : driver characteristics, understanding of the meaning of the arrows, subjective evaluation of (i) the preparatory signals, (ii) the simulated driving task, (iii) the global evaluation of the experimental session such as assessment of driving aid efficiency. Only some results are presented in this paper.

4. RESULTS

4.1. Visual tests

For the intermediate vision, all the drivers from the older group had less than 12/12 vision (minimum: 4/12 and maximum: 10/12). All the young sample had 12/12 acuity.

For the long distance vision, all the drivers had 12/12, except 2 "old" drivers (who had respectively 4/12 and 8/12) and 1 "young" driver (6/12).

Finally, the old drivers were more sensitive to the visual fatigue than the young ones.

4.2. Questionnaire

Some questions were related to the physical characteristics of the directional information (shape, colour) and the way they were understood by drivers. Answers showed that legibility and understandability of the various arrows raised no problem, except for the round-about which 30% of the drivers found ambiguous.

For the preparatory signals, the "beep" emitted before the visual display was considered as the more annoying signal by 35% of the sample, followed by the red spot HUD displayed on the road environment (20%). The more understandable signal was evaluated by the sample as being the message spoken (40%), the red spot HUD (30%), and the "beep" (25%).

Most of the drivers found the driving simulator task realistic (75%), and never forgot to put the flashing light as requested.

4.3. Visual strategies

Drivers' behaviour was recorded on video tape and the frequency of glances towards the screen on the dash-board was computed, using home-made software "Locator". The glance duration was not been taken into consideration, its average value being very small and globally equivalent among trials and drivers. As a matter of fact, in this kind of clearly legible symbolic message, perceptual and reading processes are short, information being processed in one unit, as a whole. A more precise method of data recording, such as EOG, would have certainly shown glance duration differences, especially in relation to age, but, because of their very short values, the impact in terms of screen visual demand is negligible when considering the duration of the whole experimental session. On the other hand, the glance frequency revealed when the driver was not looking at the road environment at a given time, in relation to screen happenings.

4.3.1. Visual strategies and driver's age

Generally, glance frequency towards the screen is higher for the "older group" in comparison with the "younger" group, whatever the preparatory condition and throughout the duration of the session. The "older" group adopted the strategy of checking the screen even when there was no information displayed. This behaviour has been shown in other situations, when, for example, the task was to read words in parallel with the driving task [2]. The important difference between the two groups of drivers comes not only from the fact that the "older" group checked the screen more often, on a regular basis, throughout the experimental session but also because young drivers were able to detect and to understand some of the guidance information without glancing at the screen, a situation never encountered for the "older" group. He has to be remembered that the symbolic information displayed was clearly legible and well contrasted. To illustrate this observation, the following charts (Figures 3 and 4) show the chronological events -signal happening, arrow guidance display and corresponding visual strategy-, for two drivers during a session.

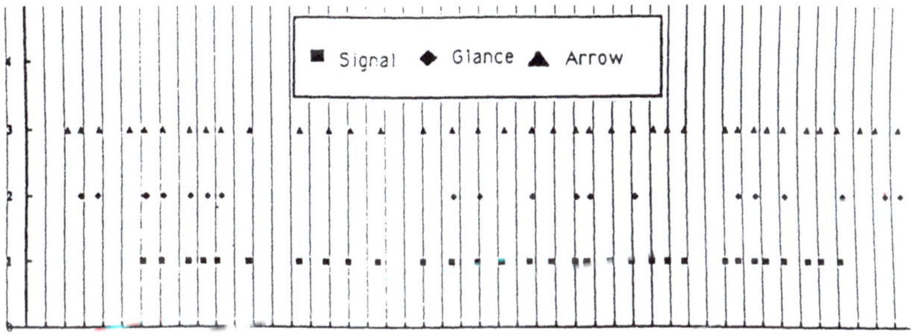

Figure 3 : Chronological sequence of signal happening, arrow guidance display and corresponding visual strategy during an experimental session : the case of a young driver.

Remark: The occurrences of the spoken message, giving prior information on guidance, were not at the origin of all the lacks of glances towards the screen for the young driver.

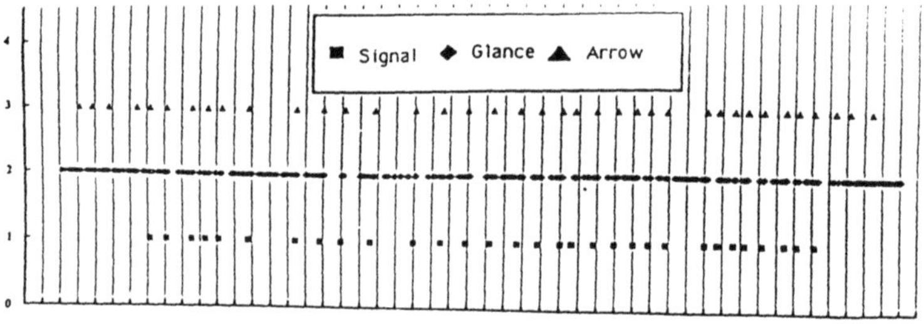

Figure 4 : Chronological sequence of signal happening, arrow guidance display and corresponding visual strategy during an experimental session : the case of an "old" driver.

Visual strategies have been also considered at the critical moment of the arrow information display, taking into account the 10 seconds before and after the event. The difference in glance frequency in this case indicated that there was also a higher visual activity for the "older" drivers during this specific period of the experiment (ANOVA, F = 5,92, p = 0,027).

4.3.2. Visual strategies and preparatory conditions

Each case of preparatory conditions was considered in connection with the driver glance frequency. An overall analysis, whatever the driver age, showed that the glance frequency values differed significantly between the preparatory conditions (ANOVA, F = 24, p < 0,001). Furthermore, there was no significant difference in use of the type of preparatory signal in relation to the driver's age (ANOVA, F = 0,07, p= 0,97).

In other words, being informed in advance about a message happening through the various proposed modalities had the same consequences on the driver's visual strategy whatever the age.

Remark: For technical experimental reasons, the time separation between preparatory information -PI- and guidance information -GI- was about 3 seconds for the "Beep" and the "on-screen signal" (Figures 5 a and 5 b) and about 4,5 seconds for the "HUD signal" and the "Spoken Message"(Figures 5 c and 5 d). As a matter of fact, it must be noted that to give a guidance message verbally, for example, required an unavoidable period of time. So, this difference explained why the maximum of glance frequency appeared later on the figures 5e and 5 f.

The main results are as follows :

- Drivers' reactions to a guidance message with an auditory message such as a beep or with a flashing red spot on the dashboard screen were very similar in terms of glance frequency. The results in both cases were very similar at each step of the process: a regular increase during the interval between PI and GI, to a maximum when the guidance message was displayed, then a decrease to finally reach the original level 3 seconds later (Figures 5 a and 5 b). In this specific experimental framework, none of the guidance information was missed whatever the preparatory signal, auditory beep or visual spot, but it must be remembered that the beep was considered by some drivers as being *annoying*. So, these results showed that for an equivalent efficiency, and for non-emergency information such as guidance messages, a visual prior signal would be recommended rather than an auditory one.

Figure 5 : Glance frequency as a function of the time for the two groups according to the type of preparatory signal -
The preparatory signal was displayed at the time identified as "t 0" on the graph.

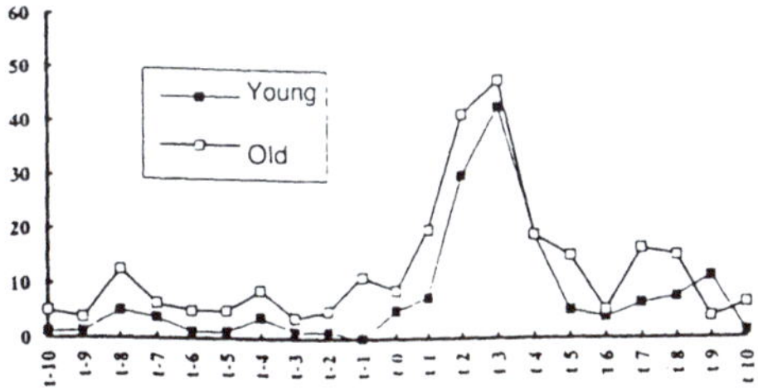

Figure 5 a : "Beep"

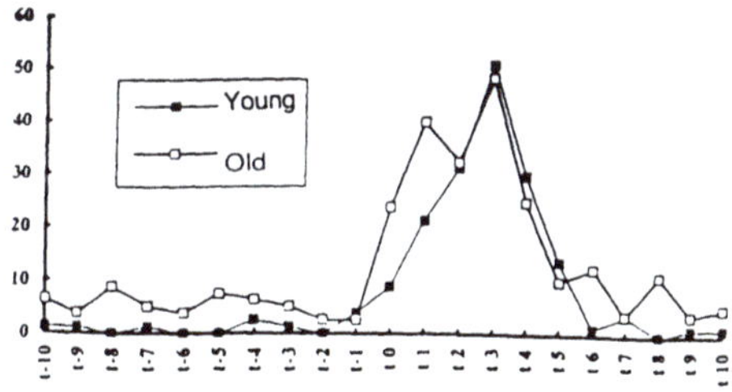

Figure 5 b : "On-Screen Signal"

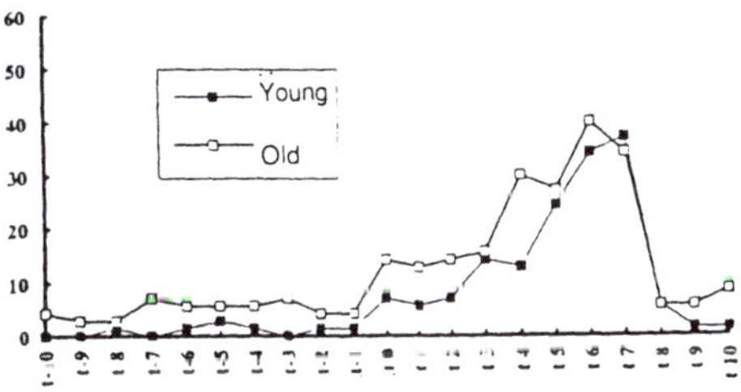

Figure 5 c : "HUD Signal"

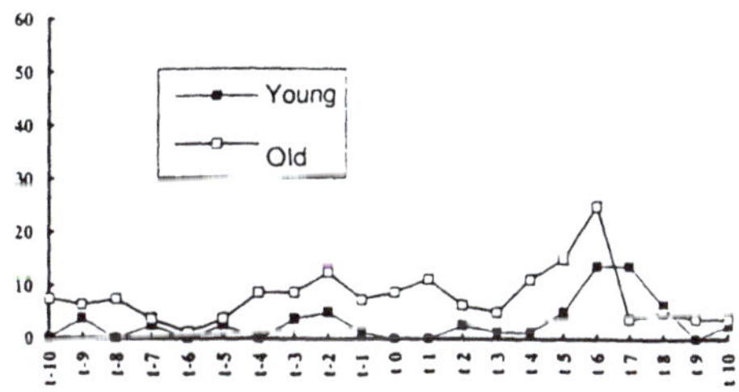

Figure 5 d : "Spoken Message"

When the preparatory information was given as a "Spoken Message" (Figure 5 d), the glances towards the screen were very much less numerous than in any other condition, and were delayed 6 seconds after the "Spoken Message". These results indicate that to give guidance information verbally is sufficiently reliable for most drivers to follow it without checking the screen displaying the equivalent information - it must be noted that in this situation, even with the noisy and varying background of the engine, were the spoken message was very easily intelligible ; it will be an aspect to take into consideration in real situations.

4.3.3. Visual strategies and guidance message

As shown previously in figure 2, the various guidance messages were divided into two sub-groups, according to the complexity of their design. If we consider the data 10 seconds before and after the display of the guidance information in these two categories, there was a relationship between the guidance message complexity and the glance frequency values.

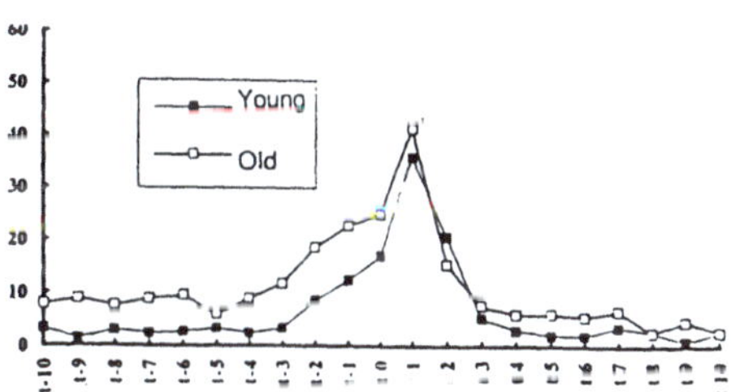

Figure 5 e : Simple Arrows

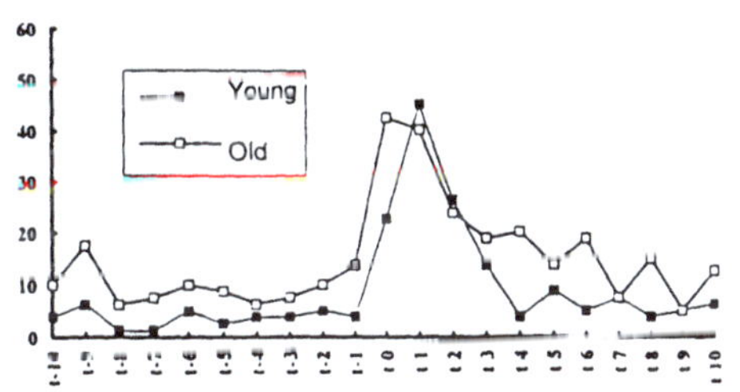

Figure 5 f : Complex Arrows

The glance frequency towards the screen increased in a significant manner in the case of a more complex design guidance arrow, in comparison with the simple one (ANOVA, $F = 38{,}29$, $p < 0{,}01$). This higher visual demand, perceptual and/or cognitive, still remained after the display event for the complex messages, higher values of glance frequency being still recorded 9 seconds after the information display, especially for the "older" group.

5. CONCLUSION

In terms of improvement of the efficiency in detecting guidance information, and according to the results of this study, the main conclusions would be the following:

- systematic prevision of advance information for drivers about guidance message events, however this information is given, does not prevent the "visual checking" behaviour usually adopted by "older" individuals.
- there is no difference in use of the preparatory information in relation to age. Presenting the information visually (centred or off-centre) and auditory (beep or spoken message) had the same consequences on visual strategies for both young and "older" group.
- simple and clear symbolic information made the "visual checking" behaviour of the "older group" less important ; by contrast, displaying a more complex symbolic information, such as roundabouts, makes the "visual checking" behaviour increase, even for young drivers.
- when the symbolic guidance information is clearly legible (large size, well contrasted), some young drivers are sometimes able to follow indications displayed on the screen without distracting the eyes from the road.
- it is better to use a visual rather than a beep preparatory information when the message does not have emergency status -these have the same efficiency but the beep might be found annoying-.
- the spoken message is considered as being reliable enough by many drivers so that they do not need to check the corresponding visual information on the screen. This information mode allows the driver to keep his eyes on the road; nevertheless, taking into account the wide range of background noise in a vehicle, and the variability in the in-vehicle acoustic quality, simultaneous use of both modes of presenting information would be useful.

REFERENCES

[1]. M. Sivak, P.L. Olson and L.A. Pastalan, (1981), Effect of driver's age on nighttime legibility of highway signs, Human Factors, 23, 59-64.
[2]. A. Pauzié, D. Letisserand and R. Trauchessec, (1992), Displayed information legibility of in-vehicle systems: focus on elderly drivers visual specificities, Proceeding of the 25th ISATA Conference, Florence.
[3]. C. Marin-Lamellet, O. Chanut and A. Pauzié, (1992), Ageing processes revealed in an attentional sharing situation, INRETS / CNRS "Vieillissement & Transport", 121-125.
[4]. A. Pauzié and C. Marin-Lamellet, (1989), Analysis of aging drivers behaviors navigating with in-vehicle visual display systems, proceedings of the "Vehicle Navigation & Information Systems Conference" Toronto, 61-67.

VISION IN VEHICLES - V
A.G. Gale et al. (Editors)
1996 Elsevier Science B.V.

A Practical Method For Comparing Driver Distraction Associated With In-Vehicle Equipment

J. Reeves and A. Stevens

Transport Research Laboratory
CROWTHORNE, Berks, RG11 6AU

Abstract

One of the major concerns surrounding the use of many advanced in-vehicle devices is additional workload and the consequent effect on driving performance. This paper reports on a practical quantitative assessment technique applicable to in-vehicle displays.

One simple measure of distraction is provided by eye glance behaviour (ie where the driver looks and for how long) while absorbing information from an in-vehicle display. It has even been suggested that designers should aim for a maximum of 2 seconds "eyes off the road" time. Whilst it may be too early to set such absolute values, (even if the driving conditions and subject groups could be specified) it is possible to add to existing data by comparing traditional and new devices.

In this paper, equipment and methods will be described to monitor a driver's eye glance behaviour during normal road driving whilst interacting with a variety of in-vehicle devices. Measurements will be reported from subjects reading a speedometer, using a radio and using a cassette player. These will be compared with similar measurements from the same subjects using a commercially available in-vehicle information system.

1. INTRODUCTION

The last ten years have witnessed an increase in the range of in-vehicle equipment available to drivers. Cassette players and radios are now standard fittings in most passenger cars. Car telephones are widespread and more recently pager systems, facsimiles, navigational and route guidance equipment have been introduced. Much work remains to be done on the effects that such equipment have on driving performance.

This study reports methods and results of a comparison between the in-vehicle attention requirements of Trafficmaster and other typical in-vehicle activities (radio tuning, cassette player operation and speedometer reading) in driving trials on public highways.

Trafficmaster is a commercially operated congestion warning device which is licensed by the Department of Transport under the 1989 Road Traffic (Driver Licensing and Information Systems) Act. It operates throughout Southern England.

The measurement used as a proxy for driver distraction (attentional demand) was chosen to be eye movement. Measurements of both the number of glances and the duration of glance were made. These measurements are relatively easy to make in an instrumented vehicle field trial but represent only one measure of the possible effects associated with in-vehicle equipment use.

2. COMPARISON OF THE IN-VEHICLE POSITION OF TRAFFICMASTER AND RADIO CASSETTE PLAYERS

One factor determining the time taken to read or use an instrument is its position in the vehicle. As background, an initial study was undertaken to compare the positioning of Trafficmaster units with that of radio cassette players. Information concerning the location of car radio cassettes was taken from 12 random copies of "Autocar and Motor" dating from January 1990 to January 1992. Details of installation were used from the 27 different vehicles with dashboards pictured in these issues. Figure 1 shows the location of the car radio cassettes. Details of the positioning of Trafficmaster displays were taken from a questionnaire administered to 108 Trafficmaster users in April 1991.

Figure 1. Radio Casette Locations

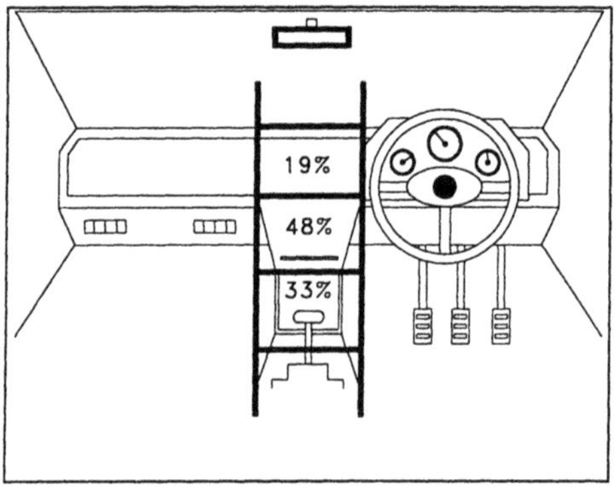

Figure 2. Trafficmaster locations

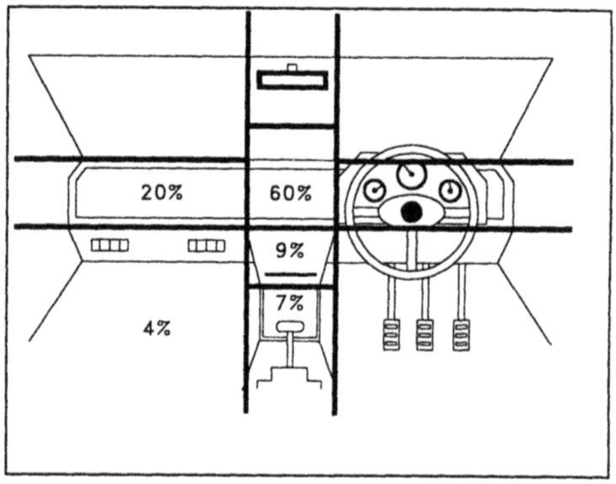

Figure 2 shows the installation positions for Trafficmaster displays. It can be seen from figure 2 that 60% of the Trafficmaster units are fitted high on the dashboard in the area recommended by the manufacturer. This compares with the 19% of radio cassettes being fitted in this position.

3. EQUIPMENT

An instrumented Ford Sierra estate was used for the field trials. A miniature CCD camera was fitted to the dashboard to record the driver's eye movements. Another camera was fitted between the front seats to record the road ahead. Both were used in conjunction with portable battery powered video recorders and monitor.

A Trafficmaster unit was fitted to the dashboard in the "high central" area and its display was controlled via a Grid Portable Personal Computer. This enabled the operator to display various scenarios to the driver at specific times.

The radio cassette player (a Ford model fitted as standard) had a digital frequency display, 4 presets, 3 wavebands, frequency lock-on facility and fine tune, fitted in the "middle central" position.

4. SUBJECTS

A total of 20 subjects, 17 male, 3 female, took part in the field trials. Ages ranged from 20 to 50 years. Subjects wearing spectacles wore appropriate lenses for driving and the in-vehicle tasks. Most of the subjects were familiar with Trafficmaster and had participated in previous experiments and trials.

5. EYE MOVEMENT ANALYSIS

The subjects' eye movements were analyzed using a video recorder with a frame-by-frame viewing facility. Time-code values generated during the journey were recorded at points where the subjects' eyes changed from looking up at the road to looking down at an in-vehicle device and vice-versa. The differences between these values were calculated to determine the duration of glances. Each glance was simply counted to determine the frequency of glances. The analyzed data was then plotted on a series of diagrams, one for each subject. The segmentation of the diagram is the result of Zwahlen's (Zwahlen 1988) research into the attentional demands of in-vehicle tasks where he proposed a segmentation into "acceptable", "grey" and "unacceptable" regions.

6. SELECTION OF IN-VEHICLE TASKS

There are clearly a number of different sub-tasks associated with using in-vehicle equipment eg.

Speedometer: This device has only one principal mode of use.
The driver simply looks at it and registers a speed.

Cassette tape: The main tasks are
- loading and playing a cassette
- rewinding a cassette
- turning a cassette over

Car radio: Tasks include
- switching radio on
- adjusting volume
- switching on and adjusting volume
- selecting pre-set station on current waveband
- selecting pre-set station on another waveband
- programming a radio station to a button
- adjusting to a frequency without a pilot tone
- scanning for a specific station on current waveband
- scanning for a specific station on another waveband

6.1. Car radio task analysis

Using the equipment and analysis method described above, the car radio task was analyzed in more detail while subjects were driving. Figure 3 shows the attentional demands of the various possible radio tasks, as described above, for a single subject who was considered representative in terms of performance.

Figure 3. Attention demands of various in-vehicle tasks involving a radio

<u>Task Key.</u>

On	- Switching radio on.
Vol	- Adjusting volume.
On/Vol	- Switching radio on, adjusting volume.
Preset C	- Selecting pre-set station on current waveband.
Preset A	- Selecting pre-set station on another waveband.
Program	- Programming a radio station to a button.
No pilot	- Adjusting to a frequency without a pilot tone.
Scan C	- Scanning for a specific station on current waveband.
Scan A	- Scanning for a specific station on another waveband.

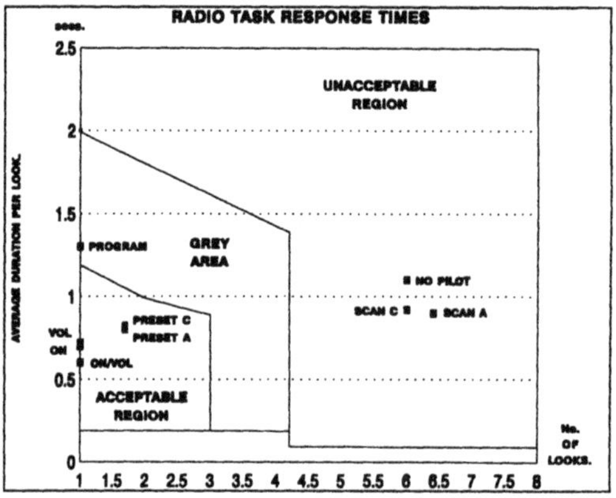

Three of the more difficult radio tasks were selected for comparison with other in-vehicle tasks in the main experiment described below.

In the main experiment 11 subjects were asked to

a) tune the radio to the Heathrow travel news station
b) tune the radio to the Capital Radio frequency of 95.8 FM.

The final 9 subjects were additionally asked to

c) select pre-set channel 2 on the current waveband

6.2 Trafficmaster Tasks

The Trafficmaster unit itself (figure 4) has a LCD display with a schematic diagram of the motorways covered by the system. During commercial operation, sensors installed on motorway bridges transmit information to a control centre about vehicle speeds. When speeds drop below a threshold value the information is transmitted over a national paging network to the Trafficmaster units. The display shows the location of any problem, the average speed at the site and the direction of travel affected.

Figure 4. The Trafficmaster in-vehicle display

Trafficmaster: There are a range of tasks involving - different locations
- different speeds
- different relevancies of information

In these experiments, each Trafficmaster scenario displayed the same section of the M25 with variations in speed shown, arrow direction and arrow location. The display complexity was approximately that shown in figure 4. According to certain criteria (described in the experimental procedure section below), each subject had to read and act on the displayed information when approaching motorway junctions. This was considered to be a typical and representative use of Trafficmaster for the purposes of this comparison.

7. EXPERIMENTAL PROCEDURE

Before the start of each circuit the subject was given a map of the route to be driven (A complete circuit of 76km: A322-M3-M25-M4-A329). The subject was then instructed to complete the in-vehicle tasks when requested by the operator during the journey and read Trafficmaster and act on the information displayed as described below.

Reading the speedometer: subjects were asked on 3 occasions to read the speedometer and state the speed.

Using the cassette player: subjects were asked on different occasions to:

a) select a tape, load it and play it

b) rewind a tape

Tuning the radio: subjects were asked on different occasions to:

a) tune the radio to the Heathrow travel news station by reading the motorway sign. This involved changing frequency band and manually scanning to a frequency without a pilot one.

b) tune the radio to the Capital Radio frequency of 95.8 FM. This involved using the automatic scan facility (locking onto intermediate stations) but from the same frequency band.

c) select the second pre-set channel on the current frequency band.

Reading the Trafficmaster: Trafficmaster scenarios were initiated by an operator and were prompted when passing under specific bridges and gantries along the journey. A series of "beeps" were emitted by Trafficmaster before each scenario was displayed and the display then remained visible until the next scenario was sent. This reflects the way that Trafficmaster operates.

The comprehension levels of the subjects were measured by asking them to leave the motorway if speeds of 0, 5 or 10 mph were displayed in the next section of motorway and the directional arrows were pointing in the direction of travel, this would constitute "relevant" information. Drivers who left the motorway were instructed to rejoin immediately at the same interchange. If the criteria were not satisfied, resulting in "irrelevant" information, the driver simply maintained his course.

8. RESULTS

The eye movements (no. of looks and duration of each look) for the 3 radio tasks, 2 tape tasks, 3 speedo tasks and the 8 Trafficmaster tasks were all averaged for each subject. These values were then plotted, resulting in a mean point for each of the four types of task. This was necessary since the spread and quantity of data was too great to plot otherwise. Figure 5 shows the results for a number of subjects. There was no correlation between a subject's glance duration or frequency and the display of either relevant or irrelevant information by Trafficmaster. The attentional demand for the 2 tape tasks (loading tape then playing, rewinding tape) were very similar and the 3 identical speedo tasks (reading speedo value) only had slight variations in attentional demand. The two complex radio scanning tasks required greatest attention, often requiring as many as 20 glances, and consequently the spread of data was very wide. The radio preset task, however, required much less attention and rarely required more than one glance.

Figure 5. Sample results of eye-glance comparison experiment

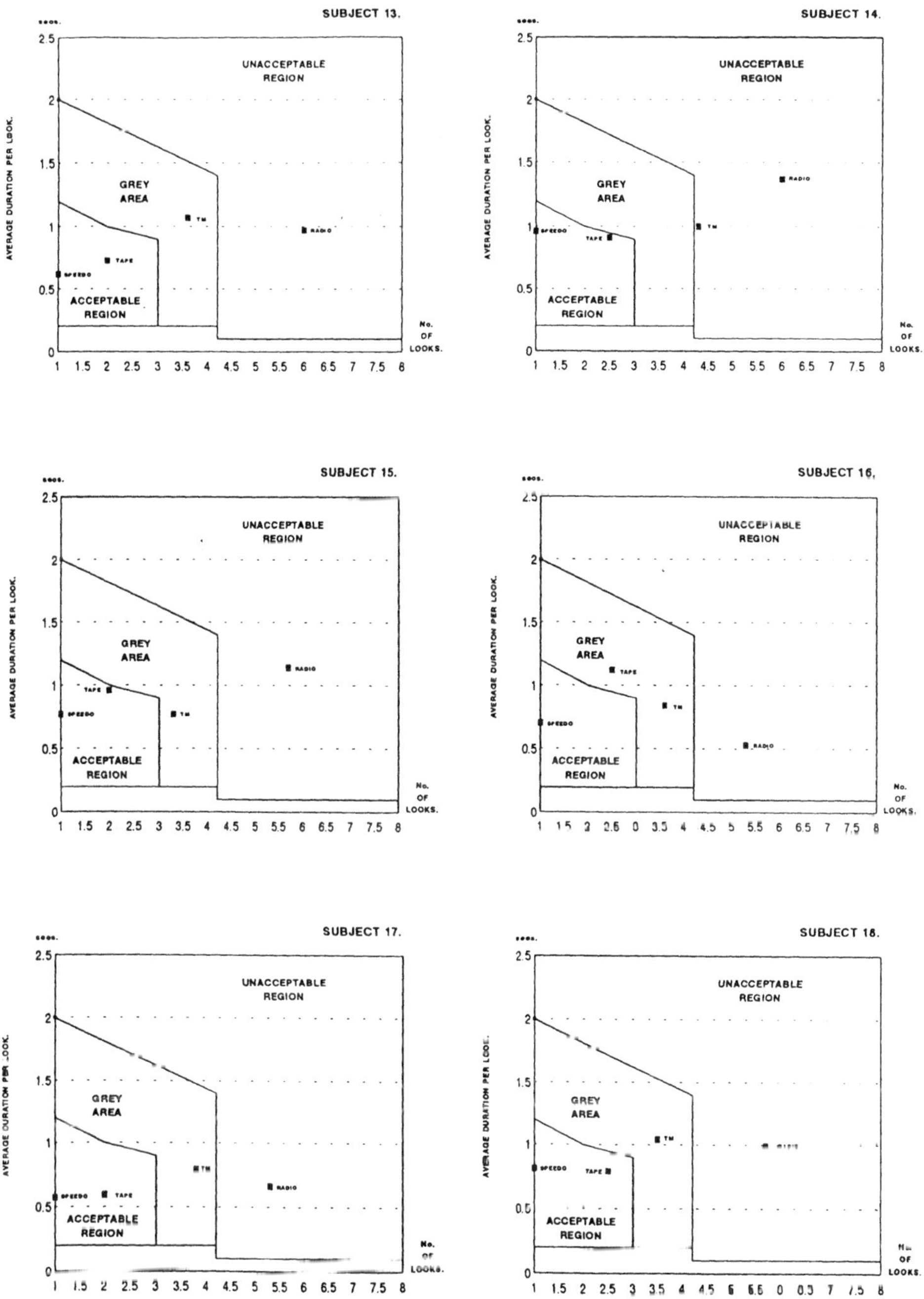

9. DISCUSSION AND CONCLUSION

One purpose of these trials was to assess the level of driver distraction caused by the new Trafficmaster congestion warning system in comparison with other, more conventional in-vehicle equipment:

- Observations suggest that car radio-cassette players are predominantly installed around the centre console although only 19% are fitted in the optimum "high central" position. Trafficmaster installations are more varied in position.

- As was expected, the simple speedometer and radio tasks required the least number of looks and the complex radio scanning tasks required the greatest. The plotted data for these tasks fell respectively in the "acceptable" and "unacceptable" regions of a Zwahlen diagram for each subject.

- Trafficmaster appeared to occupy a position between these two extremes. It is interesting to note therefore that some of these tasks associated with widely available radios, although not often undertaken, present more of a challenge than Trafficmaster observation.

- Operation of radio pre-set buttons, on/off switches and volume appears to carry a minimal distraction overhead. Similarly, operation of the cassette player does not present an unacceptable distraction risk in normal operation. However, such commonly available radio-cassette players can involve the operator in potentially distracting operations. In particular tuning the radio to a non-programmed frequency.

Another purpose was to investigate the methodology of measuring eye-glance durations and frequencies:

- The measurements reported in this paper were found to be practical to collect, although the analysis, even with a single frame "jog-wheel" video player, was somewhat slow.

- There are different possible definitions of "display reading time", but variation between subjects is a greater concern. Comparative distraction measures, or the use of one display as a "reference" are helpful, but an important consideration is the subject group for each series of measurements.

- Despite justified criticisms of the over-simplistic categorisation of the Zwahlen diagram, it is a useful way of reporting and comparing results.

REFERENCES

Zwahlen H.T. 1988. "Safety aspects of CRT touch panel controls in automobiles" in Vision in Vehicles II. A G Gale et al (Editors). Elsevier Science Publishers B. V. (North Holland).

The work described in this paper forms part of a Department of Transport funded research programme conducted by the Transport Research Laboratory and the paper is published by permission of Mr M Crompton, NMDI Division, Department of Transport and the Chief Executive of TR

VISION IN VEHICLES - V
A.G. Gale et al. (Editors)

Methodological Problems Associated with the Use of Eye Movement Measuring Techniques in Evaluating Contact Analogue Head-Up-Displays.

Leonard Stapleton, Nicholas J. Ward, & Andrew M Parkes

HUSAT Research Institute, Loughborough University of Technology, The Elms, Elms Grove, LOUGHBOROUGH, Leics LE11 1RG, United Kingdom.

Abstract

Driving involves a number of sub-tasks that are mediated by vision. Typically these sub-tasks are performed simultaneously and rely on both central and peripheral visual information (e.g. simultaneously monitoring headway while negotiating a curve). A traditional technique in driving studies has been to examine driver visual behaviour directly by recording eye movements to determine the road scene features fixated by the driver. From these measurements task specific features to which the driver is attending may be inferred.

The present paper examines the difficulties associated with the application of this technique to contact analogue head-up-displays (HUDs) which subtend a limited central field of view. An inherent problem lies in distinguishing between loci of attention i.e. features in the HUD image vs. the road scene features overlaid by the HUD image, as both image and external scene coincide in space.

A more basic concern arises from relating attentional allocation towards specific road scene features (inferred from direction of gaze) to sub-task performance where different sub-tasks may utilise similar sources of information. This difficulty is further exacerbated by the potential novelty of the overlaid HUD image, which in otherwise degraded viewing conditions (e.g. fog, darkness, etc.) might elicit novel strategies of visual behaviour.

A task description of the functions of vision in performing driving sub-tasks is outlined, with emphasis on performance under adverse viewing conditions, and the potential impact of HUD imaging. Difficulties associated with eye movement measurement techniques can be circumvented by determining appropriate performance measures to indirectly address the visual component(s) of sub-task performance. A research programme to address key aspects highlighted in the task description is outlined.

1. CONTACT ANALOGUE HEAD-UP-DISPLAYS

The present paper is concerned with methodological problems associated with evaluating Contact Analogue Head-Up-Display (HUD) technologies in automobiles. Vision Enhancement Systems (VESs) will be the most likely application to require such technology in future vehicles. These systems display an enhanced image of the road scene ahead under conditions of visual degradation, e.g. at night, in twilight, in fog, etc.. Typically the enhanced image is obtained using some form of non-visible wavelength camera and projected off the inside of the windshield (or a secondary virtually transparent screen) to the driver. The image is presented so that it overlays and matches the portion of the scene ahead that falls within the field of view of the camera. Technological limitations restrict the size of image that can be practically displayed in a vehicle, for example current fields of view of around 15 deg. (binocular) have been demonstrated publically. The image is also restricted to 2-Dimensions. However the HUD optics allow this 2-Dimensional image to appear to lie on a focal plane 3 to 10 meters in front of the driver, thus lending some appearance of depth.

The HUD image can overlay the visual scene ahead so that elements within the image subtend the same visual angle as the elements in the scene that give rise to them and occupy the same physical portions of the driver's field of view. Brightness and contrast levels of the image may be adjusted to further harmonise with the background scene. As such, the image is in *contact analogue* with the external scene. However minor mismatching occurs due to the camera's misalignment with the driver's eyes, and parallax effects due to the image being at a fixed focal distance that differs from the distances of the objects imaged. As a real time display movement of the vehicle through the road environment and of objects in the environment cause corresponding movement within the image, matching that of the external scene.

2. AN APPROACH TO EVALUATION

Initially it was hoped that the introduction of VESs into the driving task could be addressed in terms of their direct impact on drivers' visual behaviour, using photo electric viewing (e.g. NAC Eyemark equipment). Metrics for reporting visual behaviour (e.g. review by Wierwille 1993) have included: glance frequency, glance duration, glance allocation, transition and accommodation. There are problems in interpreting such metrics when used with traditional displays located in head down positions on the vehicle dashboard (Parkes and Burnett 1993). The utility of such metrics in relation to the evaluation of HUDs is more dubious. The special case of Contact Analogue HUDs renders most of these measures of visual behaviour unusable.

This paper argues in favour of a performance based framework that concentrates on the functional role of vision in mediating the driving task. This approach emphasises the driving sub-tasks that utilise visual information from the road scene and emphasises performance criteria that reflect effective uptake and use of this information. This approach holds several attractions:

- It allows a comparison of the information available under normal and adverse conditions thus offering guide-lines for outlining the visual information a VES should enhance.
- By highlighting performance criteria that reflect efficient use of such information it provides a potential framework for measuring effective uptake.
- Supplementing this approach with an account of visual factors involved in accident causation allows a formulation of criteria that a VES should meet to be safe. Furthermore safety should be determined ultimately, according to Fisher (1992) in terms of performance.

A performance based approach allows the complexity of the driving task to be addressed more readily. Typically driving involves the simultaneous performance of numerous driving sub-tasks (e.g. maintaining a constant distance from a lead car while negotiating a curve and monitoring the approach of an oncoming car). To achieve this the parallel processing of different informational sources within the driving scene may be required. Similarly more than one source of information may be utilised to perform a single sub-task (e.g. taking a curve typically requires preview, fixations of road side features - kerbs, bushes etc., and peripheral optic flow information). Again sub-task descriptions couched in terms of visual informational requirements provide performance criteria that may serve to evaluate effective uptake and use of information.

Related to the issue of sub-task interactions is the issue of task criticality. Hills (1980) observes that normally an accident results from a combination of causes rather than from one single cause. "Not infrequently, this can involve as many as fifteen or more independent factors." (Hills, p.184, 1980). As such performance criteria that reflect the multidimensional nature of the driving task and its informational requirements seem appropriate.

A HUD system constitutes a novel medium for displaying visual information. Evaluation of such systems requires a framework that enables a formulation of the potential effects of presenting visual information in this manner. Addressing purely visually based behaviours holds two fundamental problems:

- The direct measurement of eye movements may establish, for example, that a *change* in strategies of visual sampling takes place. However whether such changes imply safety benefits or costs can only be established from subsequent performance based evaluations.
- A basic assumption of the photo electric viewing technique is that the direction of gaze reflects the viewer's locus of attention. However as the HUD image directly overlays the external scene giving rise to this image, this technique is insufficient to determine the locus of attention. Furthermore, smooth rather than saccadic eye movements are likely to be more important in determining the locus of attention (see Section 3.2.).

2.1. Framework

The basis for our outline of the driving sub-tasks mediated by vision is the task analysis of McKnight and Adams (1970). Using their criticality ratings and Hills' (1980) analysis of visual factors in accident causation, a table of key driving sub-tasks and visual functions likely to be affected by VESs is listed below (Table 1).

This also borrows Leibowitz's distinction between Focal and Ambient mode visual processing (Leibowitz, et al 1983). Briefly, the focal mode of visual processing is concerned with the "what" of vision i.e. the recognition and identification of objects. It primarily utilises the central visual field and is associated with attentional allocation. In contrast ambient vision is concerned with the question of "where". This pertains to both the localisation of stimuli in the periphery, i.e. to determining where objects are relative to the environment, and to where the observer is relative to the environment. As selective degradation in visual functioning occurs at night and under adverse conditions this provides a useful framework.

Table 1
Key Driving Sub-Tasks and Associated Visual Functions.

Ambient Visual Functions
- Object detection in the peripheral visual field (pedestrians, obstacles, and traffic signs/signals, etc.).
- Monitoring peripheral optic flow information for Lane Keeping/Steering.

Focal Visual Functions
- Monitoring lead car, oncoming and stationary cars, and obstacles (speed and distance judgement).
- Previewing road curvature (curve negotiation).
- Monitoring lane features and road boundaries (curve negotiation and degraded conditions).

3. VISUAL BEHAVIOUR AND DRIVING PERFORMANCE

Focal Vision

The central placement of the HUD image within the driver's forward field of view bears directly on focal visual functions which use information from this area. Typical issues here concern detection and speed and distance judgements (e.g. monitoring a lead car, oncoming and stationary cars, obstacles, pedestrians) and the effects of environmental conditions, glare, etc.. Performance measures using reaction times, detection and judgement accuracy, etc. may be used to evaluate the HUD image effectiveness. While this appears relatively straightforward, it should be cautioned that interactive issues must still be borne in mind. For example late detection of a pedestrian outside the HUD could affect performance on a task presented within the HUD. Conversely preoccupation with a HUD task might affect non-HUD performance.

Ambient Vision

More complex methodological issues arise when evaluating the effects of this centrally-placed novel information source on performance which uses primarily the ambient visual mode or both the ambient and focal modes. The fundamental issues here are whether the enhanced central image can be integrated with the driver's use of peripheral information or whether novel strategies for information uptake and use become introduced. In particular it is important to look at (a) lane maintenance and steering which can utilise both peripheral optic flow information and focal information about road edges and boundaries, and (b) object detection.

3.1. Lane Maintenance and Steering

Lane maintenance and steering can use both ambient visual information from the optic flow in the periphery and focal information about lane boundaries and road edges. Of key interest is the effect of the centrally placed HUD on the uptake and efficient use of information from either source.

Peripheral vision plays an important role in steering. Eye movement studies provide indirect evidence supporting this role. For example Bhise and Rockwell (1971) found only slight deterioration in headway and lane position maintenance when subjects fixated a car travelling in an adjacent lane. Supplementary evidence comes from findings that more experienced drivers fixate further down the road close to the focus of expansion whilst novice drivers tend to fixate closer to their cars and to concentrate on lane markers. Furthermore when experienced drivers were instructed to increase their lateral control they increased their concentration of fixations near the focus of expansion.(Rockwell 1972, Mourant & Rockwell 1970, Shinar et al. 1977).

The supplementing of peripheral flow information with focal information is evident from concentrations of fixations on road features such as the centre line marker and road edges when peripheral information is restricted using a small aperture (e.g. Gordon 1966, Osaka 1991). Curve negotiation also shows a combination of looking down the road and at road boundaries close in for lane position information (Rockwell 1972, Shinar et al. 1977, Cohen & Studach 1977, Jurgensohn et al. 1991).

Under degraded viewing conditions a selective degradation of visual functioning occurs (Leibowitz et al 1983). While focal vision is adversely affected peripheral motion perception has been shown to be largely independent of illumination levels and optical blur (Leibowitz, Shupert-Rodemer, & Dichgans 1979). This was supported in a simulator driving study where performance on a steering task showed little deterioration due to optical blur (Merritt et al. 1978, cited in Leibowitz and Post 1982).

The effect on lane maintenance and steering of the introduction of a relatively bright centrally-placed enhanced image is thus likely to be two fold. An enhanced overlay that provides preview and road boundary information should assist focal visual functioning. The effect on ambient visual functioning however is less clear. The bright central stimulus may reduce sensitivity to peripheral stimuli.

To evaluate this effect performance measures (e.g. steering accuracy/variance in different road scenarios) are required. Establishing a change in visual scan patterns alone tells us little as novel strategies to the novel HUD stimulus may appear. These would need to be evaluated in terms of the new informational context in which they arose. Also photo electric viewing techniques only provide indirect evidence about peripheral visual functioning.

Furthermore lane keeping is generally automatic and routine and may be prone to interference from other driving tasks in emergency situations. Judicious choice of scenarios where other driving sub tasks might degrade lane keeping performance could serve to evaluate this possibility.

3.2. Object Detection

Object detection relies primarily on peripheral and para-foveal vision. Many factors influence the detectability of objects in these regions of the visual field and are highly interactive, e.g. background luminance, border gradients, location of the object in the visual field (i.e. retinal eccentricity), presence of sources of glare, clutter, object motion, size, shape, colour contrast, luminance, observer's level of adaptation, expectancy, motivation, fatigue etc. (see for example Boff & Lincoln 1988, Olson 1988).

Introducing a centrally presented image of higher brightness than the background may have several effects. Brightness contrast of background objects outside the HUD field of view will be reduced (i.e. the central image may constitute glare); levels of dark adaptation that would otherwise be realised may be impaired; and the new information source may introduce attentional allocation effects.

Two primary attentional allocation effects are likely to result from the HUD image. Firstly it has been shown that the ability to detect eccentric targets is adversely affected by performing a centrally presented task (Webster and Haslerud 1964, Leibowitz and Appelle 1969). Detection of peripheral objects may be affected by the complexity of task mediated by the HUD image. (Of course the HUD might alternatively facilitate performance of central tasks and free attentional resources for object detection).

Secondly the nature of the HUD image and the visual system's potential response to this image may elicit attentional effects detrimental to the detection of objects outside the image. While the intention of vision enhancement is to provide an image that can be integrated with the background scene, in practice small motion parallax effects partially isolate the image from the background. Research shows an intimate connection between attentional allocation and smooth eye movements (see Kowler 1990). For example objects appearing in an attended to (and smoothly tracked) array are more readily detected than objects appearing in an untracked (non-attended) array (Khurana and Kowler 1987). Thus smoothly tracking events in the HUD image may impede detection of objects in the background.

Given the complex dynamic nature of the road scene and the further complexity of a superimposed HUD image, evaluation of attentional allocation effects is particularly difficult if monitoring of smooth eye movements is entailed. Direct performance measures (e.g. detection times/accuracies) to events either within or outside the HUD, while attention is manipulated by performing HUD or non-HUD tasks may provide answers. As object detection is also likely to be prone to interactive effects (especially if the HUD captures attention in the manner suggested) appropriate choice of scenarios under which to assess these effects is important.

4. CONCLUSIONS

Driving entails complex interactive sub tasks that are mediated predominantly by vision. Evaluation of the effect of the introduction of a visual aid such as the Contact Analogue HUD requires a framework that takes this complexity into account. Several factors conspire against a direct evaluation of visual performance (e.g. Photo electric viewing techniques).

A key factor lies in the placement of the HUD so that it overlays the centre of the forward field of view. The visual system utilises information from both the centre and periphery to differing degrees for different driving tasks. Uptake of peripheral information can only be indirectly inferred from photo electric viewing techniques. Furthermore, establishing that scanning strategies are changed due to the interpositioning of the HUD during a particular driving scenario provides us with an incomplete picture. The driving sub task (or tasks) and the role of vision in its (or their) performance requires elucidation. By emphasising the performance that vision is mediating criteria for measuring visual efficiency can be outlined.

As a measure of locus of attention such techniques also suffer. The alignment of the HUD image with the background scene means that when a driver's gaze is directed within the HUD field of view, either image or background may be under regard. However a close relationship does exist between smooth eye movements and attentional allocation. Practical difficulties in measuring these in the dynamic environment of a moving vehicle suggests that direct manipulation of attentional allocation is likely to be a more profitable approach.

In conclusion the present paper advocates measuring task specific performances that reflect the efficient functioning of vision rather than rely on direct measures of visual behaviour. Our elaboration of the functions of vision in mediating driving tasks has borrowed strongly from findings that used direct visual measurement techniques. Undoubtedly such techniques will play a role in expanding our knowledge of visual functioning with such complex systems as HUDs but unless slotted into a performance based framework are of limited value.

REFERENCES

1. Bhise, V. C., & Rockwell, T. H., (1971) The role of peripheral vision and time sharing in driving. Proceedings of the 1971 Annual Meeting of the American Association for Automotive Medicine. New York: SAE. Inc.
2. Boff, K. R., & Lincoln, J. E., (1988) Engineering data compendium: Human perception and performance. AAMRL, Wright-Patterson AFB, OH.
3. Cohen, A. S., & Studach, H., (1977) Eye movements while driving cars around curves. Perceptual and Motor Skills, 44, 683-689.
4. Fisher, J., (1992) Testing the effect of road traffic signs informational value on driver behaviour. Ergonomics, 34, 231-237.
5. Gale, A. G., Brown, I. D., Haslegrave, C. M., Moorhead, I., & Taylor, S. (1991) (Eds), Vision in vehicles - III. Elsevier Science Pub., North-Holland.
6. Gordon, D. A., (1966) Experimental isolation of the driver's visual input. Human Factors, April 1966, 129-137.
7. Hills, B. L., (1980) Vision, visibility and perception in driving. Perception 9, 183-216.
8. Jurgenshon, T., Neculau, M., & Willumeit, H. P. (1991) Visual scanning patterns in curve negotiation. In Gale et al, (Eds), Vision in vehicles - III. Elsevier Science Pub., North-Holland.
9. Khurana, B., & Kowler, E., (1987) Shared attentional control of smooth eye movement and perception. Vision Research 27(9), 1603-1618.
10. Kowler, E. (1990) The role of visual and cognitive processes in the control of eye movement. Chapter 1 in Eye movements and their role in vision and cognitive processes. Kowler, E. (Ed.) Elsevier Science Publishers.
11. Leibowitz, H. W., & Appelle, S., (1969) The effect of a central task on luminance thresholds for peripherally presented stimuli. Human Factors, 11(4), 387-392.
12. Leibowitz, H. W., & Post, R. B., (1982) The two modes of processing concept and some implications. Chapter 17 in: Organization and representation in perception. Beck, J. (Ed.) Erlbaum Associates.
13. Leibowitz, H. W., Owens, D. A., & Post, R. B., (1983) Nighttime driving and visual degradation, Society of Automotive Engineers, Report No. 820414.

14. Leibowitz, H. W., Shupert-Rodemer, C., & Dichgans, J., (1979) The independence of dynamic spatial orientation from luminance and refractive error. Perception & Psychophysics, 25, 75-79.
15. McKnight, A. J., & Adams, B. B., (1970) Driver education task analysis volume I: Task descriptions. Human Resources Research Organisation (HumRRO), Alexandria, Virginia 22314, USA, HumRRO Technical Report 70-103.
16. Merritt, J. O., Newton, R. E., Sandetrson, G. A., & Seltzer, M. L., 1982) Driver visibility quality: An electro-optical meter for in-vehicle measurement of modulation transfer (MTF). Department of Transportation. (DOT HS 6-01426). (1978). (cited in Leibowitz & Post.
17. Mourant, R. R., & Rockwell, T. H., (1970) Mapping eye-movement patterns to the visual scene in driving: An exploratory study. Human Factors, 12(1), 81-87.
18. Olson, P. L., (1988) Visibility Problems in nighttime driving, Society of Automotive Engineers, Report No. 870600.
19. Osaka, N., (1991) Effects of window size and eccentricity upon eye fixation and reaction time in negotiation of curves. In Gale et al, (Eds), Vision in vehicles - III. Elsevier Science Pub., North-Holland.
20. Parkes, A. M., & Burnett, G. E., (1993) An evaluation of medium range "advance information" in route guidance displays for use in vehicles. Proceedings of Vehicle Navigation and Information Systems Conference. October 1993, Ottawa, Canada. (in press).
21. Rockwell, T. H., (1972) Eye movement analysis of visual information acquisition in driving: An overview. paper 948. 6th Conference. Australian Road Research Board. Melbourne, 6(3), 316-331.
22. Shinar, D., McDowell, E. D. , & Rockwell, T. H., (1977) Eye movements in curve negotiation. Human Factors, 19(1), 63-71.
23. Webster, R. G., & Haslerud, G. M., (1964) Influence on extreme peripheral vision of attention to a visual or auditory task. Journal of Experimental Psychology. 68(3), 269-272.
24. Wierwille, W. W., (1993) Visual and manual demands of in-car controls and displays. In Peacock, B., & Karwowski, W. (Ed.s), Automotive Ergonomics. 299-320, Taylor and Francis, London.

VISION IN VEHICLES - V
A.G. Gale et al. (Editors)

Complexity of In-Car Visual Messages and Drivers' Performances

G. Labiale

INRETS, 109, avenue S. Allende, Case 24, 69675 - Bron Cedex, France

Abstract

The present study investigates the influence of the complexity of in-car written road information messages on drivers' performances. An experimental car was fitted with a micro-computer and the equipment required to convey different road information messages and record data. During the experimental procedure the drivers had to read each in-car road information message once and to memorize it. The independent variable has taken into account the number of information units of in-car road messages and the dependent variables have taken into account the visual explorations, the memory recalling performances and indicators of the lane and the speed control. The results have shown that the number of visual explorations increase as a function of the number of units in each message, and that the mean time duration of each glance seems relatively stable (1.08 s. to 1.35 s.). The memory recalling performances are inversely proportional to the length of road information messages. The long road information messages (from 10 to 18 units) have an important impact on speed and trajectory control. Some psycho-ergonomics recommendations are proposed concerning the complexity of the in-car road information messages.

1. INTRODUCTION

Currently, a wide range of in-car information and navigational systems are under development. If the decision is taken to adopt road information systems, drivers will soon be confronted with in-car messages designed to provide road information, such as traffic jams, road accident or incident, advices for other route, weather conditions,... These messages could be presented either in short or long format, taking into account content, urgency and driving situation.

Some comparative studies have been carried out concerning the memorization of auditory and visual information messages (Gatling,1977; Labiale, 1990). The effects of the complexity of in-car maps have been previously investigated on perceptive (Wierwille & al., 1987; Parkes & al., 1991) and memory recall performances as well as on the driving task itself (Labiale, 1989, 1990) However, until now, it seems that the influence of in-car written messages on drivers' perception, cognition and driving has not been studied. So, it seems necessary to draw up some psycho-ergonomics rules concerning the road information to car drivers, taking into account the problem of safe driving as well as easy understanding and use of these messages.

The objective of the present study is to investigate the influence of the complexity of in-car written road information messages on drivers' visual explorations, memorization and driving performances, in order to make a significant contribution to the ergonomic definition of the complexity of the information system interface.

2. METHODS

2.1. The subjects

54 drivers participated in the experiment; the group was balanced for age (20 Ss. of 25-34 years, 17 Ss. of 35-44 years, 17 Ss. of 45-55 years), for gender (26 women et 28 men) and for educational level (29 Ss with school-leaving certificate : "CAP", and 25 Ss with A level + qualification : "BAC"); these drivers had normal hearing and normal sight (some of them after correction).

2.2. The experimental vehicle and the route used

The experimental vehicle, a Renault 21 GTS, was equipped for transmitting the source information and collecting the data (cf. Labiale, 1989). An on board VDU (Minitel) with a 9 inch, 625 lines, anti-glare monochrome screen fitted to the top of the instrument panel (just to the right of the steering wheel and oriented towards the driver), was used to transmit written messages.

The drivers' behaviour and glance movements were recorded by a video system, composed of a mini-camera, a recorder and a timer. A micro-computer (Canon X07) handled message presentation on the VDU, the radio-cassette and the video recorder.

The route was 2 km long, with 4 turns and very little traffic; speed was restricted to 60 kph.

2.3. The experimental variables

The independent variable took into account the length of road information messages, defined by the number of information units. Four lengths of road information message were defined concerning road conditions and alternative routes : level I (3 to 4 information units), level II (6 to 8 units), level III (10 to 12 units) and level IV (14 to 18 units). There were several categories of road information units concerning geography (region, city), type of road (road, motorway,...), event-causes (accident,...) and event-consequences (traffic jams,...), time and distance, actions proposed. This measuring method yields results rather similar to counting the words (with no article) constituting each message, however, it remains more specific since it takes account of the relevant words or groups of words of each message. In addition, for the application to road information messages, our method is more suitable than that of Kintsh (1976) and Gatling (1977). Thus twelve road information messages were constructed but only four of them (representing each level) were randomly selected for each driver.

The written messages appear on the VDU screen. The characters were double height, single width Videotex size, single line spacing with an 80 cd/m² brigthness on a 10 cd/m² grey background. Each written text was presented in a segmented format (each line consisting of 1 to 4 words spaced one from each other) because this presentation is more suitable for the driving task (indeed, the driver has to read the text in several attemps in order to keep control of the driving, and he can thus more easily pick out the place where he left the text; cf. table 1).

Table 1
Examples of road information message lengths and display types

Level I (4 units)	Level II (8 units)
Traffic jams **towards Paris**	**Work in progress** **on Road N75 along 40 km** **Take Road N85**

Level III (11 units)	Level IV (16 units)
Motorway A61 closed **between Metz and Thionville** **Go out at Metz** **and Take Road D1**	**Accident on Road N7** **at the entrance of Nevers** **Traffic stopped** **towards Paris** **Follow the road D976** **and in Guerche carry on Road D1**

Messages translated from French units (represent French equivalent).

The following dependent variables were considered :

- the visual explorations (number and duration of glances) of the in-car road information message;
- the memory recall performance : results were obtained by counting the number of information units in each message correctly memorized;
- the subjective need to slow down and to deviate from the trajectory when reading text.

2.4. Experimental procedures

Each driver was instructed to read and to memorize each road information message. On a practical level, each driver, under real driving conditions, was warned by a 3s sound bip that a specific road message was going to be displayed on the in-car screen during a specific time (display duration was calculated to enable each driver to read each message only once) and was then instructed to read the text and to memorize it. Once the text display was shut off and after a 30 or 60 second period (previous experiments have not demonstrated any significant effect of these periods on memory recall; Labiale & al.,1988), a message was screened (heralded by a 1 s buzzer) which stated "Message Repeat". Following the end of the message presentation, the driver had then to recall the road information message content. The time between the presentation of each message was around 5 mns on the VDU and message order was different for each driver tested.

In a preliminary phase, drivers were trained to drive the experimental car and to accomplish 2 successive trials with written message presentations.

3. RESULTS

The results are analysed with regard to the visual explorations and the memorization of the different road information messages and their impact on driving control.

3.1.Visual explorations

As regard each road information messages, results (cf. Figure 1) show a distribution of mean duration glances ranging from 0.3s to 2.90 s., which is not very close to a Gaussian distribution; we underline that the average duration glances = 1.15 s (0.5) and 92% of these times are less 2 s.

More precisely, the duration of each glance and the number of glances associated with the different lengths of road information messages are given in table 2 .

Table 2
Duration and number of glances for the different road information messages

Length of messages	3- 4 units	6-8 units	10-12 units	14-18 units
Duration of each glance	1.08 s (0.43)	1.18 s (0.58)	1.20 s (0.57)	1.35s (0.60)
Number of glances	3.8 (1.6)	6.9 (2.6)	9.6 (2.8)	15.5 (5.5)

Mean (s.d.); sub-sample of 14 drivers.

It can be observed that an increase in the length of road messages results in a strong and significant effect on the number of glances (one-way variance analysis; $p<0.05$), but in a very light effect on the duration of glances (one-way variance analysis; statistical tendancy: $p<0.09$).

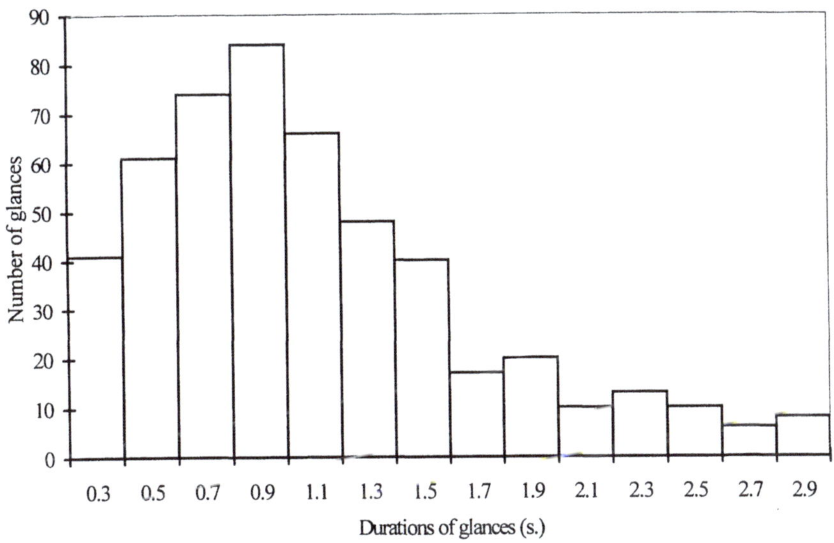

Figure 1. Distribution of glance durations

3.2. Memorization

Global results concerning memorization of the different road information messages are shown in table 3.

Table 3
Percentages of correct memory recall

Length of messages	3-4 units	6-8 units	10-12 units	14-18 units
Memory recall	100%	97.5%	75.4%	52.4%

An inversely proportional relationship can be observed between the length of information messages and memorization performance; memory recall of a level I message (3 to 4 informational units) is 100% whereas the score for a level IV (14 to 18 units) drops to 52.4%.

Moreover, we have analysed the memorization of the different parts of each road message; however, only the long road messages (III to IV levels) were taken into account, since short messages (levels I and II) gave respectively 100 % and 97.5% of correct memory recalling. Practically, messages were divided into 3 main parts : the 3 units of information beginning each message (primacy), the 3 units of information ending each message (recency) and the remaining units of information concerning the intermediate part of each message. As shown in table 4 shown, results confirmed only the primacy effects (first part /intermediate part : X^2; $p<0.05$) and not the recency effects (intermediate part / end part : X^2; $p>0.05$) on memorization of this kind of message.

Table 4
Percentages of correct memory recall for the 3 main parts of the road messages

Length of messages		10-12 units	14-18 units
	Beginning part	80 %	84.4 %
Memorization	Intermediate part	76.6 %	48 %
	End part	67.8 %	40 %

3.3. Trajectory and speed control

Following the presentation of a road information message, each driver had to specify whether he felt that he had needed to slow down or to deviate from the trajectory when reading text. Results in table 5 show that, in contrast to short messages, the long road information messages (10 to 18 units) have an important effect upon the drivers' feeling of losing trajectory and reducing speed.

Table 5
Percentages of drivers who had problems of trajectory and speed control

Length of messages	3 to 8 units	10 to 18 units
Slowing down speed	5.5 %	61.1 %
Losing trajectory	0 %	48.1 %

4. DISCUSSION - CONCLUSION

Different road information messages have been presented on an in-car screen and we have recorded the drivers' performances concerning visual exploration, memorization and control of driving. Here, we summarize and discuss the main results and we propose a few recommendations.

Concerning the visual explorations of road messages, it appears that the increase in the length of road messages results in a proportional effect on the mean number of glances (from 3.8 glances for 3 and 4 units up to 15.5 glances for 14-18 units), but in very little effect on the mean duration of a glance (from 1.08 s up to 1.35 s). Thus, it seems that drivers have favoured safe drive requirement, limiting duration of each glance. It must be noted that these mean durations of visual explorations are similar to those obtained when reading in-car navigation map (Wierwille & al., 1988; Labiale,1989). However, for reason of driving safety, it seems necessary to limit the number and duration of drivers' glances on in-car displays (Zwahlen & al.,1988); consequently, we think that the shortest road information message (3 or 4 units length) seems more appropriate to keep the driver's attention on the road scene.

Concerning memorization, the recall is inversely proportional to the length of road information messages, from 100 % for 4 units to 48.4% for 14-18 units; however, it must be noted that messages containing 6-8 units can be memorized correctly up to 93.7 %. and in that case, as a previous experiment has demonstrated (Labiale, 1990), an auditory presentation of such message would be preferable for the driver.

Results confirmed only the primacy effects and not the recency effects on memorization of the long messages. These results need to be confirmed by a further experiment which will compare the order effect of the various information units (geography, type of road, event-causes and event-consequences, time and distance, actions proposed) on the memory recall.

Concerning the trajectory and speed control, only the long road information messages (from 10 to 18 units) have an important impact on these sub-tasks of driving; however, as these variables were based on subjective feeling of drivers, these results have to be confirmed by objective measures.

Taking into account these results, two psycho-ergonomics recommendations can be made :

- for safe driving, the best perceptual and attentional solution seems to be a maximum of 4 units for written road information message, in order to minimize disturbance of visual attention away from the road scene.
- the written presentation of road information messages on an in-car screen is most useful and safe when the car is at rest; in that case, the optimal perceptual and cognitive solution seems to be 6 to 8 information unit messages.

REFERENCES

Gatling F. P. (1977). The effect of auditory and visual presentation of navigational messages, Report FWA-RD, 37 p.

Kintsh W. (1976). Bases conceptuelles et mémoire de textes, In Bulletin de Psychologie, numéro spécial : la mémoire sémantique, Ehrlich S. et Tulving T. editors).

Labiale G., Mamberti M.L., Baez D., Conus Y. (1988). Compréhension et mémorisation des messages visuels et auditifs d'information routière, Rapport de recherche INRETS n°66, 40p.

Labiale G. (1989). Influence of in-map displays on drivers performances In Vehicle/ Highway Automation : Technology and Policy issues, SAE publ. SP -791, 11-18

Labiale G. (1990). In-car road information: comparison of auditory and visual presentations. Proceedings of the Human factor society, 34 th annual meeting, 623-627.

Parkes A. M., Ashby M. C. & Fairclough S.H. (1991). The effects of different in-vehicle route information displays on drivers behaviour, SAE technical paper 912734, 61-70.

Zwahlen H. T., Adams C.C. & DeBald D.P. (1988) Safety aspects of CRT touch panel controls in automobiles, In Vision in vehicles II, Gale A.G. et al. (editors), Elsevier Science publishers B.V., 335-344.

Wierwille W. W., Dingus T.A. & Antin J.F (1988). In-vehicle attentional demands and in-vehicles information displays, In Vision in vehicles II, Gale A.G. et al. (editors), Elsevier Science publishers B.V., 305-316.

VISION IN VEHICLES - V
A.G. Gale et al. (Editors)

Locating Faults Indicated by Polygon Displays*

A. W. MacRae and S. Milligan

School of Psychology, The University of Birmingham, Edgbaston, Birmingham, B15 2TT, UK

Abstract

In a polygon display, each system parameter is indicated by the radial distance of one vertex of a polygon from the centre. Earlier results showed that the detectability of faults is enhanced by increasing the number of polygon vertices from four to twenty but a practical display-control system also requires the absence of adverse effects with more parameters. Speed and accuracy of responses when peripherally viewing a polygon display with an inset dynamic task were investigated for two tasks: detecting the presence of an out-of-limits parameter and locating the most deviant parameter. The number of vertices in the display was varied, and the vertices were permitted either a wide or a narrow range of variation. Performance was best when the deviation of the extreme vertex was outwards. As the number of parameters increased from 4 to 20, speed and accuracy in detecting a fault remained constant or improved if system variability was low but locating the most extreme parameter became poorer Ä especially when the other vertices varied widely.

1. INTRODUCTION

Polygon displays compress information that might be conveyed by an array of dials or strip gauges into a single display where each reading is represented by the distance of a polygon vertex from its centre. They may be particularly appropriate for displaying a group of parameters from a common source, such as the state of a vehicle, especially if the purpose of the display is more to give warning of an abnormal condition involving several parameters than to convey precise readings to be acted on individually. There is evidence that integrated displays such as polygons are processed holistically, allowing additional information to be conveyed without performance penalty and making relationships among the variables more accessible.

Munson and Horst (1986) tried to identify the processing of polygon displays as holistic or sequential (equivalently, parallel or serial) by measuring the time taken to identify a display as normal or abnormal as a function of the number of vertices in the polygon. Serial processing of vertices would produce longer reaction times (RTs) when polygons had more vertices but they found no sign of that; indeed RTs instead seemed to decline. Hughes and MacRae (in press) extended their paradigm by including a dynamic task at the centre of a polygon display with 4,

*We are grateful to Westland Helicopters Ltd for their support of our project.

8, 16 or 20 vertices and also found better performance with polygons having larger numbers of vertices whether the dynamic task was active or not.

However, for a practical display-control system it would also be necessary that additional parameters do not disrupt other aspects of performance. One danger is that, in a display with more parameters, the presence of a fault is better detected but its nature is not. The present study investigated that possibility by requiring not only detection of a fault's occurrence but also a response to indicate the parameter involved.

2. METHOD

2.1 Subjects

Six male and six female undergraduates aged from 20 to 39 were paid £5 to participate. All had normal or corrected-to-normal vision and were right-handed.

2.2 Apparatus

The experiment was controlled and recorded and the display was generated by an AT-compatible computer with EGA driving a NEC Multisync colour monitor. Responses were made with a Hewlett-Packard two-button mouse on a 190 mm ´ 230 mm mouse mat.

Figure 1 illustrates the display, which was based on that used by Hughes and MacRae (in press). A dynamic task at the centre of the display consisted of keeping a schematic 'spaceship' inside a coloured rectangle 38 mm x 40 mm by modifying its velocity by dragging the mouse in the desired direction. The spaceship moved a step of variable size and direction every 0.2 sec, each step being accompanied by a tone pulse which increased in pitch if any part of it passed out of the rectangle. A score displayed at the top of the screen increased on each step while the spaceship was wholly within the rectangle and decreased if any part of it strayed outside. The dynamic task required continuous control of the mouse, simulating the attention demands of the primary flying displays on a pilot.

2.3 Procedure

Green reference polygons with diameters of 97 mm and 145 mm were continuously displayed and were viewed at eye level at a distance of approximately 1700 mm, giving a visual angle of about 5 deg. Yellow test polygons appeared on the screen every 2.75 sec and remained for 2 sec. The reference polygons indicated permitted inner and outer limits for the test polygon's vertices. If all were within limits the system was classed as normal but if one was out of limits the system was abnormal. One of the vertices, randomly selected by the computer as the 'target' vertex, was always 2 mm inside or 2 mm outside one of the reference vertices. The others had random values in a band 6 mm wide (Narrow variation) or 21 mm wide (Wide variation) midway between the reference limits.

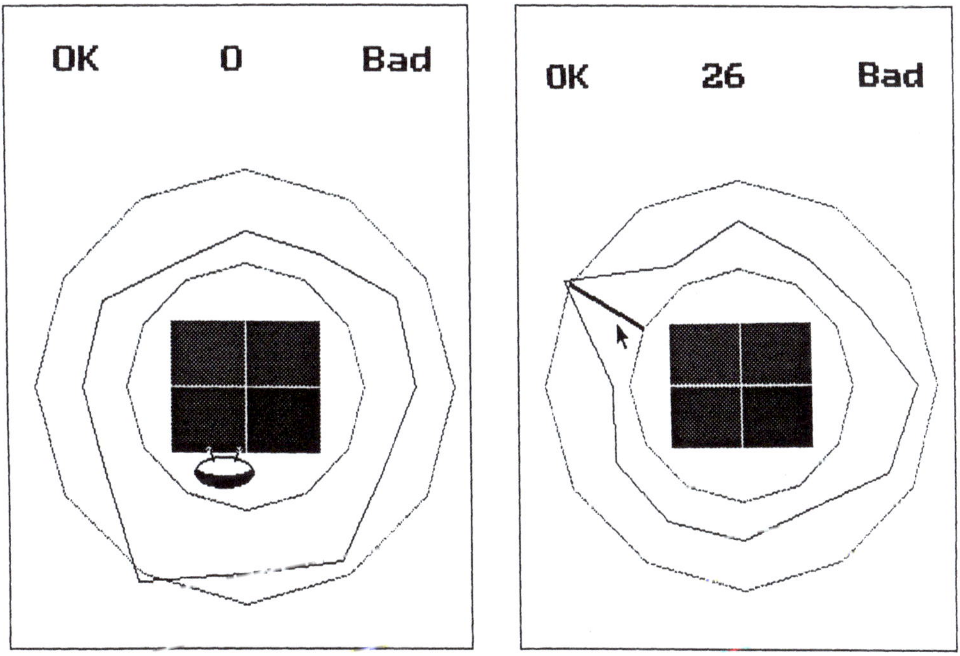

Figure 1. Dumps of the central part of the display screen showing (a) the dynamic task continuing after a test polygon appeared and (b) the most deviant vertex being highlighted prior to being recorded by a button press. Both examples have the 'wide variation' condition of the non-target vertices.

On each side of the displayed score were the words 'OK' and 'Bad' to remind subjects of the meanings of the mouse buttons. The buttons used for these responses were always the same for an individual but were in reverse order for half of them. When a mouse button was pressed, immediate auditory feedback about correctness or error was given by a rising or falling tone, the dynamic task halted and the spaceship icon disappeared. If no response was made within 2 sec, an invalid response was recorded and the feedback for an error was given. The outcome and the elapsed time since the first appearance of the test polygon were recorded.

A small arrow cursor then appeared in the centre of the display. Moving it with the mouse to any vertex of the polygon highlighted that vertex by a white bar joining the reference polygons, as shown in Figure 1b. The region around each vertex in which the cursor would 'switch' the highlighting on and off was of constant size, irrespective of the number of vertices in the polygon. The task was to highlight the vertex which was out of limits, or most nearly out of limits and then press a mouse button to record the selection. Auditory feedback was given as before, the spaceship icon reappeared and the dynamic task continued from the position at which it had been interrupted.

To begin with, subjects had at least one block of practice trials with a six-sided polygon that was not used in the main experiment and could practice further if they wished, but none chose to have more than two blocks. When they felt confident with the task, experimental trials began. Further practice was available at the start of each subsequent session but none chose to do more than one block.

They attended five experimental sessions of thirty minutes over a space of two weeks, mostly at the same time of day on successive days. In each session, subjects encountered every experimental condition. They viewed four polygons (8, 12, 16 and 20 vertices) with narrow and with wide variation of the non-target vertices, in a random sequence of eight blocks of thirty-two trials each. Within each block, the target vertex appeared eight times in each of four positions: 2 mm inside or 2 mm outside each of the reference polygons. The other vertices were randomly positioned in the relevant band of variation.

Subjects were told to respond as quickly and as accurately as possible. They were advised to attend to the centre of the display and concentrate on keeping the spaceship inside the rectangle; the polygon could be seen in peripheral vision and their responses could be guided by a general impression of its shape. After finishing the experiment, they completed a questionnaire to determine their subjective impressions of the difficulty of the various experimental conditions.

3. RESULTS

A log transformation corrected skew in the distribution of reaction times (RTs) and all subsequent calculations used log RT. The distribution of accuracy data was normalized by a logistic transformation and Analysis of Variance, with 'Subjects' as a random variable, was carried out on both sets of transformed data for each of the two responses. Scores on the dynamic task were not analyzed in detail since a high score might partly be an artefact of slow responses to the polygons allowing extra time for scores to accumulate.

3.1 Narrow and wide variation

Figure 2 shows that wide variation of the system parameters had a consistently adverse effect on both performance measures under all combinations of other conditions. Contrasting narrow with wide variation in each of the four combinations of performance measure and task yields F ratios which are all significant at 0.001 but a less predictable consequence of manipulating system variability was the way it altered the relationships among the other display conditions.

When the range of non-target variation was narrow, RTs and accuracy for the OK/Bad decision improved as the number of vertices increased, as previously found by Munson and Horst (1986) and Hughes and MacRae (in press). When the range of non-target variation was wide, accuracy and RTs deteriorated slightly with additional vertices. For the task of pointing to the most deviant vertex, both performance measures declined as the number of vertices increased, but especially so when the system variability was wide. These results are reflected in interactions between non-target variation and the other variables which are mostly significant at 0.001.

3.2 Position of the target vertex

Figure 3 shows that the value indicated by the target vertex significantly affected the speed and accuracy of 'OK/Bad' judgements. Responses were slower when the target vertex was within limits than when it was out of limits, probably reflecting its greater similarity to the non-targets. The pattern of errors was quite complex. With narrow variation in non-targets, there was little effect of target position, though accuracy was almost 100% for identification of the most deviant vertex but under 95% for identification of system status. With wide variation, there was strong dependence on the value of the target, but in opposite directions for the two responses. For the OK/Bad response, performance was better when the most extreme vertex was within limits, indicating a tendency to err in the direction of declaring the system OK. Off-limits vertices were perhaps disguised by the overall jaggedness of the display.

Identification of the most extreme vertex was essentially perfect when non-target variation was narrow. The same was true when it was wide with the target vertex out of limits. In that circumstance, the most-deviant vertex was uniquely identified by being the only one to cross a reference polygon. When variation was wide but the target was within limits, identification declined severely, because the most extreme vertex was then not distinctively different from the others.

3.3 Questionnaires

Eleven of the twelve subjects reported that they found the twenty-sided polygon in the 'wide' condition the most difficult, both for the 'OK/Bad' response and for vertex identification. Most reported that they found the eight-sided polygon in the 'narrow' condition easiest to respond to for both tasks. The next most frequent choice of 'easy' display was the twenty-sided polygon in the 'narrow' condition.

4. DISCUSSION

A quantitatively minor effect that may be of some practical importance is that response times and accuracy were generally better for vertices that deviated outwards rather than inwards, whether they were out of limits or not. If the effect is robust it may warrant designing displays that capitalize on it by coding all types of fault as outward deviations. Greaney and MacRae (in press) evaluated a polygon display in which any deviations from normality occurred outwards and found performance advantages over conventional polygons and a variant in which every alternate vertex had a fixed location.

Earlier results showing performance actually improving as additional parameters are displayed in a polygon format were replicated for the original task of identifying overall system status as OK or Bad, with a single deviant parameter and a narrow range of variation in the other parameters. When the other parameters varied widely, there was no improvement with additional parameters in the display, though the decline in performance was not great. It appears that parallel processing (holistic appraisal) was occurring because the small decline in performance was nothing like proportional to the increased information load.

When the task was to indicate the most deviant vertex Ä that is, to locate the parameter responsible for the existence of a globally-perceived fault, or near-fault, state Ä there was a clear decline in performance as the number of vertices increased, more particularly when the other vertices varied widely. The precision with which the cursor had to be positioned was kept

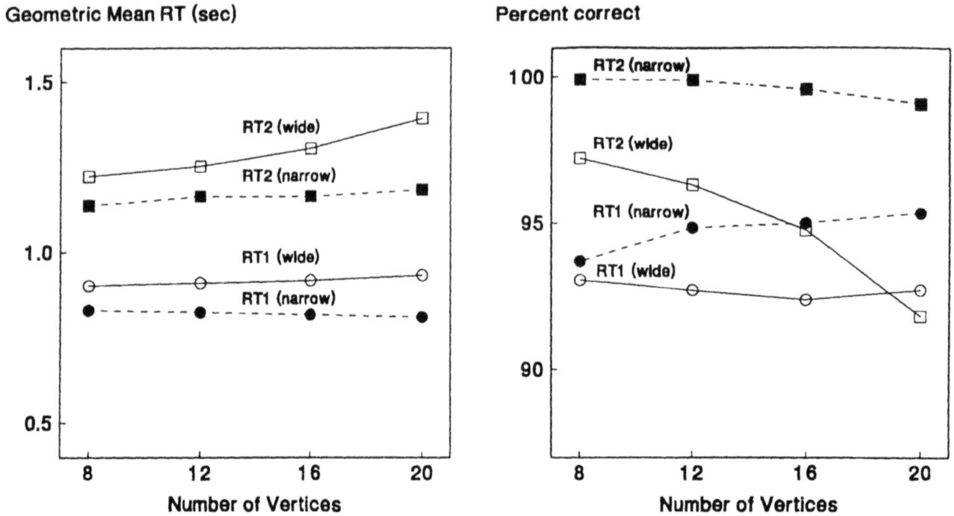

Figure 2. Performance as a function of the variability of system parameters and the number of polygon vertices in two tasks: an OK/Bad decision (RT1) about overall system status and pointing to the most deviant vertex (RT2).

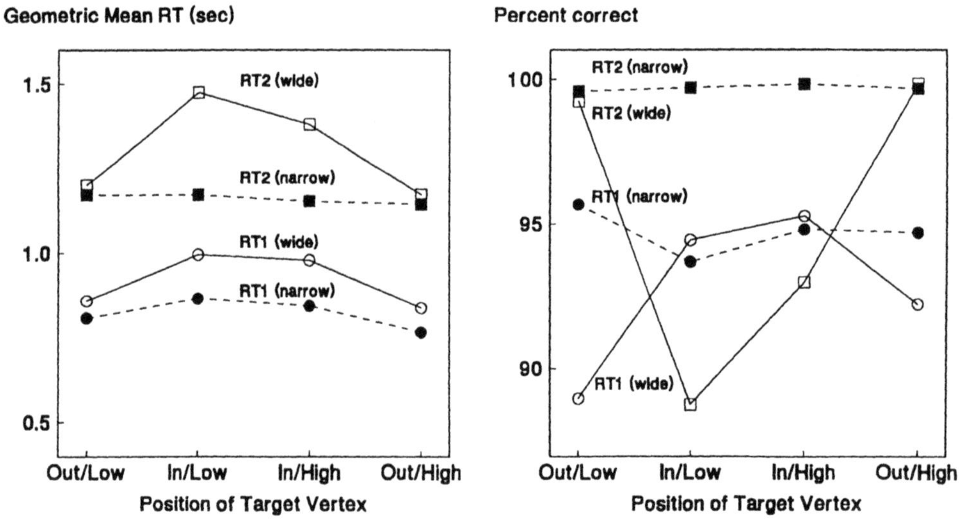

Figure 3. Performance as a function of variability in system parameters and the position of the target vertex in the same tasks as Figure 1. The label Out/Low, for example, indicates that the target was 2 mm outside the low limit of the acceptable range.

constant irrespective of the number of vertices, so the speed change was a perceptual or decision effect rather than a motor one. The dependence of RT2 on the number of vertices indicates that locating the most extreme vertex required a serial search around the polygon, especially when the polygon was irregular. Processing of the identification task therefore seems to be a serial process.

The implication for practical polygon displays is that if the purpose of a display is merely to warn of a fault or near-fault state, the number of parameters displayed can be increased at least to twenty without significant performance penalty. That may represent a benefit over two separate polygons, though that was not directly tested here. However, there would be little point in using a polygon display merely to function as a global warning indicator since the same could be done more simply with an array of lights. To justify a polygon display, some use should be made of the additional information it provides. That is, essentially, a quantitative reading for each of a number of parameters. The present study examined only the speed and accuracy with which the relevant parameter was identified, and found that there was some decline in performance as the number of displayed parameters increased. The increase in response time was of theoretical but not of great practical importance. The most worrying aspect for practical purposes was the decline in accuracy of parameter identification with increased numbers of parameters when other parameters had wide variability.

REFERENCES

Greaney, J. and MacRae, A.W. . Check-reading instrument displays in compressed formats. Proceedings of the Third International Conference on Visual Search. London: Taylor & Francis. (in press)

Hughes, T. and MacRae, A.W. . Holistic peripheral processing of a polygon display. Human Factors.

Munson, R.C. and Horst, R.L. (1986). Evidence for global processing of complex visual displays. Proceedings of the Human Factors Society 30th Meeting, 776-780.

VISION IN VEHICLES - V
A.G. Gale et al. (Editors)

A new Scientific Instrument for Vision in Vehicle Research

Dr. W. Gottlieb [a] , Dr. S. Scherbarth [b] and K. Guse [b]

[a] Daimler Benz AG, Department F1M/FM,Daimlerstraße 48, 12274 Berlin, Germany
[b] Deutsche Aerospace, Dornier GmbH, Department VF3 110, 88039 Friedrichshafen, Germany

1. INTRODUCTION

The development of a new eyetracking system specially designed for vehicle applications is reported. The system was developed by the Dornier Company, Germany and was initiated and supported by the central research section of Daimler Benz, Berlin, who contributed their application expertise in the dedicated requirements for vision in vehicle investigations.

The basic idea of the new development was to create a system to measure a car driver's visual behaviour under real ambient conditions and as far as possible undistorted by the physical and psychological experimental conditions.

The new system is a no-contact, headfree device. The pickup unit is integrated in the car's dashboard leaving the driver's environment as far as possible identical to the standard car (Fig.1). The measurement range covers all the driver's views through the windscreen, at the instruments and at the driver's rear mirrors. The ambient light conditions may vary from darkness up to full sunlight (Fig.4).

Figure 1: Mercedes car equipped with the new eyetracking system as seen by the driver

2. TECHNICAL DESCRIPTION

The system uses the pupil-centre corneal-reflection operating principle (Merchant, et al., 1974) for the remote measurement of the eye movements.

A video camera, which is hidden behind a black screen records images of the eye, which is illuminated by inperceptible infrared light (Fig.2 shows the schematic setup). A resultant eye image for the setup with two infrared light sources is displayed in Fig.3 and shows the dark pupil of an eye and two corneal reflections of the illuminators.
The distance vectors between the centres of the pupil and the reflections correspond directly to the line of sight with respect to the position of the illuminators - independent of the head position.

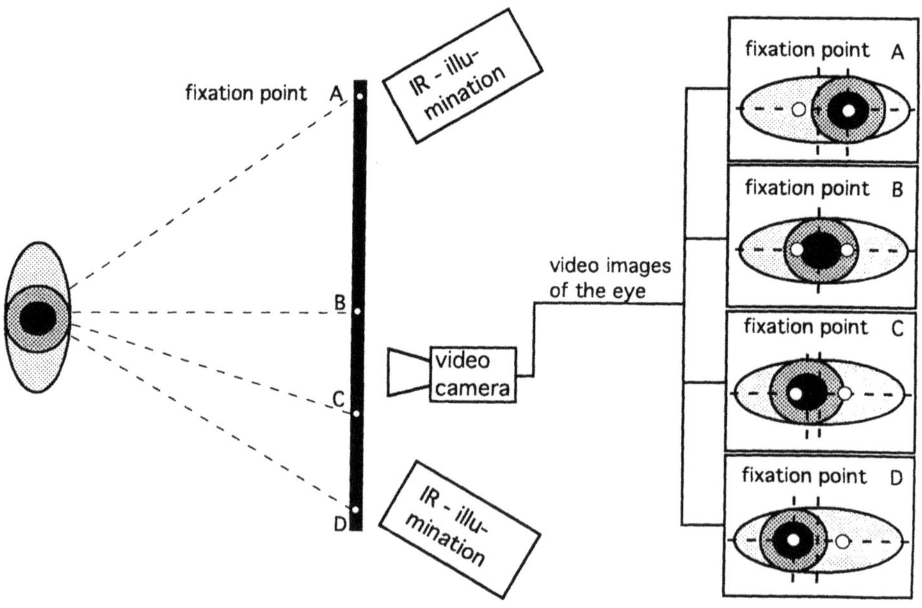

Figure 2: Schematic sketch of the setup with two infrared illuminators showing the video image of the eye camera for different lines of sight.

The main improvements with respect to remote eyetrackers so far available are achieved by the unique combination of a newly developed real time image processor for evaluation of the eye camera's picture, a patented system for suppression of ambient light, a very fast mirror system for tracking of the eye and a menu guided user software dedicated to the specific requirements and corrections necessary for vehicle applications.

The image processor extracts the positions of the centres of the pupil and the reflections using a shape recognition algorithm based on the contours of the video image (Fig.3). Therefore, no critical thresholding is needed for the identification of the pupil and no adjustment by the operator is necessary for proper operation.

The ambient light suppression system effectively eliminates any effects of ambient light on the eye image. The image evaluated by the image processor is merely produced by the light of the infrared illuminators; even reflections from car headlights or bright, sunlit objects are almost completely suppressed. The system therefore allows operation under any light condition up to bright sunlight.

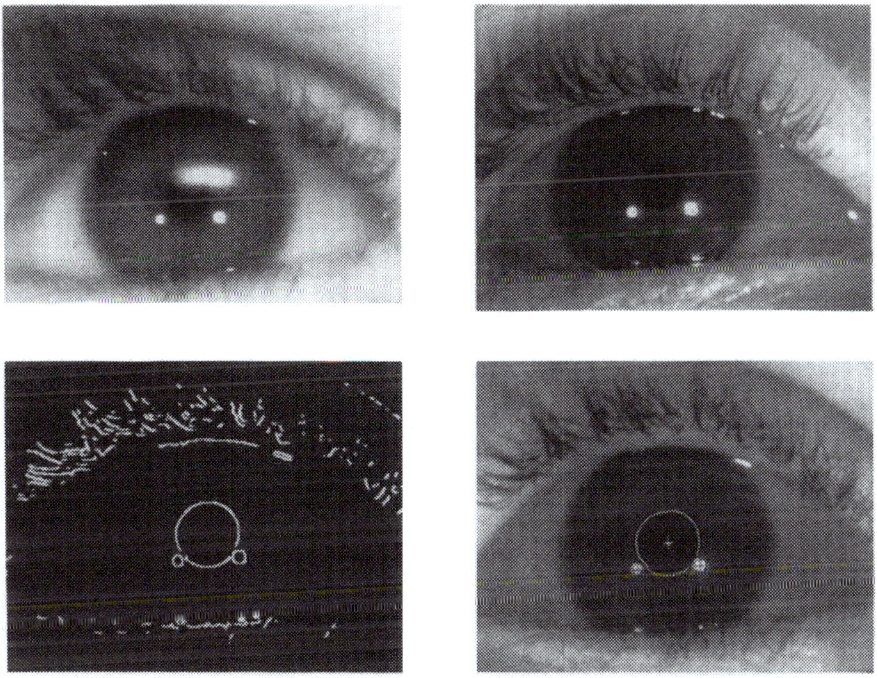

Figure 3: Different stages of the image processing:

a) Eye looking into a bright light as seen from a conventional camera (upper left)
b) Like a) but with the active ambient light suppression system (upper right)
c) Contours of b) which are used for shape recognition (lower left)
d) Contours recognized as pupil (bright) and reflections (dark) and the extracted centre positions (crosses)

The fast mirror system tracks the eye during the driver's usual head movements within $10\ cm^3$ and therefore enables operation without any physical restriction of the driver's movement. When the driver moves his head out of the measurement volume, a search routine is started which typically allows the measurements to be continued within one second after re-entering the measurement volume.

The menu guided software performs the necessary corrections to the three dimensional vehicle environment (parallax correction dependent on the viewing direction, additional corrections due to different head positions) and provides the measured point of regard as a stored numerical value and as a cursor keyed in a second camera's picture, showing the driver´s view (Fig. 4).

Figure 4: Screen photo of the scene camera´s view during a measurement with keyed in cursor showing the measured point of regard (pedestrian at the right-hand side). While the sun ahead blinds the scene camera it does not disturb the operation of the eyetracking system.

Figure 5: Complete system as used in the mercedes car with portable control unit on the rear seat, the scene camera in the middle of the car and the pickup unit integrated in the dashboard.

3. APPLICATION RANGE

The new eyetracking system provides the opportunity to perform vision in vehicle research under authentic measurement conditions. No ambiguities due to artificial laboratory setups, restricted freedom of motion, restricted field of view etc. have to be considered in the data evaluation.

Due to the ease of operation, the number of experiments necessary for statistical analysis is achievable within a reasonable time.

As the pickup unit is separated from the portable central unit, one apparatus may be used in different vehicles and in laboratory experiments. The application range in a laboratory setup covers any experiments with a video monitor, slides, computer screen or real objects as a stimulus source. In the first applications in laboratory experiments the design ergonomics of washing machines and the ergonomics of multimedia computer programs have been investigated.

4. APPLICATION EXAMPLES

4.1. Optimisation of rear-end signalling

The aim of this study was to obtain some detailed information about safety problems associated with rear end car-accidents. Previous studies showed that the frequency of rear end collisions is reduced by using a single, centre-high-mounted brake-light repeater (Malone, Kirkpatrick, Kohl & Baker 1978).

In this research study by Daimler Benz, four different rear end lighting designs were investigated:

- normal brake lights
- brake lights with added warning lights(blinking)
- normal brake lights with high mounted brake light and
- normal brake lights with high-mounted brake lights (blinking)

The study was designed to investigate the eye-fixation patterns of drivers in high speed traffic, typical of autobahn condition. As a test facility, the advantages of the Daimler Benz driving simulator (6 degrees of freedom motion simulator, real-time 180° visual plus audio simulation) and the new eyetracking system were used. The following parameters were measured:

- various vehicle dynamic parameters
- reaction time [ms],
- eye-movements (x, y)
- pupil diameter [mm].

Because in normal driving conditions the driver does not always 'fix' visually on to the lights of the car he is following, we tried to find a procedure to distract him. Therefore, during half of the trials we distracted the attention of the subjects using a special light, which was mounted in the middle of the dashboard. Forty people were tested. Compared to other studies associated with measurements of eye-fixations this is a very large number.

The results are shown in figures 6 and 7. Reaction times were computed as the interval between the lighting of the brake lights of the car in front and the use of the brakes by the subject. It can be seen that the high mounted brake lights have some advantages on the reaction time.

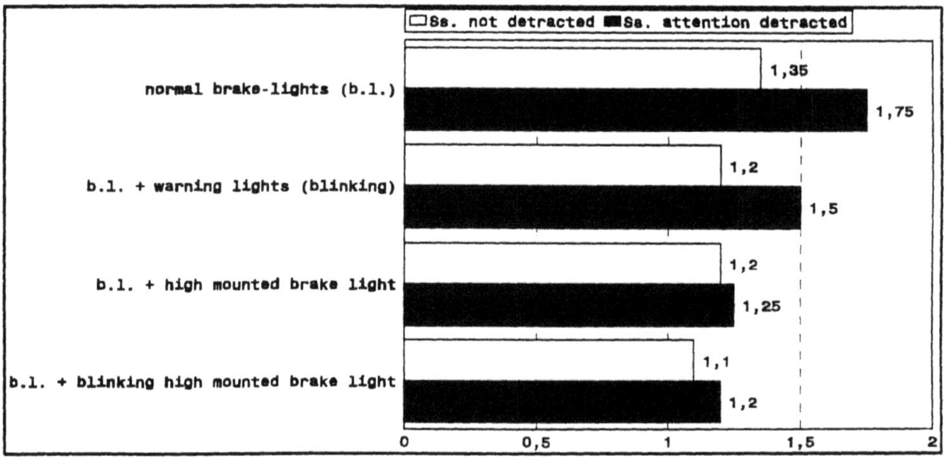

Figure 6: Results of reaction time for the four tested rear end brake-light designs for distracted and undistracted drivers.

Another reason why we used eye measurements in this study was to obtain more information about the visibility of brake lights in real traffic. For the distracted situation, we computed the interval between the shining of brake lights and the sacade from the distracting light to the car in front. The analysis of the data obtained is still going on and the results will be published soon.

Another interesting result of the eye-movement measurement is the change of pupil diameter with time. Figure 7 shows for the non-distracted situation, that the pupil diameter increases steadily (thick line), but in the distracted attention situation, the pupil diameter decreases during the first 2500 ms and then increases afterwards to the same size as in the distracted situation.

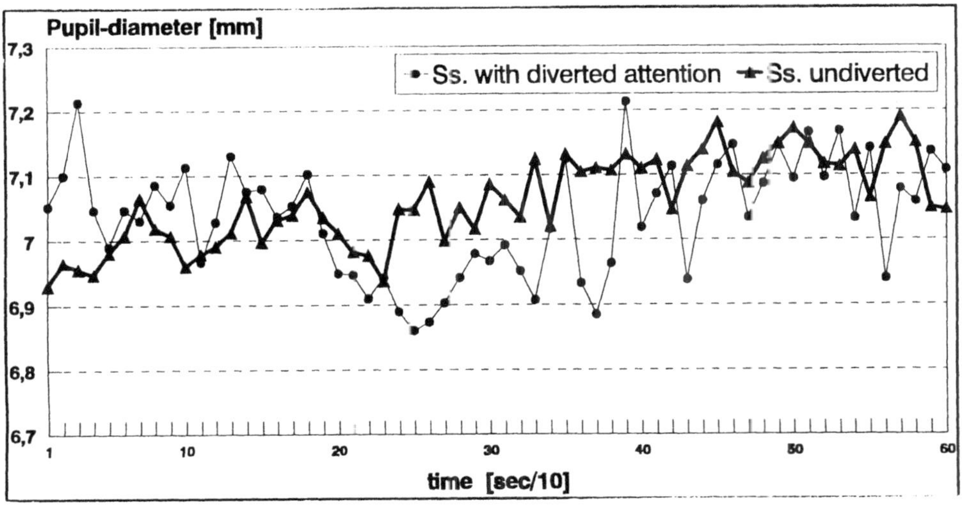

Figure 7: Pupil-diameter during the first six seconds after breaking of the car in front under distracted and undistracted conditions .

4.2. Effects of stress while collecting traffic sign information

Accident investigations have shown that intersections and junctions have many accidents that could be caused by bad traffic sign conditions. Either the number of signs is too large or the graphical design is poor.

Measurement of eye-fixations should give some information about the process of searching and information collecting strategies. The relationships between the "seen" objects, the "perceived" objects and the cognitive processes involved are still not known. (Yarbus, 1967, Höfner 1973, Sheena & Young, 1975).

In a field-study, performed with A.S.S. in Cologne, 45 subjects had to drive on a 49-km long test track with different conspicuous traffic signs.

The following parameters were measured:

- various vehicle dynamics parameters
- reaction time [ms]
- heart rate [pulse/min]
- eye-movements (x, y)
- pupil diameter [mm]

In addition, EOG-measurements (electro-oculogram) were taken. We want to compare the results from our eye-tracking system with the EOG-measurements. This includes the basic need to find an algorithm to distinguish between fixations and saccades.

This study is now going on. The data of the first six drivers have been taken. Results are currently not available but will be published.

REFERENCES

1. Merchant, J., Morrissette, R. and Porterfield, J. L. Remote Measurement of Eye Direction Allowing Subject Motion Over One Cubic Foot of Space. IEEE Transactions on Biomedical Engineering, Vol. BME-21, No. 4, July 1974
2. Malone, T.B., Kirkpatrick, M., Kohl, J.G., and Baker, C. Field test evaluation of rear lighting systems. Alexandria, VA: Essex Corporation. Prepared for NHTSA. U.S. Department of Transportation, Contract No. DOT-HS-5-01226.
3. Yarbus, A.L. Eye movements and vision, New York: Plenum Press, 1967.
4. Höfner, K. J. et al. Registrierung der Blickbewegungen beim Autofahren - bisherige Forschungen, Zeitschrift für Verkehrssicherheit, 1973, 4(19), p.221-241.
5. Sheena, D. and Young, C. R. Methods and Designs; survey of eye movement recording methods, Behavior Research Methods and Instrumentation, 1975, 7(5), p.379-429.

VISION IN VEHICLES - V
A.G. Gale et al. (Editors)
1996 Elsevier Science B.V.

Active And Passive Visual Information In Remote-Controlled Vehicles

P. Péruch[a], J.-L. Vercher[b] and G.-M. Gauthier[b]

[a]URA CNRS Cognition & Mouvement, Université d'Aix-Marseille II, IBHOP, Traverse Susini, F-13388 Marseille Cedex 13, France

[b]Laboratoire de Contrôles Sensorimoteurs, Université de Provence, Avenue Escadrille Normandie Niemen, F-13397 Marseille Cedex 20, France

1. INTRODUCTION

The nature of the available visual information for remote control of vehicles is a determining factor in the operator's knowledge of the space in which the mobile is moving [1-2]. A subject (S) moving "naturally" in space, as in locomotion, receives information on self-generated displacement from different sensory and proprioceptive receptors. Considering the respective roles of the diverse sensory modalities has suggested much research, and has shown in particular the dominance of vision for processing spatial data and acquiring spatial knowledge. The visual flow perceived by a moving observer includes not only information on the environment in which the observer is moving, but also information relative to the characteristics of his/her own displacement in this environment [3-4]. Many authors, in particular in the field of ecological psychology, have stressed the importance of active perception to extract invariants in the environment [5-6]. Thus, the active or passive nature of the displacement, on the one hand, and the dynamic or static perception of the visual information by the observer, on the other hand, may be decisive for the acquisition of spatial knowledge. In the remote control of mobiles, it may be easier for an operator to integrate the properties of the space in which the mobile is moving than for a person who only perceives the visual effects corresponding to the displacement of a mobile autodriven or driven by someone else. Likewise, it may be easier for an operator to integrate the space characteristics out of dynamic visual information (continuous sweeping) rather than static (successive fixed frames) visual information [7-9].

This experiment was aimed at evaluating the kinds of spatial knowledge gained through different conditions of visual exploration. An active exploration condition (where the S freely explored the space) was compared to two passive exploration conditions in which the S was shown a film or a series of pictures taken along a path. The acquired spatial knowledge was tested through the ability of the S to take the shortest path to reach a position which was not visible from his starting location. We hypothesised that performance would be better after active rather than passive exploration, and after dynamic rather than static exploration.

Moreover, this experiment raised questions as to the kinds of spatial knowledge required to solve such a task [10-11]: Would a survey map type of representation be necessary (cartographic), or would a route map type be sufficient (memory of explored paths)?

2. METHOD

A graphic PC-based workstation (Hewlett-Packard RS25c equipped with a Matrox SM1281 3D vectorial graphic card, 256 colours, 1280 x 1024 pixels, 10000 3D z-buffered Gouraud-shaded facettes per second) was used to produce perspective views (scenes) simulating the displacement of an observer (or of a camera mounted on a mobile). The scenes were generated as they would be seen by a 1.80 m tall observer moving through the space, and were displayed by a video projector on a 1.65-by-2.05 m screen placed 3 m in front of the S, providing a visual angle of 55_ as seen from the S's head (see Figure 1). The displacement of the simulated camera was controlled by the S by means of a joystick connected to a 12-bit analogue-to-digital converter. The joystick could be used to make left/right rotations and forward (but not backward) translations, giving the observer the impression that he was driving a vehicle through the environment and viewing the scene through the windshield of the vehicle (without a side view).

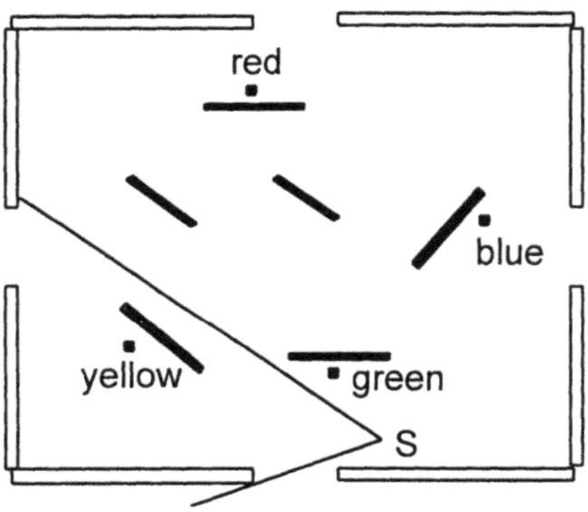

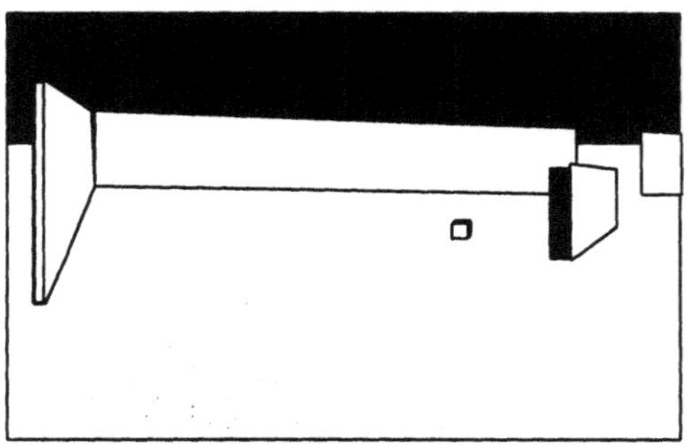

Figure 1. Map of a space used in the experiment (left) and corresponding scene (right) for an observer located at point S. Each space was composed of a 50-by-40 m rectangle bounded by four white, 3-m-high walls. There were six green, 2-m-high walls (obstacles) in the walled space, and four 50-cm cubes of different colours (blue, red, green, and yellow) placed behind some of the obstacles. On the map, the limits of the observer's visual field were indicated by two lines coming from point S.

The three exploration conditions were compared for three spaces which differed in the relative positions and orientations of the obstacles and cubes. The conditions differed in the way the S explored the environment, namely dynamic active exploration (free exploration with the joystick), dynamic passive exploration (film), and static passive exploration (a series of pictures). For each condition a 4-minute practice exploration phase in which all the obstacles and cubes in the space could be seen several times and from different points of view preceded the test phase. In the test phase, the S had to take the shortest path to reach a cube (the target) whose colour was indicated at the beginning of each trial. In a given condition, the same target was searched for twice. For each trial the starting point was set somewhere near the centre of the space at a location where no cube could be seen through a single rotation. The S did not see a map of the environment before or during the experiment. Nine female and nine male graduate students or laboratory staff members between the ages of 20 and 38 with no known visual-motor disorders participated in this 90-minute experiment.

3. RESULTS

3.1. Performance

The subject was scored on each trial according to the way the target was reached. The score ranged from 4 points if reached directly (without another cube being seen) to 0 points if all the other cubes were seen before reaching the target (see Figure 2). The analysis of these scores revealed a high degree of variability between operators [$F(17,53) = 2.47$, $p<0.01$] and an overall effect of the exploration conditions [$F(2,53) = 7.26$, $p<0.005$]. The scores were higher after dynamic active than after dynamic passive exploration [$F(1,35) = 6.67$, $p<0.05$], and higher after dynamic active than after static passive exploration [$F(1,35) = 3.99$, $p<0.05$], but the performances observed after dynamic passive and static passive exploration did not differ significantly [$F(1,35) = 0.32$]. No significant difference was observed between males and females [$F(1,53) = 0.31$, NS], nor with the order of presentation of the conditions of exploration [$F(5,53) = 0.19$, NS]. Moreover, comparison of the four first and four last trials to the same target yielded no significant difference [$F(1,431) = 1,46$, NS], suggesting that the Ss did not acquire further knowledge of the environment through practice.

These scores were used to rank the Ss and define four groups within which performance was equivalent. In group 1 the mean score was always higher than 3, in group 4 the mean score was never significantly different from a random score (1.75), and in the intermediate groups the mean score varied across exploration conditions (see Figure 3).

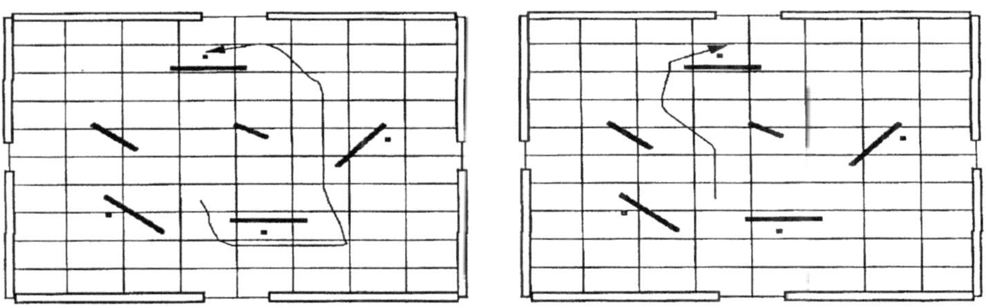

Figure 2. Examples of paths followed by a subject in the first trial (left, scored 1 point) and second trial (right, scored 4 points) to the same target.

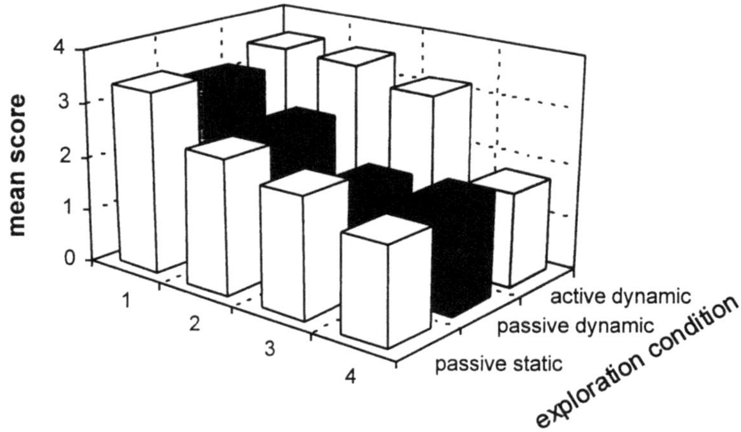

Figure 3. Mean scores by exploration condition and group of Ss.

3.2. Orientation/movement phases

For each trial, an orientation phase (during which, before translation, the S extracted spatial information by a single rotation) could be distinguished from a movement phase (moving from the starting point to the target). The results showed that the time allocated to each of these phases varied with exploration condition and subject group (see Figure 4). For group 1, orientation and movement times were equivalent in all conditions. For group 4 the time spent on the movement phase was about ten times longer than the orientation phase. The ratios for groups 2 and 3 varied through conditions.

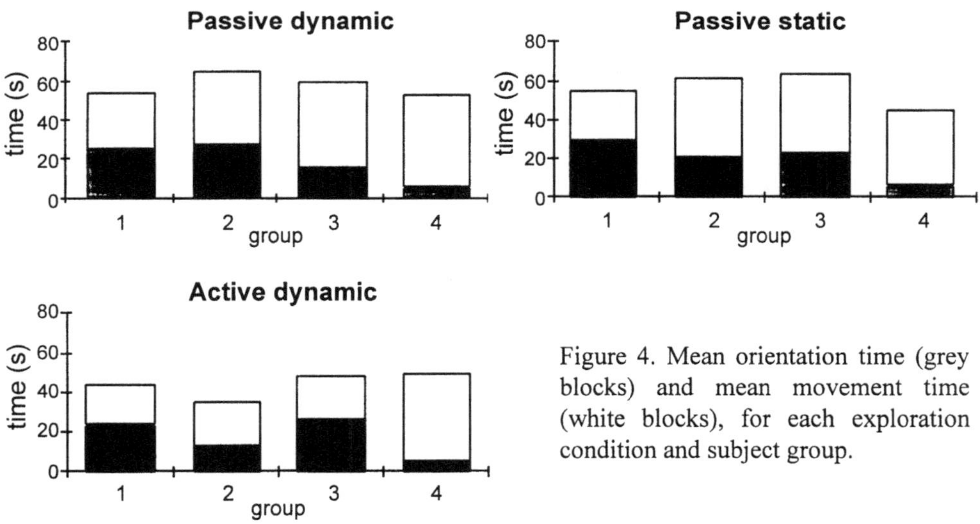

Figure 4. Mean orientation time (grey blocks) and mean movement time (white blocks), for each exploration condition and subject group.

3.3. Spatial learning

At the end of each block of trials carried out in a given exploration condition, the Ss were asked to describe how they had acquired space characteristics during the exploration phase, and what strategies they used to find the target. The correlation ($R = 0.772$, $p<0.001$ for $df = 17$) between performance and rank (defined according to the number of spatial cues used) showed that the Ss who achieved higher performance acquired better spatial knowledge (spatial cues captured during the exploration phase and used during the orientation phase).

4. CONCLUSIONS

This experiment studied the possibility for a S to learn a space under different visual exploration conditions. The active exploration condition (in which the S himself explored the space by manipulating the mobile) led to better performance than the passive exploration conditions (in which the S watched a film or saw a series of static views corresponding to the displacement of a mobile he was not driving). The performance was lower in the two passive conditions. Thus, auto-active exploration brings better knowledge of the spatial features of a given environment than passive viewing of either continuous sweeping or fixed frame views of the environment. These results are compatible with those stressing the importance of active perception to extract invariants in the environment [5-6], and should be taken into consideration when designing visual interfaces for driving remote-controlled vehicles. Moreover, although there is evidence for a link between the level of performance and the amount of spatial knowledge, it is difficult to draw any conclusions concerning the kinds of spatial knowledge required in such a situation [10-11]. Indeed the spatial cues taken into account by the Ss can either be drawn from a survey map type of representation (cartographic) or from a route map type representation (memory of paths followed), or both. The problem is to help the operator shift from one kind of representation to another.

ACKNOWLEDGEMENTS

This research was supported by a grant from the Cognisciences program (CNRS) The authors wish to thank Philippe Rivière for developing the graphic software and Marie-Dominique Giraudo, Daniel Mestre and Alain Savoyant (Cognition & Mouvement) for their helpful comments and suggestions.

REFERENCES

1. K.P. Holzhausen, F.D Pitrella, and H.L. Wolf. Vision and guidance of a telerobotic vehicle. In A.G. Gale et al. (eds.), Vision in Vehicles IV, North-Holland, Amsterdam, 1993.
2. P. Péruch, D. Mestre, J. Pailhous, and A. Savoyant. Visual interfaces in driving remote-controlled vehicles. In A.G. Gale et al. (eds.), Vision in Vehicles IV, North-Holland, Amsterdam, 1993.

3. J.J. Gibson. The ecological approach to visual perception, Houghton Mifflin, Boston, 1979.
4. D.N. Lee. Visual information during locomotion. In R.B. MacLeod and H. Pick (Eds.), Perception: Essays in honor of J.J. Gibson, Cornell University Press, Ithaca, 1974.
5. R. Held and A. Hein. Movement produced simulation in the development of visually guided behavior. J. of Compar. Physiol. Psychol., 56 (1963) 872-876.
6. J.R. Lishman and D.N. Lee. The autonomy of visual kinesthesis. Perception, 2 (1973) 287-294.
7. D.A. Gordon. Perceptual mechanisms in visual guidance. Public Roads, 34 (1966) 53-68.
8. J.J. Koenderink and A.J. Van Doorn. How an ambulant observer can construct a model of the environment from the geometrical strucuture of the visual inflow. In G. Hauske and E. Butenandt (eds.), Kybernetik, Oldenburg, Munich, 1978.
9. D. Mestre, V. Cavallo, and P. Péruch. Definition of an on-board visual aid for piloting large ships. In A.G. Gale et al. (eds.), Vision in Vehicles, Elsevier, Amsterdam, 1986.
10. R.G. Golledge. Environmental cognition. In D. Stokols and I. Altman (eds.), Handbook of Environmental Psychology (Vol 1), Wiley, New York, 1987.
11. F.N. Shemyakin. Orientation in space. In B.G. Ananyev et al. (eds.), Psychological Science in the USSR, Office of Technical Services, Washington, 1, 1962.

5: DRIVER SUPPORT SYSTEMS

VISION IN VEHICLES - V
A.G. Gale et al. (Editors)

Driving with Camera View

Pieter Padmos and Jan van Erp

TNO Human Factors Research Institute,
P.O. Box 23, 3769 ZG Soesterberg, The Netherlands

Abstract

The present study was aimed at formulating requirements for imaging systems which provide controllers of land vehicles with a view of the driving environment, for situations in which direct view is impossible. Potential applications are the driving of armoured vehicles or Remotely Piloted Vehicles.

Experiments were carried out in which an instrumented car was driven on a closed road circuit. The driver's exclusive outside view was provided by a video camera mounted on the car's roof, with a monitor mounted just above the steering wheel. The experimental variables included: camera position, field of view, and monitor markings aiding spatial orientation. Direct View was used as a control condition. For each of the conditions a fixed task battery was run. Objective driving performance measures included: lateral position, steering wheel speed, Time To Coincidence.

Results indicate that driving with Camera View is performable, be it with modest performance deterioration. The preferred Camera View condition, among the ones studied, is a camera mounting height of 2.8 m, combined with a field of view of 100° diagonal.

1. INTRODUCTION

There are two main types of (military) situations in which a direct view for drivers is impossible. Firstly, the driving of tanks or other armoured vehicles on the battlefield must be done while the driver is situated inside the vehicle's armour. Secondly, for Remotely Piloted Vehicles (RPV-s). In these situations the driver's view may be provided by a video camera at a convenient place on the vehicle and a monitor near the driver's seat. In the armoured vehicle the advantages of such a system with respect to periscopes are a larger flexibility in field of view, placement and aiming of the camera. For RPV-s the camera image must be transmitted to a monitor in the control station.

The purpose of this study (commissioned by the Royal Netherlands' Army) was to determine the human factors requirements for imaging systems which provide controllers of land vehicles with a view of the driving environment. Therefore, driving performance was assessed when the outside view was through a camera-monitor system in the car proper. This is an imitation of the armoured vehicle situation, but can also can be seen as an RPV simulation, in which the main difference with reality is that the driver is also provided with near perfect mechanical motion cues (acceleration, vibration).

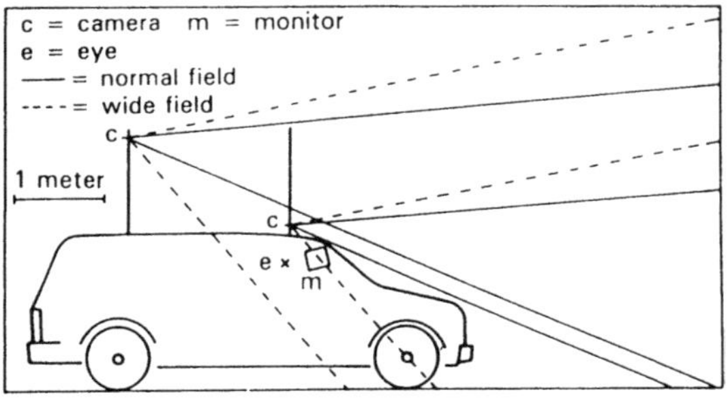

Fig. 1. Schematic side view of the car (to scale), with the two camera positions and field sizes.

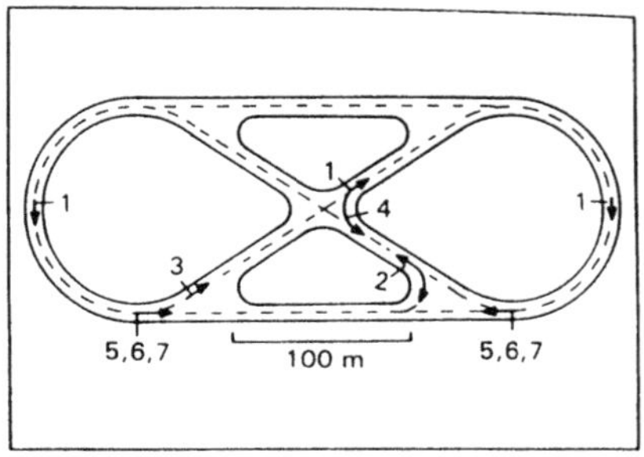

Fig. 2. Map of the driving circuit. The numbers, arrows and dashed lines refer to tasks and routes.

2. METHODS

2.1. Instrumentation

An instrumented passenger car Dodge Caravan V6 (ICACAD; Verwey e.a., 1992) was used. The driver's exclusive view on the road was supplied by a video camera (black/white, JVC type TK-S310 EG) mounted on the car's roof over it's midline, with a video monitor (Philips LDH 2152/00) mounted just above the steering wheel (Fig. 1).

The monitor's screen was 186 x 137 mm and the viewing distance 25 cm, thus providing a field size of 50 deg diagonal. The viewing conditions included: camera POSITION (front *low*; rear *high*); camera FIELD size (*normal*, 46 deg diagonal; *wide*, 100 deg diagonal) and MONIMARK, i.e. monitor markings aiding spatial orientation (*absent*; *present*). Direct View, i.e. free outside view, was used as a control condition.

Fig. 3 shows the monitor images in the four camera conditions, with the monitor markings present. The latter provide a horizon, a projection on the road of the path of the wheels' outer sides at a straight course, and a scale with distance to the front bumper in meters. These images come from video recordings obtained when the car was aligned with the right hand road marking. Only for wide field size is the car visible.

Primary driving measures were recorded digitally as a function of time (20 Hz sampling frequency) and included: speed, distance travelled (calibrated accurately by means of infra-red reflection signals from beacons at fixed positions along the route), lateral distance to the right hand road marking, and steering wheel angle. Fixed speeds could be maintained by means of force feedback on the accelerator pedal, which means that an electronic circuit increased the pedal counter force considerably if the car's speed exceeded the target speed.

2.2. Terrain and driving tasks

The driving circuit, level, covering 350 x 120 m, is depicted in Fig. 2. A 15 cm wide white line marking was painted on the right side of the road. For each viewing condition the same task battery was run, which was designed to cover many driving skills on paved roads without traffic. Below, tasks are listed according to the prevalence of lateral and longitudinal control, respectively. Tasks are divided into subtasks, indicated within brackets.

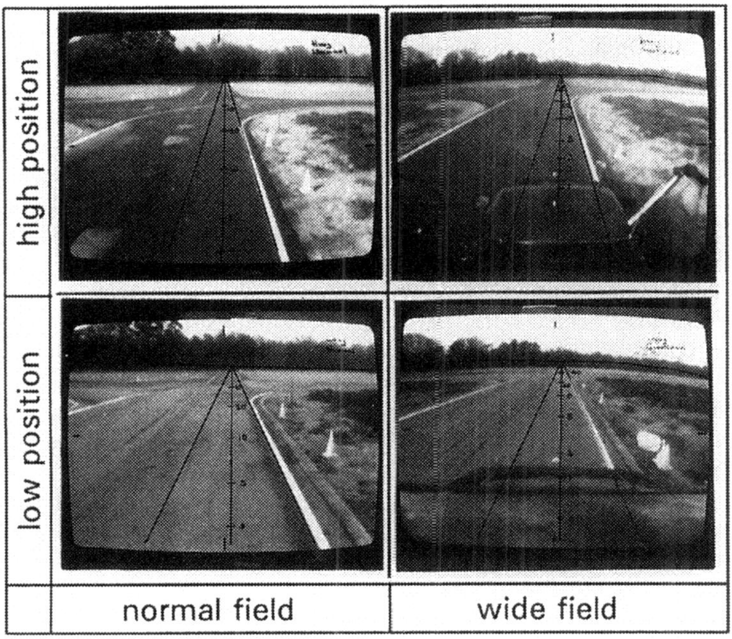

Fig. 3. Monitor images for the two camera positions and fields of view.

Lateral control tasks

1. *8-shaped circuit.* At fixed speed 40 km/h (stretches: straight, curves, transients).
2. *Sharp curves.* At fixed speed 20 km/h (curves: left and right)
3. *Lane change.* At fixed speed, on a straight section, changing from right lane to left lane and back again, according to ISO (1975) standard. (speeds: 20 and 40 km/h).
4. *Backwards.* Rounding a curve and gradually aligning with the subsequent straight road right hand road marking, at free, slow, speed (stretches: curve, and two respective straight sections.

Longitudinal control tasks (all on a straight section).

5. *Estimated speed.* Pulling up to an estimated target speed (the speedometer was blocked) and maintaining this speed for a while (target speeds: 25 and 50 km/h).
6. *Positioning.* Aligning the car's front bumper, or rear wheels, with a transverse line on the road, at free, slow, speed (parts: bumper, rear wheels).
7. *Braking.* From a fixed speed, braking at the latest moment (however, without making it an emergency stop) to stop just in front of a transverse line with side-beacons (approach speeds: 30 and 60 km/h).

For the lateral control tasks the basic instruction was to follow as closely as possible the right hand road marking, without touching or crossing it.

2.3. Dependent variables

For each (sub)task, the following objective driving performance measures were calculated from the primary driving measures.

Lateral control measures. Percentage of distance driven on or over the road marking (**MCp**). Mean lateral distance of right wheels' outer sides to road marking (**Ym**), Y is not counted if negative, i.e. if driven on or over the marking. Standard deviation of the lateral speed (**Vsd**), which is at a given speed a measure of course instability. Mean absolute steering wheel speed (**SSma**). Only for the lane change task: standard error from mid-lane (**MLse**). Only for the backwards driving task: distance travelled while rounding curve (**DT**), and distance to marking at the end of the curve (**Yec**).

Longitudinal control measures. These differ per task. For speed estimation: percentage error from target speed (**Uep**). For positioning: distance, from bumper or rear wheels, to transverse line (**DL**), negative DL means going over the line. For braking: Time To Coincidence (**TTC**). TTC is a measure for the severity of a traffic conflict (Van der Horst, 1991); the larger the value, the less severe. **TTCb** is TTC at the onset of braking; **TTCm** is minimum TTC during braking.

For each task and condition, subjects' ratings of task difficulty were recorded on a discrete scale, ranging from 1: "no problem" to 5: "almost impossible to perform". Per subject, ratings were transformed into z-scores before subjected to further analyses.

2.4. Subjects and procedures

Eight male subjects (age 23 to 38 years) participated in the experiment. All subjects were military driving instructors and had a driving experience of at least 150.000 km. All of them had normal vision; before participation they were tested with standard TNO-tests for visual acuity ($\geq$ 2.0 arcmin^{-1}), and stereovision (threshold disparity $\leq$ 60 arcsec). The subjects received no extra reward for their participation.

One pair of subjects was tested during a week. After arrival on site they received a general instruction on the goals of the experiment, followed by an instruction run with Direct View, aimed to teach car handling and performing the task battery (an instructor always sat beside the subject). Thereafter followed 10 experimental runs, one for each viewing condition. Per run each task in the battery was done three times consecutively. One run lasted about 1 hr; when one subject drove, the other rested. After each task in a run the subjective task difficulty was recorded, as well as various comments from the subjects on the task. The first and last experimental run per subject was in the Direct View condition, in between these control runs were the eight camera conditions (three factors with two levels each, balanced design, order balanced across subjects).

A short instruction run (driving only the 8-course, the sharp right curves, and 20 m straight backwards) preceded each experimental run, in order to become familiar with the particular view via the camera and with the corresponding monitor markings, if present. One part of this instruction was always "teaching the car's width", in which on a straight section the subjects had to line out the front and rear right hand wheels with the right hand road marking and watch the result on the corresponding monitor image. During instruction runs subjects received full performance feedback. During the experimental runs no feedback was given, except when the right road marking was touched or crossed, or when speed was clearly off the fixed target speed. Given this brief instruction the performance measured was almost "first shot".

2.5. Statistical methods

Analyses of variance, separate for each task and performance measure (and subjective difficulty z-scores), were run with the package SPSS® ANOVA, which enables unequal cell fillings. There were three basic designs:

CAMERA:	SUBJECT (8) × CAMERA (2) × REPLICA (3). The two levels of the factor CAMERA are *DV* (mean of the two Direct View conditions) and *CV* (mean of the eight Camera View conditions).
CAMERA FACTORS:	SUBJECT (8) × POSITION (2) × FIELD (2) × MONIMARK (2) × REPLICA (3). The three camera factors are those described in section 2.1.
LEARN:	SUBJECT (8) × LEARN (2) × REPLICA (3). The two levels of LEARN are *before* and *after*, referring to the Direct View runs before and after the Camera View runs.

These basic designs were often combined with a task dependent SUBTASK factor (sect. 2.2), which could be either SPEED (2), STRETCH (2 or 3), or PART (2).

Statistical significance of the main effects and interactions were tested against their interactions with the factor SUBJECT. For significant effects, Tukey tests were applied in order to assess significant differences between conditions.

3. RESULTS

A summary of the main results is presented. Only significant effects are reported (* = error probability $0.01 < \alpha \leq .05$; ** = $\alpha \leq 0.01$). Values reported are always means across subjects and replicas. Sections 3.1 to 3.3 treat effects on objective performance measures; section 3.4 gives the results on the scores of subjective difficulty; in section 3.5 miscellaneous observations are reported.

3.1. General findings on performance

LEARN. The Direct View runs before and after the eight runs with the camera show little or no differences in performance. This finding means that the car handling skills did not change during the experiments. It also allows using Direct View as a control condition for the runs with Camera View.

SUBTASK. Effects of subtask are often significant and in the expected directions. If interactions between subtask and viewing conditions occurred, it meant mostly that effects of viewing conditions were more pronounced for the more complicated subtasks. In the following, effects of subtask will be mentioned only if they are of special interest.

3.2. Performance of lateral control tasks

Effects of the factor CAMERA and the various camera factors on the lateral control tasks 1 (8-course), 2 (sharp curves), 3 (lane change) and 4 (backwards) will be described in this section. The performance measure MCp (marking crossing percentage) shows few and small effects. The mean is 2%, across tasks and conditions. This indicates that the instruction of not crossing the road marking was followed adequately.

Camera View (CV) vs. Direct View (DV)

Significantly differing values of performance measures Ym (mean distance to marking), Vsd (s.d. of lateral speed), SSma (steering speed) and MLse (s.e. from mid-lane), in units stated, are presented per task in the order DV-CV (significance level indicated).

task:	8-course	sharp curves	lane change	backwards
Ym (cm):	n.s.	47-58*	n.s.	38-58*
Vsd (cm/s):	10-12**	n.s.	8-12**	4- 6**
SSma (°/s):	11-13**	42-46**	43-56**	29-34**
MLse (cm):	-	-	8-14**	-

It appears that all differences point in the same direction: control of lateral position and course is worse with CV. However, differences are not always evident, and only in one instance a value in CV differs more than 50% from the corresponding DV value.

Camera factors

POSITION. A main effect of camera position (low - high) exists for the lane change task only: SSma increases (50-61* °/s). Interactions with field size are treated hereafter.

FIELD. Main effects of camera field size on performance measures, included DT (distance travelled around curve) and Yec (distance to marking, at end of curve), both defined for backwards driving only, are presented per task, in the order normal - wide field.

task:	8-course	sharp curves	lane change	backwards
Ym (cm):	n.s.	64-53**	n.s.	n.s.
Vsd (cm/s):	11-13*	20-17**	10-14**	n.s.
SSma (°/s):	n.s.	44-47**	n.s.	n.s.
DT (m):	-	-	-	32-28**
Yec (cm):	-	-	-	97-67*

These results indicate that wide field gives a larger course instability for more or less straight stretches and moderate curves (tasks 1 and 3), probably caused by the accompanying factor 0.5 image minification. Wide field gives performance improvement for sharp curves (task 2, and task 4 too), probably due to the better lateral view (the increase in SSma for task 2 is not contradictory to the simultaneous decreases in Ym and Vsd).

A typical interaction position × field on Ym in task 1**, is presented in Fig. 4. It shows that at low camera position a wide field size gives higher Ym, whereas at high position the effect of field size is just the reverse. Similar interaction effects on Ym for task 2*, and on DT for task 4*, support this finding; they show performance improvement (smaller values) for wide field, mainly at high camera position. Inspecting Fig. 3 makes this interaction plausible: at low camera position the vehicle, visible in the image at wide field, gives an overestimation of the vehicle width, whereas at high camera position it provides a better lateral reference.

MONIMARK. The presence of monitor markings has surprisingly little influence. The only effects are on the measures Ym and Vsd in task 4, which were calculated for the two straight sections exclusively. Values are (in the order markings absent-present) Ym: 67-48*cm; Vsd: 7-6*cm/s. Here the course cue of the monimark is apparently helpful.

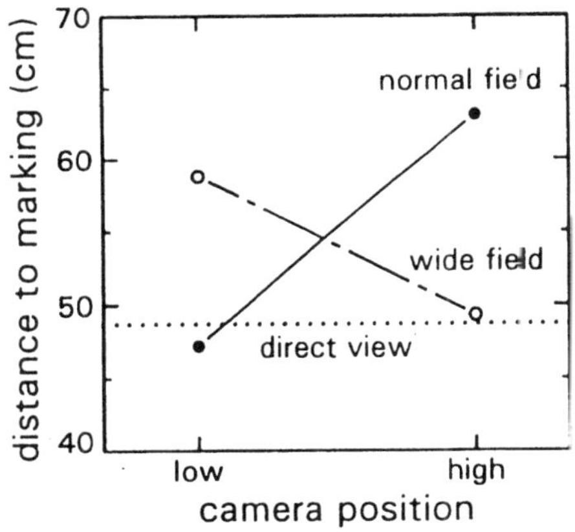

Fig. 4. Interaction position×field, on distance to marking in 8-course task.

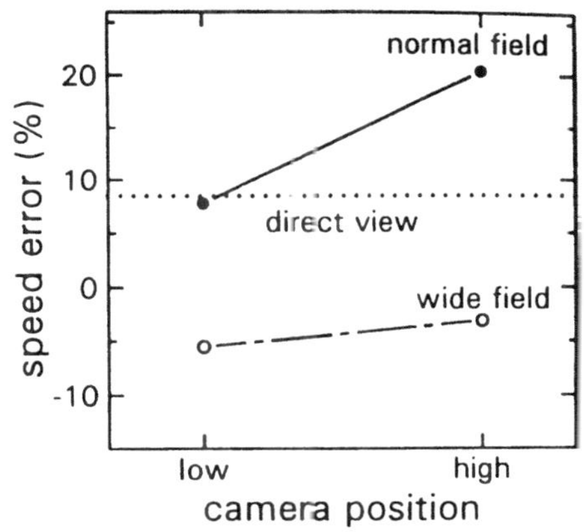

Fig. 5. Interaction position×field, on error in speed estimation task.

3.3. Performance of longitudinal control tasks

Because performance measures differ for different lateral control tasks, effects of viewing conditions are treated per task separately.

Speed estimation task

CAMERA. There is no difference between Direct View and Camera View for the performance measure Uep (speed error percent). The mean over all viewing conditions reflects a small positive error, Uep = +6%, which indicates an underestimation of speed. There is no effect of target speed, which means that speed misestimations are proportional to target speed, as expected.

POSITION and FIELD. Camera position has no significant main effect on Uep, but field size does**, and the interaction position × field is significant* too. Fig. 5 shows that for normal field there is speed underestimation, mainly at high camera position. For wide field there is relative overestimation of speed, not significantly dependent of position.

These effects are in accordance with the idea that optic flow in the image contributes to speed perception (Van der Horst, 1991). At normal field, the main flow comes from the nearest road structures; which decreases at higher camera position. At wide field the image minification decreases the flow from the road, but there is more flow from peripheral structures (immediately near the course was woodland), both at low and high camera position. These results suggest that the peripheral flow is a more effective speed cue than the flow from the road.

Positioning task

CAMERA. For the performance measure DL (distance to line), there is no main effect of Camera View compared with Direct View. However, the interaction part × camera is significant, meaning that only for the rear wheel positioning there is an effect DV-CV (0.6-1.3*m); for the front bumper positioning the mean DL value over all viewing conditions is 0.8 m. Subjects stopped too early, indicating either underestimation of distance to the line, or overestimation of approach speed, especially with camera.

POSITION and FIELD. The interaction part × position** shows that, mainly for the rear wheel part, at high camera position subjects stopped closer to the line (low-high: 1.9-0.8 m). There is no main effect of field size. However, from the interaction part × position × field it appears that, only for the rear wheels, and in camera position high, there is a field size effect normal-wide (0.4-1.2 m).

The present results can be explained by postulating that speed rather than distance was used as the primary positioning cue, especially for the rear wheels. Both for the front bumper and especially for the rear wheels the transverse line disappears from sight some time before the vehicle arrives at the target position, making speed estimation a possible alternative for distance travelled. In this case, lower DL values correspond to relative speed underestimation, and *vice versa*. With this interpretation the effects of camera position and field size on the rear wheel positioning may be described as: high position gives relative underestimation of speed, mainly for the normal field; wide field gives relative overestimation of speed, only for high position. This supports the results of the speed estimation task.

Braking task

CAMERA. A main DV-CV effect is present for the performance measure TTCm (minimum time to coincidence; 1.5-1.1**s). For TTCb (time to coincidence at braking onset) only the interaction speed × camera is significant, which means that there is only an effect DV-CV at 60 km/h approach speed (3.8-3.4**s). These effects mean that one brakes sharper with the camera than without. Given the absence of an overall camera effect in the speed estimation task, this effect suggests that with Camera View relative overestimation of distance occurs.

POSITION and FIELD. An effect of camera position low-high is present on TTCm (1.2-1.0*s). This points to relative underestimation of speed at high camera position, which is similar to the position effects in the former two tasks. Also for TTCm, the interaction subtask × field shows that only for 30 km/h there is an effect of field normal-wide (1.3-1.1**s), indicating for wide field either relative overestimation of distance, or relative underestimation of speed. However, both the speed estimation task and the positioning task indicated for wide field relative speed overestimation. Therefore relative overestimation of distance seems the most likely explanation for the wide field effect in the present braking task. Overestimation of distance for wide field was not indicated for the positioning task, but for braking relevant distances are larger. Overestimation of distance is not unlikely too, given the image minification caused by the wide field lens.

The net effect of both high position and wide field is to bring TTCm closer to zero, which is a performance improvement given the task to stop close in front of the beacons.

3.4. Subjective difficulty

Ratings of subjective difficulty are presented in terms of mean raw scores.

LEARN, SUBTASK. The before-after effects show that subjective difficulty in Direct View is almost constant. Subjective difficulty ratings are consistently higher for the more complicated subtasks. Both types of effects confirm those on objective performance.

CAMERA. For most tasks, the Camera View conditions are generally more difficult than Direct View. Mean scores across tasks are, for DV and CV respectively, 1.6 and 2.4**. This supports the generally worse performance measured for camera driving.

POSITION, FIELD, MONIMARK. Camera position does not show any main effect.

Main effects of field size (in the order normal-wide) indicate that for the lane change task wide field is more difficult (1.9-2.3*); for the sharp curves and the positioning tasks wide field is easier (2.3-1.9, resp. 3.2-2.6*). Interactions position × field indicate the following: for the backwards driving and positioning tasks wide field is easier for high camera position only (3.3-2.5*, resp. 3.3-2.5*); for the speed estimation task high camera position is more difficult for normal field only (low-high: 2.4-2.9*). The presence of markings on the monitor does not influence the difficulty ratings.

These effects of camera conditions on difficulty support the effects on performance, in the sense that higher difficulty ratings correspond to worse performance (except for the positioning task, where a larger difficulty does not correspond to a larger DL, but to a larger standard deviation of DL between replicas).

3.5. Miscellaneous observations

Motion sickness. Some subjects showed moderate signs of motion sickness after the first run with the Camera View. In the course of one or two subsequent camera runs these symptoms disappeared. Apparently, the discrepancies present between visual and vestibular stimuli, which were relatively small compared to the visuo-vestibular discrepancies encountered in simulators or in remote control stations, are able to evoke motion sickness.

Glare. Glare from the sun and the surrounding sky gave a considerable image deterioration when the elevation of the sun was lower than 15°. This was notwithstanding anti-glare measures like a hood of 25 cm depth above the camera lens, and a downward pitch of the camera of 5° for the normal field and 11° for the wide field. Glare from sun reflections from a wet road decreased visibility considerably too. Technical solutions to the glare problem are required if the Camera View is to be used in practical conditions.

Lens pollution. In one instance the camera lens was covered with dew, which ruined the camera image. This illustrates that, especially for battlefield situations, the camera must be shielded by a window with an appropriate cleaning installation.

Resolving power. Through the limited resolving power of a video image, the effective visual acuity is only 0.5 arcmin^{-1} at normal field size; at wide field acuity is only 0.25 arcmin^{-1}. In Direct View, acuity of 2 arcmin^{-1} is not uncommon, which is four to eight times better than with Camera View. In the present experiments this was not a handicap. However, for driving tasks like estimating a curve's sharpness in advance, reading signs or seeing relatively small obstacles at sufficient distance, much higher camera resolution may be required. With the present state of technology (even with the availability of High Definition TV) one may only approach the Direct View resolution at the cost of a considerable decrease of field size, or if more than one camera-monitor system is used.

4. DISCUSSION AND CONCLUSIONS

4.1 Camera View vs. Direct View

Differences between CV and DV are evident for several performance measures and tasks. If present, these differences generally show that control of lateral position and course is moderately worse with CV: lateral distance to road marking and course instability are up to 50% larger. Given the subjects' lack of experience with camera driving, with restricted field of view, different viewing geometries, and absence of stereopsis, this is not surprising. In addition, performance of the braking task suggests a relative overestimation of distance for camera driving. Subjective difficulty in CV, compared to DV, is less than one point higher on the 5-point scale.

These findings indicate that driving on flat roads without traffic, is performable with Camera View, although it is more difficult than with Direct View. For practical applications of Camera View driving one has to consider potential problems like motion sickness, glare, lens pollution, and limited image resolution, as were discussed above in section 3.5.

4.2. Effects of camera position, field size, and monimark

Markings on the monitor show only few, and modest, improvements in performance and subjective difficulty. This is against expectation, because the markings were designed to provide cues for lateral position, course and distance, which should have been especially effective for lateral control in driving straight and for the positioning task. Probably, the limited instruction runs were not sufficient to teach the proper use of the markings.

Main effects of camera position are evident in only a few instances. More evident are effects of field size and combined effects of position and field. However, effects are not quite consistent for each task and dependent variable, and the treatment here is too cursory to draw conclusions on preferable camera conditions. Taking into account all significant differences among the four combinations of camera position and field size, the following general conclusions emerge: Wide field, combined with high camera position, gives most frequently the better performance and is subjectively found easier. Next best is the combination wide field - low position, followed by normal field - low position. Worst performance and largest subjective difficulty shows the combination normal field - high position. This ranking is equally valid for the lateral and the longitudinal tasks.

Apparently, in the present experiments the advantages of wide field (better lateral view; vehicle reference in the image) outweigh its disadvantages (image minification, worse resolution), especially if combined with high camera position.

4.3. Training Camera View driving

In the present experiment, there was only a very brief familiarization period for each camera condition. It is expected that more extensive training for the preferred camera condition may improve performance considerably, enabling pupils to adapt to the particular viewing geometry, which differs considerably from Direct View. The present task battery seems a good start for training Camera View driving (both for armoured vehicles and RPV-s), covering many aspects of driving on flat roads without traffic.

REFERENCES

ISO (1975). Technical Report 3888-1975 (E), International Organization for Standardization, Geneva.

Van der Horst, R. (1991). In: Gale, A.G. et al. (eds.), Vision in Vehicles III, Elsevier Science Publishers, Amsterdam, 19-26.

Verwey, W.B., Burry, S., Bakker, P.J. (1992). Report IZF 1992 C-14, TNO Institute for Perception, Soesterberg, The Netherlands.

VISION IN VEHICLES - V
A.G. Gale et al. (Editors)

The Active Steering Wheel as a Continuous Support for the Driver's Lateral Control Task

Josef SCHUMANN[a], Jan LOWENAU[b] and Karl NAAB[b]

[a]University of the Armed Forces Munich, Human Factors Institute LRT 11
85577 Neubiberg, Germany

[b]BMW AG, Vehicle Research
80788 Munich, Germany

Abstract

The present study investigated the effectiveness of a *continuous* lateral control support via an active steering wheel during driving on a German freeway. The continuous steering support was realized as an *off-target augmented feedback* by superimposing artificial torque on the regular steering torque. A Heading Control system permitting various control strategies calculated an "optimal" steering wheel angle. If the driver's input deviated from this steering wheel angle, an additional steering wheel torque was generated proportional to this difference. This torque change indicated that the driver should re-adjust his lateral control behavior.

The field study, conducted on a 80 km stretch of a German freeway, was designed in order to evaluate the driver's lateral control performance and strategy with three different control strategy conditions for the optimal steering wheel angle under two task demand conditions. Thirty two male subjects were instructed to drive the instrumented car as normally as possible with a recommended speed of 110 km/h in low volume traffic. The results show the usefulness of a continuous steering wheel support which is due to the workload reduction when compared with driving without steering support.

1. INTRODUCTION

When driving an automobile, although different sensory cues have to be processed, the driver perceives most of the relevant information via the visual sensory modality. Since human information processing capacity is limited, an information overflow at the visual channel is apparent, which can be traced back to in-car information displays as well as to the large number of external information displays and the still growing traffic density. It needs to be shown, therefore, whether there are possibilities of reducing this information overflow at the visual channel and of providing the driver with relevant information during the driving task which is transmitted via non-visual sensory modalities, for instance the proprioceptive-tactile (or haptic) sensory modality. One way of doing this is to employ the steering wheel as an *active control device* to support lateral control at the guidance and control level of the driving task (see Schumann, Godthelp, Färber & Wontorra, 1993; Schumann & Naab, 1992).

Driver steering behavior is described in various models as a mixture of open-loop and closed-loop control processes (see e.g. Godthelp, 1984; Reid, 1983) relying mainly on visual information concerning road curvature, lateral position, and heading (see e.g. Donges, 1978). To use an *active steering wheel* as a proprioceptive-tactile display, an exact measurement of these variables has to be obtained in order to present to the driver optimal, proprioceptive-tactile information via the active steering wheel. This has been realized with the Heading Control (HC) system.

1.1. The Heading Control system

The Heading Control system (see Bastuck, Naab, Walther & Wertheimer, 1989) is based on video image processing for measurement of the vehicle's lateral deviation from the right or left lane markings. A video camera, mounted above the rear-view mirror inside the car, records the road in front of the vehicle. With a digital image processing unit, the position of the road markings are determined and the current lateral deviation of the vehicle is measured. This information is transferred to the control system. On the basis of a simplified vehicle model and a specific control strategy, a recommended trajectory in the corresponding lane, and depending on that a steering angle δ_O for the current situation can be calculated. Deviates the driver input (i.e. the actual steering angle δ_I) from this steering angle δ_O, an additional steering wheel torque will be generated by means of a torque motor which is installed at the steering column. This additional proprioceptive-tactile information via the active steering wheel indicates that the driver should readjust his steering behavior (see Fig. 1).

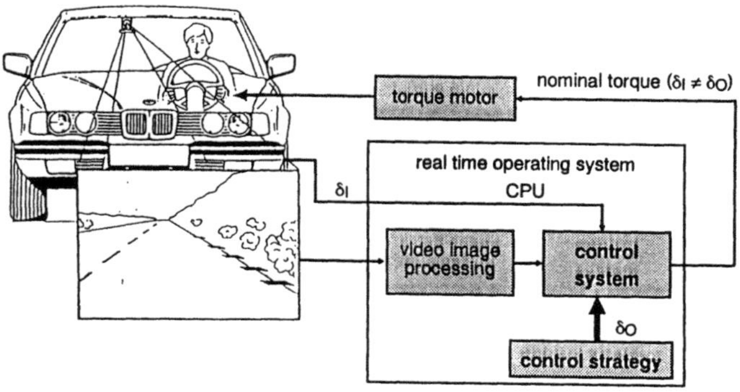

Fig. 1: The Heading Control (HC) system for an active steering wheel.

Through a restriction of the additional torque via the active steering wheel (in the range of the usual steering wheel torque), the driver always has the possibility of overruling the possible steering wheel torque with the consequence that the driver on top of that exerts full responsibility for the driving task.

Whereas previous experiments concentrated on *discrete* warnings via the active steering wheel, which showed the employment of such discrete signals during open-loop control phases of the driving task (see Schumann et al., 1993; Schumann & Naab, 1992), now the emphasis will be put toward *continuous* support via the active steering wheel, mainly during closed-loop control phases of the lateral control task.

1.2. Continuous support via an active steering wheel

Continuous support via the active steering wheel can be established as an *off-target augmented feedback*. The advantages of off-target augmented feedback could be demonstrated during tracking (see e.g. Gordon, 1968; Williams & Briggs, 1962) and also in an applied setting during a pilot's landing approach (see Roscoe, 1980). The steering support is only activated in the case of a deviation from the recommended trajectory (see also Fig. 1). The form of the continuous steering support consists of a proportionally increasing or decreasing *additional* steering wheel torque which indicates for the driver the direction of the recommended steering correction (see Fig. 2).

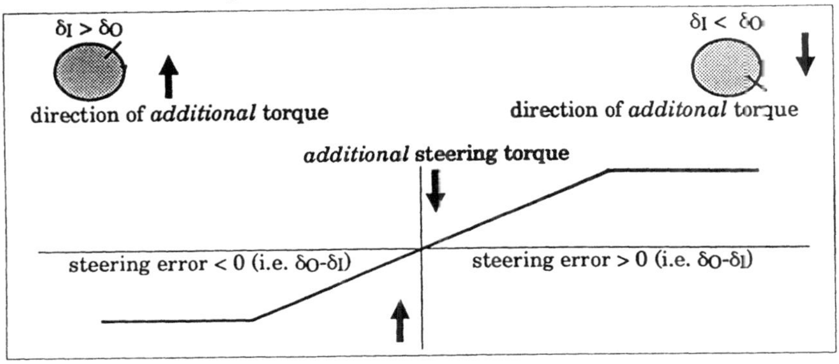

Fig.2: Implementation of the additional steering wheel torque characteristic during continuous steering support as *off-target augmented feedback* (note: minor deviations are not perceived by the driver since the signal intensity is subliminal!).

The driver-vehicle control loop for a continuous steering support is depicted in Fig. 3.

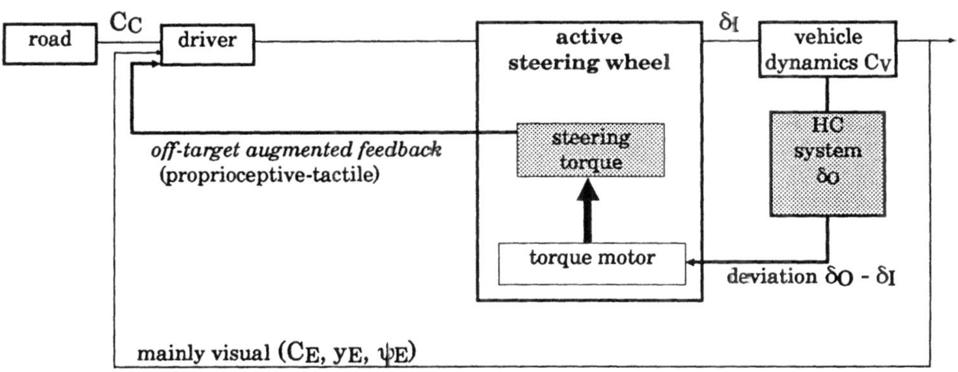

Fig.3: Schematic diagram of the driver-vehicle control-loop with an active steering wheel, which informs the driver about a discrepancy between the actual steering angle δ_I and the recommended optimal steering angle δ_O [y_E = lateral deviation, ψ_E = heading error, C_C = commanded path curvature, C_V = vehicle curvature, C_E = path curvature error].

With the augmented feedback, the driver's steering behavior should be optimized, which is restricted through misinterpretation of visual information (see for instance the "illusive curve phenomenon", Fildes & Triggs, 1985; Shinar, 1977, 1978) or human information processing thresholds (see e.g. Carson & Wierwille, 1978). Proprioceptive-tactile augmented feedback via the active steering wheel may also reduce visual loading due to improved visual sampling processes to perform in-car tasks (see e.g. Wierwille, 1993).

Crucial to the success of a continuous steering support for lateral control will be the employment of a *robust control strategy* (for the recommended optimal steering angle δ_O) which has to be adapted to the normal driver steering strategy.

1.3. Control strategies

In a series of pilot studies, different control strategies were tested to assess the possibility of adaptability in the driver steering behavior. The three best strategies have been chosen for the experiment. These are given by:

- ⇒ control strategy HC_1 as *a preview compensation* (0.6 sec, independent of speed) of lateral deviation, based on an optimal control model. The compensation is achieved by a dynamic evaluation of path curvature error, lateral deviation and heading error (see McRuer, Allen, Weir & Klein, 1977; see Fig. 1.3).
- ⇒ control strategy HC_2 as compensation of the assumed visual *"aim point errors'* of the driver at a fixed preview distance (0.6 sec, independent of speed) down the road (see Allen, Cystic & Rosenthal,1987). Although a driver continuously changes his preview distance (see Baxter & Harrison, 1979), a variable aim point was not implemented for this control strategy, since exact synchronisation to the driver's visual sampling behavior presupposes a sophisticated driver model.
- ⇒ control strategy HC_3 as a compensation of the current lateral speed change. This very simple algorithm has been chosen since it has been shown that the perception of *changes* of the lateral speed cue can improve lateral control performance (see e.g. Blaauw, 1984, p.61; Riemersma, 1981).

1.4. Objectives

This first field study investigated the effect of the continuous steering support during a drive on a German freeway. The experiment was designed to answer the following research questions:

- ⇒ How do different control strategies of the Heading Control system influence the driver's steering control performance and control strategy?
- ⇒ Is there any effect of the continuous steering support during higher driver workload conditions?
- ⇒ Are there any practice effects during the use of the Heading Control system due to learning and/or habituation?

The results will be incorporated as valuable human factor aspects into the development of a vehicle based, computer aided driver support system. This system should be able to assist the driver's lateral control task in order to enhance driving comfort and safety by reducing the driver's workload.

be perceived by the driver because of threshold limits. On the other hand a sudden change at the steering wheel, for instance triggered by additional manual control actions, results in a sudden, perceptible torque change, which might not be interpreted correctly by the driver. As a result, deviations in lane keeping have to be controlled by the driver via the regular feedback information (see Fig. 3, outer loop).

The control strategy HC_2 (compensation of the visual "aim point error") already informs the driver about minor deviations from an optimal path, but the augmented feedback via the active steering wheel does not lead to a decreasing control effort compared to driving without continuous steering support (see Fig. 4). It therefore has to be questioned whether the driver controls his lane keeping on the basis of such a strategy. Since lateral deviation is not perceived directly, but as a transformation into an angle (see e.g. Baxter & Harrison, 1979, Fig. 1), the driver has to be in a position of exactly perceiving the angle changes, in addition to the heading angle, which is at least doubtful for small angles (see the problem of perceptual absolute and difference thresholds; e.g. Baxter & Harrison, 1979; Carson & Wierwille, 1978). Moreover the fixed preview distance for the optimal control strategy plays a crucial role. If this chosen fixed preview distance for instance is too low compared to the driver's preview distance, the augmented feedback via the active steering wheel will inform possible deviations to the driver earlier, as this error would be perceived by the driver.

The control strategy HC_1, based on a preview compensation of the lateral deviation, seems to depict the driver's steering strategy in a quite robust way, since the augmented feedback via the steering wheel is supportive to the driver with respect to the reduction in the control effort (see Fig. 4). The possible dynamic, and stronger weighting of heading error compared to lateral deviation errors corresponds to observations with experienced drivers (see Smiley, Reid & Fraser, 1980). Additionally, with the calculations of possible deviations at a preview distance down the road, this control strategy is more tolerant of minor, momentary errors.

Further experiments therefore should concentrate on a fine tuning of this optimal control strategy HC_1 (e.g. concerning preview distance, weighting of heading error and lateral deviation), which as an augmented feedback via the active steering wheel should be adapted optimally to the driver's steering strategy in order to reduce the driver's workload. A further advantage of an off-target augmented feedback, implemented as a continuous steering support, lies in the possible *early and direct* warning (i.e. via the control device steering wheel) concerning perceptual errors of the main input variables for lateral control (see e.g. Shinar, 1978).

ACKNOWLEDGEMENT

This work has been partially supported by the Ministry of Research and Technology through the EUREKA project PROMETHEUS.

REFERENCES

Allen,R.W.,Szostak,H.T. & Rosenthal,T.J. (1987).*Analysis and Computer Simulation of Driver/ Vehicle Interaction.* SAE Paper *871086,* Society of Automotive Engineers.

Bastuck,R., Naab,K., Walther,C. & Wertheimer,R. (1989). *Demonstrator Project HEADING CONTROL. - Vision based autonomous system for driver assistance.*

2nd PROMETHEUS Workshop, Wolfsburg,D, May 22-23, 1989.

Baxter,J. & Harrison,J.Y. (1979). A nonlinear model describing driver behavior on straight roads. *Human Factors*, **21**, 87-97.

Blaauw,G.J. (1984). *Car driving as a supervisory control task.* Unveröff. Diss., Institute for Perception TNO, Soesterberg, Netherlands.

Carson,J.M. & Wierwille,W.W. (1978). Development of a strategy model of the driver in lane keeping. *Vehicle Systems Dynamics,* **7**, 233-253.

Cohen,J. (1988). *Statistical Power Analysis for the Behavioral Sciences (2nd Ed.).* Hillsdale, NJ: LEA:.

Donges,E. (1978). A Two-Level Model of Driver Steering Behavior. *Human Factors*, **20**, 691-707.

Fildes,B.N. & Triggs,T.J. (1985). The effect of changes in curve geometry on magnitude estimates of road-like perspective curvature. *Perception & Psychophysics, 37,* 218-224.

Godthelp,J. (1984). *Studies on Human Vehicle Control.* Unveröff. Diss., Institute for Perception TNO, Soesterberg, Netherlands.

Gordon,N.B. (1968). Guidance versus augmented feedback and motor skill. *Journal of Experimental Psychology, 77,* 24-30.

Macdonald,W.A. & Hoffmann,E.R. (1980). Review of relationships between steering reversal rate and driving task demand. *Human Factors, 22,* 733-739.

McRuer,D.T., Allen,R.W., Weir,D.H. & Klein,R.H. (1977). New results in driver steering control models. *Human Factors, 19,* 381-397.

Reid,L.D. (1983). A survey of recent driver steering behavior models suited to accident studies. *Accident Analysis and Prevention,* **15**, 23-40.

Riemersma,J.B.J. (1981).Visual control during straight road driving. *Acta Psychologica,* **48**, 215-225.

Roscoe,S.N. (1980).*Aviation Psychology.* Ames, Iowa: The Iowa State University Press.

Schumann,J., Godthelp,J., Färber,B. & Wontorra,H. (1993). Breaking up of open-loop steering control actions. - The steering wheel as an active control device. In A.G.Gale et al. (Eds.), *Vision in Vehicles - IV* (pp.321-332). Amsterdam: North-Holland

Schumann,J. & Naab,K. (1992). On the effectiveness of an active steering wheel in critical driving situations. -A proving ground experiment-. *Proceedings of the Conference Road Safety in Europa. VTI* Rapport 380A, Part 4, pp. 194-208.

Shinar,D. (1977). Curve Perception and Accidents on curves: An Illusive Curve Phenomenon. *Zeitschrift für Verkehrssicherheit, 23,* 16-21.

Shinar,D. (1978). *Psychology on the Road. The Human Factor in Traffic Safety.* New York: Wiley & Sons.

Smiley,A., Reid,L. & Fraser,M. (1980). Changes in Driver Steering Control with Learning. *Human Factors,* **22**, 401-415.

Wetherell,A. (1981). The efficacy of some auditory-vocal subsidiary tasks as measures of the mental load on male and female drivers. *Ergonomics, 24,* 197-214.

Wierwille,W.W. (1993). An initial model of visual sampling of in-car displays and controls. In A.G.Gale et al. (Eds.), *Vision in Vehicles - IV* (pp. 271-280). Amsterdam: North-Holland.

Williams,A.C. & Briggs,G.E. (1962). On target versus off target information and the acquisition of tracking skill. *Journal of Experimental Psychology, 64,* 519-525.

VISION IN VEHICLES - V
A.G. Gale et al. (Editors)

Reducing Driver's Speeds at Bends: Differential Effects of Feedback

M.J. Kuiken[a] & J.A. Groeger[b]

[a]Traffic Research Centre, University of Groningen
P.O.Box 69, 9750 AB Haren, The Netherlands

[b] M.R.C. Applied Psychology Unit, 15 Chaucer Road,
Cambridge CB2 2EF, United Kingdom

This paper presents a study which compares the effects of providing drivers with information about their speed errors at curves and at intersections, when they repeatedly drove a predetermined route under simulated traffic conditions. On each of the circuits subjects encountered a number of supported and unsupported scenarios in curves and at intersections. During the drive the actual performance of the subjects in these scenarios was compared to a criterion set by rules implemented in a support module. The effects of different types of support on the performance of drivers in curves are discussed here. Immediate auditory feedback after an error was found to reduce the incidence and size of speed errors more than any of the other types of support evaluated. The effects of feedback generalized to situations where support had not been given.

1. INTRODUCTION

The demands of an increasingly complex traffic environment place a considerable burden on the skills of the individual driver. While basic handling skills are well practised and relatively easy to master, crucial factors in accident or conflict involvement, such as correctly evaluating driving situations and the selection of the appropriate speed in these situations, receive less attention during driver training. These problems are augmented by the fact that drivers receive relatively little feedback on how well they are actually performing higher level driving tasks of this sort (see Groeger [1]). In principle at least in-vehicle instructional support could be designed in such a way as to overcome these difficulties, thereby improving the quality of feedback available to the driver. In order to ensure that such messages are perceived to be relevant by the driver, instructional messages should be contingent upon what the driver actually does. This general principle was followed in the present study. Another fundamental issue in learning relates to the nature of the contingency between error and feedback. In the study reported below, the effects of altering the timing between the erroneous behaviour, and feedback upon it, are investigated, but in each case the driver was told about every speed error they made in the selected driving scenarios.

These scenarios required repeated driving on bends and at cross-roads. They were selected on the basis of previous studies (see Groeger & Kuiken [2]). In a behavioural study of the type and frequency of errors committed by drivers under real driving conditions, Groeger and Grande [3] reported that many of the 100 or so drivers who took part in their study, required support when driving ahead at crossroads (72%) and when driving ahead on bends (41%). In a questionnaire survey of accident and error tendencies of drivers in different situations (Kuiken & Miltenburg [4]) the most frequently reported errors relating to negotiating cross-roads were errors in observing the traffic scene and the most frequently reported errors related to driving at bends were excessive speed as well as observation errors.

It was decided to use auditory support when subjects were driving in order to avoid the visually distracting effects of visual messages during driving. Thus, the interval between the error and the delivery of support may be maximally reduced, i.e. so that the support is given just after the error was committed ("immediate feedback") or maximally increased, i.e. delayed until just before the error-situation recurs ("prospective support"). Whilst both conditions are predicted to be effective for learning, what is learned may not be the same in both conditions. As these two methods of "real-time" auditory support may not be more effective than merely giving the driver a more general indication of the errors they had made in supported situations, the effects of the different types of feedback on driver performance will be assessed.

2. METHOD

2.1. Subjects

Forty four subjects, drawn from the subject pool of the Traffic research Centre, participated in this study. Subjects served in one of four conditions, to which they were randomly assigned. There were no differences between the groups in terms of their age (mean age of 26.6 years) and the extent of their traffic experience (mean of 123.000 km driven).

2.2. Materials and apparatus

Driving simulator: The TRC simulator is a fixed-based car driving simulator consisting of two integrated subsystems. The first subsystem is a conventional simulator, composed of a car that is connected to the simulator computer. This controls the visual objects in the world the driver traverses, i.e the roads, their alignment, traffic signs, traffic lights and other vehicles. The second subsystem is formed by a dynamic traffic simulation consisting of interacting cars. These cars circle independently through the world according to their own decision and behaviour rules and interact with each other and with the simulator car. For experimental purposes these cars can be instructed to do a number of things, like crossing an intersection at the same time as the simulator car does. The simulator is described in more detail by van Winsum & van Wolffelaar [5].

Road network and scenarios: The road network designed for this experiment consisted of two-lane roads with a lane-width of three meters. The route is comprised of a combination of cross-roads and curves, and is a 'rural' 80 km/h road. The curves had different radii, ranging from 30 to 140 metres, where the radius of a curve was the distance between the centre of the curve and the centreline of the road. The route driven on each trip was about 7.6 kilometres long. Each driver included in the analyses completed four trips.

Feedback and criterion for error: During the drive the actual performance of the subjects in these scenarios was compared with various performance criteria. The criteria for error free performance were based upon a descriptive model of human driving at manoeuvring level (van Winsum [6]). This model generates a number of hierarchically structured decision rules, which use the distance from objects or road configurations, the velocity of objects, and a number of other properties to calculate a required velocity or a required lateral position. In this experiment we made use of the criteria set by the decision rules for keeping speed limits (80 km/h) and velocity control when approaching and when in curves. The various rules evaluate the situation the car is in and any deviations from the requirements were regarded as an error for the purposes of the study.

While errors made during each of the scenarios were logged, support was only given in relation to speed errors at signalised junctions and for curves with radii of 50, 60, 80 and 100 metres. The "real-time" spoken messages contained information about the type of error a driver had just committed. In the Immediate feedback condition the message is spoken immediately after the error occurs. In the Prospective support condition the message is spoken the next time the driver encounters a similar (supported) situation, just before the manoeuvre starts. In the Accumulated feedback condition no messages were presented to the driver while driving. Instead all the errors made on a particular drive were counted and at the end of two trips around the circuit the subject was handed a message card with the appropriate information. For unsupported scenarios, the system logs the error that a driver makes, but does not provide feedback to the driver. No feedback was given in the control condition.

2.3. Procedure

Subjects had about 10 minutes to get used to the simulator on a separate test-track in the simulated world. After completing some rating tasks, an effort scale and a questionnaire concerning their age and traffic experience, subjects were instructed to drive ahead on the route as they would normally do. It was explained to all but the subjects in the Control group, that they would receive feedback on their errors while driving, and how this feedback would be given. The route was driven four times during the experiment. During the rest period, after two trips, subjects completed a number of rating tasks and subjects in the Accumulated Feedback condition were given message cards with an indication of the type of errors they had made.

2.4. Dependent variables

During the experiment scenario numbers were stored as an event, and in each event it was stored whether an error had been made as well as the size of the largest error.
Separately from these events and variables, velocity (m/s) was sampled with a frequency of 10 Hz. A graphical data-analysis program was used to select the appropriate variables from the datafiles for statistical analysis with SPSS. For the experiment the following variables were extracted from the datafiles.

- The lowest velocity of the simulator car during the manoeuvre in a bend
- The velocity of the simulator car at four predetermined points between scenarios

3. RESULTS

3.1. Effects of feedback on driving speed

Average speed of the vehicle while subjects were driving ahead on a straight stretch of road (measured four times in each trip) was 74.8 km/h. Although none of the drivers received support in these situations mean speeds differed in the various support groups ($F(3,40)= 4.30$; $p=0.010$). Subjects in the Control condition drove fastest with a mean speed of 81.2 km/h. Speeds reduced in the Accumulated feedback condition to 76.2 km/h, in the Prospective support condition to 72.6 km/h and in the Immediate feedback condition to 69 km/h.

The average Lowest speeds during task performance in curves differed as a function of the feedback given ($F(3,40)= 7.48$; $p< 0.001$). As expected curve radius had an effect on Lowest speeds in curves ($F(11,30)= 31.961$; $p< 0.001$), i.e. lower speeds (38.9 km/h) in curves with small radius (30 m), whilst speeds increased (to 56.9 km/h) in the curve with the largest radius (140 m).

The interaction between support group and curve size was statistically reliable ($F(33,96)=1,863$; $p=0,010$). Figure 1 shows the influence of type of support on lowest speeds in the different sizes of curves.

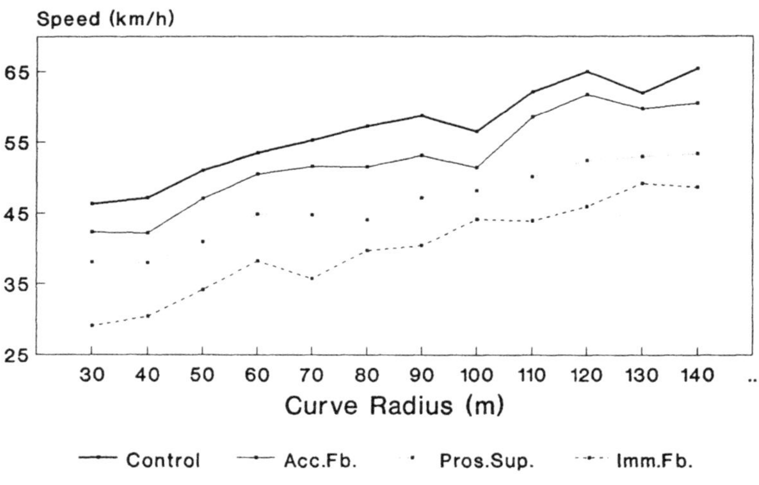

Figure 1: Effects of support on lowest speed in curves with different radii

3.2. Effects of feedback on the incidence and size of speed errors in bends

Without support drivers made speed errors on curves on 96% of the occasions. The average size of that speed error was 13.0 km/h. Accumulated feedback (81%), Prospective support (68%) and Immediate feedback (54%) all significantly reduced the error rate ($F(3,40)=7.192$; $p<0.001$). The support provided to drivers in bends also reduced the average size of the error ($F(3,40)=3.916$; $p<0.05$). With Accumulated feedback the mean error size was reduced to 11.1 km/h, and with Prospective support and with Immediate feedback mean error sizes were reduced to 7.0 km/h and 4.0 km/h respectively.

3.3. Transfer effects of feedback

Drivers received information about their speed errors only in supported curve scenarios, i.e. the four medium sized curves. Unsupported scenarios thus provided what we might term "between scenario" control. This allowed us to assess the extent to which any effects of support transfer across curve type, i.e. from supported medium curves to unsupported smaller and larger curves. Findings showed a statistically reliable main effect on error rate of curve type ($F(2,39)=14.58$; $p<0.001$). Supported medium sized curves (72%) had significantly lower error rates than unsupported smaller (83%), but similar error rates to unsupported larger (71%) curves.

The type of support influenced the error rate on the different types of curves ($F(6,78)=3.35$; $p<0.01$). For each of the support groups, each class of curves show a reduction in error rate over that observed in the control condition. In the Immediate feedback condition the effect is a general one, i.e similar levels of improvement occur for curves on which support was given, as for curves on which no support was given. In the Prospective support condition the largest improvement occurs on medium and larger curves, with the improvement on smaller unsupported curves being substantially less (see figure 2).

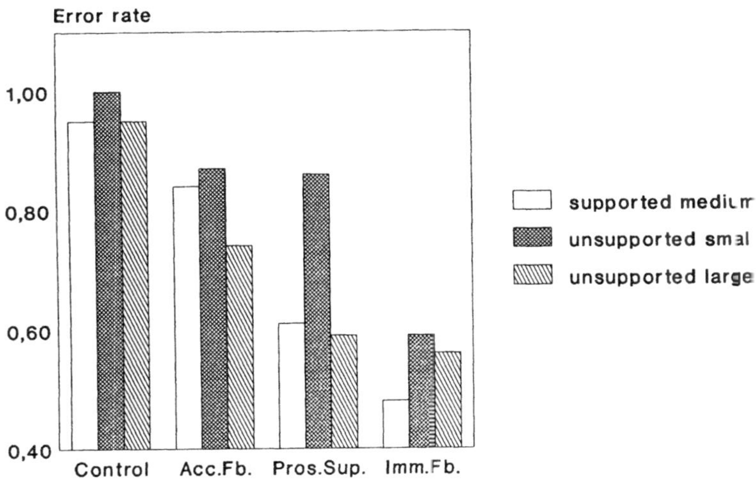

Figure 2: Effects of support on error rate per curve type

The average size of the speed errors observed differed across the three types of curves ($F(2,39)=19.841$; $p<0.001$). The average size of speed errors for the Control condition was 15.2 km/h on small curves, 12.8 km/h on the medium sized curves and 10.9 km/h on the larger curves. The average size of speed errors across all conditions was 10.4 km/h on unsupported small curves, 8.6 km/h on supported medium curves and the average error size in unsupported larger curves was 7.3 km/h.

The type of support influenced the size of error on the different types of curves ($F(6,80)=2.234$; $p<0.05$). Each of the types of support achieved a significant reduction in the size of errors observed on each type of curve. In each case the greatest reduction was achieved by Immediate feedback, its effects being significantly greater than any of the other types of support. The effects observed with Prospective support were greater than those observed with Accumulated feedback.

3.4. Effects of practice

There was a statistically reliable main effect on error size of practice ($F(3,38)= 4{,}62$; $p<0.01$). The average error size in the first trip was 10.7 km/h, reducing to 8.4 and 8.2 km/h in the second and third trip respectively, while in the last trip the average size increased again to 9.0 km/h.

The interaction between condition and trip was statistically reliable ($F(9,120)= 1.958$; $p=0.050$). In the Control condition error size increased as drivers became more familiar with the task (from 11.5 km/h in the first trip to 15.5 km/h in the last trip). Error size decreased in the Accumulated feedback condition (from 13.0 km/h in the first trip to 9.7 km/h in the last trip). In the Prospective support condition the average error size was 7.4 km/h in the first trip, and reduced to 6.2 km/h in the second trip, but increased again in the last trip (7.4 km/h). The smallest speed errors were made in the Immediate feedback condition and with practice they became even smaller (from 5.3 km/h in the first trip to 3.3 km/h in the last trip).

Practice (i.e. session and trip numbers), curve type and support condition all influence error rate ($F(6,80)=2.516$; $p<0.05$, see figures 3, 4 and 5). Post hoc tests of the components of this interaction revealed the following results. In the Control condition which has the highest error rate, performance does not improve with practice. In the Accumulated feedback condition performance improves in trips 3 and 4, after the drivers received feedback. This is generally the case for both supported and unsupported curves. In the Immediate feedback condition, performance in Trips 3 and 4 is better than for Trips 1 and 2 for all supported and small unsupported curves. With Immediate feedback error rates in large unsupported curves are higher for Trip 1 than for Trips 3 and 4. The error rate for Trip 2 is higher than for Trip 4. This is also the pattern of influence observed with Prospective Support on smaller unsupported curves. On supported curves, and larger unsupported curves, error reduces substantially later in the session from the levels observed in Trips 1 and 2. It is observed that Prospective support is slow to achieve an error reduction on small unsupported curves, since the error rate reduces reliably relative to the level in the control condition only by the second half of the study.

4. CONCLUSION

The aim of the study was to assess the effects of different types of feedback on driver performance. Driver performance was measured on the basis of speed of the vehicle in the route as a whole and of speed errors during predetermined supported and unsupported scenarios.

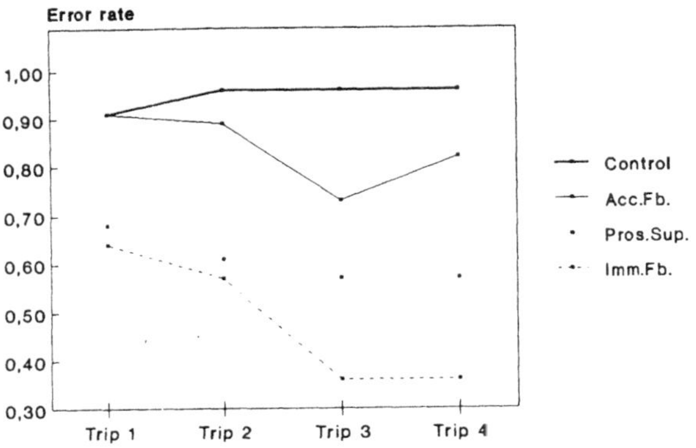

Figure 3: Effects of support and practice on error rate in supported medium curves

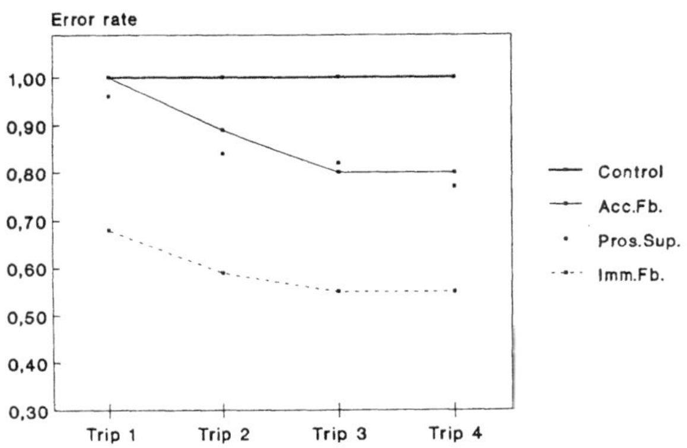

Figure 4: Effects of support and practice on error rate in unsupported small curves

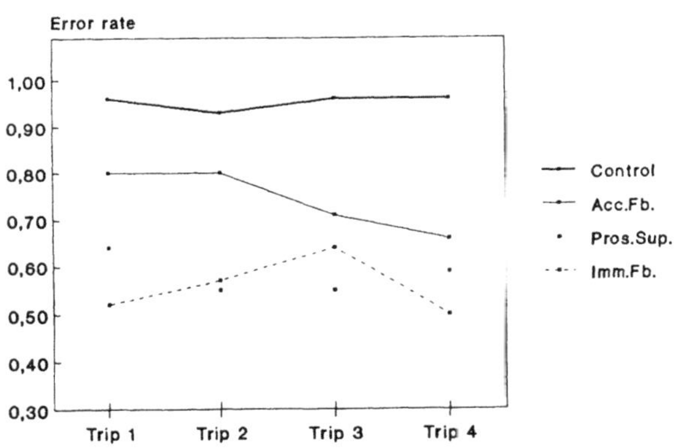

Figure 5: Effects of support and practice on error rate in unsupported large curves

The study shows that feedback on erroneous behaviour in curves has strong effects on the occurrence and the size of those errors. All types of feedback to some extent reduced the average driving speed as well as error rate and error sizes across a range of supported and unsupported situations. 'Real-time' auditory messages were, however, the most effective form of support. Of the two real-time conditions, Immediate feedback appears to have stronger and more wide-ranging effects. Immediate feedback reduces speed errors on both supported and unsupported curves. Prospective support reduces errors on curves, but not to the same extent, and seems slow to achieve an error reduction on small unsupported curves. Accumulated feedback reduces error rate and size over the level in the Control condition on both supported and unsupported curves. Although the effects are not as powerful as the effects observed with the other forms of support, it should be realized that these effects have been achieved on the basis of information given on only one occasion during the experiment.

There is considerable evidence that what has been learned in one situation transfers to other situations, where errors occurred, but on which no feedback was given. The results suggest that learning transfers to those situations (i.e. driving ahead on a straight road and driving ahead on smaller and larger bends) on the basis of their functional similarity, rather than on the basis of the perceptual similarities or dissimilarities in a scene.

ACKNOWLEDGEMENT

This study was performed as part of the ARIADNE project which is partly funded by the European Community.

REFERENCES

[1] Groeger, J.A. (in press). Degrees of freedom and the limits on learning: Support needs of inexperienced motorists. In: A.W. Parkes and S. Franzen (Eds.) Driving future vehicles. London: Taylor & Francis.

[2] Groeger, J.A. & Kuiken, M.J. (1992). Instructional support: Scenario and support definition. DRIVE Deliverable Report ARIADNE D211. Birmingham: British Aerospace.

[3] Groeger, J.A., Grande, G.E.(1992) Meeting the support requirements of drivers with different levels of traffic experience: An evaluation. DRIVE Deliverable Report GIDS/ADA3. Haren: Traffic Research Centre, University of Groningen.

[4] Kuiken, M. & Miltenburg, P.(1990) Behavioural antecedents of accidents and near-accidents. In: J. Groeger, M. Kuiken, G. Grande, P. Miltenburg, I. Brown, & T. Rothengatter. Preliminary design specifications for appropriate feedback provision to drivers with differing levels of traffic experience. DRIVE Deliverable Report GIDS/ADA1. Haren: Traffic Research Centre, University of Groningen. p.53-98.

[5] Winsum, W. van, Wolffelaar, P. van (1993). GIDS Small World simulation. In: J.A.Michon. (Ed.) Generic Intelligent Driver Support. London: Taylor & Francis.

[6] Winsum, W. van (1992). Specification of the structure of the manoeuvring level driver model. Appendix to: E.H. Piersma,, W. Van Winsum, & M. Hicks. Towards knowledge bases of traffic world, driver model and workload. DRIVE Deliverable Report ARIADNE D121. Birmingham: British Aerospace.

VISION IN VEHICLES - V
A.G. Gale et al. (Editors)

Automatic Train Protection

M. Halliday

Human Factors Team, Safety Unit, British Rail Scientific Services,
PO Box 2, London Road, Derby, DE24 8YB, England.

An account is presented of the on-going application of Human Factors in the production of The National Specification for British Rail's Automatic Train Protection system. This paper focuses on the development of the driver interface and outlines the methodology used to identify issues which the specification needs to address together with the principles applied to address them.

1. BACKGROUND.

Attempts to improve the safety of rail operation have included technological improvements in signalling equipment such as automatic route setting and also improvements to the technology in the driver's cab such as a vigilance device. Whilst these improvements have undoubtedly increased the level of safety for rail operation, the potential for driver error to result in a train passing a danger signal is still there. The development of Automatic Train Protection (ATP) is in direct response to this.

ATP systems have been under development by various European railway administrations over the last decade or so. The development of British Rail's own version of ATP started in 1988 and progressive installation of two pilot schemes, for comparative evaluation, was undertaken over the period 1991/92. The pilot schemes were set up on the Great Western Main Line (running from Paddington to Bristol) and the Chiltern Line (which runs from Marylebone to Aylesbury).

2. THE ATP SYSTEM.

The two fundamental functions of ATP are to prevent a train from passing a signal at danger and to prevent the train from exceeding the prevailing speed limit. The functions performed by ATP need to be placed in the context of existing in-cab technology.

Currently, the Automatic Warning System (AWS) is the only in-cab device which provides the driver with information about lineside signals. AWS draws the driver's attention to whether the lineside signal aspect is restrictive (yellow, double yellow, or red) or clear (green). When the lineside signal is restrictive AWS provides the driver with an audible warning which must be acknowledged in order to prevent an emergency brake application. AWS does not control the train if the driver acknowledges the warning for a restrictive signal without taking action in response to it. The ATP system addresses this shortfall because it is a supervisory system capable of *intervening* in order to control the train's speed where the driver fails to do so correctly.

3. HOW DOES ATP WORK?

The operation of ATP is complex but a simplified explanation is outlined here. Information about lineside signal aspects, train speed and local track conditions, picked up by receiver antennae located below the front end of the train, is integrated by an on-board computer with stored information about the train. A distance/braking profile is calculated and used to check whether the movement of the train is within safe limits. If the speed of the train is 3 mph in excess of the calculated safe limit then the driver receives a warning. If the train's speed reaches 6 mph above this safe limit, the ATP system intervenes with a brake application. The driver can regain control of the train's braking when the speed has fallen within safe limits.

4. THE HUMAN FACTORS PROGRAMME.

The application of Human Factors in the development of ATP was considered vital because the project concerned the large scale introduction of new technology to the driving task. It was important to take account of the driver's needs if the design of the system was to be both *correct* and *accepted*. The programme was welcomed by the drivers and the extensive participation that took place has generated a large amount of information.

The Human Factors input into the project formed part of a broader approach to establish The National Specification. A working group was set up to address all of the issues involved with the driver interface. This Driver Interface Working Group (DIWG) comprised expertise from technical areas such as Human Factors, Operational Standards, Signalling and other key areas such as the driver management from each of the pilot schemes. This multi-disciplinary group was the forum for decisions about which issues required action and how the actions would be progressed.

4.1 Methodology.

The methodology for data gathering employed by the Human Factors programme centred around a core of *subjective* techniques:-

4.1.1 Questionnaires.

Questionnaires were issued to the drivers in order to gain a broad and quick overview of their attitudes at two phases of pilot scheme implementation. Initially they were issued at the pre-training phase to establish the relationship between drivers attitudes to new technology, the railway in general, training and ATP through rated responses to questions and comments. This was followed up by a post-training questionnaire which enabled a comparative analysis of attitudes before and after training to be made. This questionnaire also provided scope for rating and commenting on training and specific equipment issues. In total, approximately seven hundred questionnaires were returned.

4.1.2 Commentary Forms.

In order to tap into a broader ATP knowledge base, Driver Leaders, who are the drivers' supervisors and have extensive experience of supervising trains fitted with ATP, were asked to provide comments on specific ATP issues. These included in-cab instrumentation, data entry, the operational issues associated with ATP's interaction with current in-cab safety devices, training, the effect on driving styles and possible improvements.

4.1.3 Structured & Informal Interviews.

Twenty six structured interviews were undertaken prior to introduction to further explore and clarify drivers' attitudes to ATP related issues. There was extensive informal discussion with the drivers and Driver Leaders during the attendance of training courses, cab rides on trial & service trains and when undertaking technical evaluations.

4.1.4 Results.

The statistical analysis of the questionnaires provided a quantitative basis with which to compare drivers' ratings of a particular statement. Comments made by drivers and Driver Leaders were used as corroborative and supplementary information to evaluate the ATP system.

4.1.5 Feedback.

Drivers were issued with an *ATP Newsletter* produced by the DIWG. Establishing a *two-way* information flow between the DIWG and the drivers was considered to be a key component of the participatory process. The feedback to the drivers provided details about any changes that were made to the pilot scheme system.

5. THE APPLICATION OF HUMAN FACTORS.

The DIWG identified issues in a number of areas that needed to be addressed, two of these are discussed in this paper:-

- The Main Display Window
- The Data Entry Device

5.1 Main Display Window.

The primary function of the Main Display Window (MDW) is to inform the driver of the ATP system's perception of track-side signal aspect information. The MDW is placed within the speedometer dial and consists of a series of LED matrices capable of displaying alphanumeric symbols. In terms of the driver interface, the inclusion of the MDW represents the largest single change to cab instrumentation. There are two features of the pilot scheme MDW that have drawn comment:

(1) Format
(2) Readability

5.1.1 Format.

The method of presentation of signal aspect information in the MDW is shaped by a two pronged display philosophy which states firstly, that the system should inform the driver what it is thinking, for both learning purposes and performance reasons. The information received by ATP is not continuously updated, rather it is intermittent, and as a result ATP's perception of lineside signal aspect may not be the same as the actual lineside signal observed by the driver. Secondly, the display philosophy requires that use of the display does not replace the driver's observation of lineside signalling.

The pilot scheme format uses abstract symbols in an attempt to provide the driver with information about ATP's perception of lineside signals without directly representing actual lineside signals to do so.

On the pilot schemes, in a four aspect signal sequence, the display progression is given to the driver as "zeros" and "dots" which are illustrated below:

= = =

ATP is not supervising to a signal at danger.

. . **0**

ATP expects the next signal to be double yellow.

. **0 0**

ATP expects the next signal to be single yellow.

0 0 0

ATP expects the next signal to be red

The abstract symbols were originally intended to represent the degree of restriction ATP is supervising to by using an increasing number of "zeros" to represent the need for the train's speed to reduce to zero. However, the drivers did not observe the "zeros" in the display, instead they observed the "dots". The drivers *converted* the "dots" into the number of yellow lineside signals to go before the red signal.

The intermittent updating of the ATP system means that a full signal progression will not always be received by the ATP system when approaching a red signal. This together with the approach to other operational situations, such as *flashing* signal aspects, means that the driver's decoding of the information is governed increasingly by the situation in which the information is received. The need for a more meaningful display format to deal with the complexity of these operational situations was therefore apparent.

In response to this a video was produced showing the behaviour of four alternative MDW options against real background footage which the drivers could then view in order to evaluate the merits of each option and indicate their preferred option overall. The options on this video adopted recommendations from the drivers themselves and advice from the DIWG. Each option was considered by the DIWG to be in keeping with the display philosophy mentioned earlier.

However, before the video was approved for presentation to the drivers, a qualitative risk assessment of the options on the video was undertaken by an independent consultancy in order to confirm that each option was in keeping with this philosophy.

Following this, a programme for the presentation of the video and the collection of data was undertaken. A total of one hundred and fifty three drivers, who represented each of the pilot schemes, were shown the video . Drivers both with and without ATP training were consulted in order to remove the effect of any pre-conceptions held about the current pilot scheme display. The data that was collected included rated responses to questions about the ease of understanding of the options and the improvement they afforded compared to the pilot scheme display. The drivers were asked to comment on the reasons for their ratings and to rank the options based on their preferences. Their comments were used as corroborative evidence to confirm that the meaning of the options had been understood and to identify the advantages and disadvantages of each option. The basic operation of the preferred option is illustrated below:

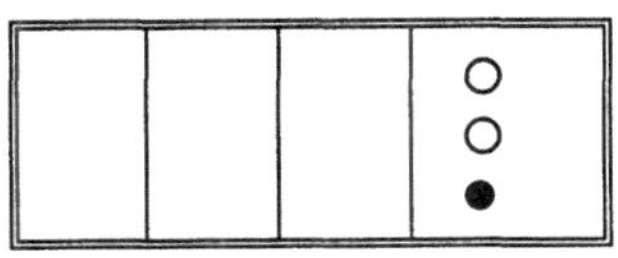

Figure 1.

● = yellow signal

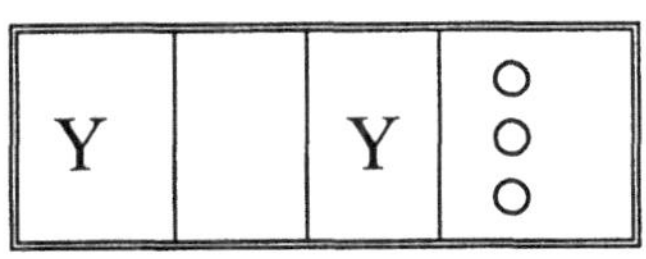

Figure 2

The principles that govern this option's display format are firstly that 'signal passed' information is given when each lineside signal is passed. If ATP receives updated information that the approaching signal is not the expected one based on the signal just passed, the 'signal passed' indication is extinguished and signal approaching information is given. A description of figures 1 & 2 is given overleaf to explain these principles more fully.

In figure 1, ATP indicates the signal *passed* was a single yellow aspect through the illumination of a yellow coloured LED on the right hand side of the main display window. ATP's perception of the lineside signals assumes a logical progression and is, therefore, expecting the next signal to be at red. The coloured LEDs would also display a double yellow and green aspect, with the appropriately coloured LEDs, when these signals are passed.

In figure 2, ATP indicates that it has received *updated* information about the signal approaching, which is not in keeping with the expected signal aspect based on signal passed information. In this example, ATP indicates that the next signal is not at red but rather at double yellow by extinguishing the signal passed indication and replacing it with the alphabetic characters "YY" to indicate this *new signal ahead.* When the new signal aspect ahead is passed, the signal approaching indication is extinguished and the display reverts to showing signal passed information. A single yellow signal aspect ahead would be indicated in the MDW by a single "Y" and a red signal by a single "R".

This option has a number of benefits which include the fact that information displayed to the driver is in a form with which they are already familiar and so facilitates rapid understanding. The display reinforces the driver's own observation of the lineside signal aspect, in keeping with the philosophy governing driver's performance. By displaying signal passed information the predictive function of the display is minimised. Where the ATP system receives accurate information about a *change* in the expected signal sequence, the new signal ahead is indicated in a format that is readily distinguished from signal passed information. This helps to address the performance problems associated with the intermittent nature of the information received by the ATP system by providing accurate information about ATP's perception of the lineside signals at all times.

5.1.2 Readability.

The problems associated with readability are, in part, due to the overall build of the speedometer and the effect of the in-cab environment. The problems encountered were principally those of glare, reflection and washout caused by sunlight entering the cab. Washout is caused by sunlight hitting the LEDs of the MDW display making it difficult to distinguish between which LEDs are self-illuminated and those which are "phantom" lit by sunlight.

In order to minimise in-cab sunlight, blinds and reflective external cab-window coatings were proposed. To minimise the effect of the sunlight that did enter the cab, recommendations were put forward for the optimal mounted position of the speedometer, shrouding around it and for the use of non-reflective glass and surface coatings. Also the use of polarising filters was suggested to minimise "phantom" illumination.

Whilst the design of in-cab instrumentation is well covered by existing British and BR Standards, the incorporation of LEDs as part of the design is not. To specify the design and use of LEDs in the MDW, evaluation trials were carried out in order to establish the required range of luminance needed to ensure readability in all ambient light conditions. It has been recommended that the range of luminance levels should either be manually adjustable by the driver or an optimal level maintained through automatic adjustment.

5.2 Data Entry Device

The Data Entry Device (DED) is used by the driver, once at the beginning of each journey, to enter information about the train that is not permanently stored but which is required by the ATP system.

There are three main issues related to the DED that were studied, the results of which were used to establish a general specification:

(1) Anthropometrics
(2) Readability
(3) Dialogue Design for the HCI

5.2.1 Anthropometrics

Anthropometric data was examined in order to examine the position of the DED within the cab. This evaluation confirmed that although the drivers of the two pilot schemes could read the DED screen and operate the keypad, the positioning was not optimal. Recommendations were put forward for optimal placement of the DED in new locomotive builds where existing build constraints could be overcome. On the existing pilot schemes, the Great Western Main Line drivers were required to lean forward on the edge of the co-driver's (second man's) seat and the Chiltern Line drivers needed to stand up, with their driving seat restricting their leg room and tilt their heads upwards in order to use the DED.

Anthropometric data was also used to examine the construction and layout of the DED controls, this time to specify the size, travel, resistance and separation of the buttons used to input the data. The layout of numeric data keypad was considered with respect to the keypads which drivers typically use. It was recommended that a 'telephone' format,

123
456
789
0

be adopted by all in-cab numeric keypads to avoid negative skill transfer from keypads with a different layout.

5.2.2 Readability

The physical characteristics of the DED display (size & contrast etc.) were examined with respect to existing British and BR Standards addressing 'readability' in keeping with the measures adopted for the specification of the MDW and speedometer.

Having to stand up to operate and read the DED exacerbated problems of operability and readability on the Chiltern Line. The forced proximity of the DED screen caused problems for near-sighted drivers requiring spectacles for reading at close distances. That is, the design of near-sighted glasses incorporates the corrective focal element at the base of the lens which meant that drivers had to tilt their heads back much further to read the DED display.

Recommendations were put forward for the screen's mounting to be adjustable. This would permit the users to angle the screen to suit individual reading requirements imposed by their height and need for spectacles. This would serve the additional function of enabling the driver to block-out unwanted sunlight thereby reducing problems with glare, reflection and washout.

5.2.3 Dialogue Design.

A task analysis of the data entry process of each of the pilot schemes was undertaken which formed the basis of establishing a formal specification for the method of data entry.

The driver's ability to check for errors made in manually entering data and the procedure to correct them was an issue that the DIWG had identified as needing to be addressed. Informal interviews with drivers clarified which elements of the data entry task required modification. Recommendations to address these issues were put forward that made it possible to alter either only the software for possible retrograde changes on the pilot scheme or for combined software and hardware changes that could be incorporated in the National Specification. Further work is required to establish the language structure of the drivers' prompts. The prompts on the pilot schemes use terminology which the drivers do not ordinarily use as part of their work and the prompts are therefore not matched to the drivers' needs.

6. SUMMARY

This paper has only been able to present a limited account of the involvement of Human Factors in the on-going development of the Automatic Train Protection system. It is hoped that this paper has demonstrated the success of the Human Factors programme in providing the drivers with an interface that meets their requirements and which has gained their acceptance through their participation at all stages of the evaluation process. Moreover, valuable lessons about the practical application of Human Factors in a large scale industrial organisation have been learned and will be of benefit for further ATP implementation and other similar projects in the future.

7. ACKNOWLEDGEMENTS

The author thanks the ATP Project Team, the staff who co-operated in the Human Factors programme and the Managing Director of British Rail Research for permission to publish this paper.

VISION IN VEHICLES - V
A.G. Gale et al. (Editors)
1996 Elsevier Science B.V.

The Human Factors of Cameras for the Civil Cockpit

J.A. Baird and H.J. Dudfield

Centre for Human Sciences, Defence Research Agency, Farnborough, Hampshire GU14 6SZ.

1. INTRODUCTION

In the event of an incident occurring on a civil aircraft, aircrew have standard procedures and instrument checks to follow. In most situations, this is sufficient for them to analyse the situation properly and carry out corrective action. It is inevitable, however, that in times of high stress indicators may be missed. The information required may simply be absent, or be inadequately presented. One possible approach to this problem may be to train cabin crew for better communication, since they may be able to observe signs on the airframe that would enhance interpretation of the situation.

Cabin crew could be trained to tell aircrew if they can see a problem that the aircrew cannot view from the cockpit. However, social psychology studies on the 'bystander effect' suggest that a member of a group who can attribute responsibility for action to another member will stand by and take no action (Latané and Darley, 1970). Where one of the parties has a higher status, the situation may be worsened because, as many studies have shown, people will readily defer responsibility to those who appear to have some form of authority (Milgram, 1974). Thus, the cabin crew would be likely to defer responsibility to the aircrew. Formally assigning responsibility to one of the cabin crew could help overcome this (Moriarty, 1975), but it has to be borne in mind that the cabin crew have their own job to do. When a problem has arisen that can be viewed by the cabin crew, the passengers are likely to have seen the same signs and may have become distressed. Cabin crew workload will increase under these circumstances since it is part of their duties to keep passengers calm in an emergency.

As an additional source of information, external camera systems for civil aircraft have been recommended by the Air Accident Investigation Branch (AAIB) in the report on the British Midland Boeing 737-400 crash on the M1 (1989) when the wrong engine was shut down. Camera systems provide a facility for aircrew to visually examine the outside of the aircraft and may reduce aircrew error, since they will provide additional information to the normal cockpit displays, thereby aiding decision making. In these systems, miniature cameras are mounted on the outside of aircraft and the imagery is relayed to a display in the cockpit. As yet, no operational system has been defined. Hence, it is not yet known how the system will be used, and whether it will be part of routine checks or consulted after action has been taken to correct a problem. Little human factors work has been carried out in this area to establish recommendations about these issues.

One human factors study was carried out in this area by Dudfield, Baird and Naish (1993), who considered a range of issues pertaining to such systems. A review of the ergonomics literature was carried out, with particular emphasis on recommendations about the visual characteristics of the display. The majority of current display standards relate to the conventional CRT display, although the slim design of the liquid crystal display (LCD) has enhanced its potential as a candidate for the limited workspace of the civil cockpit. Thus, evaluation of the LCD from a human factors standpoint is required. Dudfield *et al.* concluded that issues relating to the display of alphanumerics and distances from the screen would be generalisable from past work, but that many human factors issues pertaining to this new system had yet to be resolved.

This paper discusses the human factors of external cameras for civil aircraft. The following areas are considered:

* generation of a tentative list to be used in the evaluation of a system's potential to display visually evident incidents
* the positioning of cameras on the airframe
* the location of the monitor in the cockpit
* the display format of the imagery, and
* the control of the system.

2. DISPLAY CONTENT

A survey of incidents recorded in the UK Civil Aviation Authority database (Dudfield, Baird and Naish, 1993) was carried out to assess those in which camera systems might have been of benefit. This search confirmed that there are many incidents for which external cameras would provide no assistance, such as explosions or overshooting the runway. However, the question is whether external camera systems can be of use for *any* kind of incident rather than for all incident types. Dudfield *et al.* (1993) concluded that the system could be of use for some incidents and suggested that certain areas of the airframe should be displayed (see Table 1).

Table 1 List of areas that require display

Aircraft Area	**Questions on displayed information**
Gear	Is it possible to tell from the display whether the gear is down and locked?
Wheels	Is it clear from the displays if all the wheels are intact?
	Could smoke from a wheel be viewed on the display?
	Could flames from a wheel be viewed on the display?
Engines	Could smoke from the engine be seen clearly on the display?
	Could flames from the engine be seen clearly on the display?
Flaps	Is it possible to tell from the display whether the flaps are down?
(leading edge/ trailing edge)	Is it possible to tell from the display whether the flaps are correctly positioned?
	Is it possible to tell from the display whether the flaps are intact?
Doors	Can doors be seen to ensure that they are properly sealed?

The areas selected for display by the system were tentative and should be revised in the light of experimental findings on an operational system.

The resolution of the camera and display influences the incidents that can be viewed. It has been assumed that only visually obvious incidents could be viewed since the size of the monitor is likely to be small. Thus, fatigue cracks and the security of bolts would still be a matter for ground maintenance crew. In addition, only airborne incidents have been surveyed. Cameras may have a use on the ground, such as ensuring wing clearance or checking for the presence of ground crew when manoeuvring. Table 1 shows a list of questions that could be asked of a camera system display to ensure that it was able to show useful areas of the airframe. The kinds of incidents in which an external camera may be of use are those in which part of the aircraft is on fire, the gear is not properly extended or retracted, the flaps are not at the correct position, a door has not been closed properly, or part of the airframe has broken off.

Although the flight instruments alone have previously been considered sufficient warning of any of these incidents, in some circumstances indicators may be difficult to interpret. For example, the displays may show the flaps to be down and at the correct angle when the handling of the aircraft indicates otherwise. Another advantage of a camera system is that crew should be able to check from the cockpit whether the gear is down and locked, thereby avoiding the current practice of flypast inspections where air traffic control have the responsibility for a visual examination of the gear from the tower. Similarly, although normal checks were performed by the crew of the Boeing 737 that landed at Casper, Wyoming on 23 March 1983, the wheels of the aircraft had not been extended and a passenger was killed. Were camera checks to be included in before landing procedures, accidents like this might be less frequent.

Implications of external cameras for overall air safety should be examined, since it is now well recognised in the human factors literature that failure to design for the complete system can leave gaps that allow for system breakdowns. Hence, the effects of the installation of cameras for civil aircraft on ground maintenance, air traffic control, crew procedures and crew training must all be taken into account when designing the system. Camera systems may decrease the workload burden of air traffic control by placing some of the responsibility for visual examinations with aircrew. If fires break out on take-off, this is sometimes reported to aircrew by air traffic controllers. Pilots on the Boeing 737 that caught fire on the runway at Manchester airport in 1985 thought that the problem, whose only indication was a thud, might have been due to a tyre burst or a bird strike. Only 9 seconds later was the left hand engine fire warning shown in the cockpit and aircrew had to confirm this diagnosis with air traffic control. Again, a more rapid response might be possible with the use of external cameras to assess the situation.

3. POSITIONING OF THE CAMERAS

The positioning of the cameras determines the kind of incident that can be viewed, and should be an iterative process since an exhaustive list of all possible incidents is not viable. More than one camera will be required to display all of the airframe areas listed in Table 1. It has been suggested that four cameras may be used, displaying the front gear, the wings and the fin. Figure 1 shows the suggested positioning of cameras where four are used.

The area viewed by each camera is influenced by a number of factors such as weather, lighting conditions, glare, the type of camera lens used and whether static or panning cameras are used. Bad weather conditions have to be accepted as being detrimental to the utility of an external camera. However, it may be possible to lessen the effects of poor lighting conditions and glare. Military aircraft already use infrared cameras in low light conditions. One potential problem associated with the use of infrared is the transition from daylight to darkness and how the transition between ordinary television cameras and infrared should be managed. The technical feasibility of such a system, as well as how it should be controlled, should be assessed through simulator trials. Another possibility is that glare could be dealt with by providing a polarised filter over the lens[1]. Whether normal or wide angle lenses are used should also be decided through simulator trials. These trials should primarily investigate which lens produces least error in subjects' performance on an incident identification search task, and response time should be considered a secondary issue. That is, in an operational system, it is more important that aircrew diagnose the situation correctly than diagnose it quickly but incorrectly. Of course, whether a panning or static camera should be used should also be examined before the system becomes operational. An issue that has been highlighted is that a panning camera could become fixed in one position due to a malfunction, and that to avoid this potential problem more than one static camera could be used effectively to display the same area. However, the presentation of imagery from one camera is less complex than that from several cameras.

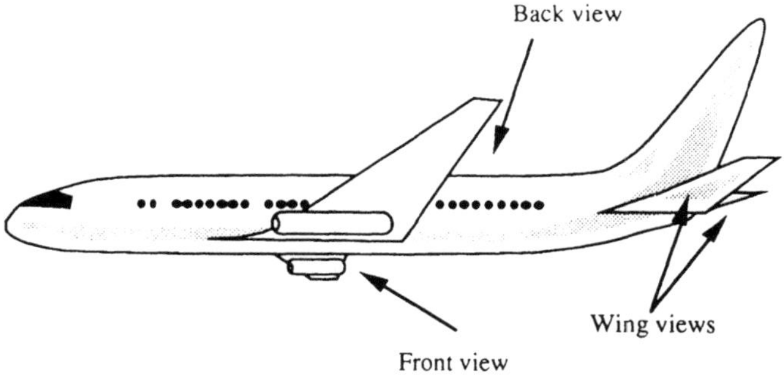

Figure 1: Camera positions

4. POSITIONING OF THE DISPLAY IN THE COCKPIT

The positioning of the display in the cockpit is dependent upon whether it is considered to be a primary or a secondary instrument. Primary instruments are those that are critical to the safe running of the aircraft, and should be located within a thirty degree visual angle of the normal line of sight. Figure 2 shows the recommended positioning of primary and secondary flight instruments given in the Defence Standards. Secondary instruments are to be located within a sixty degree cone, the rationale being that they are of less importance and it is therefore less critical if it takes longer to scan the cockpit for them. The camera system could be considered as a primary instrument if it had to be observed as part of routine checks when

[1] Roger Green (Army Personnel Research Establishment), personal communication.

an incident occurred. Were it to be consulted only after diagnosis of the situation and corrective action had been carried out, then it would be regarded as a secondary instrument and could be placed more peripherally.

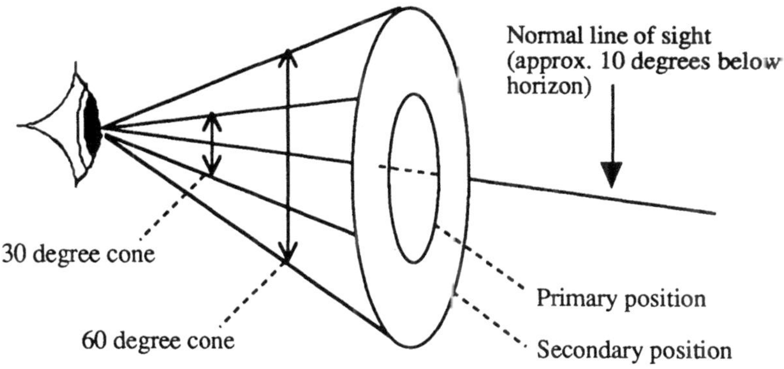

Figure 2: Position of display in relation to the visual cone

One solution to this problem may be to place the camera on a semi-flexible mounting such as those that have been suggested for passenger entertainment systems. A monitor would be attached by a semi-flexible mounting to the chair, and users could move the displays into their lap whilst operating the system and stow it at the side at other times. A liquid crystal display is an ideal candidate for such a monitor, due to its slim design.

Dudfield, Baird and Naish (1993) examined current fleet aircraft to identify suitable positions in which a monitor could be placed. The general conclusion from this work was that there was a lack of available cockpit space and free space was often in awkward positions such as behind and above the crew's heads. It should be noted that the size of the monitor may be defined by the amount of space in the cockpit. Some aircraft present less of a problem than others in this respect. On Concorde, for example, there is a space 7x4.75 inches on the central panel that would allow use by two viewers. The 747-400 series, on the other hand, has a potential location of 6x8 inches above and behind both crew on the overhead panel. Clearly this is not ideal, but if external camera systems become an accepted tool then future aircraft manufacturers will be able to design the location from the outset. Indeed, some companies are suggesting that one monitor could be used to display both an electronic library system (ELS) and external camera imagery (for example, see *Flight International*, July 1993). Although this may reduce the difficulty of locating the monitor, there can be no doubt that the complexity of the issues associated with displaying are increased when they are used for two systems.

5. THE DISPLAY AND CONTROL OF IMAGERY IN THE COCKPIT

The display of cockpit information is complicated by the likelihood that there will be more than one camera in such a system. One method would be to present the different camera views in sequence, with the system scrolling through each view. This has the advantage of maximising the screen space available. However, an obvious problem with this type of presentation is that it may take a long time for the user to scan each presentation for indications of a problem. Another possibility is that the four images could be displayed concurrently on a split screen, but there would be a poorer resolution for each image in comparison with the sequential display. Yet another suggestion is that the images could be displayed on a staggered screen in a manner that is physically congruous with the layout of the aircraft: the front camera view to the top of the screen, the left to the left, and so on. This may aid the user to analyse correctly the area in which the incident has occurred and, for example, turn off the correct engine when there is an engine fire. Additionally, there is the advantage with a staggered display that all screens can be viewed at once, but resolution of this display will be poorer than both the sequential and split displays since some of the display area is not utilised.

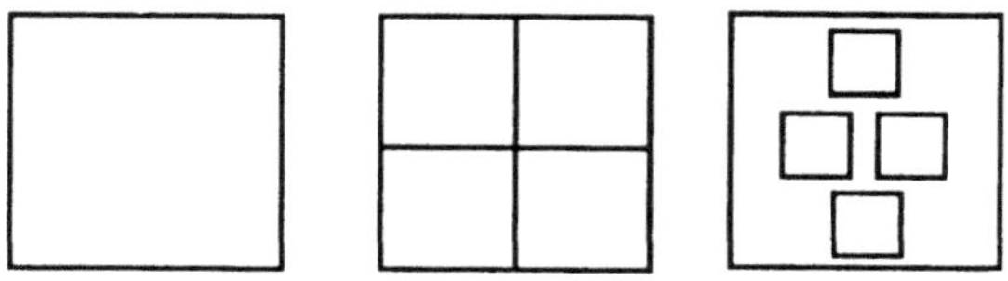

1 Full screen 2 Split screen 3 Staggered screen

Figure 2: Possible display formats

The simultaneous display of information from more than one camera will be possible only where the resolution and monitor size are adequate. Where the resolution is not high enough for simultaneous display, a serial display of each camera position should be provided. If more than one camera's imagery is to be displayed at one time, pilots should be provided with a control facility that allows them to select the camera from which they would like to view the aircraft, and this imagery should then fill the screen. Labels should be provided for each screen in a further attempt to circumvent confusion over location of the incident on the airframe.

The ability to review an incident after it has occurred, by running through a video tape recording of the last few minutes (the length of this buffer is undetermined), could help to identify the sequence of events leading to and during an incident. Although a visual replay would be of immense use to accident investigators, it could also benefit the crew in the identification or confirmation of unusual noises or events. However, crew could be distracted by the system if it were available during critical phases of flight when workload is highest. One suggestion is that the video monitor could be inhibited during these phases. A replay facility could be particularly useful after monitor inhibition times, such as when committed to take-off, where at a safe altitude the crew could review the tape to confirm the nature of the incident and use the live visual scene to assist in the decision of what to do next.

As home video users are aware, finding a particular part of a video tape is time-consuming and not straightforward. Indeed, on home videos one often has the advantage of searching for the start or end of a programme where the content of the part of the tape one is looking for is easy to identify. On an external camera system the context that the crew member is looking for may not be so obvious. In this case, he or she will be searching through a series of views that are similar, trying to spot a change from one frame to the next. In some circumstances this might be obvious (e.g. if an engine catches fire) but in others it may be easy to miss the consideration of the operation of the system is necessary. One possibility could be to 'event' mark the tape. Users could press a button to stamp the tape with a visually obvious mark so that searching for the relevant area is easier. The video replay controls need to reflect conventional systems. The imagery would need to be correctly labelled in common with the real time video and the two would need to be easily discriminable. That is, on replay an appropriate label 'REPLAY' would be displayed. It would be necessary to have a digital time display that would permit the user to rewind to the point at which he or she recalled the event occurring. All of this will be time-consuming, hence the ease of operation is critical. The length of time that the user can review is as yet unspecified. However, it is likely that the need for a timely analysis of an incident will influence this.

6. OPERATIONAL PROCEDURES

As well as controlling the system, the operational procedures should be considered. One issue is which crew member will be responsible for replay, and when he or she will review an incident. It seems reasonable that the flight engineer could control this facility from a monitor and controls on the engineer's panel. As many aircraft are currently two-crew, it is recommended that the individual responsible for analysing the incident takes this role. Procedures to incorporate this into emergency routines need development and analysis. It is crucial that the system does not become so absorbing that decision time and accuracy are degraded. How realistic these concerns are can be assessed only through experience. Eventually, computer processing of the imagery may assist in the identification of an incident by carrying out a frame by frame comparison and displaying the imagery when a significant difference is detected, drawing attention to the area in question.

Human decision makers have various biases that limit the optimality of the conclusions that they reach (see Evans, 1990). A possible misuse of this system would be merely to confirm the hypothesis that the crew had already reached. With such confirmation bias, it is unlikely that contradictory evidence will be processed fully. That is, humans tend to seek out evidence that supports their conclusion and ignore evidence to the contrary. Woods (1990, p255) states that

> "The results of several studies ... strongly suggest that a major source of human error in dynamic domains is a failure to revise situational assessment as new evidence comes in. Initial assessment tends to be accurate, in the sense of being consistent with the partial information available early in the event. Errors become manifest later, in the evolution of the event, as people fail to revise their assessments in response to new evidence which indicates a deviation of the event from the expected path (e.g. due to multiple failures)."

To avoid this problem, it may be necessary for a list of possible failures to be run through when using the system. An active search for evidence about specific incident types is required. This may be achieved by use of the list and training to make aircrew aware of the possible problem of confirmation bias. The task should be for users to make negative as well as positive tests of their hypothesis, searching for both confirmatory and disconfirmatory evidence.

7. CONCLUSIONS

An externally mounted camera system could have some utility in incidents where a visual check of the airframe could clarify a situation, but many human factors issues associated with this system have yet to be resolved. It is suggested that simulation studies should examine the ergonomics of the display and control of the system, the benefits of the system for various incident types (which affects the positioning of the cameras) and the integration of the system into operational procedures. This paper has highlighted some of the research issues that should be addressed and has discussed possible solutions to some of the problems. It is concluded that operational procedures should circumvent potential cognitive biases. Hence, it should not be assumed that camera imagery will not be used to re-affirm conclusions already reached by the users. This may simply perpetuate error, instilling a higher level of confidence in the wrong diagnosis of a situation.

REFERENCES

DEF STAN 00-25 (PART 7)/1 6.1 HMSO.

AAIB. *Report on the accident to Boeing 737-400 G-OMBE near Kegworth, Leicestershire on 8 Jan 1989.* Department of Transport, Air Accident Investigation Report Published by HMSO.

Anon. Sextant/CDI explore airline ELS needs. *Flight International.* (1993) 7 - 13 July page 10.

Dudfield, H. J., Baird, J. A. and Naish, P. N. L. (1993) *A human factors investigation into the use of airborne external video view camera systems.* Defence Research Agency Technical Report TR 93021, May 1993.

Evans, J. St. B. T. (1990) *Bias in Human Reasoning: Causes and Consequences.* Essays in Cognitive Psychology, Lawrence Earlbaum Associates, Hove, East Sussex.

Latané, B. and J. M. Darley (1970) *The unresponsive bystander: Why doesn't he help?* New York, Appleton-Century-Crofts.

Milgram, S. (1974) *Obedience to Authority.* Tavistock: London.

Moriarty, T. (1975) "Crime, commitment and the responsive bystander: Two field experiments." *Journal of Personality and Social Psychology* 31: 370 - 376.

Woods (1990) Chapter 19: Modelling and Predicting Human Error. *Human Performance Models for Computer-Aided Engineering.* Academic Press, Ltd., London.

ACKNOWLEDGEMENTS

The authors would like to gratefully acknowledge the assistance of Mr. Les Anstey of British Airways for his assistance in gaining access to fleet aircraft and of the Civil Aviation Authority for providing funding for the work upon which this paper is based.

6: VISUAL PERFORMANCE IN DEGRADED VISIBILITY

VISION IN VEHICLES - V
A.G. Gale et al. (Editors)

Effects Of A Vision Enhancement System On Drivers' Ability To Drive Safely In Fog

Lena Nilsson and Håkan Alm

Swedish Road and Transport Research Institute (VTI) S-58195 Linkoping, Sweden

1. INTRODUCTION

Car driving is to a large extent a visual task. Therefore, poor visibility conditions like fog may impose severe demands on drivers, because the possibility to collect necessary information is markedly degraded. If, however, car driving is seen as a self-paced task, the drivers should be able to adjust their behaviour in accordance with the increased demands.

Speed reductions have been reported for driving in fog on rural roads and highways [1] Using a fixed base simulator, Tenkink [2] found that poor visibility not only resulted in speed reduction, but also introduced lane keeping problems. He concluded that the lateral position becomes more uncertain and inconsistent with reduced sight distance. Tenkink [3] has also pointed out the importance of the presence of obstacles, and of the behaviour of leading vehicles, for the speed choice in poor visibility conditions. Using a moving base simulator, Harms [4] found that sight distance influenced drivers' mean speed, whereas their lateral position and variation in lateral position were not systematically influenced, implying that reduced sight increases the amount of random variation in lateral position. The speed adjustments obtained under poor visibility conditions have often been insufficient, in the meaning that the stopping distance has remained longer than the actual visibility distance. For example, more than half the number of drivers were exceeding the speed. at which they could stop within the sight distance, in an English motorway study of fog effects [5].

Fog is a relatively rare event, and the accidents occurring in fog constitute a small proportion of the total number of accidents. But, the percentage of fatalities and seriously injured persons, as well as the number of vehicles involved in each fog accident are higher than average [5]. One way to reduce the number of accidents in fog, or at least their consequences, may be to develop a Vision Enhancement System (a VES), that facilitates road following and speed choice, and that helps the driver to detect obstacles and information in time to take appropriate actions.

Using sensors, for the detection of what drivers are unable to see, and presenting the information in the form of a picture directly on the windscreen (a Head Up Display, HUD) has been suggested as one VES solution. A small but "clear" representation of the traffic environment, shown on a monitor placed on the bonnet of the car, can be used as a simple simulation of a HUD for vision enhancement. The purpose of this study was to investigate if it was possible to drive safely in heavy fog when such a simulated VES was available. Because the study focused on traffic safety, the effects on driver behaviour (in terms of speed, lateral position, reaction time and distance) and on workload were investigated, and compared to driving in clear sight and in fog without VES support.

2. METHOD

2.1 Subjects

Twenty-four subjects, 12 men and 12 women, participated in the study. They were between 23 and 46 years of age (mean 33.5, sd 7.5 years). All were experienced drivers, meaning that they had had a driving licence for at least five years *and* that they drive at least 10,000 km per year. Many of them were also experienced "simulator drivers", from participating in simulator studies before. The subjects were paid 250 SEK.

2.2 Apparatus

The study was conducted in the VTI driving simulator [6, 7]. It consists of six subsystems: a computer system with the simulation model, a moving base system, a 120° wide visual system, a vibration-generating system, a sound system, and a temperature-regulating system. The subsystems are controlled to evoke impressions, reactions and actions which are very similar to those experienced by a driver during real driving. The additional time delay introduced in the simulator is extremely short (40 ms).

2.3 Driving task

Road. The road type presented to the subjects was a two-lane, high friction asphalt road, 7 m wide and with shoulders. A 15 km long practice route and a 40 km long test route with the given characteristics were used. Both routes were rather straight, imposing very low workload on the subjects from road following.

Visibility. Two visibility levels, fog and clear sight, were used in the study. They were characterised by their maximum theoretical sight distances, which were 50 and 480 m, respectively, and generated by the fog function available in the simulator. The two maximum sight distances were absolute sight limits, beyond which the subjects could not see anything at all. From these limits towards the driver's position the sight was exponentially improved with distance.

Car. An ordinary Saab 9000 with a manual gearbox was used. The simulated physical environment corresponded to that in modern passenger cars.

Visual stimulus. A red square was used to simulate an unexpected event in the traffic environment outside the car. It appeared four times along the test route, at a fixed position, slightly to the left of the road. When the subjects passed certain specified route positions, the red square was presented 400 m ahead.

Obstacles. A van standing still ahead of the subjects' car was used as a stationary obstacle. It was positioned on the right road markings, occupying 1.5 m of the right lane and 0.4 m of the right shoulder. The obstacle appeared four times along the test route. When the subjects passed certain specified route positions, the van was presented 400 m ahead. The subjects had to overtake the vans to reach the destination.

Oncoming traffic. Oncoming vehicles appeared, and were controlled to drive with the subjects' speed. The meeting positions were fixed along the test route, and the oncoming vehicles never appeared in such positions that they disturbed overtaking of the vans.

2.4. Vision Enhancement System (VES)

The VES generated a "clear", black and white picture of the traffic environment (a copy of the "clear sight" video picture generated in the simulator's visual system). It was 17x12 cm in size, and presented on a monitor positioned directly on the bonnet of the car, in the drivers' central line of view, approximately 1.4 m in front of their eyes. The visual stimulus, the obstacle, and the oncoming traffic all appeared "clearly" on the monitor.

2.5. Design

A between-subject design was used. The varied factor was visibility. Three visibility conditions were studied: 1) a *clear sight* (control) condition with 480 m sight distance, 2) *a fog* condition with 50 m sight distance, and 3) *a fog plus VES* condition with 50 m sight distance supported by the VES. The 24 subjects were randomly assigned to the different conditions, with the only restriction of an equal number of men and women in each condition.

2.6. Measures

The *speed* was recorded, and its standard deviation (sd) was used to estimate the *variation in speed*. The *lateral position* on the road was measured in relation to a zero-position, defined as the position where the centre line of the road coincides with the centre line through the driver's body. A more negative value indicates a position more to the right. The standard deviation was used to estimate the *variation in lateral position. The brake reaction time* was calculated as the time elapsing from the onset of the red square until it was put out by a sufficiently hard braking (brake pedal depressed approximately 10 mm or more). The resolution was 20 ms. If no driver reaction (sufficiently hard braking) had been detected within 400 m after the red square presentation, the stimulus was regarded as unanswered and put out. Correspondingly, the *brake reaction distance* was calculated as the distance driven from the onset of the red square until it was put out by a sufficiently hard braking. The subjects' *workload* was measured using the Task Load Index (NASA-TLX) [8]. The subjects had to rate the six factors mental demand, physical demand, time pressure, performance, effort, and frustration level on continuous scales, ranging from very low to very high. They also had to rate the relative weights of the different workload factors.

2.7. Procedure

Firstly, the subjects answered a questionnaire about background variables. Then, written and verbal instructions were given, describing the experimental task, and how to handle the car. The subjects were asked to drive as they would normally drive, on a real highway with corresponding traffic and visibility conditions. They were informed that they had to brake as fast as possible when the red square appeared, and that they had to overtake the stationary vans. The function of the VES was explained to the subjects in the fog plus VES condition.

Then the subjects were introduced to the driving simulator. The handling of the car was practised. For the subjects in the fog plus VES condition, the function of the VES was repeated. The subjects drove the practice route, to get used to simulator driving, the traffic condition, and the respective visibility condition, in order to avoid learning to influence the results. The red square appeared four times, and the subjects could practice to "brake it away". Also the stationary vans appeared four times, so the subjects could practice to overtake them. The experiment leader made sure that the subjects noticed what was shown on the VES monitor, and that they got familiar with the overall functioning of the system.

After a brake, the real test phase took place. The subjects performed the driving task, including the specific reaction (red square) and interaction (van) subtasks. Driving performance data were recorded via the simulator's main computer. When the test route was completed, the subjects rated their workload on the NASA-TLX scales. The running of each subject took 1 to 2 hours in total.

3. RESULTS

3.1. Speed and speed variation

The mean speed levels and the variations in speed level for the three visibility conditions are listed in Table 1. When the VES was available while driving in fog, the speed level was markedly higher than that for driving in fog without the VES, but did not fully reach the speed level chosen when driving in clear sight (control). A one-way ANOVA showed a significant effect of visibility condition on speed ($F(2,21)=36.13$, $p= .0001$), and the posteriori test Tukey HSD revealed that all three visibility conditions differed significantly in speed level. A one-way ANOVA failed to show any difference in speed variation between the visibility conditions. Mean speed was thus affected by visibility, but the variation in speed was not. Using a help system, presenting a small but "perfect" representation of the road and its closest environment while driving in fog, seems to lead to a speed choice that is a compromise between the speed choices in clear sight and in heavy fog conditions, respectively.

Table 1
Mean speed levels and speed variations (sd)

Condition	Speed	
	Mean (km/h)	sd (km/h)
Fog	60.5	9.2
Fog plus VES	90.9	12.3
Control	104.6	10.1

3.2. Lateral position and variation in lateral position

The mean lateral positions for the three visibility conditions are shown in Table 2. Small differences can be seen between driving in fog without the VES, and the other two conditions. The subjects in the fog condition drove closer to the centre line of the road. The positioning of the car was similar in the clear sight (control) condition and the fog plus VES condition. A one-way ANOVA showed a significant effect of visibility condition on lateral position ($F(2,21)=4.64$, $p= .0215$), and the posteriori test Tukey HSD revealed that the lateral position when driving in clear sight (control) differed significantly from the lateral position when driving in fog without the VES. The differences in lateral position between the fog plus VES condition and the other two conditions did not reach statistical significance.

Table 2
Mean lateral positions and variations (sd) in lateral position

Condition	Lateral position	
	Mean (m)	sd (m)
Fog	-1.39	0.21
Fog plus VES	-1.66	0.41
Control	-1.70	0.32

Also for the variation in lateral position (Table 2), a significant effect of visibility condition (F(2,21)=14.91, p= .0001) was obtained using a one-way ANOVA. According to the posteriori test Tukey HSD, all three conditions differed significantly. Table 2 shows that the subjects in the fog plus VES condition varied their lateral position most, followed by the subjects in the clear sight (control) condition, and the subjects in the fog condition, who varied their lateral position least.

3.3 Brake reaction time and brake reaction distance

Table 3 shows how fast the subjects reacted (by braking), when a simulated unexpected event (the red square) appeared 400 m in front of them. It also shows how far the subjects drove, from that the red square appeared until they reacted by braking.

The much longer reaction time in the fog condition reflects the fact that the subjects had no possibility to detect the red square until it came out of the fog, 50 m in front of them. The difference in reaction time between the clear sight (control) condition and the fog plus VES condition is more interesting. A one-way ANOVA showed that reaction time was significantly influenced by visibility condition (F(2,21)=362.32, p= .0001). The posteriori test Tukey HSD revealed, however, that only the differences between the fog condition and the two other conditions were significant. The 0.25 s prolongation of brake reaction time, when driving in fog with the VES available compared to driving in clear sight (control), was thus not found to be statistically significant.

Table 3
Mean reaction times (4 stimulations) and mean reaction distances (4 stimulations)

Condition	Reaction time	Reaction distance (m)
Fog	23.14	385.0
Fog plus VES	1.07	27.6
Control	0.82	24.6

Also the much longer distance travelled, before the subjects in the fog condition reacted (braked) to the presented red square, results from the fact that these subjects had to drive appr. 350 m to the sight distance limit, before they could possibly discern the red square in the fog. Thus, again the difference in reaction distance between driving in clear sight (control) and VES supported driving in fog is more interesting. A one-way ANOVA showed that reaction distance was significantly influenced by visibility condition (F(2,21)= 8756.53, p= .0001). The posteriori test Tukey HSD revealed, however, that only the differences between the fog condition and the two other conditions were significant. The 3 m prolongation of brake reaction distance, when driving in fog with the VES available compared to driving in clear sight (control), was thus not found to be statistically significant.

3.4. Workload

For each subject, the scale values for the workload factors mental demand, physical demand, time pressure, performance, effort, and frustration level were multiplied with their corresponding weights. Table 4 shows the resulting means of the workload ratings, associated with driving under the various visibility conditions.

Table 4
Mean ratings of six workload factors

Workload	Visibility condition		
factor	Fog	Fog plus VES	Control
Mental demand	297.9	190.9	125.4
Physical demand	121.0	59.9	32.0
Time pressure	59.8	59.6	13.9
Performance	151.8	149.1	202.5
Effort	131.9	212.3	102.8
Frustation	95.1	155.9	105.1

Using one-way ANOVAS, only the workload factors mental demand ($F(2,21)=4.56$, $p= .0226$), and physical demand ($F(2,21)=3.63$, $p= .0443$) showed significant effects of visibility. The workload factors time pressure, performance, effort, and frustration level, did not show any statistically significant differences between the three visibility conditions.

From Table 4 it is obvious that the mental demand was rated highest for driving in fog without the VES, lower for VES supported driving in fog, and lowest for driving in clear sight (control). The posteriori test Tukey HSD revealed that mental demand ratings differed significantly between the fog and clear sight (control) conditions, whereas the differences between the fog plus VES and the other two conditions were found to be non significant.

For physical demand, the highest rating was again obtained for the fog condition, followed by the rating for the fog plus VES condition and the clear sight (control) condition, in that order. The posteriori test Tukey HSD showed that a significant difference was present between the fog and clear sight (control) conditions. The differences in physical demand ratings between the fog plus VES and the other two conditions were not found to be significant.

4. DISCUSSION

The use of a VES, presenting a small black and white picture of the road and its closest environment on a monitor in front of the driver, has been shown to influence driver behaviour, or more precisely speed choice, variation in lateral position, and reaction time.

As reported for real driving [1], and more or less self-evident, the *speed* decreased in the fog condition. The mean level (60.5 km/h) was of the same order of magnitude as that in another simulator study [4], with comparable visibility, but with a more curved road. Introducing the VES when driving in the fog, increased the speed level by 30.4 km/h to 90.9 km/h, which still was 13.7

km/h below the speed level obtained in clear sight. This result indicates that drivers still could have experienced some problems when they used the VES. Even though the VES presented a true representation, the road and the traffic were not equally easy to see on the monitor as through the windscreen; especially not the far away sections, as the small size of the monitor picture probably lead to a reduction of the actual sight distance. The speed results therefore partly support the hypothesis that drivers adjust their speed so the sight distance remains constant in time [2]. Another explanation may be that the obtained speed reductions were caused by lane keeping problems.

The *variation* (sd) *in lateral position* on the road was increased when the VES was used, indicating that these drivers seem to have larger problems than the other drivers to keep a steady course. Also, large deflections in lateral position during overtaking of the vans imply that it was difficult to control lateral manoeuvres by looking at the monitor. The problems may have been caused by the strategy for system use. Most drivers moved their eyes between the VES monitor and the real road. An additional reason could have been the fact that the bonnet was not reproduced on the monitor, leading to the picture "floating around" without a stationary reference. That unsupported driving in fog shows the smallest variation in lateral position is in disagreement with earlier results [2], but indicates that these drivers probably kept to the centre line as a reference. The increase in lateral position was not so large, that the drivers using the VES spent more time in the left lane, compared to other drivers.

The differences in *reaction time* and *reaction distance* between the fog plus VES and the clear sight conditions were not significant, meaning that the drivers' ability to react quickly to an unexpected event was not negatively influenced by the VES. Instead, this ability was strongly improved compared to unsupported driving in fog. But, in the fog condition it was impossible to perceive the stimulus until it came out of the fog, ca 350 m after presentation. To overcome this design restriction, the reaction times and reaction distances for the fog condition were *theoretically* recalculated, assuming that the red square was presented at the fog limit, 50 m ahead of the drivers. The resulting mean values were 2.1 s and 35 m, respectively. The compensated reaction time for unsupported driving in the fog was still longer than the reaction time when the VES was used (one-way ANOVA; $F(2,21)=76.24$; $p= .0001$). The compensated difference in reaction distance did not reach statistical significance. An explanation for the reaction time improvement can be that the VES gave the drivers the opportunity to detect the red square at the moment it occurred, that is to detect a distinct change which humans are good at. In the fog condition, the red square appeared more like a gradual change growing out of the fog. Such changes are more difficult to detect.

Different *strategies* for system use were adopted among the drivers using the VES. Some reacted very quickly to the red square (mean reaction time 0.76 s), indicating that they looked at the monitor most of the time, while others seemed to be more uncertain about how to divide their attention between the monitor picture and the real road, and therefore reacted somewhat slower (mean reaction time 1.25 s). The strategy for VES use also varied for the same individual, in different situations along the test route. Especially in more critical situations like overtaking and meeting oncoming vehicles, the drivers tended to look more through the windscreen. Thus, introduction of the VES probably made the driving task somewhat more complicated, because the two sources for visual information acquisition resulted in a choice situation for the driver, making divided attention a potential risk factor.

It is desirable that a driver can stop within the sight distance, making *stopping distance* an important factor. Assuming a deceleration near maximum (7 m/s2), and using the speeds and reaction times obtained in the study, the theoretical stopping distances were: 84 m in clear sight, 56 m (compensated) in fog, and 74 m in VES supported fog driving. For a more moderate deceleration of 3 m/s2, the corresponding values were: 165 m, 82 m, and 135 m, respectively. Thus, in clear sight and when the VES was used in fog, the drivers could easily stop within the sight distance, for both deceleration levels. The margin seems to be large enough, for the interpretation to hold, even if the sight distance on the monitor is somewhat reduced because of picture size. In the fog condition, drivers seem to have driven too fast, or reacted to slow to be able to stop within the sight distance.

The subjective assessment of *workload* did not reveal any significant effects of the VES, even though tendencies towards higher workload rates compared to clear sight rates, and lower workload rates compared to unsupported driving in fog, could be seen.

5. CONCLUSIONS

Use of the VES when driving in fog
- resulted in a speed level between the speed levels in clear sight and in fog.
- resulted in a larger variation in lateral position than in clear sight and in fog.
- improved the ability to react quickly, compared to unsupported driving in fog.
- did not degrade the ability to react quickly, compared to driving in clear sight.
- did not influence the workload level.

It seems both possible and acceptable to use a small representation of the traffic environment, in order to support drivers in poor visibility.

Further studies are necessary concerning long-term effects, MMI aspects, and effects of varying driver strategies for information acquisition.

ACKNOWLEDGEMENTS

The authors are most grateful to Saab Automobile AB, especially Bertil Ilhage, who provided a special bonnet and the monitor. Our colleagues Maria Berlin, Håkan Jansson, Mats Lidström, Helen Pettersson, and Tommy Pettersson assisted in planning, realising, conducting and interpreting the study. We are also indebted to the subjects, without whom the study had been impossible. The study was financially supported by Saab Automobile AB.

REFERENCES

[1] White, M.E., and Jeffery, D.J. (1980). Some Aspects of Motorway Traffic Behaviour in Fog. Report LR 958, TRL, Crowthorne, Berkshire.

[2] Tenkink, E. (1988). Lane Keeping and Speed Choice with Restricted Sight. In: T. Rothengatter, and R. de Bruin (Eds.) Road User Behaviour: Theory And Research, van Gorcum, Assen/Maastricht, the Netherlands.

[3] Tenkink, E. (1991). The Effect of Lead Vehicles on Speed Choice under Restricted Sight Distances. In: A. Gale, et al. (Eds.) Vision In Vehicles Iii, Elsevier Science Publishers B.V., North-Holland.

[4] Harms, L. (1991). The Influence of Sight Distance on Subjects' Lateral Control - A Study of Simulated Fog. VTIsärtryck 173, Swedish Road and Traffic Research Institute, Linkoping, Sweden.

[5] Sumner, R., Baguley, C., and Burton, J. (1977). Driving in Fog on the M4. Supplementary Report No. 281, TRL, Crowthorne, Berkshire.

[6] Nordmark, S. (1990). The VTI Driving Simulator - Trends and Experiences. Proceedings of Road Safety and Traffic Environment in Europe, Gothenburg, Sweden, September 26-28.

[7] Nilsson, L. (1989). The VTI Driving Simulator - Description of a Research Tool. DRIVE Project V1017 (BERTIE), Report No. 24 (VTIsärtryck 150).

[8] Hart, S.G., and Stave land, L.E. (1988). Development of NASA-TLX (Task Load Index): Results of Empirical and Theoretical Research. Ref in P.A. Hancock, and N. Meshkati (Eds.) Human Mental Workload, Elsevier Science Publishers B.V., North-Holland.

Night-Time Gap Acceptance and Time-To-Coincidence Judgements Based on Visible Wavelength and Infra-Red Imaging

Nicholas J. Ward, Leonard Stapleton, and Andrew M. Parkes

HUSAT Research Institute, Loughborough University of Technology, The Elms, Elms Grove, LOUGHBOROUGH, Leics LE11 1RG, United Kingdom.

Abstract

A gender and age balanced sample of subjects viewed video footage which necessitated the judgement of the acceptability of gaps between two obstacles, as well as time-to-coincidence (TTC) estimates in relation to a stationary vehicle. Approach time was held constant while approach speed, gap size, and period of occlusion (for TTC) were systematically varied. Judgement accuracy was compared for footage obtained with a visible wavelength camera in darkness with the images from an infra-red thermal camera. Results indicated that approach speed, gap size, period of occlusion, and type of image affected judgement accuracy.

1.0 INTRODUCTION

There are a number of European and North American based research ventures dedicated to the enhancement of traffic safety, comfort, and efficiency. These goals are to be achieved through the research, development, and introduction of new and advanced technological systems into motor vehicles and transportation networks.

One such application is denoted *Vision Enhancement.* It is the intent of this application to enhance the visibility of the forward driving scene under conditions of restricted visibility (e.g., night-time, fog) so that the motorist is better able to detect and identify hazards affecting safety. As an example, infra-red sensors can be applied to direct enhanced collimated images to the motorist through a head-up display mounted in line with the forward line of sight. The question arises, however, as to whether these infra-red images - independent of the presentation medium - do convey their intended advantage.

Night-time driving is the most commonly experienced condition of impaired visibility. The most advanced and accessible technology for enhanced night-time viewing is infra-red thermal cameras. These cameras can be selected to record images in either black-hot mode (with relatively 'hotter' elements appearing darker in the scene) or white-hot mode (with relatively 'hotter' elements appearing lighter in the scene). The present study was undertaken to determine the basic effect of thermal enhanced imaging upon a number of visual tasks related to the focal vision mode within a driving context. This demonstration compared task performance using visible wavelength images of driving scenes with performance using currently available (and accessible) state-of-the-art (far) infra-red thermal imaging.

2.0 METHOD

2.1 Subjects

Sixteen subjects were recruited through advertisement for paid participation (mean age :41 years, range: 20 to 70 years). An even number of male (8) and female (8) subjects were recruited. These numbers included eight young subjects under 25 and eight older subjects over 55, balanced across subject sex. A seventeenth subject (female, under 25) was also included with data only for the gap acceptance task.

2.2 Viewing simulator

Subjects were seated in the driver seat of a test vehicle. The vehicle was parked facing a projection screen (4.95 m diagonal) inside a black-lined cubicle. Heavy black curtains covered the cubicle opening and covered the vehicle to darken the space and simulate night-time conditions.

The positioning of the vehicle in front of the screen facilitated a 25.5° vertical by 38.2° horizontal viewing angle consistent with the field of view of the lens used to record the video image. Subjects remained inside the darkened vehicle for the duration of the study session to maintain dark adaptation levels.

2.3 Video imaging

Subjects viewed two types of night-time driving scenario footage projected onto the screen by an overhead multiscan projector. These scenarios were simultaneously recorded during vehicle manoeuvres on a test track by a visible light video camera (COHU) and a far infra-red thermal camera operating between 8 and 13 microns (Barr and Straud IR-18). The cameras were parallel and adjacent to each other mounted above the eye position at the driver seat of the test vehicle. The thermal infra-red footage was recorded in white-hot or black-hot modes, each with its own matched visible wavelength footage.

2.4 Driving scenarios and subject tasks

Two driving scenarios were derived which could be easily orchestrated for video recording. These examples of driving tasks relying on the focal mode of visual processing to acquire high fidelity information about specific identified objects within the set driving environment.

The first scenario was filmed with visible wavelength and black-hot thermal infra-red imaging. The first scenario involved an approach toward two dark blue foam obstacles (200 mm deep x 400 mm wide x 800 mm high) facing the vehicle and separated by a specified distance. The footage depicted approaches at 20 and 40 mph, with a constant temporal approach distance of approximately 20 seconds. Within each speed, the size of the gap was varied (+200 mm, +100 mm, 0 mm -100 mm, -200 mm) in reference to the width of the vehicle (1.75 m). Thus, the range of gaps meant that the vehicle could pass between the two obstacles in some cases, but not in others.

The task of subjects was to judge whether the vehicle in which they were seated (i.e., the same one used to obtain the footage) could fit between the gap defined by the two obstacles. They were instructed to press the brake pedal if they judged the gap to be too small, and the accelerator pedal if they judged the gap to be large enough. Subjects were directed to indicate their judgement as soon as they had reached a confident decision.

The second scenario was filmed with visible light and both black-hot and white-hot thermal infra-red imaging. The second scenario involved a pass-by approach to a stationary vehicle. The footage depicted approaches at 20, 30, and 40 mph, with a constant temporal approach distance of approximately 20 seconds. Within each speed, the view was occluded (by a full black screen) 1, 2, or 3 seconds preceding the instant of coincidence between the rear bumper to the stationary car and the front bumper of the approaching vehicle. There were two trials of each episode.

The task of subjects was to judge the instant of coincidence (with an occluded view). They were instructed to press the brake pedal at the instant of judged coincidence.

Each episode clip for both scenarios was preceded by a numeric display of a 5 second countdown on a blackout screen and concluded with a blackout screen after the obstacle(s) were passed. A single randomised ordering of clips within each task was prepared for presentation to subjects. Subjects first completed the gap acceptance task, and after a short rest break, then completed the TTC task.

The scenarios used the brake and accelerator pedals to transmit subject responses. The brake pedal and accelerator linkage were linked by switches to a PC-computer which read and recorded the time-stamp of the current video frame. The video operated at a frame rate of 25 frames per second, allowing a resolution to 40 msec per frame. Reaction time values were calculated by comparing these recorded time values with those known to correspond to the actual events in the footage.

3. RESULTS

The results of the analyses for the gap acceptance and time-to-coincidence tasks will be presented separately. Due to missing data resulting from equipment faults, the all within subject design meant that not all subjects were included in every measure analysis. The reported mean values for conditions should be taken as comparative values rather than absolute indicators given the sources of unsystematic error accrued in the determination of event times from the video frame images.

3.1 Gap acceptance - correct decisions

The number of *correct* gap acceptances (+100 mm, +200 mm) and rejections (-100 mm, -200 mm) were summed for each subject across approach speed. The 0 mm gap was not considered as an accepted or rejected gap because of its intermediate value. The total correct decisions were analysed within a 2 (DECISION: accept/reject) x 2 (IMAGE: visible/infra-red) design (ANOVA).

Neither the main effect for IMAGE [$\underline{F}(1,16) = 1.74$, ns.] nor DECISION [$\underline{F}(1,16) = 2.06$, ns.] were significant. However, the interaction between IMAGE and DECISION illustrated in Figure 1 was statistically significant [$\underline{F}(1,16) = 10.40$, $\underline{p} < .01$]. Compared with the visible wavelength images, the infra-red (black-hot) images promoted a greater number of correct decisions for gap rejections, but fewer for correct gap acceptances.

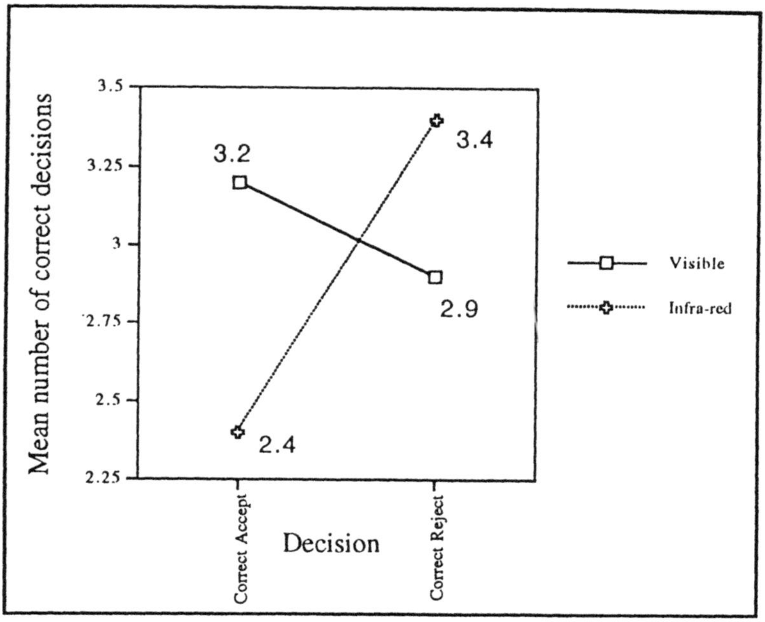

Figure 1: Mean number of correct decisions for visible wavelength and thermal (black-hot) images.

There was an interaction between AGE group and IMAGE [$F(1,15) = 4.53$, $p < .05$): whereas both age groups evidenced comparable performance with the visible wavelength images, the performance of the older group (> 55 years) was worse with the infra-red images.

3.2 Gap acceptance - decision response times

The response time for each *correct* decision was converted to the time preceding the moment of contact with the gap plane (excluding 0 mm gap). In order to maximise the sample size within the repeated measure analyses, response times were averages across the approach speed and gap size categories. The resultant times were analysed with a 2 (IMAGE: visible wavelength/infra-red) x 2 (DECISION: correct accept/correct reject) design.

There was a significant main effect for IMAGE [$F(1,13) = 36.48$, $p < .0001$]. Correct decisions were made sooner with the infra-red camera (mean = 5.2 seconds) than with the visible camera (mean = 1.91 seconds). There was a marginally significant interaction between subject SEX and DECISION [$F(1,12) = 4.47$, $p < .06$]: Whereas both genders evidence comparable performance with the visible wavelength images, males responded considerably sooner with the infra-red images.

When decision times were re-calculated within each GAP size category (excluding 0 mm gap), GAP size and IMAGE type interacted significantly [$F(3,26) = 5.98$, $p < .01$].

As shown in Figure 2, the superiority of the infra-red image was most predominant at the extreme gap sizes (±200 mm).

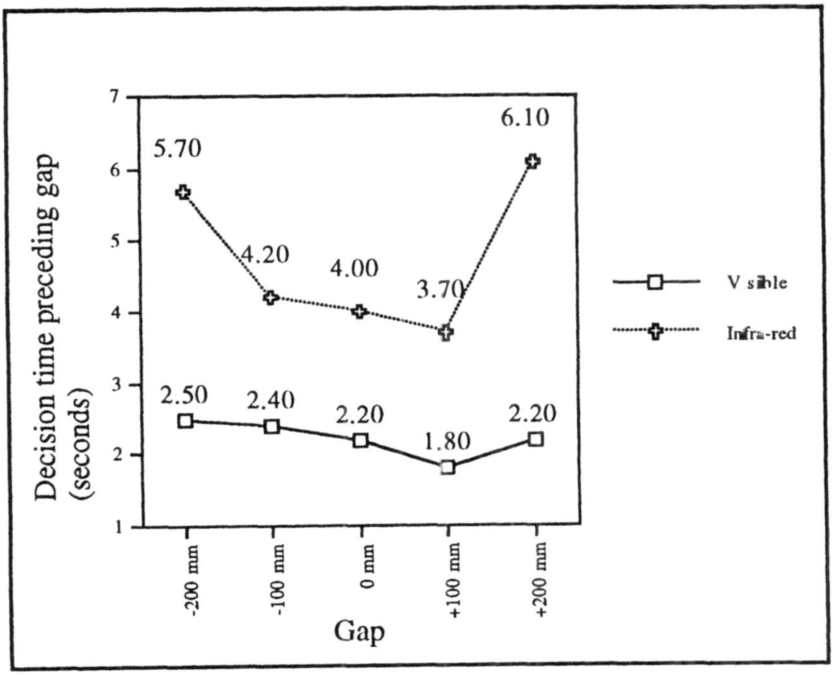

Figure 2: Correct decision times preceding gap in relation to gap size and image type.

3.3 Time-to-coincidence judgements

Each TTC judgement time was converted to reflect the time preceding the actual moment of coincidence with the plane of the rear bumper of the stationary target vehicle (i.e., underestimation error). These times were analysed within a 4 (IMAGE: black-hot infra-red/matched visible for black-hot/ white-hot infra-red/ matched visible for white hot) x 3 (SPEED: 20 mph/ 30 mph/ 40 mph) x 3 (occlusion; 1s/ 2s/ 3s) x 2 (TRIAL: 1st trial, 2nd trial) design (ANOVA).

The main effect for IMAGE was significant [$F(3,42) = 7.81$, $p < .0001$]. Subjects were comparably accurate for the black-hot setting (mean = .81 seconds) and the visible matched scenes (mean error = .87 seconds), but were less accurate for the white-hot setting (mean error = 1.08 seconds) than for the visible matched scenes (mean error = .89 seconds). The main effect for SPEED was significant [$F(2,28) = 7.81$, $p < .0001$]. Judgements were more accurate at higher speeds [mean (20 mph) = 1.09 seconds; mean (30 mph) = .90 seconds; mean (40 mph) = .76 seconds]. The main effect for OCCLUSION was also significant [$F(2,28) = 75.19$, $p < .0001$]. Judgements were more accurate for shorter occlusion periods [mean (1 second) = .50 seconds; mean (2 second) = .85 seconds; mean (3 second) = 1.39 seconds].

The only significant two-factor interaction was between IMAGE and OCCLUSION [$F(6,84) = 2.70$, $p < .01$]. As depicted in Figure 3, judgements became consistently less accurate for all image types as occlusion times increased. However, whereas the TTC underestimation error for the two visible scenes and the black-hot scenes converged at the longest occlusion period, the white-hot scenes consistently incurred greater inaccuracies throughout all occlusion periods.

TRIAL did not interact with any of these reported effects.

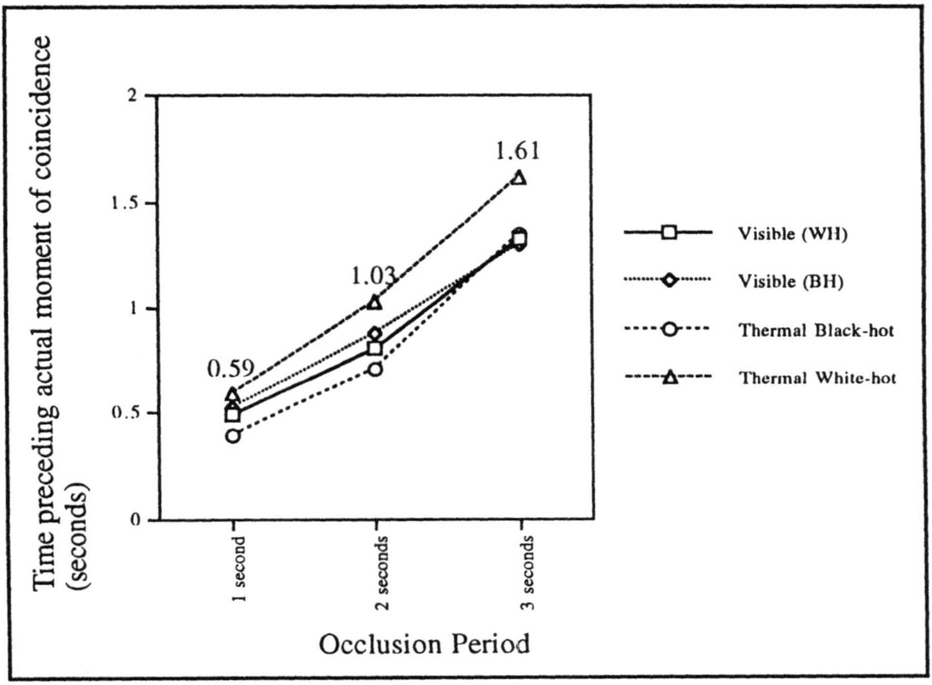

Figure 3: Judged moment of coincidence preceding actual moment of coincidence in relation to image type and occlusion period. [Note: Visible (WH) and Visible (BH) refer to the matched visible wavelength footage for the Thermal White-hot and Black-hot images, respectively]

4.0 DISCUSSION

There are a number of pertinent findings from this study that will be summarised.

4.1 Gap acceptance

1) Thermal imaging (black-hot) produced more correct rejections of gaps too small for safe passage, but fewer correct acceptances of sufficiently wide gaps.

2) Thermal imaging (black-hot) resulted in earlier correct decisions, particularly with gaps of greatest magnitude. The obstacles were, in fact, seen sooner upon approach with the 'enhanced' thermal images in comparison to the point at which the the obstacles entered the headlight beams within the visible wavelength images. To account for this, future studies could hold the preview time of obstacles constant by requesting responses at a point at which the obstacles were in view for both image types for equal periods. This procedure would address the issue of image quality enhancement apart from the precedence of relative viewing time.

4.2 Time-to-coincidence (TTC)

3) Subjects were generally premature with judgements of time-to-coincidence; that is, TTC was typically underestimated. This finding is consistent with earlier findings reported by Cavallo and Laurent (1986), Groeger and Brown (1988), Groeger and Cavallo (1991), Groeger, Grande, and Brown (1991), and McLeod and Ross (1983).
4) TTC judgements were also progressively more premature (i.e., less accurate) for longer occlusion periods (Groeger et al., 1991).
5) TTC judgements were more accurate (i.e., judged TTC shifted toward the actual TTC) at higher approach speeds (Cavallo & Laurent, 1988; Groeger & Brown, 1988; McLeod & Ross, 1983).
6) Whereas the black-hot imaging mode of the thermal camera and the visible wavelength camera produced similar TTC judgements (particularly as occlusion times increased), the white-hot imaging mode consistently resulted in substantially larger underestimation of TTC.

Although correct decisions were reached sooner with the 'enchanced' thermal image. Rather, differences in the type of error committed differentiated the two image types. Thermal image presentation resulted in a greater number of correct rejections but fewer correct acceptances (i.e., more incorrect rejections) than presentation as visible wavelength images.

This pattern of results suggests that the thermal image presentation resulted in a shift in decision criteria (b) towards greater conservativeness in the determination of gap acceptability . Indeed, although there were too few instances of each stimulus to permit a meaningful analyses of signal detection parameters using individual subjects as the unit of analysis, comparisons on grouped data indicate that judgements based on infra-red images operated with a decision criterion (b = 1.74) more than twice as conservative as for visible wavelength images (b = 0.87) . There was comparatively little difference in terms of sensitivity between thermal imaging (d' = 1.3) and visible wavelength imaging (d' = 1.4). Thus, thermal infra-red imaging appeared to affect the decision making criteria more than the perceptibility of gap width per se.

Interestingly , thermal imaging, while not improving stimulus sensitivity, resulted in a larger safety margin because of the greater conservativeness at no expense in terms of decision deliberation time. In this case, the thermal images facilitated judgements 2 to 3 times sooner than visible wavelength images. Although an artefact of the distinction in image quality, this temporal precedence is a direct safety advantage given that greater temporal latitude is provided in which to identify obstacles, and decide upon and complete an appropriate course of action.

It may be that the conservative shift in decision making is attributable to the novelty of the thermal image. If so, it is foreseeable that repeated exposure to thermal imaging would result in familiarity with its unique perceptual quality, and hence, lead to a return shift to more moderate decision criteria. This possibility further demonstrates the need for long-term field analyses of automotive vision enhancement systems which present unfamiliar image formats.

Evidence that thermal infra-red images are beneficial for TTC judgements with occlusion was not apparent. If any effect could be attributed to the 'enhanced' imaging, it appears to be that TTC judgements based on thermal imaging in white-hot mode again lead to more conservative responding. In the case of TTC judgements, it would seem to be quite a conundrum whether such conservative responses can be framed as "safer" in terms of perceptiveness despite quantifiable less accuracy in relation to the actual moment of coincidence.

5.0 CONCLUSION

It was apparent from this study that the effect of visible wavelength and infra-red imaging are not equivalent; that is, the types of information conveyed by the two types of imaging are not synonymous. Thus, in terms of technological implementation, it is not a straightforward issue of whether one image type is superior to another. Rather, it is the case that the image types are different - not only in terms of how they are perceived and the information they convey, but also in their impact upon decision-making and concluded responses. It is apparent, therefore, that researchers and designers must be cautious in inferring the relative merits of either type of image within any given application domain.

REFERENCES

Cavallo, V. and Laurent, M. (1988) Visual Information and skill level in time-to-collision estimation, Perception, 17, pp 623 - 632.

Groeger, J.A. and Brown, I.D. (1988) Motion perception is not direct with indirect viewing systems. In A.G. Gale et al. (Eds.) Vision in Vehicles II, Elsevier Science Pubs B. V., North Holland.

Groeger, J. A. and Cavallo, V. (1991) Judgements of time-to-collision and time-to-coincidence. In A.G. Gale et al (Eds.) Vision in vehicles III, Elsevier Science Pubs B. V., North Holland.

Groeger, J. A., Grande, G., and Brown, I. D. (1991) Accuracy and safety: Effects of different training procedures on a time-to-coincidence task. In A.G. Gale et al (Eds.) Vision in vehicles III, Elsevier Science Pubs B. V., North Holland.

McLeod, R. W., and Ross, H. E. (1983) Optic flow and cognitive factors in time-to-collision estimates, Perception, 12, pp 417 - 423.

VISION IN VEHICLES - V
A.G. Gale et al. (Editors)

An Examination Of The Influences Of Vehicle Design For Adverse Weather Condition Operation On Driver Behaviour

M Fowkes and H S Storey

Motor Industry Research Association, Watling Street, Nuneaton, Warwickshire, CV10 OTU England

Abstract
The design of a road vehicle, and its various systems, should enable the driver to control that vehicle safely in a wide range of traffic environments. For example adverse weather conditions can directly affect external driver vision and various systems are commonly provided on vehicles to counteract the effects of these conditions. The design of these windscreen clearance systems are influenced by national and international legislation. These legal requirements define specific engineering standards that systems have to meet before the vehicle can be offered for sale. This paper describes how these systems are controlled by describing the current international standards and development methods used and typical practical results achieved. Issues related to the subsequent characteristics of these systems and their possible influence on driver behaviour are discussed.

1. INTRODUCTION

Modern road vehicles have to operate under a wide range of environmental conditions. Therefore the automotive industry designs its products to maintain function within a wide but defined environmental envelope. Typically vehicles are developed to operate within a target temperature range of -40 to +80 degrees centigrade in association with other specified environmental conditions such as icing, humidity and/or rainfall.

These environmental conditions can have a direct effect upon the drivers field of view by obscuring the view through the vehicles windows by icing, rainfall, contamination and/or misting. All vehicles therefore have some means of clearing the effects of this obscuration generally by a combination of mechanical wipers and some means of applying localised heating or ventilation to the vehicle glazing. In order that some minimum level of performance is available on vehicles various legal standards exist that specify both standardised evaluation methodology and performance requirements. Vehicle manufacturers have then to ensure that their designs comply with this requirement. An overview of the vehicle standards relating to driver vision has already been given (Fowkes 1985). This current paper seeks to describe in more detail how the requirements applicable to windscreen clearance systems are applied in vehicle systems development.

2. LEGISLATIVE STANDARDS

Within the European Community passenger car design is effectively controlled by a series of EEC directives operating under a vehicle type approval system. The capabilities of the vehicle in giving the driver clear and adequate vision in adverse weather conditions is contained in two of these directives. These are :-
78/317/EEC Motor Vehicles - Defrosting and Demisting Systems, and
78/318/EEC Motor Vehicles - Windscreen Wiper/Washer Systems
These directives outline the practical test procedures and minimum performance requirements of the vehicle in these two specific respects. In both cases the directives utilise the concept of specifying areas of the windscreen in front of the driving position as vision "zones" that, in subsequent environmental testing, must be cleared of any obscuring contamination.

2.1 Determination of Vision Areas

The vision areas specified in EEC Directives are zones of the vehicle windscreen that are defined by their geometrical relationship with other landmarks within the vehicle structure. This geometrical definition applies to a number of planes projected at specified angles and orientation from locations termed V-points. These points are themselves referred to the drivers seat of the vehicle and can be considered to represent the location of the driver's eyes. Several alternative methods exist for practically determining the position of these vision points and the vision areas. However the method adopted at the Motor Industry Research Association is based upon the installation of a three-dimensional manikin into the driver's seat of the vehicle under test. This enables the practical determination of the location of the seating reference position of the drivers seat (R-point) from which the V-points may be subsequently referenced. There are two V-points defined in the directives, both located above and slightly outboard of the driver's seat centre-line. In a typical driving seat having a back-angle of 25 degrees these points are located relative to the three co-ordinate axes relevant to the vehicle and the R-point as shown in Figure 1.

V Point	X-axis	Y-axis	Z-axis
V1	68mm	-5mm	665mm
V2	68mm	-5mm	589mm

The exact location of the V-points in a practical test is calculated by reference to a table of correction factors that modify the quoted V-point locations above dependant upon the actual seat back angle for that particular vehicle. These corrections effectively move the V-points further back and lower in respect of the windscreen with seat back angles of more than 25 degrees rake, and the converse for more upright seating positions. A light projection system is then installed within the vehicle with the light sources placed in the location of the V-points. This system projects a controlled geometric pattern of light onto the windscreen of the vehicle whose boundaries comply with the technical requirements of the directive. Figure 1 below illustrates these boundaries for Vision Areas A and B.

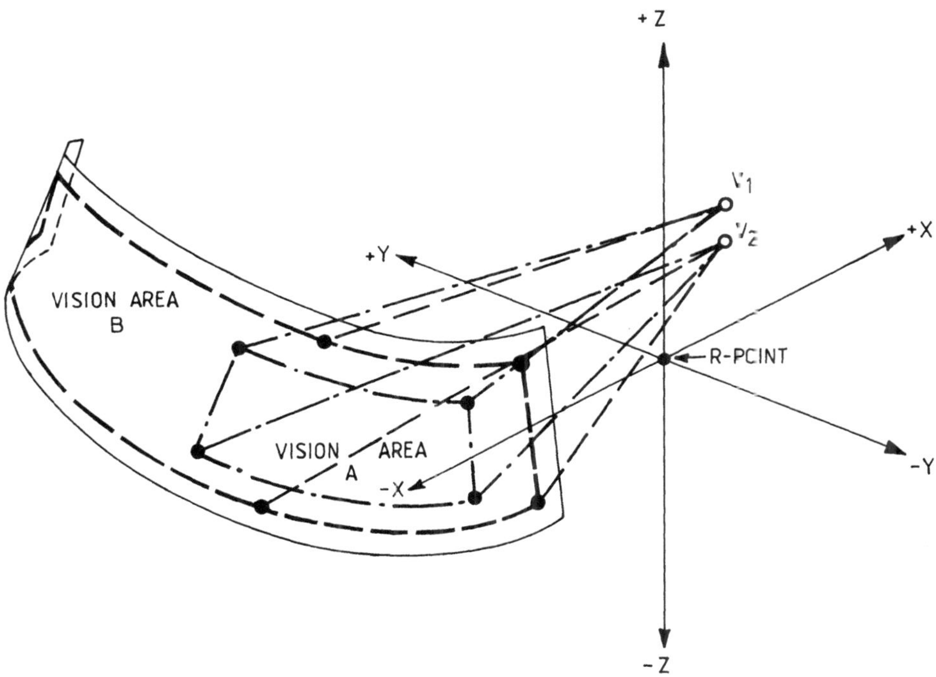

Figure 1 : The projection of Vision Areas A & B from V-points

In practical trials a translucent overlay is then placed over the external surface of the windscreen and the location of the vision zones relative to entire glazed area can be marked. This overlay is then used in the subsequent assessment of the performance, ie areas cleared, of the windscreen clearance system.

2.2 Performance Requirements for Defrosting and Demisting Systems

To satisfy the windscreen defrosting and demisting aspects of the EEC Directive 78/317 the following conditions must be met under specific environmental conditions:-

After 20 minutes 80% of the vision area A must be *defrosted.*

After 25 minutes a comparable area to vision area A on the passenger side should also be 80% *defrosted.*

After 40 minutes 95% of vision area B must be *defrosted.*

After 10 minutes 90% of area A and 80% of area B should be *demisted.*

2.3 Practical evaluation of Defrosting and Demisting Systems

In the case of the defrost test the test vehicle windscreen is cleaned and then placed in a climatic chamber and soaked for a minimum of 10 hours at the chosen test temperature. This temperature is selected by the vehicle manufacturer from either -8 +/- 2 degrees centigrade or -

18 +/- 3 degrees centigrade. The external surface of the glass is then sprayed with a water gun to achieve a uniform layer of ice. The supply of water is regulated to attain an ice density of 0.044 grammes per square centimetre over the windscreen. The defrosting test can then commence with either one or two observers entering the vehicle and starting the engine.

The defrosting system is then activated in an attempt to clear the ice layer. The observers inside the vehicle mark the boundary of the defrosted pattern of the screen every 5 minutes up to a maximum period of 40 minutes. The areas cleared, relative to the vision zones are then assessed after the test period by transferring the outline of the defrosted boundaries to the translucent overlay.

For demisting performance assessment the inside surface of the vehicle windscreen is again thoroughly cleaned and the vehicle placed in a climatic chamber maintained at a temperature of -3 +/- 1 degrees centigrade. A steam generator is placed in the vehicle and adjusted to give an output equivalent to 70 +/- 5 grammes per hour of steam for each seating position in the vehicle. After 5 minutes one or two observers enter the vehicle and the output of the steam generator is reduced accordingly. The engine is then started and the demisting system operated. After 10 minutes the boundary of the demisted zone is marked on the windscreen and subsequently compared with the previously plotted vision zones on the translucent overlay.

2.4 Performance Requirements for Wiping and Washing Systems

To satisfy the windscreen wiping and washing aspects of EEC Directive 78/318 the following conditions must be met:-

> The *wiped area* of the screen must cover at least 98% of vision area A and 80% of vision area B.
>
> The *washer system* must be capable of delivering enough liquid to clear 60% of vision area A.

A secondary requirement for the wiping system is that the system must have at least 2 sweep frequencies for compliance with this standard. One of not less than 45 cycles/minute and one of either not less than 10 or not more than 55 cycles/minute. In addition, this directive also specifies a number of thermal durability cycling performance requirements on the components of the wipe/wash systems. These test for leakage and actuator efforts as well as thermal stability. However as these do not directly have consequences on the visual performance of the system they are not detailed here.

2.5 Practical evaluation of Wiping and Washing systems

The practical evaluation of the efficacy of the wiping and washing system is considerably more complex that that for defrosting and demisting. It has been noted that several component level tests are also required however the whole system is evaluated fitted to the vehicle when a defined test contaminant is applied to the external surface of the glass and allowed to dry. This contaminant mixture is an aqueous solution of salt and a complex test dust mixture having defined particle size distribution. After drying the wiper/washer system operated in an attempt to clear the windscreen to the required visual efficiency.

This clearance test is carried out statically. A road or track test of wiper effectiveness is also carried out at a speed equal to 80% of the vehicles maximum speed (but not exceeding 160 kph) to assess the efficiency of the system under the influence of aerodynamic forces.

3. ADDITIONAL VEHICLE CLEARANCE CAPABILITIES

Vehicle manufacturers therefore have to engineer systems exceeding these performance levels to comply with current EEC vehicle construction directives which may be considered to be the minimum acceptable safety standards in a consumer product. However these requirements only apply to direct forward vision through the windscreen under specified environmental conditions. There are no current legal requirements for side or rear window clearance systems but manufacturers routinely supply such systems on current vehicles. How then are these additional systems and capabilities specified, developed and assessed?

Test methods based on those described in the EEC directives above, and others such as ISO standards, are utilised by manufacturers to assess the ultimate performance and quality of the additional systems provided. However there is considerable variation in the practices adopted by different manufacturers in this area reflecting perhaps different perceptions of the importance of this aspect of vehicle design.

In general terms side screen clearance assessments utilise similar practical test procedures, applying icing layers (external) or condensation (internal). Clearance over specified time and external environmental conditions follows those used for forward vision. There is little common practice in specifying vision areas for vehicle side screens, however overall area clearance over time and the time-to-clear for areas adjacent to external rear view mirror are basic indicators that can be used. Rear screen clearance of both defrost/demist and wash/wipe again follow closely that for front windscreen test environments and assessment methods. Similar contaminants and surface application methods are used but once more overall indices are commonly of percentages of the overall screen area rather than targeted evaluation of specified vision areas.

Recent trends in the assessment of both front, side and rear screen clearance systems revolve around two principal areas. Firstly at a practical level more sophisticated laboratory tests are being developed to evaluate the detailed performance of all components and systems under investigation. For defrost/demist systems this can mean widening the scope of the environmental conditions under investigation, ie by introducing repeat testing at lower and intermediate temperatures to those specified in EEC directives. In this case a closer examination of the characteristics of flow through the vents and heater matrix up to and beyond the fascia/door vents onto the glazing can be carried out.

This level of detail also facilitates a second area of methodological change where predictive modelling of the thermal performance of vehicle systems is now possible. These computational fluid dynamics (CFD) techniques and models can also be utilised to assess the effects of a wider variety of external factors on the efficiency of windscreen clearance systems. For example this can apply to windscreen wiping performance where the effects of interactions of airflow over the external surface of the vehicle, and wipers, can be modelled. These extended investigations in the vehicle development cycle are attempts to develop systems of higher quality which will commonly involve the use of subjective ratings evaluations as part of controlled laboratory and/or road development tests. Frequently the target performance for the systems are set by a prior assessment of competitor vehicles to provide a class benchmark that must be met or exceeded.

4. PRACTICAL TEST RESULTS

Practical development programmes on the driver vision attributes of new passenger cars are regularly carried out at MIRA. The detailed engineering of the defrost/demist systems and the wiper/washers varies between vehicles and specific comparisons in characteristics are therefore difficult. However some similar general characteristics exist for the results obtained from vehicles that employ similar design philosophies for windscreen clearance systems. The commonly adopted design philosophy for *defrost/demist* systems utilises a forced heated airflow directed at the windscreen from vents at the base of the screen. The characteristic pattern of screen clearance is therefore "bottom-up", ie the base of the screen is cleared first. This is illustrated by some typical anonymised results shown below for demist performance of both front windscreen (figure 2) and side glass (figure 3) as examples. These show the boundaries of the defrosted areas of the glass relative to time in minutes from the start of test. It should be noted that these results represent defrosting tests carried out at -18 degrees centigrade having icing layers applied as described in the appropriate EEC directive.

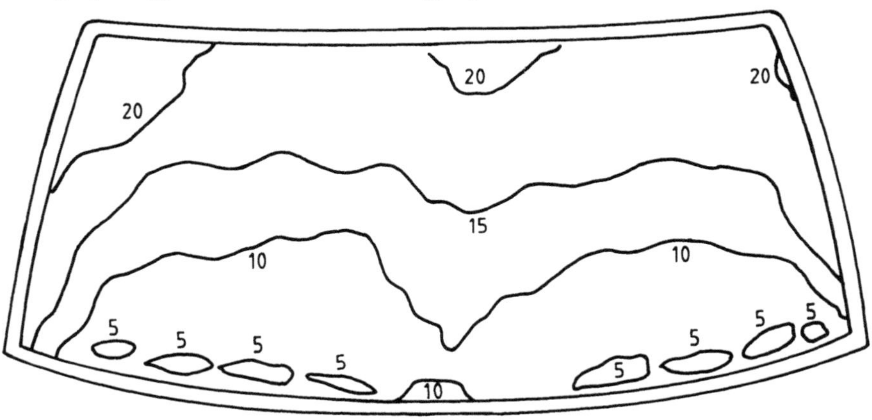

Fig 2 : Typical Results of Passenger Car Windscreen Defrost Test

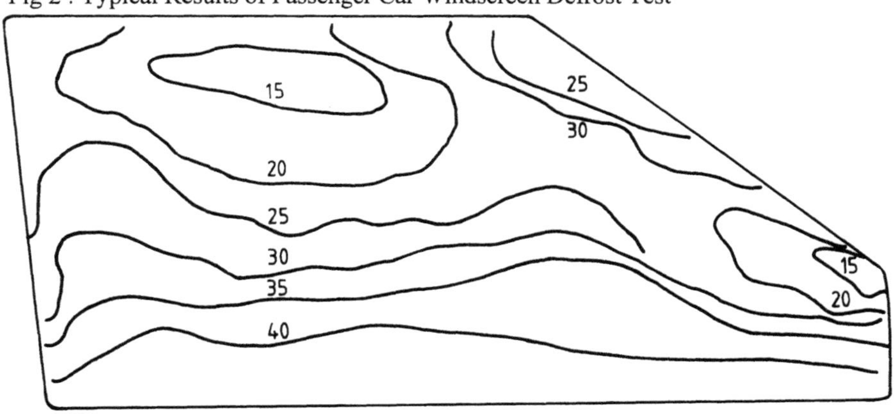

Fig 3 : Typical Results of Passenger Car Side Screen Defrost Test

5. DISCUSSION

Legal requirements and extended product development testing therefore ensure that vehicles are provided with tested and approved vehicle glazing clearance systems. Results from practical testing of a sample of current production cars carried out to EEC and manufacturers own standards have been re-assessed and are described below. There are also some combinations of real world environments, not covered by current development regimes, that can still produce driver visibility problems. Examples of these conditions and their effects on windscreen clearance systems are also outlined below.

The typical windscreen *defrosting* performance for a modern passenger comfortably exceeds the minimum legal requirements. Clearance of 100% of central vision area A is achieved within the 20 minutes test period maximum. However the 80% "minimum level" is commonly only achieved after 13-17 minutes from a cold start at -18 degrees centigrade.

The typical *demisting* performance also exceeds those legally required targets by a considerable margin, clearing screens completely in under 5 minutes from a cold start at -3 degrees centigrade.

Therefore there is some considerable time delay in *defrosting* a central vision area of the windscreen without additional intervention by the driver under low temperature conditions. Similar clearance characteristics obviously occur at more moderate icing temperatures where screens are cleared faster but where central forward vision areas are still only cleared after the systems have been in operation for some time, eg 4-9 minutes at -8 centigrade. However these are results gained in laboratory conditions. Real world environments also present additional loads to be cleared. Snow and thicker external screen icing layers can lengthen these screen clearance times markedly without any additional manual clearance of the screen by either manual scraping and/or the application of chemical solutions. Indeed the application of some commercial de-icing solutions can contribute to these problems by causing internal screen icing under certain conditions. It should not therefore be surprising to observe vehicles being driven with only partially cleared windscreens as weather conditions deteriorate in the winter months. Drivers therefore seem willing to trade-off restricted direct forward and peripheral vision against their desire to be on their journey. In contrast to defrosting however, *demisting* clearance is performed relatively quickly in the laboratory but under test conditions utilising chemically cleaned internal screen surfaces. Vehicles in real-world conditions are more likely to have some contamination of the screen as they age and encounter a range of environmental and usage conditions which can therefore compromise speed of demisting clearance.

As to *wiping and washing* capabilities these also necessarily exceed the legal minimum requirements. However the evaluation of the efficiency of the windscreen clearance system in dealing with more likely realistic environmental contaminating conditions is not commonly performed. Oil based contaminants common in road spray for example can cause localised distortions and streaking in the wiped field. The sweep frequencies offered by wiping systems allow accommodation to different levels of rainfall. However the effects of partially degraded vision by either streaking or intermittent obscuration in heavy rainfall on driver vision is unclear.

In summary the performance of current windscreen clearance systems appear to offer levels of performance that comply with legal minimum performances and exceed them but that still show some compromised performance when in "normal" operating conditions. Competitive market pressures are leading manufacturers to extend their evaluation and performance targeting beyond the legal standards. More complex evaluation tools such as CFD modelling enable the cost-effective evaluation of a greater range of conditions in vehicle development but systems still employ similar design philosophies and therefore performance characteristics lead by the necessity to comply with safety standards at the most basic level. Have these standards now become irrelevant? Should new standards be required that raise the required performance level and cover other vehicle glazing areas?

This could be a possible path for the future but several issues should be evaluated before such an action could be pursued. The needs of the driver would have to researched and specified in this respect in greater detail. Some research questions may be posed. Do drivers adopt their visual search patterns when restricted, distorted or partially obscured view of the road is given? Do such reductions in visual capabilities affect driving behaviour? What is the evidence for interpersonal variability in this respect? In addition there are questions surrounding how performance targets could be drawn up that would allow for the wide range of environmental conditions likely to be encountered and the costs of carrying out further extended testing in a vehicle development programme. Finally we would also have to consider the effectiveness of legislation in providing a structure for enhancing vehicle safety standards. Legislation provides a minimum level of performance perhaps but it also may be seen as inflexible and liable to influence and potentially constrain vehicle designers.

6. CONCLUSIONS

Vehicle manufacturers provide systems to clear the glazed surface of the vehicle under adverse weather conditions. Legal performance requirements are applied to front windscreen clearance systems only. Vehicle systems can provide performance that exceeds minimum legal requirements and is increasingly led by competitor performance targeting. However it is not clearly understood what drivers require both subjectively, in terms of speed and efficiency of operation, and objectively, in performance characteristics that complement drivers visual needs. Research activity in defining the required performance for future windscreen clearance systems is required in order to guide subsequent performance standards oriented towards drivers needs.

REFERENCES

1. M. Fowkes, The legislative determination of the drivers field of view, In A.G. Gale et al (Eds) Vision in Vehicles (1986), p305-312, Elsevier Science Publishers B.V.
2. Council of the European Communities Directive 78/317/EEC Defrosting and Demisting of glazed surfaces of motor vehicles.
3. Council of the European Communities Directive 78/318/EEC Wiper and Washer systems of motor vehicles.

VISION IN VEHICLES - V
A.G. Gale et al. (Editors)
1996 Elsevier Science B.V.

Influence of Distribution of Luminous Fluxes of Car Headlights on Night-time Signalling Visibility

Yannick Guillard[a], Genevieve Loos [a], Michele Colomb[b], and Victor Carta[b]

[a]Laboratoire Regional des Ponts et Chaussees, 11 rue Jean Mentelin, B.P. 9, 67035 Strasbourg Cedex, France

[b]Laboratoire Central des Ponts et Chaussees, 58 Boulevard Lefebvre, 75015 Paris. France

1. INTRODUCTION

In night-time traffic in zones that are not illuminated, the only light sources allowing obstacles and road signalling to be seen are the headlights of vehicles. Since most signalling devices are not themselves luminous, their luminance depends on the quantity of light that reaches them. The spatial and energy distribution of the luminous flux of the beams from vehicle headlights is therefore an important parameter both for the detection and legibility of road signalling devices (horizontal and vertical) and for the perception of various obstacles.

A measurement device based on the principle of the headlight tester associated with a CCD camera and image processing software was developed to perform the photometric survey of the luminous beam from the vehicle headlights. This device was used to investigate the influence of a number of parameters, such as the type of lamp, the adjustment of the headlights, and dirtiness, on:

- the spatial and energy distribution of the luminous flux;

- the predicted legibility and detection distances of vertical signalling;

- the detection distances of horizontal markings.

These last were calculated using the EVADIS software. This is a program for evaluation of the legibility and detection distances of road equipment that takes account of the interaction of three main factors:

- the driver, characterised by his position of observation and, more importantly, by his visual performance;

- the vehicle headlights with their photometric characteristics;

- and the equipment (signs, markings) characterised by their geometry of location on the road and their retroreflecting properties.

2. MEASUREMENT DEVICE AND METHODOLOGY

2.1. Measurement device

This consists of a headlight tester, an acquisition system (CCD camera), and an image processing system (digital card and microcomputer) [1].

2.2. The optical principle of the headlight tester

A convergent lens is used to produce, on a plane relatively close to the headlight, located at a distance d' that is less than the focal distance f, an image of the beam at a distance d (the distance d in question is generally 25 metres). We used a translucent screen to represent the true image of the headlight beam in order to avoid any angular deformation in information acquisition by the CCD camera.

2.3. Image acquisition and processing

These operations are performed by an assembly including:

- an IBM PC compatible microcomputer;

- a CCD camera with a type V (λ) filter and an objective having a notched diaphragm;

- a video image digitising card.

This card digitizes the image in 255 x 255 elementary points (or pixels). To each of these pixels is assigned a value directly proportional to the luminous intensity of the point in question.

The intensity ratio between the centre of the screen and its edges is relatively large, of the order of 1000. It is therefore necessary, given the small dynamic of the CCD camera, to perform two surveys with different diaphragm openings.

The two images are then combined into one and a file of the levels of luminous intensities is created. This file can be read directly by the EVADIS software for calculation of the road signalling legibility and detection distances, or processed in the form of intensity profiles, or represented as in figure 1.

3. THE EVADIS CALCULATION PROGRAM

The EVADIS calculation program is a research tool of the network of Laboratoires des Ponts et Chaussees having the object of evaluating the detection and legibility distances of night-time signalling [2].

The first objective of this program is to process the detection and reading of retroreflecting road signs and the detection of markings.

The night-time detection of road equipment results from interaction among three factors:

1) the driver, characterised by his position of observation and, more importantly, by his visual performance,

2) the vehicle headlights with their illumination characteristics,

3) the equipment, characterised by their geometry of location on the road and their photometric retroreflection characteristics.

The deterioration of one of these three elements with respect to a mean level (lights poorly adjusted, or sign dirty, or observer having defective vision) destroys the equilibrium and satisfactory conditions of visibility cease to exist.

Knowledge of the performances of drivers, entered in the form of models of visibility, serves to establish, for the situations studied, a contrast threshold Cs that governs the detection of an object and a luminance threshold Ls that governs the reading of a message on a sign at a given distance.

Knowledge of the geometrical and photometric characteristics of the vehicle headlights, of the signs or of the markings, and of their interactions, is used to calculate, for a given distance, the true luminance Lr and the true contrast Cr of the equipment being studied.

The maximum detection or legibility distance is determined by comparing the true value to the threshold value for each distance step. When the true contrast becomes less than or equal to the threshold contrast, the maximum detection distance is reached, and when the true luminance becomes less than or equal to the threshold luminance, the maximum legibility distance is reached.

4. INFLUENCE OF VARIOUS PARAMETERS

4.1. Study of different types of headlights

The measurements were made with a supply voltage of 12V. It should be recalled that the illumination varies with the 3rd power of the voltage.

There are currently four families of vehicle headlights based on different technologies:

- headlight with parabolic reflector equipped with type H4 lamp (yellow, white, or gold);
- headlight with discharge lamp and parabolic reflectors;
- headlight with reflector having complex surface;
- headlight with elliptical reflector.

In this study, different headlights belonging to these families were examined [3. 4]. The comparisons covered the 16 characteristic points generally used to qualify headlights, together with the levels of the maxima and of the means of the fluxes on the whole image.

It would seem tricky to classify headlights according to photometric performance, especially since the distributions of their low-beam intensities are different. In effect, see below the representation in isocandela curves of a headlight with a complex surface, compared to a conventional headlight. The cut off is clearly sharper in the case of the former, and the isocandela curves are more effloresced.

This first point is confirmed by the very low values in the glare direction of a vehicle travelling in the opposite direction. The luminous intensities in this direction reach about a hundred candelas, whereas for headlights of the 1st family, they are between 200 and 500 candelas.

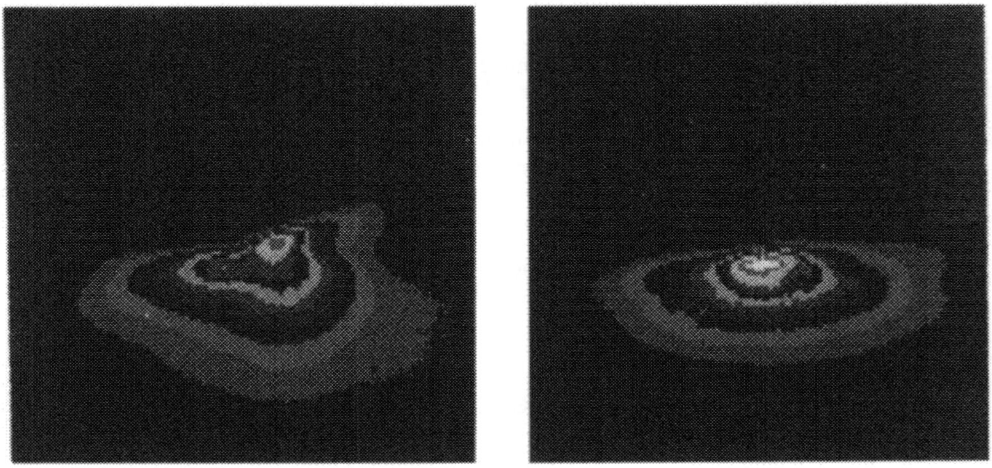

Figure 1. Comparison of intensity distributions of parabolic and complex-surface headlights with an H4 lamp. The scale for intensity is from 0 to 16.000 cd.

4.2. Calculation of legibility and detection distances

The legibility and detection distances of three roadside and overhead signs were calculated (table 1).

- sign 1 is located on the roadside at 2,30 m height, the text is composed of letters of 12.5 cm on a whole surface of 1 x 1 m^2;
- sign 2 is located on the roadside at 4 m height, the text is composed of letters of 20 cm on a whole surface of 1 x 1 m^2;
- sign 3 is located overhead at 6 m height, the text is composed of letters of 32 cm on a whole surface of 2 x 2 m^2.

The type of headlight (in new condition) has a relatively small influence on the legibility distance, the letter height influence is preponderant.

On the other hand, variations in detection distance are larger; the range is from 500 to 1200 m.

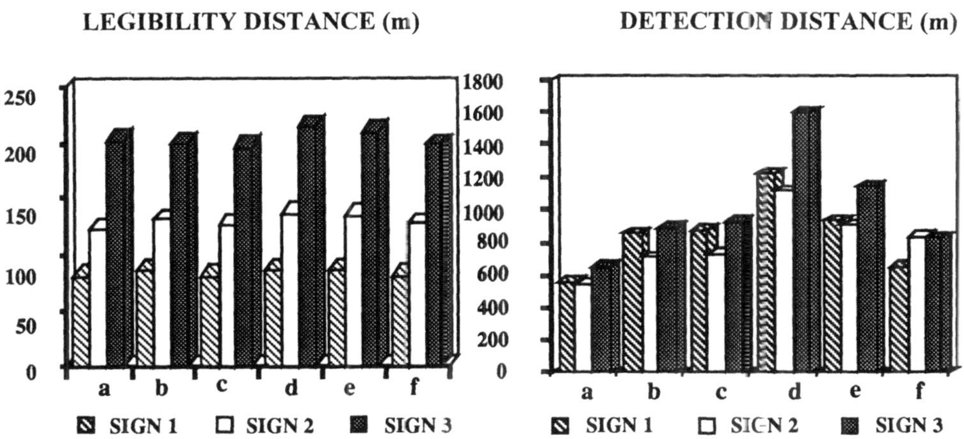

Table 1. Result of calculations of legibility and detection distances of signs with class II films, located on the roadside (signs 1 and 2) and overhead (sign 3) and illuminated by different headlights (a, complex surface yellow; b, complex surface white; c, elliptical; d, halogen; e, discharge; f, parabolic).

4.3. Influence of positioning of optical units

To study the influence of different positionings of the optical units, we examined a new parabolic reflector with a yellow H4 lamp, with the following adjustments:

- in the "normal" position, in other words with the low beam cut-off 1 % below the horizontal;
- with different height adjustments: at +2 %, +1 %, -1%, and -2 % from the normal position.

The influence of the positioning was examined starting from the predicted legibility and detection distances of the horizontal and vertical signalling.

The calculations were performed for different sign configurations and several types of marking, with low beams only.

It was found:

- that there is no significant variation of the legibility distances of the signs versus the height of the headlight;
- that the detection distances of vertical signalling can vary by about twenty percent;
- that the high position of the optical unit leads to a small increase of the detection distances of the markings (~ 4 %), while a low position rather substantially decreases these distances, especially if the retroreflection level of the lines is low (figure 2).

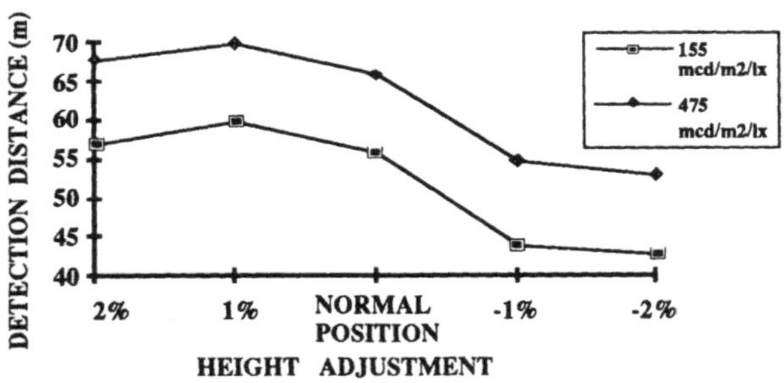

Figure 2. Examples of detection distances of two different markings illuminated by the parabolic headlight of a passenger car, in low beam mode

4.4. Influence of dirt on the optical unit

Given the great variety of vehicle headlights and the difficulty of obtaining different degrees of dirtiness for a given type, we approached this study by dirtying three headlights artificially, by spraying a suspension of clay. The position of the headlight studied in front of the measuring device was not modified during the tests and successive sprayings of water containing clay served to produce different levels of dirtiness. Following the photometric survey, we found that a given degree of dirtiness on the optical unit of a headlight does not have the same influence on the spatial and energy distributions of the beam in the low and high beam modes. In the high beam mode, the attenuation found is related to the intensity of the dirtiness, whereas in the low beam mode, in addition to a global attenuation, the distribution of luminous intensities is modified (figure 3). In this last case, for small dirtiness gradients, we sometimes observed very substantial increases of the luminous intensities in some directions.

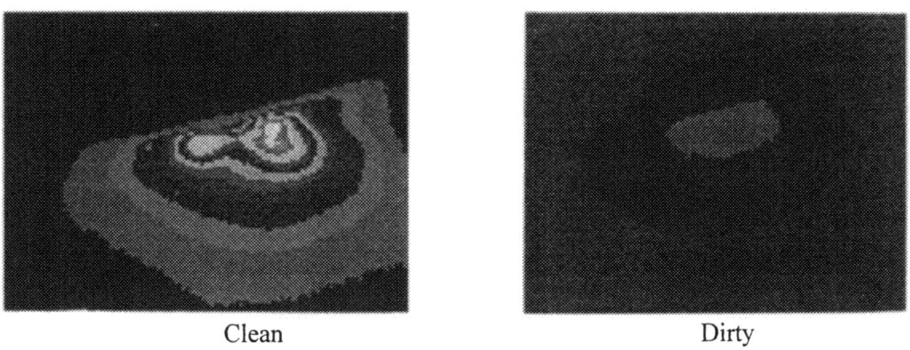

Figure 3. Spatial distribution of the luminous intensity from a headlight, in the clean and dirty conditions, in the low beam mode [Scale for intensity is from 0 to 3000 cd]

Concerning the legibility and detection distances of the vertical and horizontal signalling, we may make the following remarks:

Vertical signalling (figure 4)

- dirtiness clearly has a larger influence on the detection distances than on the legibility distances;

- substantial dirtiness rather strongly decreases the detection distances of the vertical signalling. The poorer the photometric performance of the retroreflecting films, the larger the variations seem: in a given configuration, these variations are larger for class I than for class II films.

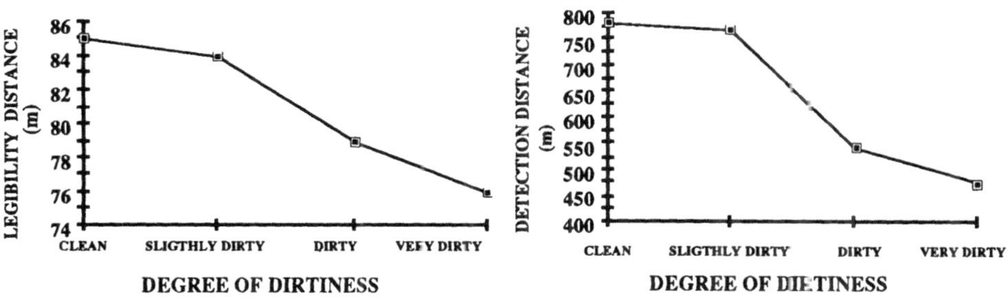

Figure 4. Example of legibility and detection distances of a sign with a class II film, illuminated by the parabolic headlight of a passenger car, in the low beam mode, for different levels of dirtiness.

Horizontal signalling (figure 5)

- for all dirtiness gradients and lighting modes (low or high beams), the lower the level of retroreflection, the larger the variations of the detection distances of marking lines;

- on the whole, for a given dirtiness and marking, the variations in relative value of the detection distances are greater with high than with low beams.

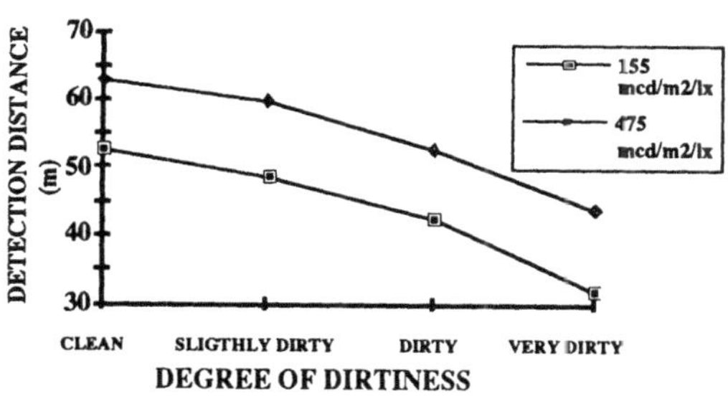

Figure 5. Example of detection distances of different markings illuminated by the parabolic headlight of a passenger car in the low beam mode

5. CONCLUSION

The measurement system used, in conjunction with the EVADIS software, makes it possible to compare headlights and the parameters of influence of the detection of nighttime signalling from the road user's viewpoint.

The effectiveness of the different families of headlights (parabolic, complex surface) with incandescent, halogen, or discharge lamps, was studied by calculation of the legibility and detection distances of several signs. The first remark is that there is no significant difference in legibility distances. On the other hand, depending on the headlight and the lamp, the detection distances may vary by a factor of two.

The position of the headlights has a truly significant influence, especially on the detection distances, but only when the position is low.

Dirt very clearly modifies the spatial distribution of luminous intensity together with its amplitude. The detection and legibility distances are substantially attenuated.

REFERENCES

1. Guillard Y. and Loos G.: Photometric survey of the luminous beam from vehicle headlights using a CCD camera, Report, LR of Strasbourg, April 1990.
2. Colomb M. and Guillard. Y.: Prediction of detection and legibility distances in road traffic at night: EVADIS program, Bulletin de Liaison des Ponts et Chaussees, no. 176, Nov./Dec. 1991, pp. 29-42.
3. Loos G. and Guillard. Y.: Vehicle headlights: various types of lamps, various positioning adjustments, degrees of dirtiness, Report, LR of Strasbourg, January 1992.
4. Guillard Y. and Loos G.: Study of various types of headlights, Report, LR of Strasbourg, January 1993.

7: DEALING WITH DRIVERS' VISUAL IMPAIRMENT

Visual Impairment and Driving

J. M. Wood[a] and R. J. Troutbeck[b]

[a]Centre for Eye Research, Queensland University of Technology, Brisbane 4001, Australia.

[b]Dept of Civil Engineering, Queensland University of Technology, Brisbane 4001, Australia.

Abstract

The effect of simulated visual impairment on the driving performance of 14 young and 10 old normal subjects was investigated. Visual impairment was induced using goggles to simulate the effects of cataracts, visual field restriction and monocular vision. Driving performance was assessed on a closed-road circuit free of other vehicles. Visual performance was assessed using Divided Attention Visual Fields (DAVF), Useful Field of View (UFOV) and the Pelli-Robson letter contrast sensitivity (CS) chart.

Visual impairment significantly reduced performance for all driving tasks ($p<0.05$). Cataracts resulted in the greatest decrease in driving followed by visual field restriction, even though all drivers satisfied the visual requirements for driving. Monocularity did not significantly affect performance for any of the driving tasks assessed. The reduction in driving performance was greater for the old subjects. Visual impairment significantly decreased the DAVF, UFOV and Pelli-Robson letter CS ($p<0.05$) A significant correlation between driving and DAVF, UFOV and Pelli-Robson letter CS was demonstrated ($p< 0.05$).

Ongoing studies of a large group of subjects with true visual impairment are being undertaken. Preliminary data supports our finding that visual impairment can reduce driving performance, even when the visual requirements for driving are satisfied.

1. INTRODUCTION

It has been estimated that vision comprises up to 90% of the sensory input for driving and this has led to the suggestion that visual impairment reduces driving performance. Most visual impairment arises subsequent to eye disease, whose prevalence increases significantly with age. Thus the problem of the visually impaired is likely to become a major concern in the future, as the driving population ages.

If visual criteria are used to determine driving eligibility, there should be strong evidence that those who fail to meet the given vision standard do have poorer driving performance leading to an unacceptably high risk of accidents. Although there is some evidence to support this there have also been a number of studies which have failed to show any direct relationship between vision and driving performance. For example, only weak correlations have been shown between accident rates and visual acuity, even when the sample was stratified for age (Hills and Burg 1977), and studies have found no relationship between visual fields and accident rates (Council and Allen 1974). Conversely, other studies have shown a strong relationship between accident rates and the extent of the binocular visual field (e.g. Johnson and Keltner 1983).

The inconsistencies in these findings are likely to arise in part from the variation in the methods employed in the studies, both for assessing driving performance and in the assessment of visual function. For example, Council and Allen (1974) in their study of the relationship between visual fields and accident rates used a relatively crude technique to assess the visual fields, taking account only of its temporal extent, whereas, Johnson and Keltner (1983), used a visual field testing instrument which has been shown to be more accurate and reliable. Similarly, the measures employed to assess driving performance vary widely between studies. With the exception of studies such as that of Wood and Troutbeck (1992), driving performance has been assessed by laboratory simulations or by self-reported or state registered accident rates. Laboratory simulations may bear little relationship to actual driving conditions and do not simulate the risks incurred in driving on road systems. Whilst, accident rates are only a partial index of driving ability as many accidents remain unreported, the correlation between self reported accident rates and state registered accidents is poor (Owsley et al 1991).

The aims of this study were to determine which types of visual impairment cause the greatest detriment to driving performance (measured on a driving course) and to identify those tests of visual function which can best predict driving performance. This was undertaken in two stages. In the first, the effect of simulated visual impairment on the driving and visual performance of young and old normal drivers was measured. In this way factors other than vision, known to have an influence on driving performance, such as experience and level of risk taking were constant for all visual conditions. In the second stage, driving and visual performance were measured for subjects with true visual impairment arising from cataracts and compared to that of an age-matched control group.

2. SUBJECTS

The subjects were divided into two groups: young and old normal subjects with simulated visual impairment and those with true visual impairment arising from cataracts and their age matched controls. The subjects with simulated visual impairment comprised 14 young (mean age 23.6 yrs; SD 4.5 yrs) and 10 old (mean age 64.5 yrs; SD 5.2 years) normal subjects. Visual impairment was induced using modified goggles to simulate the effects of cataracts, visual field restriction and monocular vision, and compared to a baseline condition, where subjects wore the goggles without any visual impairment in place. The subjects with true visual impairment comprised 18 old subjects with a range of early cataracts (mean age 68.6 years; SD 6.2 years) and 9 old subjects with normal vision (mean age 66.8 hyrax; SD 4.95 hyrax). All subjects had distance visual acuity of 6/12 or better and were holders of a current drivers license.

3. METHODS

3.1. Assessment of Driving Performance

Driving was assessed on a closed circuit driving course, which has been employed in previous studies of vision and driving (Wood and Troutbeck 1992). The nature of the visual impairments necessitated that, in the interests of safety, the circuit was free of other vehicles The circuit has been modified to permit the assessment of specific aspects of driving performance including:

Peripheral awareness - ability to detect and recognise standard road signs and people positioned at the road side
Manoeuvring - driving through a narrow line of cones (recorded as an error score for each cone touched or knocked over)
Reversing - reversing into a parking bay (scored by angle and centrality within the white lines delineating the parking bay)
Reaction time - in response to LEDs linked to the brake pedal and a control box operated by the examiner
Road positioning - assessed by video camera positioned in the rear of the vehicle and scored as a mean of values taken at 9 points on the course
Speed estimation - whilst the speedometer is occluded
Driving time - to complete the circuit (not including the manoeuvring and reversing tasks)
Driving score - calculated as the time taken to complete the course with a time penalty of 5 s for each error on the peripheral awareness task.

The test car was instrumented to record its location and assess various aspects of driving performance and contained video cameras for recording the road position of the car. The car also had two LEDs mounted on the windscreen to provide the stimuli for the reaction time task. These were linked to the brake pedal so an accurate measure of the time between the onset of the LED stimulus and the onset of braking could be made.

3.1.2 Procedures

Each subject was given a number of practice runs around the circuit (each circuit took approximately five minutes to complete) in order to familiarise them with the car, the road circuit and the driving tasks. The normal subjects with simulated visual impairment drove around the circuit once for each visual condition (a total of four times) in alternate clockwise and anti-clockwise directions. The order of conditions for each subject was randomised to avoid order effects. The subjects with true visual impairment and their age-matched controls were required to drive around the circuit only once following their practice runs.

3.2. Assessment of Vision

A battery of tests of visual function were employed in order to determine which tests best predict driving performance. All tests were undertaken binocularly.

3.2.1. Useful Field of View (UFOV)

A measure of the functional field for peripheral search and localisation, known as the

Useful Field of View (UFOV) was determined. This involved a computer-generated task to measure central and peripheral information processing. Targets were presented centrally and then in a given peripheral location for a duration of 90 ms. The central task provides a stimulus for fixation, as well as creating various levels of central demand. The peripheral component measured localisation of targets in the periphery when the targets were either presented against an empty field or within a distractor array. Subjects were required to detect the central targets and at the same time determine the location of the peripherally presented targets, which also tested the ability of the subject to recognise relevant targets within a cluttered array.

3.2.2. Divided Attention Visual Fields (DAVF)

Functional visual fields were also measured whilst the subjects performed a concurrent central task throughout the test, representing a divided attention measure. The DAVF test was undertaken using a standard static automated perimeter, the Humphrey Field Analyser (HFA) which was adapted for this purpose. Subjects were required to respond to conventional perimetry spot targets of different contrasts presented across the visual field whilst undertaking a central task. The central task comprised a flashing LED which was placed in the central fixation aperture of the perimeter bowl and linked to a control box and separate response button. Subjects were required to press the LED response button whenever the LED flashed off in order to maintain constant illumination of the LED. The response time between the LED flashing off and activation by the response button was recorded as a series of reaction times. At the same time perimetric sensitivity was measured across the visual field.

3.2.3. Pelli-Robson Letter Contrast Sensitivity (CS)

A measure of low contrast letter sensitivity was determined using the Pelli-Robson Letter CS chart as described by Pelli et al (1988), in which letters decrease in contrast from the top left to bottom right of the chart in 0.15 log unit steps, but the size of the letters remains constant. Letters are arranged in triplets, where contrast is constant within a triplet. Subjects were instructed to identify the letters starting with the highest contrast letters in the top left hand corner and working down the chart until all the letters in a given triplet were incorrectly identified. Subjects were encouraged to look at each line of letters for 20-30 s and forced to guess when they were not sure as the scoring depends upon a forced choice paradigm.

4. RESULTS

A two way ANOVA demonstrated that visual impairment significantly reduced driving for all tasks except manoeuvring score (Table 1).

Table 1
Results for the two way ANOVA with main effects of visual impairment and age on driving. The dF for the visual impairment was (3,66), age (1,22) and for the interaction effect (3,66).

Task	Visual Condition		Age		Interactions	
	F	p	F	p	F	p
Driving time	24.38	0.0001	2.43	NS	1.99	NS
Driving score	35.59	0.0001	2.59	NS	2.63	0.05
Central reaction times	11.24	0.0001	7.89	0.01	0.89	NS
Peripheral reaction times	16.52	0.0001	16.67	0.0005	2.74	0.05
Speed estimation	6.51	0.0006	0.87	NS	0.25	NS
Peripheral awareness	19.34	0.0001	1.43	NS	1.69	NS
Road position	13.94	0.0001	0.00	NS	3.01	0.04
Reverse score	3.86	0.01	11.64	0.0025	1.9	NS

Post hoc analysis showed that these differences were between the cataract simulation and the other visual conditions, except for the reaction time task where the differences were between field restriction and the other visual conditions. Monocularity did not significantly affect performance. The differences between the old and young subjects reached significance for central and peripheral (represented in Figure 1) reaction times and reversing score and there were also significant interactions between age and the type of visual impairment.

Figure 1. Histogram representing the group mean results for peripheral reaction times for the three impairments compared to baseline (vertical line) for the young (left) and elderly (right) subjects.

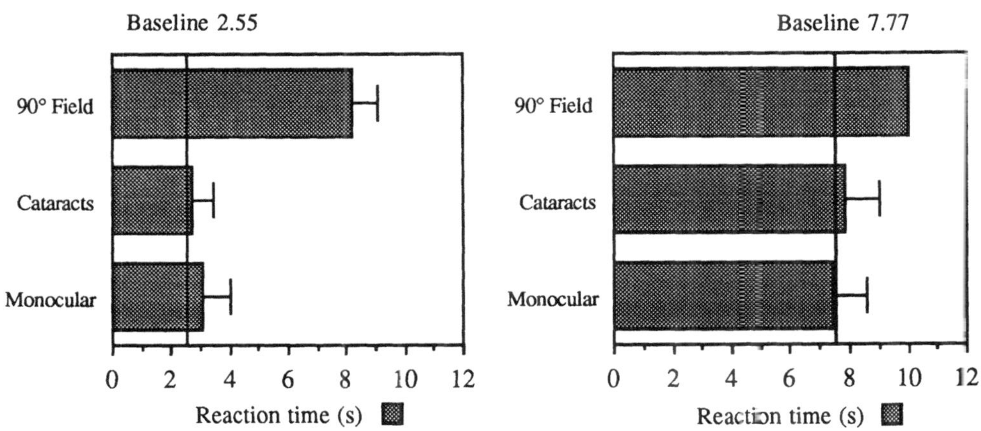

These findings were supported by the results of the cataract subjects, whose driving performance was worse compared to the age-matched controls. These differences were significant for driving time (dF 1,26; F 10.94; p=0.002) and score (dF 1,26; F 6.59; p=0.01).

A two way ANOVA demonstrated that visual impairment significantly reduced vision for all measures except the reaction time task on the DAVF test (Table 2). Significant differences between the old and young subjects were recorded for the UFOV under the high level of difficulty and for the summed sensitivity on the DAVF test.

Table 2

Results for the two way ANOVA with main effects of visual impairment and age on vision. The dF for the visual impairment was (3,66), for age (1,22) and for the interaction effect (3,66).

Task	Visual Condition		Age		Interactions	
	F	p	F	p	F	p
UFOV low central	3.07	0.03	0.42	NS	1.40	NS
UFOV low peripheral	58.70	0.0001	0.22	NS	3.18	
	0.02					
UFOV high central	8.97	0.0001	4.08	0.05	2.84	
	0.04					
UFOV high peripheral	9.45	0.0001	34.71	0.0001	4.62	
	0.005					
DAVF summed sensitivity	462.55	0.0001	5.88	0.02	5.61	
	0.0001					
DAVF reaction time	0.59	NS	0.10	0.NS	0.82	NS

These results were supported by the subjects with true cataracts who had poorer visual performance than the age-matched controls and these differences were significant for the UFOV (p=0.02) under the high level of demand and Pelli-Robson Letter CS (p=0.0001).

The correlation between visual function and three summary measures of driving performance was also determined. Significant correlations were demonstrated between total driving score and Pelli-Robson Letter CS (p<0.001), and the UFOV at the high level of demand (p<0.005). Significant correlations (p<0.05) were also demonstrated between manoeuvring score and PelliRobson Letter CS, and between manoeuvring score and reaction time on the HFA test. There was no correlation between reversing score and any of the measures of visual function.

5. DISCUSSION

The results demonstrate that imposing simulated visual impairment on young and old subjects reduced driving and vision performance, despite the fact that all subjects satisfied the visual requirements for driving for all conditions of testing; these effects were greatest for the cataract condition except for the driving reaction time task. These findings were supported by the results for the subjects with true visual impairment.

5.1 Cataracts

The reduction in contrast and increase in glare induced by the cataract simulations resulted in the greatest reduction in driving performance. These findings were supported by the results for the subjects with true cataracts, who had poorer driving performance compared to the age-matched controls. These results have important implications in terms of road safety, since all elderly people have some degree of cataract as part of the age-related process, yet the cataract must be relatively advanced to reduce visual acuity below the level required for driving. This arises because vision is measured using high contrast letters in the driving test centres, which do not reflect the decrement in visual function experienced by cataract patients. These results are supported by the fact that cataracts are given as one of the reasons that elderly persons self-regulate their driving and surrender their driving license (Kosnik et al 1990).

5.2 Binocular visual field restriction

When the binocular visual field was restricted to a maximum horizontal and vertical extent of 90° subjects drove slower and driving reaction times were increased. Indeed, it has been shown that the binocular field restriction has to be relatively severe before it has a significant effect on the other aspects of driving measured (Wood and Troutbeck 1992). This finding that driving performance appears to be related to the extent of the binocular field concurs with studies of patients with retinitis pigmentosa, where patients with mild field loss did not have significantly different accident rates to those of normal subjects (Fishman et al 1981), whilst those with severe field loss had higher accident rates and poorer driving performance (assessed in a driving simulator) relative to patients with less severe loss and those with normal fields (Szlyk et al 1992). Similarly, Johnson and Keltner (1983) reported that drivers with severe binocular field loss had twice the accident and conviction rate of those drivers surveyed with normal fields.

5.3 Monocular vision

Monocular vision had no significant effect on any of the driving measures except road position, despite the fact that monocular vision was imposed without adaptation. This finding of a minimal effect of monocular vision on driving performance is in accord with previous studies (Edwards and Schachat, 1991; Johnson and Keltner, 1983; McKnight et al, 1991). Johnson and Keltner (1983) found no significant difference in the accident and conviction rates for drivers with monocular visual field loss as compared to a control group. Similarly, McKnight et al, (1991) reported that monocular drivers were not significantly worse than binocular drivers in the safety of day-to-day driving functions and Edwards and Schachat (1991) demonstrated that most patients who had lost an eye through enucleation retained their ability to drive. A number of less recent reports have suggested that monocular drivers are more dangerous and have more accidents than binocular drivers (e.g. Keeney, 1968), however, the experimental design of these studies and the analysis and interpretation of results has been questioned.

5.4 Overall comments

Imposition of visual restrictions without adaptation is an artificial situation and would produce a greater impairment to performance than for a person whose visual impairment has developed slowly and to which they will have adapted to some extent. The first part of the study was conducted with simulated visual impairment imposed without adaptation, to examine the worst possible effect that visual impairment could impose on driving performance and to isolate the effect of visual restriction on driving performance in the absence of contaminating factors. The results from the subjects with true visual impairment from cataracts did, however, support the findings for the subjects with simulated visual impairment, even though all the participants had a current driving license. As predicted, for the subjects with true cataracts in whom visual impairment had developed slowly, some adaptation had occurred and the decrement to driving was not as marked as for those subjects in whom visual impairment had been suddenly imposed. In addition, the subjects were selected to have only relatively early cataractous changes which ranged from very early lenticular haze to more defined lenticular changes and none had cataracts which reduced their visual acuity to a level below 6/12. The decrement in driving for subjects with cataracts compared to the controls is thus significant and is of great importance for the increasingly elderly driver population, as most persons aged 65 years and over have some degree of cataract.

It is also important to note that the results of this study may only be applied to driving on a closed road circuit free of other vehicles. These conditions were selected in the interests of safety as the effect of visual impairment on driving were unknown. It is acknowledged that driving in the presence of other road users is a far more complex task than that involved in the study. However, the number of signs and their information content was relatively high and the reaction time task was included to increase the degree of information processing for the driving task in an attempt to compensate for the lack of other vehicles on the road.

5.5 Correlation between driving performance and visual function

The results demonstrate highly significant correlations between driving performance and measures of functional vision. Not surprisingly, these correlations were highest for overall driving score which took into account driving time and the number of errors made during the course.

The finding of a correlation between driving performance and functional visual fields is supported by the work of Sloane et al (1991), who reported a significant correlation between UFOV scores and accident rates in elderly drivers. Interestingly, the relationship between the UFOV and driving scores only holds when the UFOV task involves a high level of demand. Similarly, the divided attention visual fields measured on the HFA did not reflect changes in driving performance as well as the high demand UFOV task. This is likely to have arisen because the peripheral targets were presented against an empty field in the HFA test, whereas in the driving situation, relevant targets appear against a background of clutter or irrelevant objects.

Significant correlations were demonstrated between overall driving score and Pelli-Robson letter CS for all visual impairments. Such a relationship has not been previously reported. This finding of a significant relationship between Pelli-Robson Letter CS and driving together with the fact that the test is rapid and easy to administer, indicates its potential as a predictor of driving performance.

5.6 Differences between old and young subjects

The impact of visual impairment was greatest for the elderly compared to the young drivers. These differences were significant for reaction time and reversing score. The finding of increased reaction times for the elderly subjects is in agreement with previous studies which have reported that a general slowing of information processing speed (Salthouse 1985) and increased reaction times (Korteling 1990) are part of the aging process. These changes may contribute to the reduction in driving performance reported with age and this is supported by the study of Wolfelaar et al (1991), who demonstrated that speed of judgement in a traffic merging task was significantly related to four choice reaction times measured in the laboratory.

The visual performance of the elderly subjects was also significantly reduced compared to the young subjects. For the UFOV test, elderly subjects had more problems as the level of demand was increased and when they were required to locate a target within a cluttered array. These results are in accord with the findings that the age-related decline in the UFOV, demonstrated in the presence of distractors (Walker et al 1992), reflect the problems experienced by older adults with visual distractors in real life situations, such as reading a sign surrounded by other street signs (Kosnik et al 1988).

These effects are important, as they highlight areas that elderly drivers have difficulty with and emphasize the significance of visual impairment (particularly cataracts) on driving. The importance of these differences will become more evident over the next decades as the driving population ages.

6. CONCLUSIONS

Simulated visual impairment had a significant effect on the driving and vision performance of young and old normal subjects. The effects being greater for the cataract condition. The subjects with true visual impairment supported the results of the simulations and demonstrated that subjects with true cataracts had significantly poorer driving and vision performance compared to an age matched normal group. The elderly subjects also had significantly longer reaction times and poorer ability to detect targets within a cluttered array compared to the young subjects.

7. ACKNOWLEDGEMENTS

We gratefully acknowledge the cooperation of the Queensland Department of Transport and the Queensland Police for providing the Mt Cotton Complex for the driving studies in the field. This study was funded by a Federal Office of Road Safety seeding grant.

REFERENCES

Council FM and Allen JA (1974): A study of the visual fields of North Carolina drivers and their relationship to accidents. Chapel Hill, University of North Carolina, Highway Research Safety Centre.

Edwards MG and Schachat AP (1991): Impact of innucleation for choroidal melanoma on the performance of vision-dependent activities. Arch Ophthalmol 109: 519-521.

Fishman GA, Anderson RJ, Stinson L and Haque A (1981): Driving performance of retinitis pigmentosa patients. Br J Ophthalmol 65: 122-126.

Hills BL, and Burg A (1977): A reanalysis of California driver vision data: general findings. Report LR768, Department of the Environment/Department of Transport, TRRL, Crowthorne, Berks.

Johnson CA and Keltner JL (1983): Incidence of visual field loss in 20,000 eyes and its relationship to driving performance. Arch Ophthalmol 101: 371-375.

Keeney AH (1968): Relationship of ocular pathology and driving impairment. Trans Am Acad Ophthalmol Otolaryngol 72: 737-740.

Korteling JE (1990): Perception-response speed and driving capabilities of brain-damaged and older drivers. Hum Fact 32: 95-108.

Kosnik W, Winslow L, Kline D, Rasinski K and Sekuler R (1988): Visual changes in daily life throughout adulthood. J Gerontol 43: 63-70.

Kosnik W, Sekuler R and Kline D (1990): Self-reported visual problems of older drivers. Hum Fact 32: 597-608.

McKnight AJ, Shinar D and Hilburn B (1991): The visual and driving performance of monocular and binocular heavy-duty truck drivers. Accid Anal Prev 23: 225-237.

Owsley C, Ball K, Sloane ME, Roenker DL and Bruni JR (1991): Visual/cognitive correlates of vehicle accidents in older drivers. Psychol Aging 6: 403-415.

Pelli DG, Robson JG and Wilkins AJ (1988): The design of a new letter chart measuring constrast sensitivity. Clin Vis Sci 2: 187-199.

Salthouse TA (1985): Speed of behaviour and its implications for cognition. In: Birren JE and Shaie KW (eds). Handbook of the psychology of aging (2nd Ed. pp 400-426) New York.

Sloane ME, Owsley, C and Ball K (1991): Visual correlates of vehicle accidents in older drivers. In: Non-invasive Assessment of the Visual System, Technical Digest 1991. Optical Society of America, Washington DC. Vol 1: 50-53.

Szlyk JP, Alexander KR, Severing K and Fishman GA (1992): Assessment of driving performance in patients with retinitis pigmentosa. Arch Ophthalmol 110: 1709-1713.

Walker J, Sedney CA and Mast TM (1992): Older drivers and useful field of view in a part-task simulator. Transport Research Board, 71st Annual Meeting, Washington DC.

Wolffelaar PC van, Rothengatter JA and Brouwer WH (1991): Elderly drivers traffic merging decisions. In: Vision in Vehicles III. Cunningham GR (ed.) pp 247-255.

Wood JM, Troutbeck R (1992): The effect of restriction of the binocular visual field on driving performance. Ophthal Physiol Opt, 12: 291-298.

VISION IN VEHICLES - V
A.G. Gale et al. (Editors)

Vision and the Signing Needs of Older Drivers

T. McGarry

Safety Resource Centre, Transport Research Laboratory, Old Wokingham Road, Crowthorne, Berkshire RG11 6AU, United Kingdom

Abstract

The average age of the driving population is increasing. It is therefore likely that the proportion of drivers whose visual and cognitive abilities have started to decline will also be increasing. This awareness has prompted research which seeks to evaluate the appropriateness of current traffic sign standards, especially for the older driver.

The ability of older drivers to extract information from signs has been studied and measurements made of the legibility of signs manufactured with different retro-reflective materials. Some of the newer sign materials were included in these studies to determine the effect of their greater brightness on legibility distances. Volunteer subjects in the 50-75 age group were invited to participate in a series of four experiments:

(1) A test to examine reading times for direction signs of various complexities (using the TRL vehicle simulator).

(2) A test to investigate the ability of older drivers to recall information from arrays of warning signs (also using the TRL vehicle simulator).

(3) A full scale night-time legibility experiment using different signing materials and levels of ambient brightness (on the TRL research track).

(4) A full scale day-time experiment assessing sign legibility (on the TRL research track).

1. INTRODUCTION

This research has been prompted by the steadily increasing proportion of older drivers in the driving population over the period since the current regulations governing signs were introduced. It was thought necessary to determine whether current signs meet the needs of older drivers, both in terms of the amount of information presented and the distance from which the signs are legible. A number of different retro-reflective signing materials were tested including some of the brighter materials recently developed.

Visual changes of various types which take place in older people can cause a degradation of their visual ability. Depending on the precise condition, the ability of an individual might be improved or worsened by brighter signs. It is necessary to decide whether present signs are still appropriate and if not whether brighter signs are likely to be beneficial to older drivers. Notwithstanding the signs themselves, it is also necessary to ask whether older drivers have sufficient time to react to the signs and to make safe decisions whilst driving. This paper seeks to study these questions and provide some provisional results from the experiments.

2. NATURE OF THE EXPERIMENTS

Four experiments were carried out - two of the experiments used the TRL simulator and two used the TRL research track. Fifty-one volunteers were invited into TRL to participate in the research. The experiments were designed to test the cognitive abilities of subjects, through response time and recall measurements, and also their visual abilities in terms of their performance in legibility tests with full-scale traffic signs. A number of other measurements were made to help in the interpretation of the main results. These were measures of individuals' static visual acuity (using a Snellen chart), contrast sensitivity and colour vision.

3. RECRUITMENT OF SUBJECTS

Subjects were recruited by advertising in local newspapers and through contacts established with local groups and associations. Approximately 340 people applied to participate in the research. Information about each individual was obtained from a postal questionnaire which incorporated open and closed questions. Forty-five individuals were chosen to participate in the project and an additional six volunteers were selected to act as replacements should selected individuals have chosen to drop-out (see Table 1). Subjects were primarily selected using the information obtained on their age, annual mileage and also on details which they supplied concerning their vision and particular eye problems (myopia, cataracts, astigmatism etc). The ratio of males to females invited to participate directly reflected the proportion of licensed older drivers according to the National Travel Survey's 1988/90 figures. The figures were also proportional to the number of males to females who responded to the advertisement.

Table 1
Age and sex of selected subjects

AGE		MEN	WOMEN
50-54		4	3
55-59	Younger	6	2
60-64		6	1
65-69	Older	10	5
70-75		1 1	3
TOTAL		37	14

4. TRL VEHICLE SIMULATOR

The response time experiment and the recall experiment used the TRL vehicle simulator. The TRL simulator is a stationary life-sized manually controlled car. Images of a moving-belt representing a 3-lane carriageway are projected onto a screen in front of the car. Two vehicles are shown travelling along in the inside and middle lanes in front of the driver. These vehicles brake and accelerate unpredictably and the subjects are required to 'drive' the car appropriately. The severity of this driving task can be adjusted to meet the requirements of the experiment. In this instance it was reasonably demanding.

5. RESPONSE-TIME EXPERIMENT

The first experiment was designed to test the response times of individuals when asked to locate a specific destination on a direction sign. The signs were on 35mm slides and were projected for fixed periods of time onto the main screen while subjects were driving the simulator. The slides were in two different carousels - 'A' and 'B'. Whilst each subject saw both carousels, half of the subjects saw carousel 'A' first and half saw carousel 'B' first. The order of the slides in each carousel was randomised in a stratified way so that subjects were unable to anticipate the next sign to be projected.

The projection of the slides was controlled by a computer program which was co-ordinated with the driving task, in which the vehicles in front of the driver braked and accelerated at pre-defined times. The computer was programmed to allow the subject sufficient time to view the sign, make an appropriate response and regulate the driving of the car before any further movements from the vehicles in front prompted the drivers' attention.

Before each slide was projected, a target destination was read aloud by the experimenter. The time between calling out the destination and the sign appearing was varied to ensure that subjects could not predict when the signs would appear on the screen. The subject then had to find the stipulated destination as swiftly as possible and indicate accordingly. Using the car's indicator stalk, they indicated left if the destination was to the left; right if the destination was to the right; and they pulled the indicator towards them if the destination was straight ahead. On some occasions the destination did not actually appear on the sign. In these cases, subjects pulled the indicator towards them and said 'Missing'. This answer was then noted by the experimenter. Each sign remained on the screen for 8 seconds.

In order to ensure that the target destinations were distributed evenly over the positions on the signs, nine different sets of target destinations were used for different subjects. Each series of target destinations was carefully selected to ensure that individual destination names were positioned either left, right or straight ahead an equal number of times.The sequences were subdivided equally among the 5 age groups shown in Table 1, and between both sexes, to eliminate possible bias. Furthermore, the respondents in each age grouping were chosen from a range of driving experience and visual abilities as stated in the questionnaires.

5.1 Subject preparation for the response-time experiment

Upon arrival subjects were permitted adequate time to practise driving the simulator. Initial instructions were read out to each volunteer which specified only how the car was controlled. During this practice phase, slides of map and stack signs were projected onto the screen in front of the car to enable subjects to get used to the images to which they would have to react. This practice run could be repeated if necessary. Volunteers were then given a further practice run prior to the actual experiment. This was a 'dummy-run' for the real experiment. Further instructions were read out informing the subjects about how to respond to each sign.

This run entailed the subject driving the car whilst maintaining 'a safe distance' behind the other vehicles, listening for each destination name to be called out, and responding appropriately.

In this practice run the subjects were shown 10 slides in total. From the control room behind the simulator the subjects were observed to ensure that they were indicating correctly and that their driving was controlled, not haphazard. This run could be repeated.

5.2 Experimental procedure

For the experiment itself the subjects were shown 42 signs with a short break after the twenty-first sign. Their response times were stored automatically by the computer and calculated from the time at which the signs appeared on the screen to the time the subjects responded. If a respondent realised they had made a mistake they were advised that they could correct this before the next destination name was called out. Their reaction time was then calculated on the last response given for any particular destination.

5.3 Results of the response-time experiment

For all analyses, subjects were grouped in either the younger (50-64) or older (65-75) age category. The initial results for the response-time experiment illustrated that the most important main effect is the number of names on a sign. This is followed by the sex of a subject and their age. The statistical probabilities (i.e. the probability that there is not an effect due to this factor) are <0.001, 0.012 and 0.055 respectively. The type of sign, whether map or stack, does not appear to affect response times. Figure 1 shows that men in the younger age group had the shortest response time. The time taken by subjects in the other groups was very similar. For both age groups and both sexes the response time steadily rises the more destination names there are on a sign.

Figure 1. Mean response times for both age groups and both sexes (Y=Younger, O=Older)

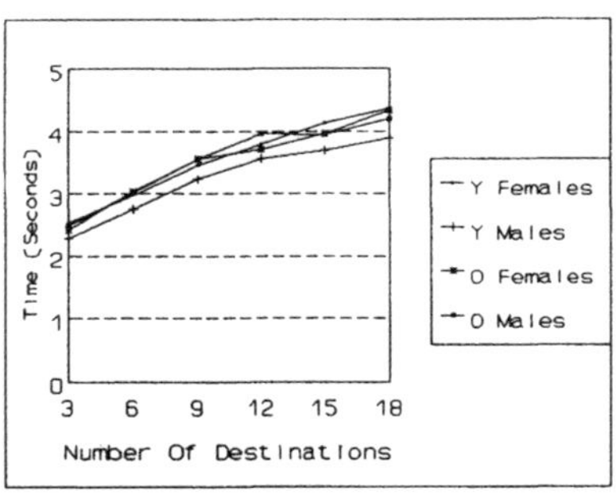

6. RECALL EXPERIMENT

The recall experiment investigated the ability of older drivers to recall information from arrays of warning signs. In this experiment slides showing arrays of 2, 3 or 4 signs were used. There were eight 2-sign clusters, six 3-sign clusters and eight 4-sign clusters. Two different exposure times were used - either 2 or 4 seconds. Subjects were shown each array in turn and after the exposure ended, were asked which sign had appeared in a given position. Again a number of different sets of target positions were used (in this case 8) and, within each, target positions were arranged to ensure they were balanced in terms of equal numbers of requests for recall of signs in different positions on the screen.

6.1 Subject preparation for the recall experiment

A picture of each warning sign and the corresponding definition was sent to each subject in advance so that they could familiarise themselves with the signs that were to be used. This was to ensure that any problems with recall were due to an inability to remember the signs rather than lack of knowledge of the signs. This experiment followed the response time experiment after a 20 minute break. Subjects were offered refreshments and during this period they were questioned to ensure they understood each of the warning signs. Any signs they had problems understanding were explained until it was certain the subject fully comprehended the meaning of the sign. The subjects were again given a short test run to ensure they felt confident with the sign designs and with the sign arrays.

6.2 Experimental procedure

Subjects were presented with twenty-two arrays of signs. The first eleven clusters were present on the screen for 2 seconds, the remainder were displayed for 4 seconds. After each clusters' removal from the screen, the subject was then asked to recall the sign in a given location. The possible positions were, top or bottom for a two sign cluster; top, middle or bottom for a three sign cluster; top left, bottom left, top right or bottom right for a four sign cluster. The subjects' responses were recorded manually.

6.3 Results of the recall experiments

In choosing the best 'Goodness-of-fit' model for the data a loglinear analysis was performed. Here the dependent variable was the number of answers correct, while the independent variables were age, time and cluster size. The data is presented in Figure 2. The loglinear analysis showed that the 'best-fit' model for the data, i.e. the model which came closest at the 0.05 level of significance to describing the data simply, derived from main effects only. This model indicated that the most important factor explaining the probability of correct recall was cluster size, then exposure time followed by age. The statistical probability for each of the above factors was <0.001, 0.002 and 0.011 respectively. Time by cluster size(0.043) was a statistically important interaction.

Figure 2. Percentage of signs recalled correctly by each age group, cluster size and time

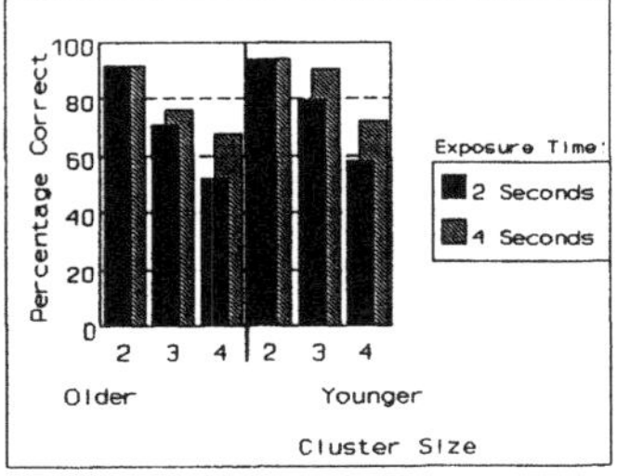

On average the younger group retained approximately 6% more images correctly than the older group. The effect of exposure time was especially pertinent when there were more signs in a cluster to remember. For both age groups there was a decline in the number of correct responses as the cluster size increased.

7. NIGHT-TIME LEGIBILITY EXPERIMENT

The night-time legibility experiment determined the distances from which older drivers could read signs under night-time conditions. For this (and the subsequent daytime legibility experiment) a left hand drive car was used following several tests which demonstrated that sign brightness, at night-time, as viewed from the driver's seat of a car appeared to differ substantially from that observed from the passenger's seat under certain viewing conditions. For both experiments therefore one of the experimenters drove the car while the subject occupied the position of the driver of a right-hand drive car.

7.1 Experimental Design

In total 15 signs were shown to each subject. These signs were shown in 3 'runs'. Three different grades of materials were used - Engineering grade, High Intensity and Diamond grade. Both black on white and white on blue signs were used. The first 2 'runs' consisted of 6 signs, 3 blue and 3 white, whilst the 3 remaining signs, which were white, were shown in the final run. The lighting conditions differed for each set of signs. For the first 'run' street lights were switched on and the car headlamps were dipped. For the second run the street lights were off while the headlamps remained dipped. The remaining 3 signs were shown with no street lighting but with head lights on main beam. The signs were placed sufficiently far apart to avoid interaction effects.

7.2 Experimental procedure

Subjects were first given instructions and then driven individually at a slow walking pace towards each sign in turn. They were asked to read the destination name or road number in a given position. Each sign incorporated 2 destination names, one above the other, and below these a road number. Individual signs had destination names that were either 7, 8 or 9 characters long with similar ascenders or descenders. Subjects did not therefore receive a cue from the length of the destination name as to what it might be. Subjects were advised not to call out an answer unless they felt 'reasonably sure' that they knew the answer. When the correct answer was called out, the car was stopped and the distance of the car from the sign was noted. If the subject called out an incorrect response they were asked to try again. For each sign a legibility distance was calculated with an estimated accuracy of half a metre. The track had been marked out at 1 metre intervals prior to the experiment.

7.3 Results of the night-time legibility experiment

A sequential MANOVA was performed on the data to determine which of the factors was most important in explaining the distance from which subjects could read the traffic signs. The independent variables considered were sex, age of the subject, subject's visual acuity, grade of material, colour of material, whether the destination to be read was a name or a road number and lighting conditions (street lights on or off, with dipped or main beam). This test demonstrated that at the 0.05 level of significance there were five statistically significant main factors. The factors and their statistical probability were, the subjects' age (0.002), visual acuity(<0.001), the lighting conditions(<0.001), destination type (<0.001), and the grade of material (<0.001). Colour of material and the sex of a subject were found to be statistically non-significant. There were no statistically significant interactions between these variables. Overall subjects with better acuity can read signs at a greater legibility distance than those with a lower acuity. The means here are 84 metres for 6/4 acuity and 62 metres for 6/6 acuity. Furthermore, the younger group have a longer legibility distance for each acuity level than the older age group. (With a Snellen chart the standard visual acuity is 6/6. The first number is the viewing distance in metres, the second number is the distance at which the letters just read subtend 5 minutes of arc). For both age groups, destination names were read at greater distances than destination numbers. Lighting conditions and grade of material will need further analysis.

Figure 3. Legibility distance of signs summarised by age group and visual acuity

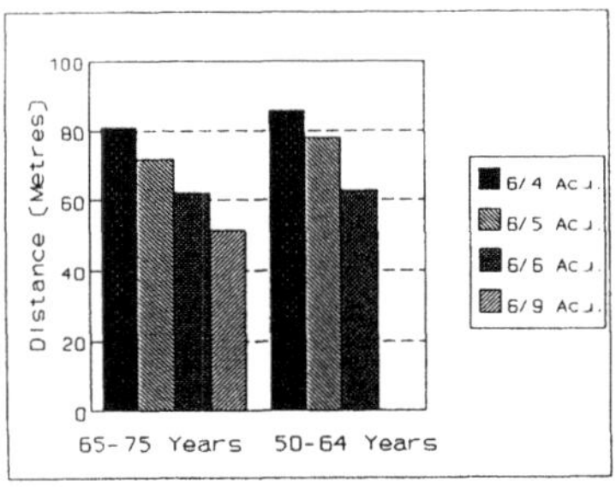

8. DAY-TIME LEGIBILITY EXPERIMENT

This experiment was similar to the night-time experiment. For this experiment subjects were shown only six signs. Of these 2 signs were Engineering grade, 2 were High Intensity and 2 were Diamond grade. Again both black on white and white on blue signs were used for each material. Target destinations were again randomised in order to address any problems of bias.

8.1 Experimental procedure

Subjects were given instructions and then driven individually towards each sign in turn after being given a particular target position. When the correct answer was called out the car was stopped immediately and the distance of the car from that sign was noted manually. This was repeated for each sign in turn.

8.2 Results from the day-time legibility experiment

A sequential MANOVA was performed on the data from this experiment. The independent variables considered were sex, grade of material, subject's visual acuity, whether the destination to be read was a name or a road number, colour of material, age of the subject and weather (either dull or bright). The dependent variable was the distance from which a sign could be read. This test demonstrated that at the 0.05 level of significance, in terms of main effects, those factors which influenced the distance from which a sign could be read (see Figure 4) and their statistical probability are, destination type (<0.001), visual acuity (<0.001), age (<0.001) and weather (0.004). Grade of material, colour of material and the sex of a subject were found to be statistically nonsignificant. Figure 4 illustrates the importance of age and visual acuity for reading distance. Furthermore, as in the night-time legibility results, destination names perform better than destination numbers for all acuities over both age groups. In general, the brighter weather also improves legibility distance.

Figure 4. Legibility distance of signs in dull weather for destination numbers according to age and visual acuity

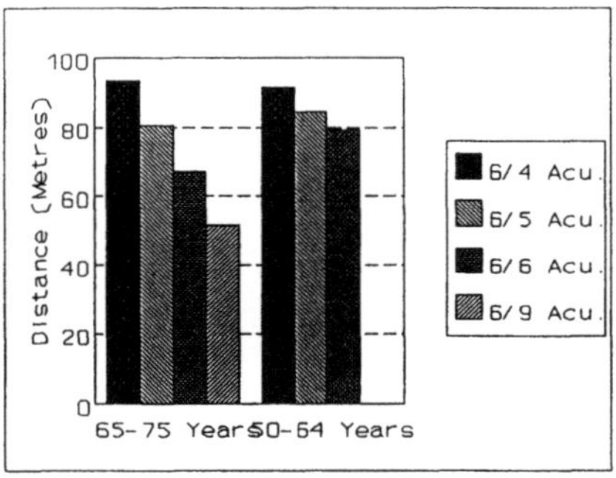

9. SUMMARY

Preliminary results from these four experiments indicated that drivers in the younger age group (50-64) took less time to read direction signs and were more successful in recalling sign information than those in the older age group (65-75). For the night-time legibility tests, visual acuity and age were both statistically significant determinants of reading distance, as was the grade of sign material, destination type and the lighting conditions under which the signs were viewed. In day-light, age, visual acuity, weather conditions and destination type were important main factors, but sign material, sign colour and sex of subject were not statistically significant as main factors. The results from the response time experiment will also be compared with the results from another TRL experiment involving younger drivers.

VISION IN VEHICLES - V
A.G. Gale et al. (Editors)

Use Of The Esterman Visual Field Test In Diabetics Following Pan-Retinal Photo Coagulation With Respect To DVLA Recommendations

S.W. Mackie*, T. Barrie+, E. McClure+, and G.Walsh*

*Department of Vision Sciences, Glasgow Caledonian University, Cowcaddens Road, Glasgow G4, UK. +Glasgow Eye Infirmary, Sandyford Place, Glasgow G3.

Abstract

The Esterman visual field test (EVFT) is now available on the Humphrey field analyser. In 25 patients with treated diabetic retinopathy we have compared the EVFT with other forms of perimetry currently accepted by the UK Driver and Vehicle Licensing Authority (DVLA). Twenty-four patients passed and one patient failed the DVLA field recommendations. Our data indicates that the EVFT has the potential to be used for reliable field assessment and guidelines are given relating to EVFT score.

1. INTRODUCTION

Laser pan-retinal photo coagulation (PRP) is now the preferred choice of treatment for diabetics with proliferative retinopathy. Its value in inducing neovascular regression has been established (The Diabetic Retinopathy Research Group, 1978), albeit at the expense of detectable losses in visual function (Sieberm, 1987). More recently the use of reduced burn size has been shown to reduce the risk of DVLA field test failure (Hulbert, 1992).

A standard PRP initial treatment protocol at the diabetic retinal clinic, Glasgow Eye Infirmary, consists of up to 3000 argon burns at the 200 micron setting avoiding major vessels within the temporal arcades, and the superior and inferior retina within 20 degrees from the horizontal midline. Following laser treatment each patient is legally obliged to inform the DVLA (Road Traffic Act, 1988), who in turn request a formal acuity and field test from the patient's medical attendant to assess their fitness to drive.

* All correspondence should be addressed to Mr S W Mackie.

DVLA recommendations include:

a) Reading a number plate, letter height 3.125 inches at 25 yards (i.e. binocular VA~6/10) (Drasdo, 1981).

b) A minimal visual field of at least 120 degrees along the horizontal and of at least 20 degrees above and below the horizontal measured by perimetry using a 3mm white test object at l/3m (or equivalent perimetry) (Form CLEW 1060, 1992).

The standard does not define the use of one eye only or both eyes together since either condition is allowed.

The Esterman Visual Field Test (EVFT) (Esterman, 1968; Esterman, 1982; Esterman,1985; Mills, 1986; Choy, 1986) as adopted by the International Perimetric Society, and used by the American Medical Association (AMA) in its guides to visual impairment (American Medical Association ,1988), is now available on the Humphrey field analyser. In order to assess the EVFT we have compared it with other forms of perimetry currently accepted by the DVLA in patients with treated diabetic retinopathy (Form CLEW 1060, 1992).

2. METHOD

The Esterman test is scored using a relative value scale which is divided into unequal units of 100 for monocular tests and 120 for binocular tests. Each unit is equated to one test point and is given a value of 1 in the monocular field, and 0.83 in the binocular field. The inequality in size and distribution of the units, with greater unit density in more important areas makes this scale functional (Figure 1). The field analyser yields the functional score automatically as a percentage and prints it in the lower right hand corner of the printout. Monocular tests extend 75 degrees temporally and 60 degrees nasally; binocular tests extend 150 degrees laterally. Each stimulus duration is 400ms with a Goldman stimulus of III4e.

Since the binocular test requires central head positioning, the video eye monitor is aligned on the bridge of the nose and therefore the usual automatic controls of fixation cannot be employed. Fixation was therefore monitored by operator observation. If the patient needs spectacles whilst driving, the test is performed using the patient's own correction and not trial lenses. If the results are equivocal, the test is performed without the patient's correction to assess whether the frame is obstructing the field of vision.

3. SUBJECTS

We studied 25 patients who had received bilateral PRP for proliferative retinopathy using an argon laser; 200 micron target. All retained a central visual acuity sufficient to pass the DVLA requirements (Drasdo, 1981).

All had visual acuity of at least hand movements in their poorer eye, and as such were deemed binocular with respect to DVLA field testing. I n each patient, 3 separate visual field assessments were performed in random order: binocular EVFT (Humphrey static); binocular custom test (Humphrey static) and binocular Goldmann test (Topcon kinetic). All tests measure a minimum field of 120 degrees horizontally, 40 degrees vertically. The binocular

EVFT was also performed on 10 patients on two separate occasions under identical conditions to assess its repeatability.

4. RESULTS

Results were compared by: a) using a customised Esterman grid overlay for the Goldmann recording chart to obtain Esterman field efficiency scores, and b) using the meridian method adopted by the AMA for the Goldmann recording chart to obtain traditional field efficiency scores.

Method a)
The sum of dots on the overlay lying inside the isopter is multiplied by 0.83 to yield a manual score,
and
Method b)
The sum of the eccentricities (visual field angles) of the isopter in the eight principal meridians is divided by 500 to yield a manual score.

Calculation for method a) was made by subtracting any dots lying within a scotoma and for b) by subtracting any scotoma's width from the values of the meridians crossing through it.

One way ANOVA revealed no significant variation between groups ($p=0.005$). Good sensitivity (Goldmann overlay / Esterman correlation $r=0.843$ and Goldmann meridian / Esterman correlation $r=0.850$) and reliability (Esterman / Esterman correlation $r= 0.943$) of results gained using the binocular EVFT were achieved. Good agreement was also noted between the EVFT and the Custom test (see Table.1). Only one patient who had received the most extensive PRP treatment, and subsequently developed retinal detachments, failed the DVLA field requirements (see Figure 2 a,b,c).

5. DISCUSSION

Published data shows no significant correlation between vision defects and accident rate, with the exception of data pertaining to side collisions (Council, 1974). However, it has been widely accepted by ophthalmologists, neurologists and medical advisors to the DVLA in this country that significant homonymous, quadrantanopic and bitemporal field defects may be hazardous for driving (College of Ophthalmologists Guidelines, 1990). Although the eyes scan constantly during driving, the benefits of this are not easily quantified, whereas a field deficit is measureable evidence of potential danger to other road users.

Fig. 1 Customised Esterman Grid Overlay

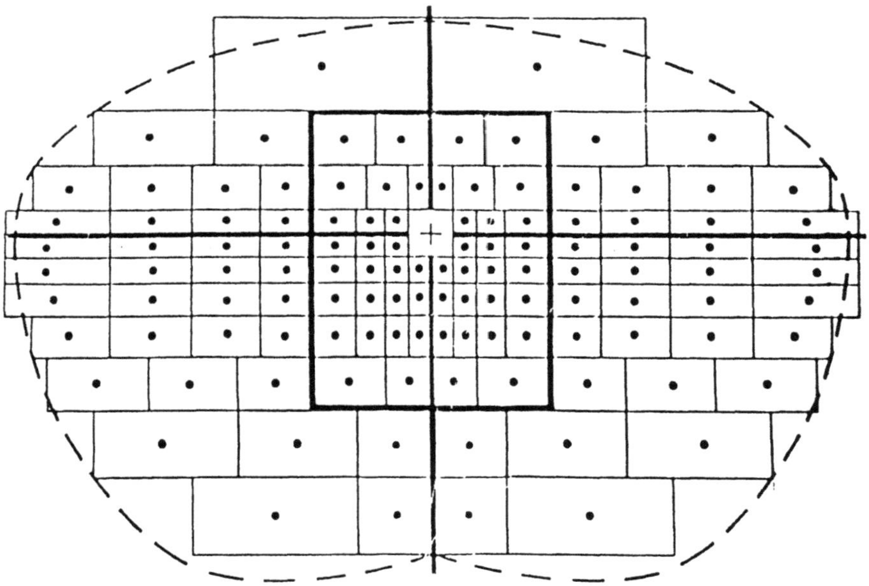

Table 1

Correlation Coefficients between each test

Type of test	Correlation (r)	Gradient (m)
Esterman / Esterman	0.943	0.91
Goldmann overlay / Esterman	0.843	0.85
Goldmann meridian / Esterman	0.850	0.87
Goldmann overlay / Goldmann meridian	0.976	0.96
Goldmann overlay / Custom	0.778	0.77
Goldmann meridian / Custom	0.780	0.77
Custom / Esterman	0.857	0.83

Fig.2 a) b) c): Field plots for the only patient that failed to meet the DVLA recommendations.

Type of test	Field score (%)
Esterman	46
Goldmann overlay	44
Goldmann meridian	46
Custom	48

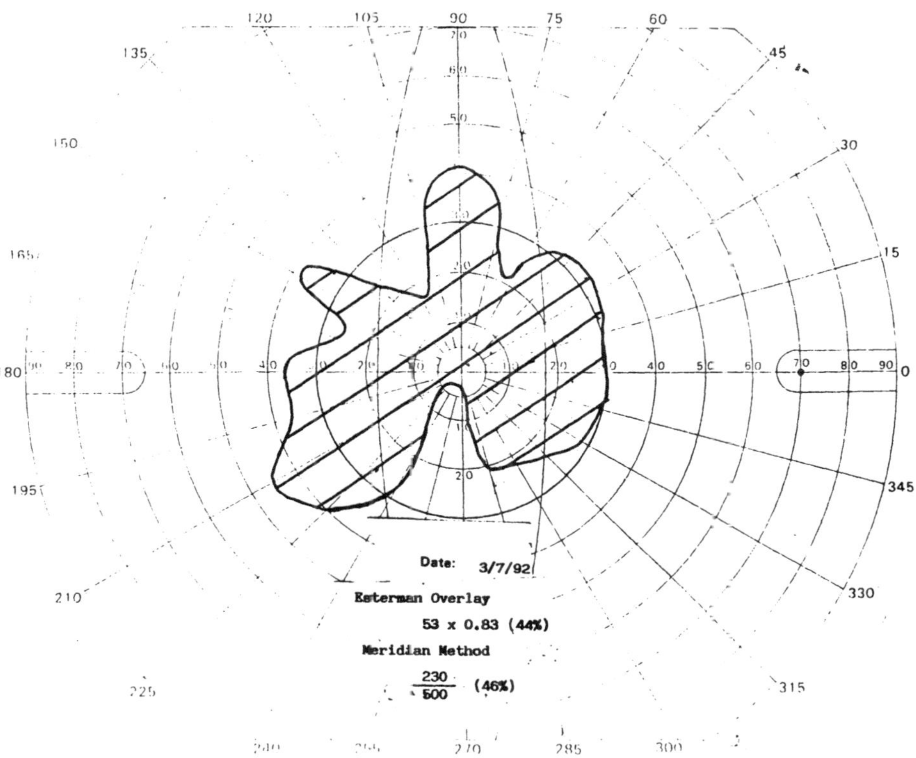

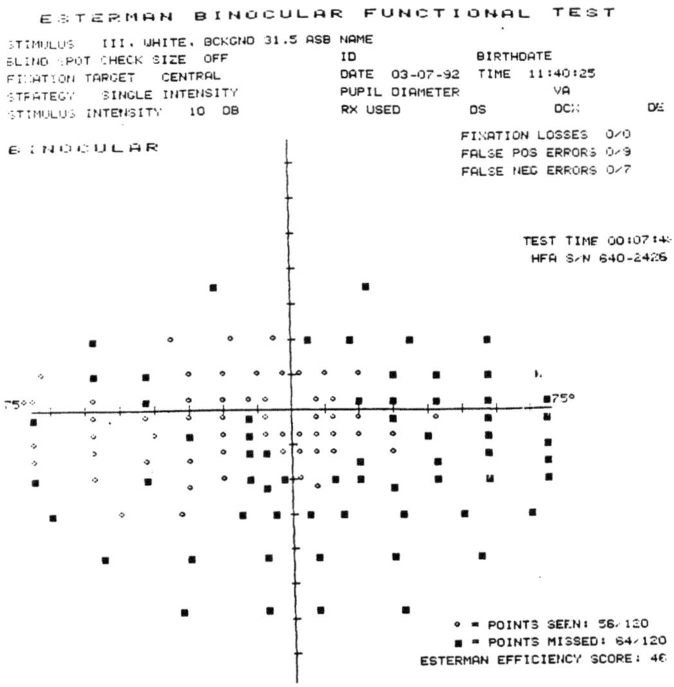
ESTERMAN BINOCULAR FUNCTIONAL TEST
STIMULUS III, WHITE, BCKGND 31.5 ASB
BLIND SPOT CHECK SIZE OFF
FIXATION TARGET CENTRAL
STRATEGY SINGLE INTENSITY
STIMULUS INTENSITY 10 DB
NAME
ID
BIRTHDATE
DATE 03-07-92
TIME 11:40:25
PUPIL DIAMETER
VA
RX USED
DS
DCX
DS
BINOCULAR
FIXATION LOSSES 0/0
FALSE POS ERRORS 0/9
FALSE NEG ERRORS 0/7
TEST TIME 00:07:4
HFA S/N 640-2426
75°
75°
• = POINTS SEEN: 56/120
■ = POINTS MISSED: 64/120
ESTERMAN EFFICIENCY SCORE: 46

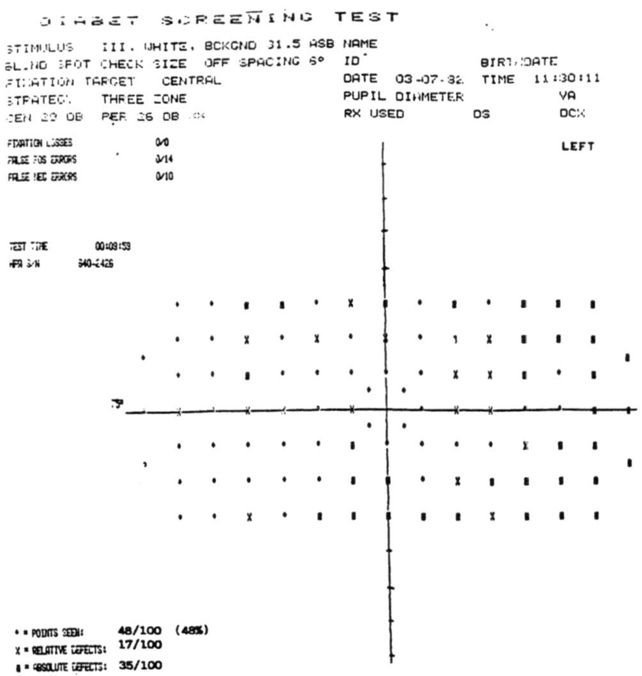
DIABET SCREENING TEST
STIMULUS III, WHITE, BCKGND 31.5 ASB
BLIND SPOT CHECK SIZE OFF SPACING 6°
FIXATION TARGET CENTRAL
STRATEGY THREE ZONE
CEN 29 DB PER 26 DB
NAME
ID
BIRTHDATE
DATE 03-07-92
TIME 11:30:11
PUPIL DIAMETER
VA
RX USED
DS
DCX
FIXATION LOSSES 0/0
FALSE POS ERRORS 0/14
FALSE NEG ERRORS 0/10
LEFT
TEST TIME 00:09:53
HFA S/N 640-2426
• = POINTS SEEN: 48/100 (48%)
X = RELATIVE DEFECTS: 17/100
■ = ABSOLUTE DEFECTS: 35/100

In 1988 the Faculty of Ophthalmologists (now the College of Ophthalmologists) and its Visual Standards Sub-committee made recommendations to the DVLA and Minister of Transport that the minimum safe field for driving should be at least 120 degrees horizontally and 40 degrees vertically using the simplest apparatus then available (e.g. Lister, Aimark). Although this standard defined the angle subtended by the target to the eye, and brought the UK in line with European Community Law, it was apparent that the standard was not scientific as it failed to define luminance, contrast etc. Subsequent review included the Goldmann bowl perimeter, an apparatus which could perform field testing under controlled and repeatable conditions and equivalent standard parameters for this equipment were introduced. In order to establish these parameters it was assumed that the bulbs illuminating the original perimeters were only 50% efficient and for ~20dbs of contrast with a subtended angle of 0.7 degrees, the setting closest to the previous was a target size III4e, with a target / bowl luminance of l5db (Munton). Adoption of this standard has fortuitously brought us into line with current American and European guidelines. The Visual Standards Sub-committee, College of Ophthalmologists, reviews this standard regularly and is currently evaluating the EVFT for consideration as an approved test.

We have shown that the EVFT results are compatable with those obtained from Goldmann testing despite differences in testing methods. For example the EVFT is a static test and is 0.5 log units brighter. However we are advised that the Committee does not wish the standard to be unduly restrictive. Thus the EVFT is a non-stringent test "which will not disbar too many from the important civil liberty of the right to drive" (College of Ophthalmologists Guidelines, 1990)

5. CONCLUSION

The EVFT has the potential to be used for reliable field assessment although it is not yet recognised by the DVLA for this purpose. It is quick to administer, easily understood and can be used by ancilliary staff. In its binocular mode it encloses the recommended minimum field for safe driving which corresponds to an Esterman functional score of 71% + 3% (variation of performance).

As a result of our study we suggest the following guidelines:

Binocular Esterman Score	DVLA Recommendation
>74%	Pass
68-74%	Borderline
<68%	Fail

In borderline cases and field plots which look suspicious reassessment using another recognised field test are advised.

REFERENCES

1. American Medical Association (1988). Guides to the evaluation of permanent impairment (3rd Ed.) 153-163. American Medical Association, Chicago.
2. Choy ES, Mills RP, Drance SM (1986). Automated Esterman testing of disability in glaucoma. Seventh International Visual Field Symposium, Amsterdam.
3. Council FM, Allen JA (1974). A Study of the visual fields of North Carolina drivers and their relationship to accidents. Highway Safety Research Centre, University of North Carolina .
4. Drasdo N, Haggerty CM (1981) A comparison of the British number plate and Snellen vision tests for car drivers. Ophthal Physiol Opt. 1 :39-54.
5. Esterman B (1968). Grid for scoring visual fields. II. Perimeter. Arch Ophthalmol. 79:400-406.
6. Esterman B(1982). Functional scoring of the binocular field. Ophthalmology. 89: 1226-1234 .
7. Esterman B, Blanche E, Welsh M, Bonelli A (1985). Computerised scoring of the functional field: preliminary report. Doc Ophthalmol Prick Ser. 42:333-339.
8. Form CLEW 1060. DVLC Drivers Medical Branch, revised September 1992.
9. Hulbert MFG, Vernon SA (1992). Passing the DVLC field regulations following pan-retinal photo coagulation in diabetics. Eye. 6:456-460.
10. Mills RP, Drance SM(1986). Esterman disability rating in severe glaucoma. Ophthalmology. 93:371-378.
11. Munton G, Visual Standards Sub-Committee, Personal communication.
12. Redefinition of the minimal field of vision for safe driving, (1990). College of Ophthalmologists Guidelines.
13. Road Traffic Act 1988 Provision of information etc. relating to disabilities. HMSO
14. Sieberm V, Alexandrides E, Feng W (1987). Function of the diabetic retina after pan-retinal argon laser coagulation. Graefes Arch Clin Exp Ophthalmol. 225:385390.
15. The Diabetic Retinopathy Research Group (1978). Photo coagulation treatment of proliferative diabetic retinopathy: the second report of diabetic retinopathy study findings. Ophthalmology. 85:82-106.

VISION IN VEHICLES - V
A.G. Gale et al. (Editors)
1996 Elsevier Science B.V.

Contrast Sensitivity with Coloured Windscreens*

B. Rassow

Medical Optics Laboratory, Department of Ophthalmology University of Hamburg, Germany

1. INTRODUCTION

The relatively high incidence and the gravity of traffic accidents at night raises the question whether in addition to other factors like e.g. over-tiredness, visual problems might be responsible. This has led to investigations into a possible reduction in visual acuity (VA) and contrast sensitivity from oblique and tinted windscreens.

2. SCOPE

So far studies on how vision is affected by oblique and tinted windscreens have by and large used the attainable VA as a criterion (Rompe & Tupova 1980; Arnold 1981; Chmielarz et al. 1992; Waetjen et al. 1993). But visual problems in reduced lighting conditions (driving at dusk and at night; fog) are caused by a reduced contrast in the visual object rather than anything else.

Another point is that the influence of windscreens on visual ability has so far usually been tested on healthy, normal subjects. A question of equal or greater importance is how oblique and tinted windscreens affect the visual ability of those drivers who have an already reduced VA and are only just fit for driving (V=0,5 on both eyes) under normal conditions.

3. METHOD OF TESTING

Letter optotypes (Pelli et al. 1988) with variable contrast were shown from a distance of approximately 3 m under standardized conditions (luminance 1.0; 0 1 and 0.03 cd/m^2). Testing conditions were - as far as possible in this experiment - in accordance with those laid down by ISO (1994) for testing VA. The optotypes were shown in a seven-second rhythm (3 seconds display, followed by a 4 second pause), and test persons had the task of naming the letters (C, D, H, K, N, O, R, S, V and Z), which were known to them, within those 7 seconds. Answers like "not recognised" or "don't know" were not admissible (forced choice method).

The test persons had to look through three types of windscreens (clear-transparent, blue, and green), which were mounted at an angle of inclination of 60 °. We tested five normal subjects and five persons with V=0.5. The ten letters (v.s.) were available in 12 contrast steps. The relative change in contrast from one step to the next was 20-30%. Five optotypes could be offered at each contrast level. A contrast level was considered as recognised when at least three of the five different optotypes were correctly named. In order to precisely determine the contrast threshold the optotypes were offered on at most 5 to 7 contrast levels in such a selection that some of them were above and some below the threshold.

Each test person took part in five sessions, during which he was offered approximately 30 individual tests at each of the luminance levels mentioned above and for each of the three different types of windscreen.

* Supported by *Forschungsgemeinschaft Auto - Sicht - Sicherheit*, Cologne, Germany

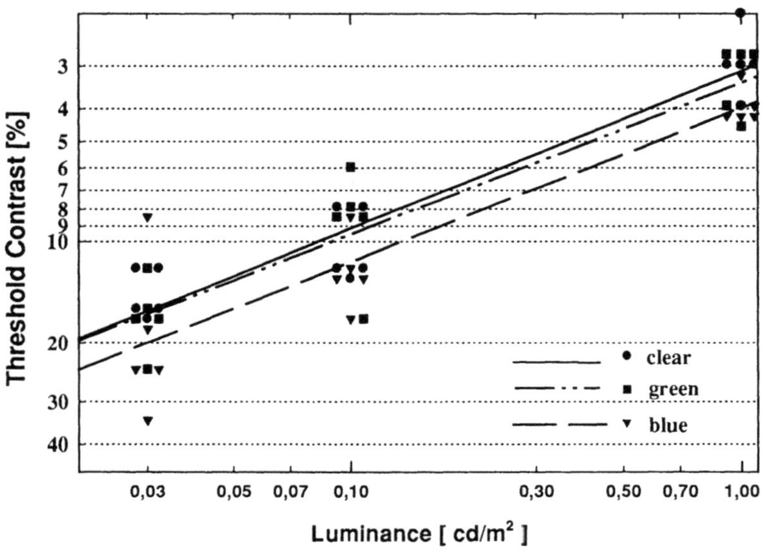

Fig. 1a: Correlation between threshold contrast and luminace for one person with normal VA (results of 5 sessions).

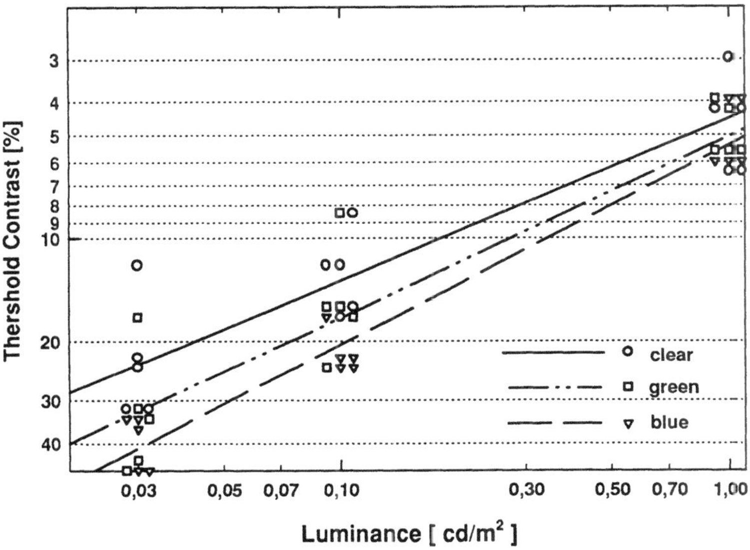

Fig. 1b: Correlation between threshold contrast and luminance for one person with reduced VA (results of 5 sessions).

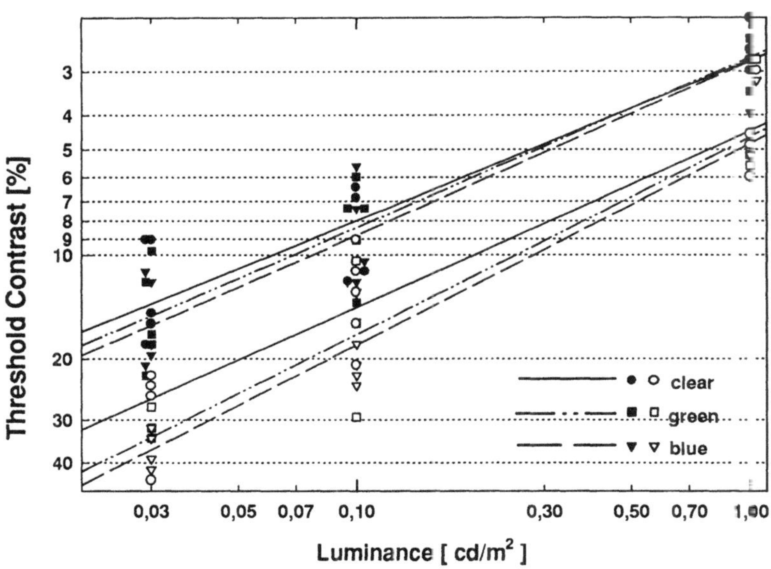

Fig. 2: Correlation between threshold contrast and luminance for 5 persons with normal VA (filled symbols) and 5 persons with reduced VA (empty symbols).

4. TEST RESULTS

Fig.1a shows the results for one normal test person and fig. 1b for one test person with reduced VA over the five sessions. The various symbols denote the five individual test sessions and the straight lines the mean results for the three different windscreens. A spread of approximately +/-1.5 contrast steps results. Fig.2 is a synopsis of the diagrams of the five normal test persons and of the five with reduced VA.

5. DISCUSSION

Test results show that the mean contrast sensitivity of the test persons with VA=0.5 is 3% at the maximum level of luminance used (1 cd/m^2), i.e. already one unit below that of normal persons (4%). At this level of luminance the spread of the two groups of test persons is relatively small. No difference can be found for the various types of windscreen in either group.

A reduction in luminance entails a marked reduction in contrast sensitivity for both groups. The spread within the group of normal test persons goes up slightly at a luminance of 0.1 cd/m^2; for test persons with reduced VA it goes up considerably. The mean value for all subjects and all three types of windscreen is 8-9% for normal test persons and 15-19% for those with reduced VA, i.e. double the value for healthy subjects. A statistically significant if minor difference between contrast sensitivity values for the transparent windscreen on the one hand and the coloured ones on the other exists for persons with reduced VA.

At a level of luminance of 0.03 cd/m^2, which corresponds approximately to the border of the area illuminated by normal front driving lights, the difference becomes more marked. While the spread in both groups of test persons does not increase further, the mean value for all types of windscreen is approximately 15% for healthy test persons, whereas test persons with V=0.5 require a mean contrast of approximately 30%. The reduction in contrast sensitivity compared with the transparent glass is higher for blue than for green and in both cases on the 5% level of significance.

From a comparison of the curves in fig. 2 it can be seen by what factor luminance would have to be increased for a person with VA=0.5/0.5 to have the same contrast sensitivity as one with normal vision. This factor is approximately 3. On a level of luminance of 0.1 cd/m^2 the group of test persons with reduced VA has approximately the same contrast threshold as the group with normal VA has at a luminance of 0.03. Differences between the green and the blue tinted glass are not statistically significant (although a mere look at the illustrations might produce a different impression). There is, however, a clear indication that at a low level of luminance the blue glass causes a greater reduction in contrast sensitivity than the green. This can be explained from the relative values for light transmission (transparent: 90.6%; green: 80.4%; blue: 75.6%).

Before practical conclusions are drawn from these results it has to be taken into account that the tests were done on unused samples of windscreen glass. Research has shown (Hartmann 1965; Allen 1969; Timmermann & Gehring 1986) that windscreens which are soiled and scratched by long usage not only cause a higher level of stray light and thus increase glare sensitivity but also reduce contrast sensitivity. Another factor to be considered is age (Hartmann 1989): reduced transparency of the ocular media with advancing age can reduce contrast sensitivity even though VA might still be good.

REFERENCES

Allen M.J. (1969) *Automobile Windshields - Surface Deterioration,* Am.J.Optometry 46, 594-598

Arnold R. (1981) *Einfluß der Leuchtdichte verkehrsrelevanter Sehobjekte auf die Erkennungsentfernung des Kraftfahrers,* Diss. Univ. Tübingen

Chmielarz M., Derkum H., Schneider W. *Zu Effekten unterschiedlicher Transmissionsgrade in Windschutzscheiben auf die Wahrnemung,* in: Reinschild K. W. *Berwertung von Windschutzscheiben, Anzeige- und Blickregistrierungstechniken,* Köln 1992

Hartmann E. (1965) *Windschutzscheiben selten sauber, und das ist gefährlich*, Motor-Rundschau 23

Hartmann E. *Sehen,Wahrnehmen und Erkennen in Abhängigkeit vom.Alter der Fahrzeugführer*, in: *Sicht aus Kraftfahrzeugen,* TÜV Rheinland, Köln 1989

ISO International Organization for Standardization, *Optis and optical instrumentation - Visual acuity testing - Correlation of optotypes,* ISO 8596/8597 (1994)

Pelli D. G., Robson J. G.,Wilkins A.J. (1988) *The Design of a New Letter Chart for Measurring Contrast Sensitivity,* Clin.Vis:Sci. 2, 187-199

Rompe K., Tupova J., *Zum Einfluß eingefärbter Scheiben auf die Sehweite bei Dunkelheit*, in: *Sicht aus Kraftfahrzeugen,*TÜV Rheinland, Köln 1980

Timmermann A., Gehring G. (1986), *Oberflächenschäden an Windschutzscheiben,* Zeitschr. f. Verkehrsicherheit 1/32, 31-35

Waetjen R., Schiefer U., Gaigl A., Aulhorn E. (1993) *Der Einfluß von Windschutzscheiben "-Tönung" und "Neigung" auf den Erkennungsabstand unter mesopischen Bedingungen,* Zeitschr. f. Verkehrsicherheit 1/39, 17-23

VISION IN VEHICLES - V
A.G. Gale et al. (Editors)

The Effectiveness of Multi Anti Reflection Coated Spectacle Lenses in the Presence of Glare

W Poplar[a], G Mouat[a] and M Dunne[b]

[a]Lancaster & Thorpe, 42 Friar Gate, Derby, UK

[b]Department of Vision Sciences, University of Aston, Birmingham, UK

Abstract

Multi anti reflection coatings have become popular additions to spectacle lenses to aid in the reduction of glare in various situations. There is little published study on the effect of anti reflection coats in such situations. The paper investigates subjective views on the performance of these coatings and uses contrast sensitivity measurements to quantify the glare reducing effect of the coatings.

1. INTRODUCTION

In the past few years, lens coatings have become increasing popular additions to spectacles in the UK. Of these coatings, the multi anti reflection coating (MAR) has had increasing amounts of publicity. The anti reflection coating was pioneered by Zeiss and originally applied to lenses in instruments such as cameras, binoculars etc.

The original anti reflection coatings use only a single layer of the coating material, and reduce reflection from the lens to about 4%, producing a transmission of 96% of incident light. More modern multi layer coatings increase transmission to as high as 99.5% of incident light, which compares with approximately 90% transmission for an uncoated lens.

Many lens manufacturers promote their coatings with claims of improved vision when night driving, under artificial lights and when working with VDU's; claiming better performance in the presence of glare.

The aim of this study was to investigate the effectiveness of MAR coated lenses on vision in the presence of a glare source. Two approaches were adopted. Firstly the subjective opinions of wearers of MAR coated lenses was sought via a questionnaire. Secondly, a more objective investigation was carried out by measuring contrast sensivity of subjects with and without an anti reflection coating in the absence and presence of a glare source.

2. SUBJECTIVE IMPRESSIONS OF MAR COATINGS

2.1 Methods

Data for subjective views on the effectiveness of MAR lenses were collected in the form of a questionnaire which was distributed to members of Aston University Vision Sciences Department. Thirty six questionnaires were completed, all by subjects who wore and who had worn MAR coatings on their spectacle lenses.

2.2 Results

Responses to the questionnaire are shown in Figure 1. Most respondents felt that in each of the conditions investigated they gain some or much improvement from their lens coating. Although the major improvements most people gained from such a coating was in the cosmetic appearance of their lenses, the majority of people claimed at least some improvement in vision with an anti reflection coat for VDU use and under artificial lights and a large minority (10 from 36) of people felt a major improvement with night driving. Most of the people questioned said they would have such a coating applied to their next pair of spectacles.

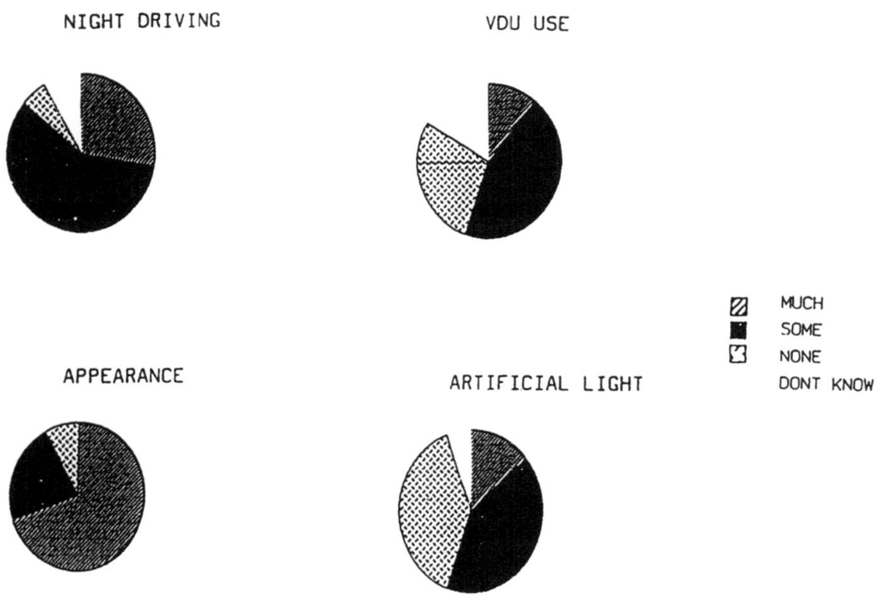

Figure 1. Subjective improvements in spectacle lens performance under different conditions.

3. EFFECT OF MAR COATED LENSES ON CONTRAST SENSITIVITY

3.1 Methods

Contrast sensitivity for nine subjects was measured. All subjects were emmetropic with no ocular abnormalities and uncorrected visual acuity of 6/9 or better. No refractive correction was worn for any part of the experiment.

A sine - wave grating was generated by a Venus visual simulator under computer control. Black and white horizontal gratings were produced in one of four quadrants of the display screen. A 4 forced choice staircase method was used to assess contrast sensitivity, with the subject required to identify in which quadrant the grating appeared. If the response was correct, contrast was reduced for the next presentation, if incorrect it was increased. Steps used were 20% of present contrast level.

Contrast threshold was determined for 3 spatial frequencies, 0.75 cycles/degree, 3.0 cycles/degree and 12.0 cycles/degree with frequencies presented at random, screen angular subtense was 25.5 degrees square and mean luminance 60 cd/m^2 . General luminance was 2 cd/m^2 and subjects viewed the display monocularly with the right eye.

The glare source took the form of an illuminated bowl with a central aperture through which the screen was viewed. The bowl was positioned 25mm from the eye and luminance was 1200 cd/m .

Spectacles worn were glazed with plano CR39 lenses. One pair were uncoated, the other had a Dollond & Aitchison XTE 5 layers MAR coating, with a maximum transmission of 99.2%.

Contrast sensitivity for each subject was measured in randomised order with and without the glare source, with no spectacles, with uncoated or with the coated lenses.

3.2 Results

The results of this experimental study are shown in figures 2 and 3. These data suggest that spectacle lenses made only a marginal difference to contrast sensitivity in the absence of glare, whereas in the presence of a glare source uncoated spectacle lenses reduced contrast sensitivity at all spatial frequencies. Multi anti reflection coated lenses made very little difference in the absence of glare; in the presence of a glare source the coated lenses resulted in higher contrast sensitivity than uncoated lenses.

So are coated lenses better than no lenses at all? Figure 2 shows that in the absence of glare a coated spectacle lens gave a marginal, but not significant improvement in contrast sensitivity, but in the presence of glare contrast sensitivity was marginally better with no lens at all at low and mid spatial frequencies and marginally better with the coated lens at high spatial frequencies. Overall though there was wide inter subject variability in the data, multi anti reflection coated spectacle lenses would appear to restore the losses in contrast sensitivity under conditions of glare caused by spectacle lenses to close to the position without lenses.

The data for glare disability show a similar picture. Glare disability appeared greater at high and least at low spatial frequencies; uncoated lenses performed worse than no lenses and the addition of the multi anti reflection coating to the lenses restored this reduction in performance to close to the no lens situation.

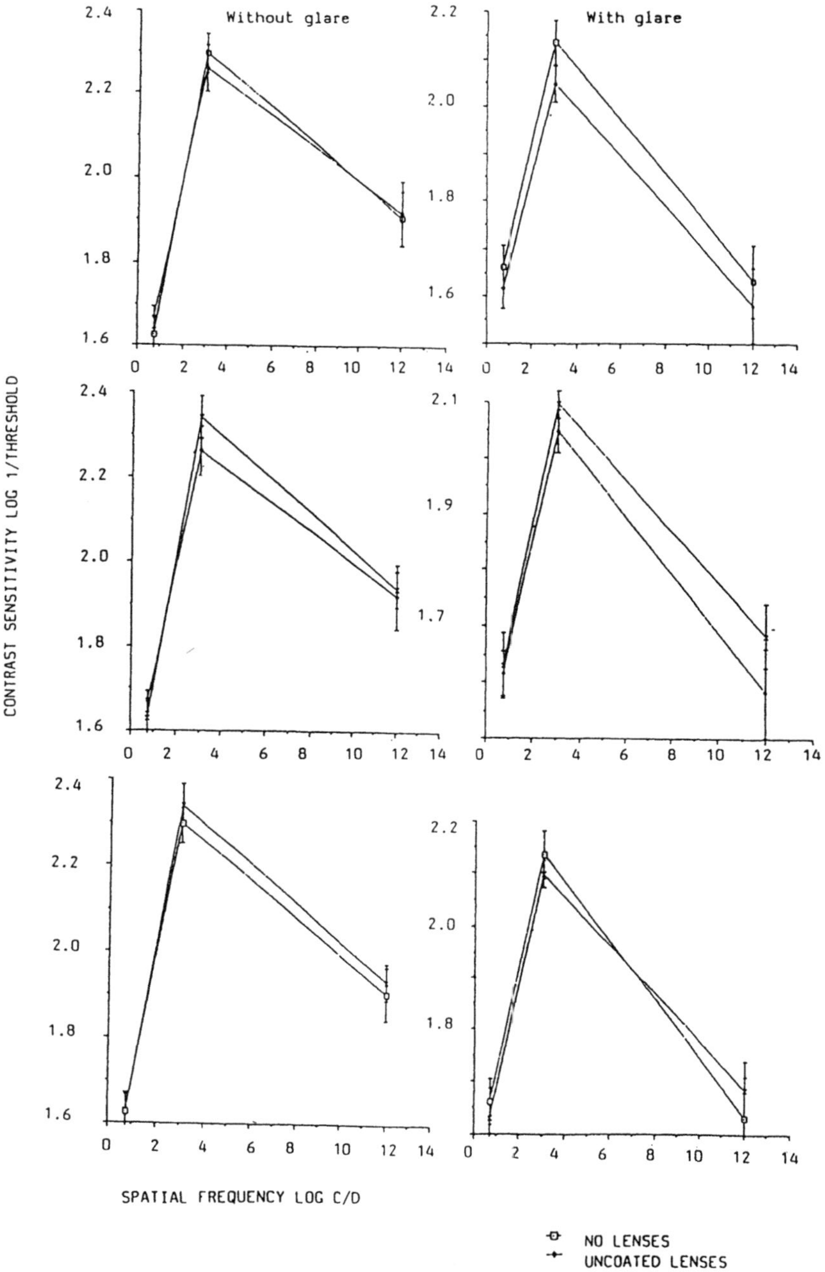

Figure 2. The effect of uncoated and coated spectacle lenses on contrast sensitivity in the presence and absence of glare.

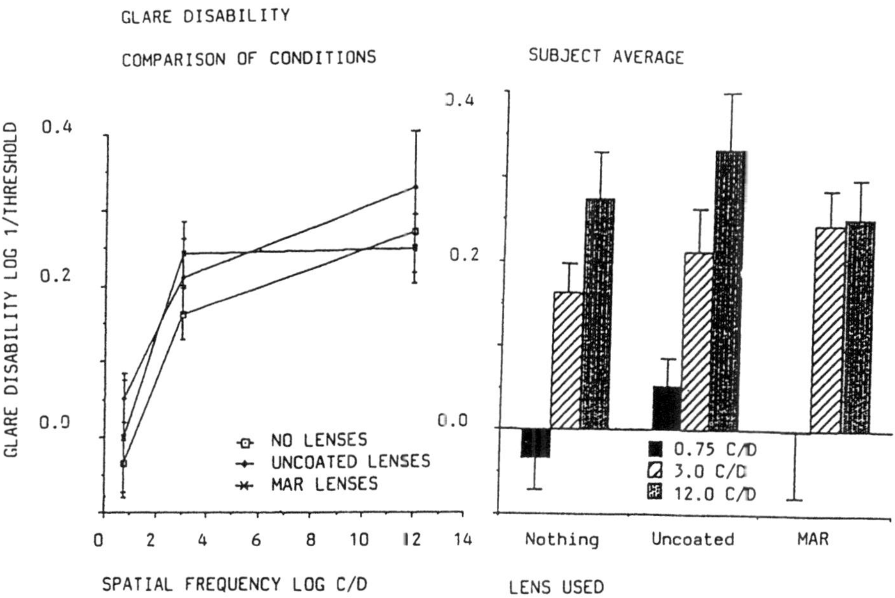

Figure 3. Do MAR coated lenses reduce glare disability?

4. DISCUSSION

These results suggest that MAR coatings do improve contrast sensitivity, though the differences are smaller than those found by previous studies (Coupland & Kirkham 1981). Small improvements were found both in comparison to without lenses and with uncoated lenses.

Glare was, not surprisingly, seen to reduce contrast sensitivity; and this reduction is greatest at mid and high spatial frequencies. This confirms Coupland & Kirkham's (1981) data that the effects of glare are spatial frequency dependent. This reduction of contrast sensitivity was greatest when wearing uncoated lenses; performance with MAR coated lenses in the presence of glare was less reduced.

The results obtained when wearing MAR coated lenses were quite similar to those found with no lenses worn. Without lenses performance was marginally better at low and middle spatial frequencies, but MAR lenses aided peformance slightly at high spatial frequencies. These data suggest that wearing MAR coated plano lenses in the presence of a glare source is unlikely to improve vision compared to wearing no lenses at all. There would appear to be little argument in favour of prescribing coated, plano lenses to patients who suffer glare problems when driving or using VDU screens. However since glare disability was greatest with uncoated lenses, the data would suggest that for an ametropic patient where spectacles will be worn the addition of a MAR coat will improve vision under glare conditions.

During this study, individual results showed wide variability between subjects. This would appear to confirm the findings of the questionnaire most subjects found the coatings to be of some benefit, but the extent of this benefit was quite variable.

This study suggests that MAR coatings have advantages to spectacle wearers. Cosmetically the appearance of the lenses is improved, and subjectively wearers found they made conditions involving glare more acceptable. In terms of visual performance, they would appear to improve a situation in which the introduction of a lens has reduced contrast sensivity, but their assistance to the normal unaided eye in a glare situation is not significant.

REFERENCE

Coupland S.G. and Kirkham T.H. (1981), Improved contrast sensitivity with anti reflective coated lenses in the ppresence of glare. Can. J. Ophthal., 16, 136-140.

VISION IN VEHICLES - V
A.G. Gale et al. (Editors)

Traffic Safety Aspects of High-Intensity Discharge Headlamps; Discomfort Glare and Direction Indicator Conspicuity

J.W.A.M. Alferdinck

TNO Human Factors Research Institute
P.O. Box 23, 3769 ZG Soesterberg, The Netherlands.

Abstract

A laboratory study was conducted for evaluating the effect of size of High-Intensity Discharge (HID) headlamps and the separation from the direction indicator on discomfort glare and direction indicator conspicuity, respectively.

The discomfort glare was subjectively rated on the nine-point De Boer scale. In addition to the expected effects of glare illuminance and glare angle on the discomfort rating, a small, but statistically significant effect of headlamp size was found. Reducing lamp dimensions by a factor two (a factor four in area) increases the discomfort glare by only 0.1 points. This effect can be compensated for by a 11% reduction in the luminous intensity of the headlamps.

The conspicuity of the front direction indicator as a function of its separation from the HID headlamp was measured by determining the maximum eccentricity of the line of sight at which the direction indicator was just perceptible. A strong effect of separation was only found for low indicator intensities. When the separation is defined as the distance between the lamp centres, there was no effect of lamp size. A minimum centre-to-centre distance of 22 cm is recommended, based on the criterion of a minimum conspicuity angle of 25°.

1. INTRODUCTION

Due to the recent development of very small High-Intensity Discharge (HID) lamps, it is now possible to considerably reduce the size of motorcar headlamps. To preserve sufficient luminous intensity, the luminance of such headlamps has to be rather high. It is expected that the luminous intensities of HID headlamps will be two to three times higher than those of halogen lamps. This may have at least two adverse effects, the first being an unacceptable increase of discomfort glare. Secondly, small lamp sizes designs are possible with a relatively small separation between headlamp and direction indicator, and thus could cause a decrease in the conspicuity of the latter. The goal of this study was twofold: to evaluate the extent of this discomfort glare as a function of lamp size (Experiment 1), and to measure the conspicuity of the front indicator as a function of its distance from the HID headlamp (Experiment 2).

2. EXPERIMENT 1

2.1. Methods

The experiment was carried out in the laboratory, with (spatial) reality scaled down by a factor five. The subjects were seated at five metres in front of a white plywood screen (2.5 m x 3 m) in which the lamps were mounted. The mean luminance of the screen was 0.2 cd/m^2. The luminance of the side walls of the 3.8 m wide laboratory was about 0.05 cd/m^2. These background values are representative for nighttime luminance conditions on a road with public lighting.

Subjects were instructed to perform two tasks, a tracking task and the evaluation of the discomfort glare produced by simulated HID headlamps. The tracking task, shown on a VDU-screen located at five meters in front of the subject, was executed with a steering wheel. To the left from the VDU-screen a glare source was mounted, which was switched on during the tracking task. After completing the tracking task the subject rated the discomfort glare on a nine-point scale (see below).

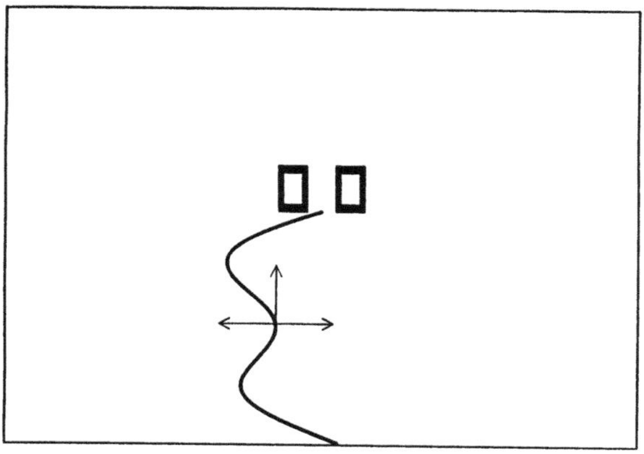

Figure 1 The tracking display. The vertical arrow indicates the direction of the waving track. The horizontal arrows indicate the directions of the control actions by the steering wheel. The two rectangles were stationary. Black in this drawing was white on the VDU-screen.

Figure 1 shows the picture generated on the tracking display. A wavy track continuously moved downwards over the screen with a speed of 7.3 mm/s (see also [1]). Using the steering wheel, the subject could move the whole track in the left-right direction. The subject's task was to align the lower end of the track with the gap between the two stationary rectangles. The rectangles were kept stationary to minimize eye movements of the subjects. Eye movements cause variation in the glare angle, and would thus introduce variance in glare rating. When the track was outside the gap, an irritating beep warned the subject to pay attention to the tracking task. The mean luminance of the rectangles and the track was 27 cd/m^2.

Rectangular headlamps of three sizes (3x6 cm, 6x12 cm and 12x24 cm) were simulated at three distances, 25 m, 50 m and 100 m, resulting in five different glare source areas of 0.00059 deg^2, 0.0024 deg^2, 0.0095 deg^2, 0.038 deg^2, and 0.151 deg^2.

The glare source was located at 1.72°, 3.43° or 6.84° to the left of the fixation point (the gap in the tracking task). These glare angles are representative for oncoming passenger cars approaching at 25 m, 50 m and 100 m, on a two-lane road, with lanes of 3 m width. Using a slide projector in combination with a computer controlled diaphragm/filter wheel, 25 different stimuli (5 sizes x 5 glare illuminances) could be generated and presented in random order to the subject. The halogen lamp of the projector was exchanged for a HID bulb. The five glare illuminance values used had average values of 0.0286 lx, 0.0974 lx, 0.298 lx, 1.023 lx and 2.952 lx (standard deviation 5%), as measured at the eye of the observer.

The discomfort glare was rated with the de Boer [2] nine-point scale, with naming of the qualifiers for the odd points (1 = unbearable; 3 = disturbing; 5 = just admissible; 7 = acceptable; 9 = inappreciable). The naming of 7 and 9 was slightly modified. (see also [3]). The use of this rating scale, which is quite common in public and automotive lighting [4-6], was explained to the subjects in a short training session of about 10 minutes. In this session, covering the full range of glare illuminances and sizes, the subjects also practised the tracking task. After this introduction, the glare source was set at one of the three possible glare angles. Each of the 25 size/illuminance-combinations was presented for 10 seconds, in random order, until all combinations had been displayed twice. Discomfort glare was rated after each presentation. A session was completed after this procedure was repeated for the other two glare angles. This took about one hour. After a 10 minute break, a session was repeated. Every subject participated in three sessions. The presentation order of the glare angles was different for each session, and randomized over subjects. So, every subject made six assessments of all angle/size/illuminance-combinations. Sixteen paid subjects, eight males and eight females in the age range from 20 to 74 years, all with normal visual acuity, participated in this study.

2.2. Results

The results, in terms of the mean discomfort glare ratings of the six replications, were tested for statistical significance with an analysis of variance (ANOVA) and a post hoc Tukey test.

Glare illuminance (E_G) appeared to be the most important factor. With increasing (log) glare illuminance, the discomfort glare rating (D) decreased linearly (more discomfort), according to $D = 3.42 - 2.19 \log E_G$. This result corresponds rather well with other studies [4-6].

Compared to what is reported in the literature [6], a rather large effect of glare angle was found. With increasing (log) glare angle (q) the discomfort glare rating increased linearly (less discomfort), according to $D = 3.69 + 1.62 \log q$.

A small, but significant effect of size (A) was found, just as shown by other authors [6]. That is, the discomfort glare rating decreased with decreasing glare source size (more discomfort). The best fit regression line, averaged over all illuminance levels and angles, was $D = 4.90 + 0.169 \log A$. Figure 2 shows the discomfort glare rating as a function of the glare illuminance, with the glare source area (in deg^2) as a parameter. The near coincidence of the functions illustrates the small effect of the size of the glare source area, especially for the moderate glare illuminances

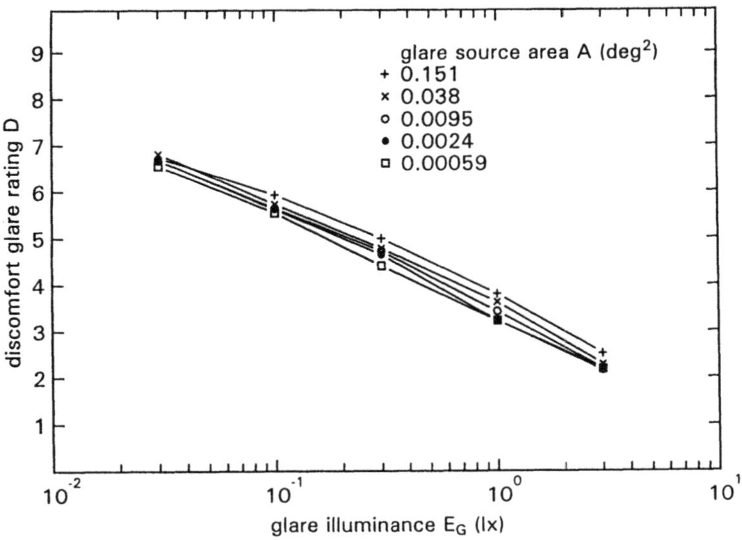

Figure 2 Discomfort glare rating as a function of glare illuminance, with the glare source area as a parameter. High rating implies low discomfort glare.

An interaction was found between glare angle and glare area. At large glare angles, the influence of the glare area was smaller than at small glare angles. This can be explained by the lower resolving power of the retina in the periphery compared to the centre of the retina.

No significant effect of sex was found, which contradicts an earlier study [6] reporting that only the male subjects were responsible for an effect of size on the discomfort glare rating, although this effect could not be reproduced. Also, no significant effect of age was found. However, as reported elsewhere [1], an (expected) age effect was found for *disability* glare, the effect produced by light scattering in the eye [7,8]. About twice as much disability glare (in terms of estimated straylight) was measured at 70 years as compared to age 20 years. This finding confirms the view that discomfort and disability glare are caused by different mechanisms.

An equation was derived which describes the discomfort glare D as a function of glare source area A (deg^2), glare illuminance E_G (lx), and glare angle q (°).

$$D(E_G,\theta,A) = 3.15 - 2.19 \log(E_G) + 1.138 \log(\theta) + 0.298 \log(A) - 0.242 \log(\theta) \log(A)$$

2.3. Discussion

The small effect of the area of the glare source on the discomfort glare rating, as shown in Figure 2, is of little practical consequence. Halving the size of the headlamp (factor four in area) results in a decrease in the discomfort rating of 0.1 points, which can be compensated for by 11 % lower glare illuminance. An earlier study reported a decrease of 0.2 points [6]. This is still a rather small effect in comparison with the influences of headlamp aiming, aging and dirt [9]. Paying more attention to aiming and cleaning the headlamp can easily compensate for smaller headlamp sizes.

3. EXPERIMENT 2

3.1. Methods

The laboratory and lighting conditions were the same as in experiment 1. Three independent variables, lamp size, separation, and intensity ratio, were simulated for a distance of 25 m, with the subjects seated at 5 m distance. As for lamp size, the first variable, three lamp size combinations were simulated, as shown in Figure 3. The smallest combination represents a possible miniature design for HID headlamps.

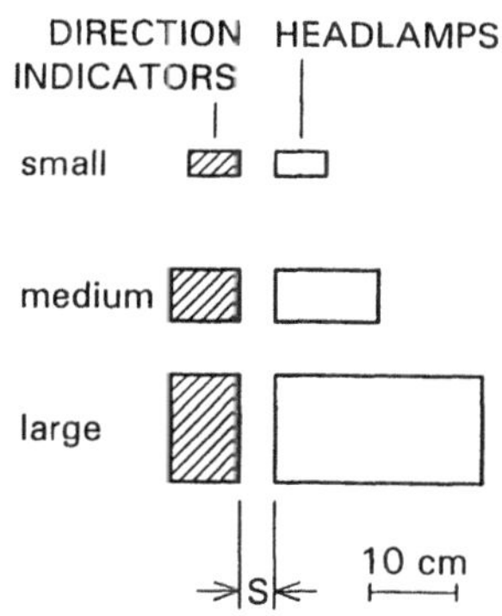

Figure 3 Simulated lamp/size combinations used in the experiment. S is the separation between the direction indicator and the headlamp.

The second independent variable, the simulated separation S between the two lights, was varied over a range from 0 to 40 cm. As will be discussed, the centre-to-centre separation (to be referred to as "distance between centres") turned out to be a more useful variable, in that it allowed for a simpler description of the results.

The ratio between the luminous intensities of the direction indicator and the headlamp, the third independent variable, was varied as follows. The simulated minimum luminous intensity of the headlamp was 250 cd, which is the ECE's limiting intensity of halogen headlamps in the direction of an oncoming car driver's eye [10]. A luminous intensity of 6250 cd was taken as the maximum. Drivers may be exposed to these high HID intensities, when overtaken on straight roads or encountered or followed in curves by other cars. The simulated minimum and maximum luminous intensities of the director indicator were respectively set at 175 cd and 860 cd, the limiting values for these lamps in the ECE regulations [11]. The "high" intensity ratio was the combination of the maximum direction indicator intensity and the minimum headlamp intensity. For the "low" ratio the minimum indicator intensity and the maximum headlamp intensity were combined. The "medium" ratio was the geometrical mean of the "high" and "low" ratios. The resulting three indicator/headlamp ratios for "high", "medium" and "low", thus took values of 3.44, 0.31, and 0.028.

The headlamp was simulated by the same slide projector as used in Experiment 1. An additional projector with a halogen bulb and amber filter was installed, for simulating the direction indicator. The chromaticity coordinates of the latter, i.e. x = 0.588, y = 0.411, conformed to ECE regulations [11]. Its flicker frequency, produced by a chopper in the light beam, was 1.5 Hz, which is within the prescribed ECE frequency limits of 1 to 2 Hz [12]. The luminance distribution over the lamp areas was quite homogenous, the maximum standard deviation occurring for the largest headlamp, being 14%. A movable mirror system was used for adjusting the separation between "headlamp" and "indicator".

The conspicuity of the direction indicator was expressed in degrees of eccentric perceptibility [13], that is the angle defined by the lines passing through the central fixation point (the centre of the indicator) and the most eccentric fixation point, respectively. The latter is defined as the fixation point (to the left of the indicator) at which that light is just visible. A measurement started by fixation on a point far to the left from the flashing stimulus (>90°). From that position the fixation was moved slowly towards the stimulus until the flashing stimulus could just be detected. The subject was seated on a rotatable chair, on which a pointer and a He-Ne laser were mounted. The light spot of the laser on the screen or the wall served as a fixation point for the subject. The conspicuity angle could be read by the experimenter from a scale on the floor. The subject was instructed to use a fixed criterion for making the decision "visible" or "not visible". This criterion was: a *flashing* light point should be visible from the corner of the eye. The subjects were allowed to look with two eyes.

Every subject rated the indicator conspicuity at the intensity ratio "low", with five different separations (0, 10, 20, 30, and 40 cm), the intensity ratio "medium", with three separations (0, 20, and 40 cm), and the intensity ratio "high", with two separations (0 and 40 cm). Five subjects were used, four males and one female, between the age of 20 to 50 years, all with normal vision (Landolt-C visual acuity between 1 and 2).

3.2. Results

Figure 4 shows the conspicuity angle as a function of the distance between the two lamp centres. Note that this distance is not the separation (S) as depicted in Figure 3. Statistical analysis (ANOVA, with five replications per subject), showed the effect of the intensity ratio to be clearly significant. The higher the ratio, the greater the conspicuity. A significant effect of separation was found for the "low" and "medium" intensity ratios. For the "high" intensity ratio, the flashing indicator was so conspicuous, that it could be seen at the limit of the field of view, at an angle between 90 and 100° Due to this ceiling effect, there was no effect of separation.

An effect of size was found only when the lamp separation was defined as the gap between the lamp edges (S in Figure 3). However, when the separation was defined as the distance between lamp centres, the conspicuity was independent of the separation. This is illustrated in Figure 4, where the data relating to the different sizes all fall along a single line (for a given intensity ratio).

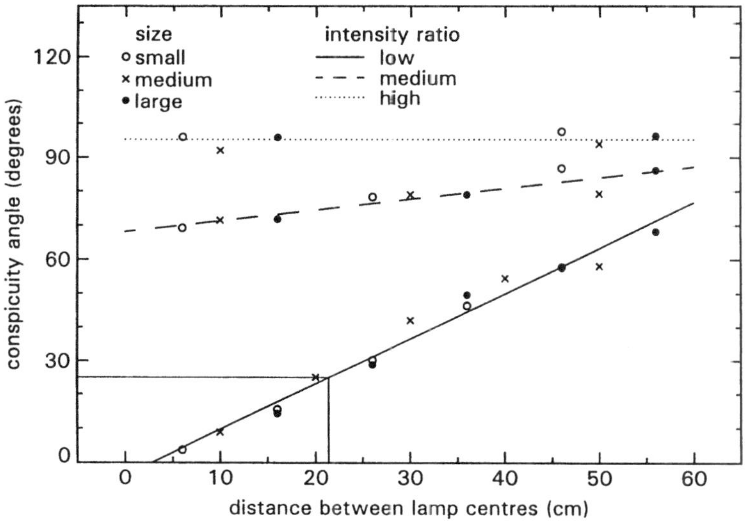

Figure 4 Conspicuity angle of the direction indicator as a function of the centre-to-centre distance between direction indicator and headlamp, with intensity ratio and lamp size as parameters. Linear regression lines are shown for each set of data.

3.3. Discussion

A relationship was found between the conspicuity angle of the direction indicator as a function of intensity ratio, separation, and lamp size. But what is the minimum conspicuity angle needed in practice? On straight roads, the most relevant information for the driver is located within an arc of 10° from the line of sight [14]. For curved roads, this easily increases to 15°. Thus, we need a conspicuity angle of at least 15° (conspicuity threshold). For an adequate safety margin, the angle should be far above the threshold, say 10°. We thus arrive at a minimum conspicuity angle of about 25°. In an additional experiment in a real traffic situation with a typical car in *daylight*, we measured angles between 13 and 32° when the car was located respectively in sun and shadow [3]. Therefore, a minimum of 25° seems to be a reasonable value. When the 25° criterion is applied to Figure 4 (as indicated by thin lines), a minimum allowable distance between the lamp centres of 22 cm can be derived, regardless of lamp size.

4. CONCLUSIONS

a) Headlamp size has a minor effect on the discomfort glare rating. Halving the size (a factor four in area) decreases the discomfort glare rating by 0.1 point on the nine point de Boer scale (more discomfort glare). This effect can be compensated for by an 11% lowering of the glare illuminance.

b) Taking 25° as an estimate for the minimally required conspicuity angle for direction indicators, the minimum distance between the centres of headlamps and direction indicators should be 22 cm, regardless of lamp size.

5. REFERENCES

1. J.W.A.M. Alferdinck and J. Varkevisser, Discomfort glare from D1 headlamps of different size. Report IZF 1991 C-21, TNO Institute for Perception, Soesterberg, The Netherlands (1991).
2. J.B. de Boer, Visual perception in road traffic and the field of vision of the motorist. Public Lighting, Philips Technical Library, Eindhoven, The Netherlands (1967).
3. J.W.A.M. Alferdinck and J. Varkevisser, Conspicuity of the front direction indicator in combination with a D1 headlamp. Report IZF 1991 C-20, TNO Institute for Perception, Soesterberg, The Netherlands (1991).
4. H.J. Schmidt-Clausen and J.Th.H. Bindels, Assessment of discomfort glare in motor vehicle lighting. Lighting Research and Technology 6 (1979) 79-88.
5. M. Sivak and P.L. Olson, Toward the development of a field methodology for evaluating discomfort glare from automotive headlamps. Report No. UMTRI-87-41, The University of Michigan, Transportation Institute, (1987).
6. M. Sivak, C.J. Simmons and M. Flannagan, Effect of headlamp area on discomfort glare. Lighting Research and Technology 22 (1990) 49-52.
7. J.J. Vos. Disability glare - a state of the art report. CIE-Journal 3/2, 39-53 (1984).
8. J.K. Ijspeert, J.K. Waard, T.J.T.P. van den Berg, and P.T.V.M. de Jong. The intraocular straylight function in 129 healthy volunteers; Dependence on angle, age and pigmentation. Vision Research, 30, 699-707 (1990).
9. J.W.A.M. Alferdinck and P. Padmos, Car headlamps: Influence of dirt, age and poor aim on glare illumination intensities. Lighting Research and Technology 20(4) (1988) 195-198.
10. ECE, Agreement concerning motor vehicle equipment and parts. Economic Commission of Europe, Regulation 20 (H4 halogen lamps), United Nations, Geneva (1976).
11. ECE, Agreement concerning motor vehicle equipment and parts. Economic Commission of Europe, Regulation 6, Revision 1 (Uniform provision concerning the approval of direction indicators for motor vehicles and their trailers), United Nations, Geneva (1987).
12. ECE, Agreement concerning motor vehicle equipment and parts. Economic Commission of Europe, Regulation 48, Revision 1 (Uniform provision concerning the approval of installation of lighting and lighting signalling devices), United Nations, Geneva (1982).
13. F.L. Engel, Visual conspicuity, directed attention and retinal locus. Vision Research 11 (1971) 563-576.
14. CIE, Roadsigns. Publ. CIE nr. 74, Int. Commission on Illumination, Vienna (1988).

6. ACKNOWLEDGEMENT

The work was sponsored by VEDILIS (VEhicle DIscharge LIghting System) in the context of a European Eureka project.

8: VISIBILITY RESTRICTIONS AND VEHICLE CONTROL

VISION IN VEHICLES - V
A.G. Gale et al. (Editors)

Risks related to visibility restrictions in vehicles used in materials - handling and construction

F. Hella, J.F. Schouller and M. Tisserand

Institut National de Recherche et de Sécurité, BP 27, F 54501 Vandoeuvre les Nancy, France

1. INDUSTRIAL APPLICATIONS AND STANDARDIZATION

The driving of a forklift truck in a workshop, or of earth moving machinery at a construction site represents a complex industrial situation in which the driver of the vehicle, the vehicle itself, the task undertaken, the environment and other people at the site are all simultaneously involved. The driver must continuously monitor the external environment in order to obtain any information needed to adapt to a situation which can change rapidly. Thus anything that can hinder this gathering of visual information can impede the driver' s appreciation of the situation and thus present a safety risk.

Machine manufacturers have made progress on most of the ergonomic aspects of the driver' s stand of such vehicles. However, the overall characteristics of a large number of these vehicles are such that visibility is still quite restricted (Soued et al., 1983 ; Mouret, 1988). It is therefore very important that visual imperatives be taken into consideration by the manufacturers from the very first stages of the vehicles' design. In order to do so, the manufacturer must be able to rely on well defined and validated standards and regulations.

The current standards and standardization projects include methods for the measurement of the field of vision from the driver' s stand of motorized forklifts (European Directive 89/240/EEC) (EEC, 1989) or from earth-moving equipment (standardization project ISO/DIS 5006 (ISO, 1988). It can be considered that the standards, or norms, for forklift trucks are well-founded, but could still be perfected. In contrast, the principle on which the measurement in the standardization project for earth-movers is based can be contested, and in no way guarantees that the field of vision from such a vehicle will be clear enough to provide the driver with the required visibility (Hella et al., 1991).

It is therefore necessary to identify and define criteria which will allow the people concerned with the development and implementation of different standards and norms to establish rules based on the requirements imposed by both safety and ergonomic aspects of the problem. The current study is a contribution to the identification of the quantitative criteria that could be integrated into the regulatory procedures for the measurement of visibility.

2. THEORY

It is generally thought that the driver of a vehicle controls its displacement on two levels (Neboit, 1984) :

- a regulation, or control, by temporal anticipation that consists of collecting information in the distant regions of the environment in order to be able to predict the vehicle' s trajectory, and that brings central vision into play above all else,
- a closed-loop, or "feed-back" regulation that consists of minimizing, little by little, the deviation between the predicted and real trajectories, and that relies on the peripheral perception of lateral indicators such as the edge of the route, ground markings, etc.

One could suppose that the driving of an industrial vehicle brings into play the same type of spatial and temporal evaluations, even at low speeds.

3. METHODOLOGY

In order to attempt to prove the existence of these mechanisms, the following methodology was employed :

- the simulated driving of an industrial vehicle on a closed circuit, composed of both straight and curved sections,
- a comparison between the drivers' performances in situations of total visibility and other situations where the field of vision is partially masked.

The simulation station consists of a seat, a steering wheel, two pedals (accelerator, brake), a personal computer and a large video screen to display the road image and the background landscape. The road scene, the dynamics and geometry of the simulated vehicle can quickly be adjusted. This station hardly looks like a real driver's cabine, but it aims at reproducing situations enabling drivers to carry out some of the activities he performs in real driving.

The performance levels were evaluated using the following criteria :

- recording of the deviation from the proposed trajectory and of the speed as indications of the adjustments, or regulation made by the subject,
- recording of any lateral head motions made by the driver in order to avoid the restrictions imposed by the visual masks interposed between the driver and the target zone.

Twenty drivers participated in two experimental sessions which took place one month apart. During each session, the drivers were made to drive twice around the circuit at high speed, and in different experimental modes, these being defined by the level of visibility of the simulated scene :

- total visibility : the images presented on the screen covered a 30° area and were 1.25m from the subject.
- masking of the middle of the field of vision : two series of five masks of different size blocked from 12.5 to 75 % of the middle section of the field of vision (Masks A1 through A5 and B1 through B5).
- masking of the peripheral vision : the two lateral zones (vertical = C, and horizontal = D) were blocked by masks of different size which allowed one to see from 12.5 to 75 % of the middle part of the field of vision (Masks C1 through C5 and D1 through D5).

The subjects were required to keep the vehicle in the middle of the path, the latter being indicated by a dashed white line. The maximum possible speed was 37 km/h.

The visual masks consisted of black bars superposed on the image. The lateral position of these bars was linked to and controlled by the drivers' head movement. In order to get a clearer field of vision, the subjects could cause the bars to move laterally by moving their head to one side or the other (Figure 1). This was intended to simulate head movements that are possible in a real situation.

4. RESULTS

The analysis of the collected data shows that three types of strategies were used by the drivers in order to obtain the information necessary for the proper driving of the vehicles when obstacles restrained, or blocked, their field of vision.

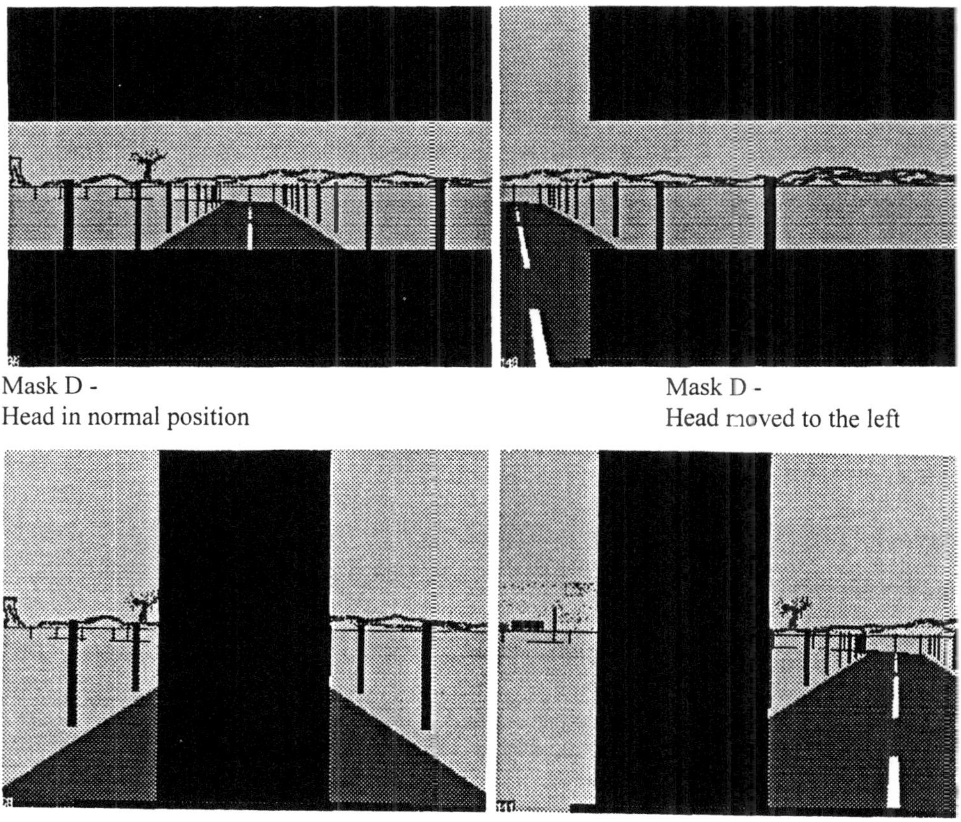

Mask D - Head in normal position

Mask D - Head moved to the left

Mask A - Head in normal position

Mask A - Head moved to the right

Figure 1 - Examples of the effect of lateral head movements on the position of the masked areas.

a) Lateral head movements in order to avoid the mask and to gather the missing visual information. (It was considered, by convention, that there was head movement when the amplitude of the lateral motion was greater than the average value in situations where the vision was not obstructed)

b) Modification of the speed in order to maintain a constant level of precision while steering the vehicle,

c) Use of visual information available in the windows defined by the masks without any additional head motion.

4.1. Lateral head movement

The proportion of subjects that moved their heads laterally in order to gain a clearer field of vision depended significantly on the type of mask used (Figure 2). For example, in the case of the obstruction of the vertical portion of the middle of the field of vision (Mask A), only 45 % of the subjects moved their heads, whereas 60 % of them moved their heads when there was a central opening in the field of vision in the vertical plane (Mask C).

The results shows that the subjects were less inclined to move their heads laterally with masks A and B than they were with masks C and D.

A comparison of masks B and D would seem to indicate that the horizontal "window" of vision is better placed for mask B (downward vision) than it is for mask D (horizontal vision). This could underline the importance of downward vision (some few degrees below the horizontal) in the control of the trajectory of the vehicle.

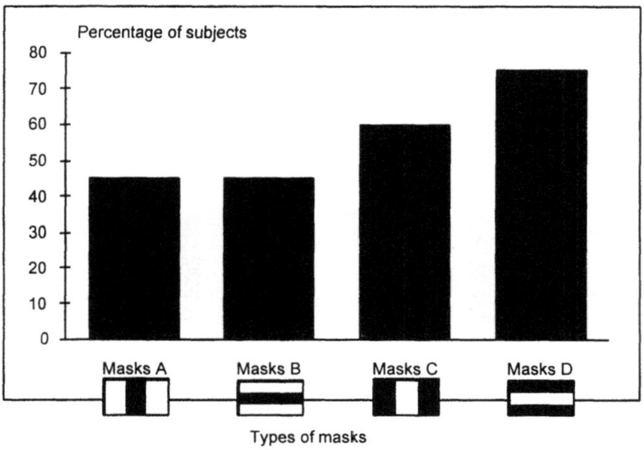

Figure 2 - Proportion of subjects showing lateral head movements as a function of the type of mask.

Furthermore, the experimental set-up did not include the capacity to create situations where obstacles were randomly introduced in the path of the vehicle, and therefore head movement was not motivated by any requirements of systematic surveillance, but only to carry out the task of steering the truck.

The average amplitude of the head movements increased as the portion of the field of vision masked was increased, but did not seem to depend on the configuration of the mask. Nevertheless, the dispersion in the absolute and average amplitudes of the head movements increased with the amount of surface obscured by the masks.

4.2. Control of vehicle speed

The capacity of a driver to control the vehicle's speed depends on the visual information gathered from the immediate environment.

The constraints placed on the visibility by the experimental masks caused the subjects to slow down as the percentage of the surface masked by the bars was increased (Figure 3, masks A and D). The speed also varied as a function of the location on the circuit. The average speed of the drivers in the curves was lower than that in the straight-sections. This corresponds to a safety-oriented type of behaviour on the part of the drivers, which goes to prove that the objectives of the simulated tasks were well understood by the drivers.

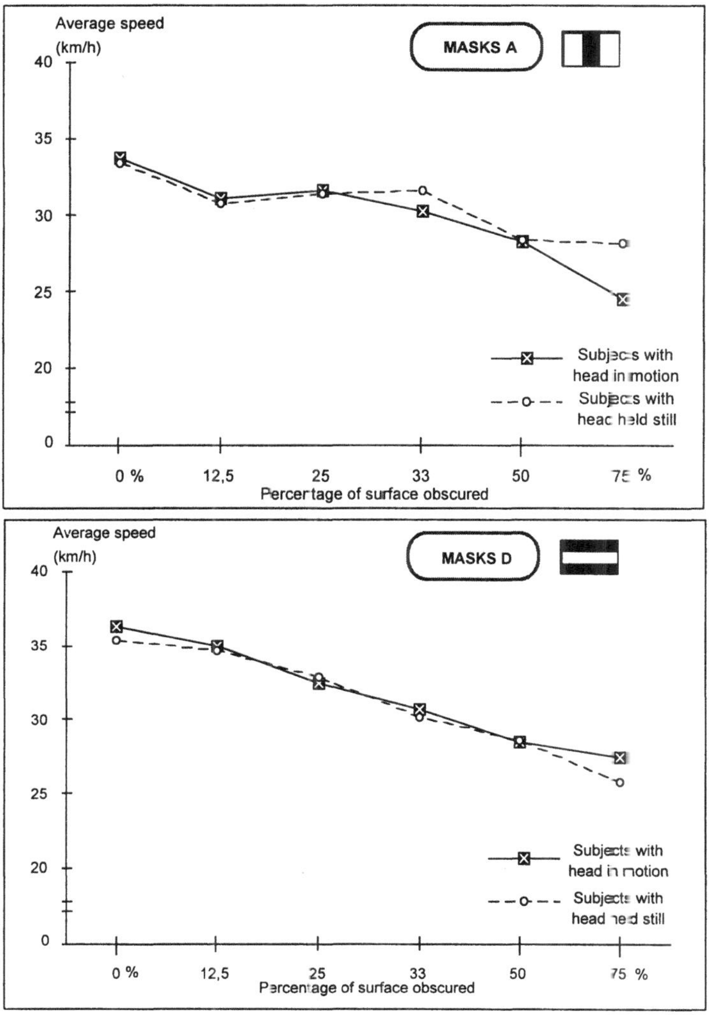

Figure 3 - Average speed as a function of the surface obscured and of head mobility for masks A and D.

Figure 3 shows that this reduction of the average speed is the same in the case of drivers who did and who did not move their heads. One could thus suppose that the strategy of moving the head to compensate for a reduced field of vision was not efficient. If, in moving their heads, the drivers found a method of gathering visual information identical to that which they used with a clear field of vision, then they should be able to maintain a speed similar to that observed with unobstructed vision. Given that this is not the case, it could then be believed that, in terms of controlling the speed, looking laterally around the edges of the mask is not at all equivalent to gathering visual information under maximum visibility conditions.

4.3. Use of available information

The subjects who did not move their heads could not exploit the visual information obscured by the masks, only that information which was available in the clear window. A comparison of the ability of this group of drivers with those who did move their heads gives an indication of the influence of these two strategies on the quality of the steering of a given machine.

The data on the steering level as a function of the type of mask appears to depend to a large extent on the unfolding of the circuit (Figure 4). It can be seem that when the visual field is partially masked, all the subjects tend to come into the curves at relatively high speed because the masking leads them to underestimate the real speed at which they are driving (Malaterre et al., 1991). However, once in the curve, they tend to slow down rapidly because the deviation from the median stripe becomes quite significant. In this circumstance, moving the head allows the drivers to better appreciate the degree of curvature of the corners and to adapt their reactions (brake, steering) to the form of the circuit more rapidly. In contrast, not moving the head when the vision is masked limits the distance to which the driver can see in the curve, and as a consequence, has a negative impact on the driver' s ability to anticipate any changes in the curvature of the course and to follow the required trajectory.

The situation is completely the opposite in the straight sections of the circuit where head movements that are too big reduce the steering quality.

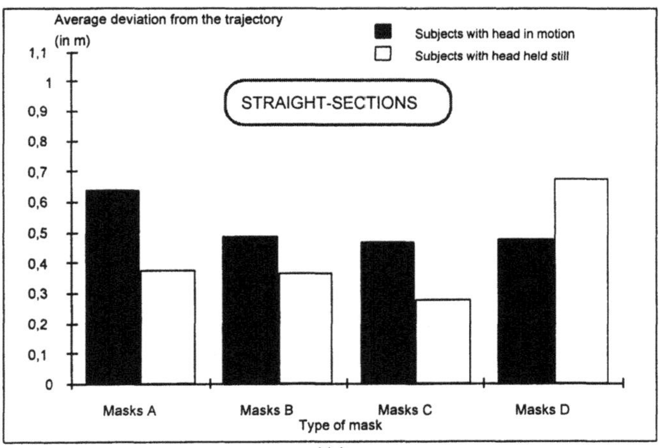

4(a)

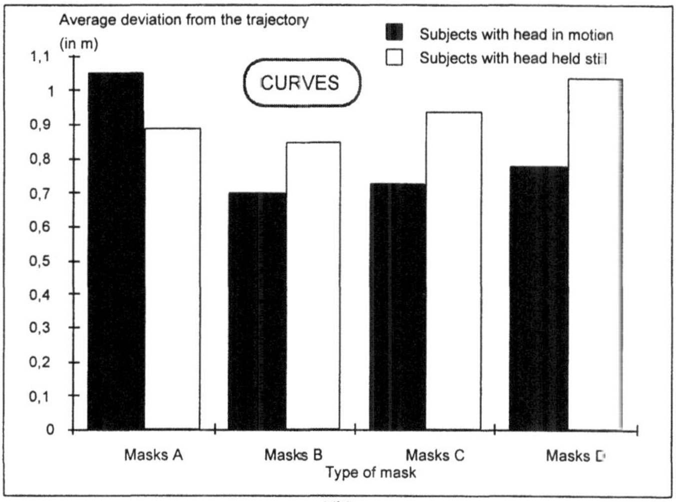

4(b)

Figure 4 - Average deviation from the trajectory
as a function of the nature of the circuit and of head mobility
for the different types of masks.

5. DISCUSSION AND FUTURE WORK

From the results of this study, the following three points should be emphasised :

- lateral head mobility, undertaken to avoid the visual masks, is not systematically seen in all of the subjects (it is present in only 45 - 75 % of the subjects depending on the type of mask). The absence of the use of this type of strategy could be taken as an indicator of the level of obstruction imposed by the visual restrictions studied, and corresponds to the adoption of a more rigid posture,
- the stability of the head in a certain proportion of the subjects in different masking situations seems to indicate that these drivers favour a strategy of correcting their trajectory (based on near visual clues) rather than on an anticipation of the circuit (based on the use of distant information.) However, this type of behaviour could prove to be quite dangerous in real situations since it would lead to a non-detection, or at best a delayed detection, of obstacles that are like to get in the way of the moving vehicles,
- finally, lateral head movement does not automatically guarantee an improvement in the ability to follow the proposed trajectory or to control the speed of the vehicle, and is thus not equivalent to the gathering of visual information under conditions of maximum visibility. This would lead to the recommendation that the field of vision should be enlarged in order to allow the drivers to improve their steering performance, as well as to anticipate the unfolding of the path on which they are driving and to detect any moving obstacles that may be in their way without having to move their heads.

If the above results are confirmed, they should have positive repercussions on the procedures for the assurance of good visibility from the driver' s stand of earth-moving equipment covered under the standardization project ISO/DIS 5006 (ISO, 1988). They would also lead to an examination of the importance attributed to lateral head movements in the visual evaluation of the driving environment.

It is clear that further studies are necessary in order to confirm these data in situations where risks linked to visibility restrictions in the driver' s stand are more realistic (random appearance of a pedestrian for example) and that include head movement in three dimensions.

REFERENCES

EEC : Méthode de mesure de visibilité pour les chariots de manutention automoteurs, Directive Européenne 89/240/CEE, Annexe 13 (1989).

F. Hella, M. Tisserand, J.F. Schouller and M. Englert, International Journal of Industrial Ergonomics, 8 (1991) 135-145.

ISO : Earth Moving Machinery. Operator Field of Vision, ISO Draft Proposal ISO/TC 127/SC 2 (1988).

G. Malaterre, A. Hary, F. Quere, Recherche-Transports-Sécurité, 30 (1991) 52-56.

M. Mouret, Cahiers des Comités de Prévention, du Bâtiment et des Travaux Publics, 2 (1988) 36-37.

M. Neboit , Convergences Médicales, 3, No. 2,(1984) 169-171.

A. Soued, C. Beuneux and A. Grosjean, Travail et Sécurité, 5 (1983) 252-261.

VISION IN VEHICLES - V
A.G. Gale et al. (Editors)
1996 Elsevier Science B.V.

The problems of restricted visibility from free-steered mining vehicles.

M. G. Boocock[a], A. K. Weyman[a], T. C. Corlett[a] and J Naylor[b].

[a]Health and Safety Executive, Health and Safety Laboratory, Broad Lane, Sheffield S3 7HQ, England.

[b]Health and Safety Executive, HM Inspector of Mechanical Engineering in Mines, Silver House, Silver Street, Doncaster DN1 1HR, England.

Abstract

During a routine operation, the driver of a free-steered vehicle (FSV) received fatal crush injuries to the chest whilst apparently adopting a posture to improve his line of sight. An ergonomics computer-aided design package (SAMMIE) was used to construct visibility charts and evaluate the existing design and proposed modifications to the vehicle. Visibility charts demonstrated significant improvement to the all-round visibility afforded to the driver of the FSV. Modifications were evaluated with respect to ergonomic constraints.

The new design was implemented and feedback from drivers of the converted vehicle suggests that modifications have improved the ease with which the vehicle can be operated. This investigation showed the benefits of computer-aided modelling for the assessment of visibility during vehicle design or prior to retrofit modifications being undertaken.

1. INTRODUCTION

Free-steered vehicle (FSV) is the phrase used to describe self propelled, rubber-tyred vehicles introduced into coal mines in the 1980's. Since their introduction the number of FSVs in use at British coal mines has increased considerably; 460 were reported to be in operation in 1991, compared with 188 in 1986 (HSE, 1991). The increased mobility and flexibility of FSVs over more conventional transport systems (e.g., rope and locomotive haulage systems) was the main reason for their introduction. Originally intended only as a load-haul-dump machine FSVs now carry out a number of functions, including material transport, manriding, dinting and roadway maintenance.

The Health and Safety Executive (HSE) reported that, between 1986 and 1991, FSVs were the primary cause of 4 fatal and 38 major injuries in British coal mines (HSE, 1991). Over half these accidents involved pedestrians being run over or struck by an FSV, or drivers striking or becoming trapped against the sides of the roadway. In the majority of cases, the accidents were reported to stem from either poor visibility or limited roadway clearances.

Typically, FSVs consist of two major units supported on one axis running on rubber-tyred wheels. These two units articulate around a central pivot arrangement controlled by hydraulic rams which enable the vehicle to be steered. The driver is seated on either of the two main units, close to the pivot, in a 'sideways' position, with his back adjacent to the roadway wall. This allows the vehicle to be driven in both directions.

The centrally located driving position, combined with a need to maintain a low vehicle height and carry large and awkward loads, inevitably places considerable restrictions on the driver's field of vision. Frequently, drivers are forced to adopt awkward and uncomfortable postures to improve their line of sight, which may ultimately place the driver at risk from injury or inhibit his ability to control and operate the vehicle. Designs, therefore, need to be assessed to ensure that they do not affect the safety of the driver or pedestrians.

2. TECHNIQUES FOR ASSESSING DRIVER VISION

Numerous approaches have been developed to assess the field of vision afforded to drivers of mobile machinery ranging from simple line of sight techniques to more complex photographic procedures. For example, the ISO 5006-1 standard (ISO, 1991) for recording the operators field of vision for earth moving machinery requires the measurements of shadows cast by two light sources on to a circle, 12 m in radius, placed at ground level. The length of shadows and the distance separating shadows cast on the perimeter of the circle are used to derive a rating of acceptability of visibility for designated regions around the vehicle. A criticism of this technique is that it is insensitive to structural differences between different designs of vehicle. Hella et al (1991) stated that field of vision can only be defined by considering a solid angle or, in projection, by a surface, and not by a single length as ISO 5006-1 (ISO, 1991) proposes. Using planimetric photography, Hella et al (1991) replaced the two light sources with a special photographic camera producing images without angular distortions. Comparison of obstructions measured by the ISO technique bore little relation to those measured using the photographic procedure.

A similar photographic procedure was used on selected mining vehicles by Sanders and Kelley (1981), the primary difference being that photographs were taken from outside the vehicle looking towards the driver's cab. To accommodate movement of the driver's trunk and head, an adjustable manikin was seated in the cab. Photographs were taken from selected 'visual attention locations' (VALs) around the vehicle which had been identified following interviews with drivers and observing vehicles in use. By combining a score for visibility observed from each location with the importance of each VAL during a particular task, an overall visibility score was derived for each vehicle and the task being carried out.

Limitations of line of sight and photographic procedures are that they require access to vehicles, they tend to be labour intensive, and do not lend themselves to assessing vehicle redesign. Glowacki et al (1992) sought to overcome these difficulties by using a computer-aided design system. The computer is used to generate a three dimensional model of the vehicle and visibility assessment are based on the VALs defined by Sanders and Kelley (1981). The software determines the location of each VAL, the corresponding line of sight vector and whether the sight line intersects with the machine geometry. Validation of the technique against the procedure used by Sanders and Kelley (1981) showed good correlation except in certain instances where imprecise digitisation of the machines geometry resulted in error.

Computer-aided design would seem to provide a more flexible and cost-effective approach to assessing driver vision and the implications of redesign. However, it is felt that such an approach should view visual requirements in conjunction with other ergonomic criteria. On this basis it was decided to investigate the suitability of using a standard ergonomics CAD system to evaluate vehicle visibility. A case study, involving a fatal accident to the driver of an FSV is used to illustrate the value and limitations of this approach in assessing vehicle design with a view to retrofit modifications.

3. INCIDENT INVESTIGATION

A driver of a FSV received fatal crush injuries to the chest whilst carrying out a routine back grading operation (levelling a roadway floor) in an underground fluorspar mine. In the opinion of the investigating inspector the accident occurred as a result of the driver reversing the FSV whilst concentrating on the position of the bucket at the front of the machine. It was felt that in order for the driver to view the angle and position of the bucket, the driver must have leaned outwards thereby placing his upper torso and head outside the confines of the protective cab. The FSV involved in the accident and the presumed driving posture are depicted in Figure 1. In adopting this posture when reversing the FSV, it was concluded that the driver misjudged the contours of the roadway and became trapped between one of the FSV canopy support pillars and the side of the roadway, at a point where the roadway narrowed and curved.

Figure 1. The FSV involved in the accident and presumed posture.

To prevent a similar accident from occurring it was recommended that an ergonomic evaluation should be conducted on the FSV, with emphasis being placed on the visibility and protection afforded to the driver. The intention was to identify modifications which would improve the safety of the driver.

4. VISIBILITY CHARTS CONSTRUCTED USING THE ERGONOMICS COMPUTER-AIDED DESIGN SYSTEM

A commercially available ergonomics software package, SAMMIE (System for Aiding Man Machine Interface Evaluation), was used in the investigation. A description of the computer modelling approach is detailed elsewhere (Case and Porter, 1980), along with its application for assessing a driver's field of vision (Porter et al, 1980).

Technical drawings were obtained of the FSV involved in the accident and, together with direct measurements (to account for modifications made by the mine), used to derive three dimensional co-ordinates of each major body component. These 3 D co-ordinates were manually input into SAMMIE to construct a computer model of the vehicle (Figure 2).

Visibility charts were constructed by taking perspective views from a manikin seated within the driver's cab. A horizontal grid, with 1 m squares, was first placed at ground level. Looking from the manikin, co-ordinates were recorded for the edges of the vehicle within each grid. These were then transcribed on to a scaled plan view of the vehicle. A similar process was repeated for horizontal grids at 1 m and 1.7 m above the ground, heights considered to represent a stooped and upright worker, respectively (Mason and Simpson, 1990).

Throughout the investigation several variables were controlled in order to reduce the complexity and time taken to conduct the analysis. Visibility charts were constructed with the vehicle positioned so that it was not articulated and with the bucket lowered, typical of the position adopted when transporting material (transport configuration). A further chart was developed with the FSV in an identical position to that found at the time of the accident. The driver manikin used throughout the visibility assessment was equivalent to a 5th percentile male (approximately 5% of the male population are considered to be smaller) with a balanced soma-

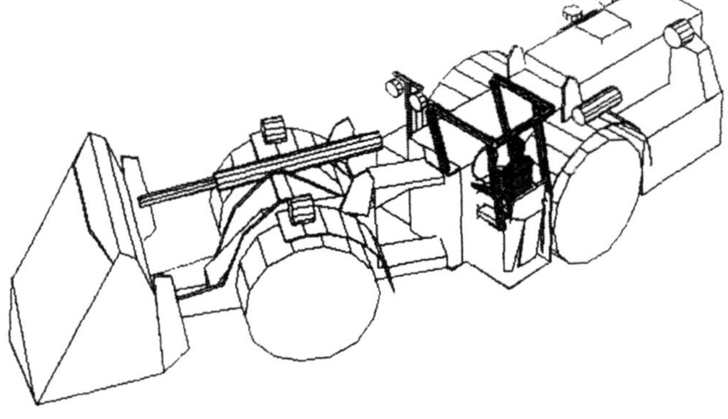

Figure 2. A 3D computer representation of the FSV involved in the accident.

totype. This was based on the assumption that a 5th percentile male driver would in practice experience the greatest all-round restrictions on visibility due to low eye height. Perspective views from the driver's eye point were taken from a central eye location, the line of sight being perpendicular to a line joining the two eyes. Clearly, this introduces some error as it does not take account of the benefits gained through binocular vision. Although, SAMMIE does enable views to be taken from either eye it was not felt that the benefits gained from this approach would significantly influence the judgements made during this study. The long axis of the head and trunk remained vertical, with the head rotating only about its long axis. A visibility chart considered the full 360 degrees about the driver's seated position, ranges of acceptable head and eye movement being 160 degrees for sustained periods of time (comfort limit) and 190 degrees for maximum head and eye rotation (Mason and Simpson, 1990).

5. VISIBILITY AND ERGONOMIC SPECIFICATIONS OF THE FSV INVOLVED IN THE ACCIDENT

For the FSV involved in the accident a visibility chart, with the vehicle in the transport configuration, was constructed using SAMMIE (Figure 3). The shaded segments represent areas where objects with a height of less than 1.7 m (black) and 1 m (dark grey) cannot be seen by the driver. Light grey segments show the areas where visibility is restricted at ground level. All non-shaded regions represent unrestricted visibility. Forward vision is impaired by the height of the bucket which restricts the point at which the driver is able to see the ground, approximately 75 m ahead of the driver. A similar restriction on vision (50m from the driver's seated position) was found to the rear of the vehicle, this arising from the height of the diesel engine. These have implications for judging roadway floor conditions and whether obstacles are present in the roadway. The narrow arc of unrestricted vision down the side of the vehicle on which the driver is seated, seems to be the only critical area of unrestricted vision open to the driver. In practice, this would be enhanced through the effects of binocular vision and head and upper body movements. However, the chart illustrates how the driver's line of sight is impaired by the position of the canopy support pillar (76 mm in diameter) and side of the bucket. Given the severely restricted view over the top of the bucket,

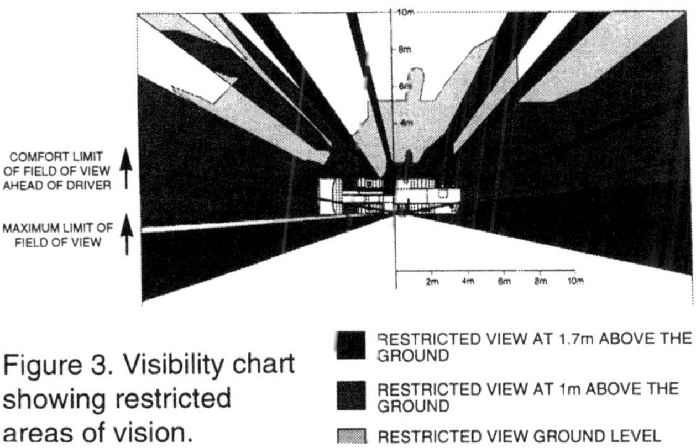

Figure 3. Visibility chart showing restricted areas of vision.

evidence suggests that the driver is forced to adopt postures that take his head and upper torso beyond the safe environment of the protective canopy, outside the vehicle envelope. This was further underlined when the FSV was articulated into a position similar to that found at the time of the accident.

Evaluation of a 5th percentile operator showed that the driver would be capable of positioning his upper torso and head outside the protection afforded by the canopy and side of the vehicle. Ergonomic specifications stipulate that a minimum distance of 150 mm should separate the outer most edge of the seat back rest and the side of the vehicle (Mason and Simpson, 1990). Measurements taken from the model found this distance to be approximate 20 mm. This investigation highlighted that inadequacies in design ergonomics may well have contributed to the accident and, given the restriction placed on driver vision, the operator is likely to have positioned his body between the canopy support pillar and roadway side, so that he became trapped. There was a clear need to instigate modifications to prevent a similar accident from occurring.

6. ASSESSMENT OF VEHICLE MODIFICATION AND ITS ERGONOMIC IMPLICATIONS

Following consultations with the vehicle manufacturers and the mining company, potential modifications to the design of the driver's seat and cab were evaluated. Consideration was given to mounting the seat on a section of the vehicle's main body, directly in front of the present seat position and towards the centre of the vehicle with driving controls adjusted accordingly. A suitably designed canopy needed to meet height restrictions imposed by the mine, to be suitable for range of drivers of different sizes, not to interfere with visual requirements and to provide adequate driver protection.

The height of the canopy was fixed at 2.44 m, the maximum permissible by the mine. Seat height was determined by positioning a 95th percentile manikin in the driver's seat. The clearance between the top of the manikin and the roof of the canopy set at 100 mm to allow for seat vibration and the wearing of a helmet. The incident investigation identified restrictions imposed on forward and rear vision by the placement of canopy support pillars. A central pillar directly behind the driver was used in preference to supports directly in line with the left and right shoulder. Guidance for the design of canopy supports suggest they should have a diameter less than interpupillary breadth (Mason and Simpson, 1990). The new canopy pillars were 60 mm in diameter. Additional modifications involved removing the protective covers of the redundant headlights and shortening the mud guards, permitting improved vision towards the rear and base of the bucket. The width of the roof canopy was increased to improve protection over the driver's left shoulder.

The eye height for a 5th percentile male was found to be 455 mm higher than before and this resulted in improvements in all-round visibility (see Figure 4). Compared with the original vehicle design, it was now possible for even small

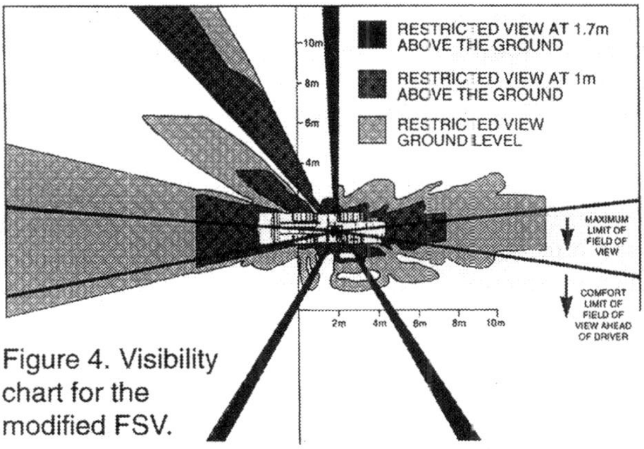

Figure 4. Visibility chart for the modified FSV.

drivers to view a 1.7 m high object at all four corners of the machine, with the vehicle in the transport configuration. Similarly, the roadway floor surface could now be viewed at a distance of 15m and 13m from the driver's seated position, in the forward and rear directions, respectively.

It was felt that the modified driving position may present two potential drawbacks. Firstly, certain tasks may require the upper body to be rotated in order to aid vision over the left and right shoulders. Secondly, difficulties could be encountered when gauging the relative position and articulation of the bucket. However, the considerable improvements to driver vision and protection were felt to outweigh these potential limitations. Consequently, the FSV was modified and placed back in service (Figure 5). Feedback from drivers' suggests that the modifications have considerably improved the ease with which they can operate the vehicle. Further work is necessary in order to re-evaluate drivers perceptions of the modified vehicle.

Figure 5. The FSV following modification

7. CONCLUSIONS

Underground roadways present unique problems to vehicle designers which inhibit machines meeting optimum ergonomic specifications. Parameters which are important to designers of mining vehicles include:

i) overall height, width and length of the machine;
ii) operator's seat configuration;
iii) canopy design;
iv) adjustability of the cab; and
v) lighting.

(Sanders and Kelley, 1981)

The effects of these parameters on the vision afforded to drivers has been assessed for an FSV involved in a fatal accident using the ergonomics design package, SAMMIE. It is concluded that SAM-

MIE provides a cost-effective approach during vehicle design or when seeking to instigate modifications. In addition, it enables a driver's field of vision to be evaluated in conjunction with other ergonomic constraints. Improvements in the technique are necessary in order to improve its efficiency and reliability. These include:

i) automated input of vehicle specifications;
ii) enhanced facilities for deriving and mapping visibility charts; and
iii) developing a suitable approach to account for postural changes and the effects of binocular vision.

Investigation of the validity of the technique will be undertaken by conducting physical measurements on a number of different machines and comparing with information obtained from SAMMIE. Further work to assess a number of FSVs in use in British coal mines is now underway.

REFERENCES

Case, K. and Porter, J. M. (1980). SAMMIE. A computer-aided ergonomics design system. Engineering, 220: 21-25.

Glowacki, A. F., Unger, R. L. and Rossi, E. W. (1992). A computerized approach for assessing the visibility from underground mobile mining equipment. In Society of Mining Engineers Proceedings. New Publications, 29-41.

Hella, F., Tisserand, M., Schouller, J. F. and Englert, M. (1991). A new method for checking the driving visibility on hydraulic excavators. International Journal of Industrial Ergonomics, 8: 135-145.

HSE (1991). The safety of free steered vehicle operations below ground in British coal mines. HSE Topic Report, HMSO, London.

ISO (1991). ISO 5006-1. Earth-moving machinery - Operator's field of view.

Mason, S and Simpson, G. C. (1990). Ergonomics principles for the design of free-steered vehicles. British Coal Corporation, Scientific Services - Ergonomics Technical Department, Report No SSL/90/173.

Porter, J. M., Case, K. and Bonney, M. C. (1980). A computer-generated three dimensional visibility chart. In Human Factors in Transport Research -Vehicle Factors: Transport Systems, Workspace, Information and Safety, Vol 1 (edited by D. J. Oborne & J. A. Levis), Academic Press, London, 365-373.

Sanders, M. S. and Kelley, G. R. (1981). Visibility attention locations for operating continuous miners, shuttle cars, and scoops. Report No. Bu Mines OFR 29(1)-82, Bureau of Mines, Washington.

VISION IN VEHICLES - V
A.G. Gale et al. (Editors)

Effects of Motorcycle Helmets on Task Performance and User Acceptability

Halimahtun M. Khalid[a] and P.C. Ooi[b]

[a] Faculty of Social Sciences, Universiti Malaysia Sarawak, Kota Samarahan, Sarawak, Malaysia.

[b]Department of Psychology, Universiti Kebangsaan Malaysia, 43600 Bangi, Selangor Darul Ehsan, Malaysia.

Abstract

The incidence of motorcycle accidents in Malaysia is a growing public health problem. A majority of the accidents incur head injuries to victims despite wearing safety helmets. This study attempts to investigate the usability and acceptability of full face and open face helmets as protective devices. Subjects performed three basic skill competency tasks that differed in complexity levels while using both helmet types. A baseline condition was included for control purposes. The results indicated highly significant effects of helmet wear on task performance, with greater performance decrement when using full face than open face helmets. This may be attributable to restriction of the vertical visual field as established in past studies. Also, there were significant effects of helmet use on design suitability and comfort, with full face helmets being less ergonomically effective relative to open face. The findings imply the need for adequate enforcement of quality standards in the design and manufacture of safety helmets.

1. INTRODUCTION

Motorcycle accidents pose a serious problem to road safety in Malaysia. About 53.92% of all road accidents that result in death or injury involve motorcyclists (Road Accidents Statistical Report, 1991). A MAAP analysis of accident data suggested that the risk of death and injury faced by motorcyclists is 9 times and 17 times greater, respectively, than other road users, especially drivers (Radin Umar and Aminuddin, 1991). This is because motorcyclists and pillion riders are more exposed than drivers; the latter being protected by the body of the vehicle. The analysis also showed that side or lateral collision appears to be the main type of vehicular collision (about 30.7%), indicating that motorcyclists may be less sensitive to other vehicles in their visual environment.

There is evidence to support the hypothesis that the use of safety helmets may be restricting the field of vision. Hayward and Marsh (1988) demonstrated that a full face/ integral helmet caused a 38% reduction in vertical visual field and this was increased to 60% when wearing a jet helmet with sun shield and ventilation mask attachments. Other past studies too have shown that vision is restricted when the head is in the static position and this restriction is offset when assisted by eye, head and bodily movements. Also, there is a tendency for peripheral visual performance to degrade when the central task is complex, resulting in the perceptual narrowing phenomenon (Halimahtun, 1983).

In addition to vision. the risk of hearing impairment when using full face helmet has been raised by Ross (1989). This relates to the design of the interface between the user and the helmet which prevents effective information processing via the auditory system. Given the more important role of vision in motorcycle accidents, it becomes necessary to identify the locus of injury in accident victims.

1.1. Locus of in Jury

An analysis of motorcycle accidents in Seremban and Shah Alam, Malaysia, between January 1991 and April 1992 revealed that 32.9% of the total casualties (26 cases from a total of 79) suffered head injuries (Radin Umar, 1993). Similarly, Chen (1985) reported about 31% (127 cases from a total of 409) of motorcycle accident cases in Kuala Lumpur involved head injuries. In all cases, the victims were in fact wearing open face helmets. A series of studies by Mclean, Chen, Wong and Ukai (1990) in Adelaide found 13.9% of total motorcycle accidents resulted in head, face and chin/throat injuries. In this instance, the motorcyclists were using the full face helmet. Although the data is not conclusive, more diagnostic investigations are required to ascertain further the locus of injury in motorcycle accidents involving the use of such helmets. Nevertheless, the effectiveness of helmets as protective devices becomes an issue of concern.

The advent of full face helmet in Malaysia generated much interest as it was perceived to be relatively safer and protective in terms of design and functionality. However, its use was banned which spurred a series of controversial debate on aspects of usability and safety, thus resulting in the lifting of the ban on 7 November 1991. Therefore, the use of full face helmets in Malaysia is still in its infancy, relative to other advanced countries which have used it since the 1970s. As such, evaluative ergonomic studies have not been conducted rigorously to investigate its use on motorcyclist riding performance in the local context. Since motorcyclists represent the largest population of safety helmet users world-wide, this study seems warranted and timely.

1.2. Study aims

Generally full face helmets are worn by racing motorcyclists in circuit races where the tracks are generally straight, unidirectional and wide. Such conditions, however, do not prevail in the real-world environment; ordinary motorcyclists operate in road environments that are usually narrow, two-way and congested with multi-vehicle traffic, particularly in urban and city roads. Thus the use of full face helmets may have consequences on task performance under real and simulated riding conditions. This study is an attempt to analyse and identify usability issues concerning the use of full face helmet in relation to task performance that might have implications on aspects of design. Comparisons are made with open face helmet to provide information on the nature of the problem.

Clearly, the design of a product should fulfil usability functions in order to avoid risk taking during product usage. Also, it should meet specific ergonomic criteria, that is, safe in relation to user-product relationship, providing physical comfort, benefiting the user during prolonged use, satisfying, and beneficial as well as product-worthy to society. In order to evaluate the safety of products, testing should be made on product characteristics, user response and usage environment in sequential stages from analysis, identification, synthesis to evaluation (Schoone-Harmsen, 1990). Given time constraints, this study involves analysis and identification of problems at two levels of analysis, product usability and user acceptability. The main hypothesis predicts possible effects of helmet wear on task performance, with decrement being a function of task characteristics.

2. METHOD

The study employed two data collection methods, namely, field experiment and questionnaire.

2.1. Experimental design

Subjects were assigned randomly to the experimental conditions using a 3 x 3 x 2 factorial design with repeated measures (that is, 3 conditions, 3 types of task, 2 levels of helmet wear experience). There were three conditions: no helmet wear, full face helmet only, and open face helmet only. Subjects performed three tasks that differed in levels of complexity. Task complexity is determined according to Donder's formula:

Task 1 = Ps I v1 [T]
Task 2 = Ps [T(v1+v2+v3+... v7) x2]
Task 3 = Ps (3) [T(v1+v2)]

where, Ps denotes pathway size, T is time taken, v is variable.

A third variable was subject's experience in using full face helmets. The order of presentation was counterbalanced across the subjects so as to offset potential order and learning effects.

Task performance was measured in terms of speed (response time) and accuracy (task errors), while user acceptability was measured in relation to importance of helmet use, design suitability and usage comfort. To provide a measure of performance decrement, the following is used:

Pd= (Mean performance using helmet - mean performance in the baseline condition) I (mean performance baseline) x 100%

where, Pd is performance decrement.

2.2. Experimental tasks

The tasks to be performed by subjects were simulated tasks so as to be representative of real-world tasks. They involved riding on straight narrow plank (referred to afterwards as Test 1), riding between pylons (Test 2), and negotiating curves (Test 3). For these purposes, three types of motorcycle skill test scales from the Road Transport Department, Malaysia, were selected for use in this study. The aim of the first test was to evaluate control and body balance in the most optimum time without the subject's feet touching the plank or road. The minimum time was set at 7 seconds; a longer time indicates the subject's ability to balance properly on the plank, measuring 0.05m x 0.3m x 15 m.

The second test was aimed at evaluating subject's skill in manipulating the vehicle from left to right, as well as maintaining it upright while riding between 7 traffic cones in a space measuring 3m x 27m. For this test, the subject was required to complete the trial as fast as possible without touching the cone or knocking down the barrier nor stepping on the ground. In the third test, the subject was required to negotiate two sharp curves and three straight lanes in the shortest distance. The lane was 2m in width and 14 m in length in the form of the letter Z. This test in particular measures a subject's competence in negotiating two curves in a narrow lane. The subject was also required to complete the task in the shortest time possible without committing similar errors as in the second test. All three tests have been proven to measure basic competency levels in separate test trials at the testing ground of the Department of Road Transport, Petaling Jaya, Malaysia.

2.3. Equipment

The equipment for the field experiment involved two full face helmets and two open face helmets of sizes X and XL, and with clear visor shields. A 150cc motorcycle, model Suzuki TXR was used. This vehicle is popular because of its compatibility with the physical dimensions of the Malaysian motoring population. The remaining equipment comprised measuring tapes, whistle, stop watch, traffic cones, plank and bricks. In addition to these, the study employed a checklist, test evaluation form, and questionnaire for recording information concerning the subject's performance.

2.4. Subjects and location

About 48 male students, aged between 20-26 years, with normal vision, of height ranging from 1.60-1.75 m, weight and bodily size between 55-65 kg., were selected using a purposive sampling technique. All subjects owned a 100cc motorcycle and a valid motorcycle licence, Class B2, for a period of at least 3 years. Half of the subjects had used the same or a similar model of the full face helmet for about 3 months. All subjects were familiar with the open face helmet in use.

The field experiment was conducted at the parking ground of the Universiti Kebangsaan Malaysia, Bangi, in the vicinity of the Cultural Theatre. This place is considered ideal given its openness and in particular meeting the requirements of the specific tests. Figure 1 shows the layout of the testing arrangements for the three tasks.

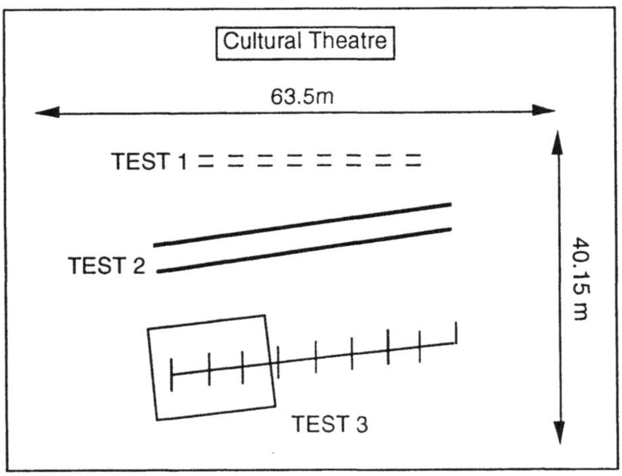

Figure l. Testing arrangement for field experiment.

2.5. Procedure

The experiment was conducted from 9.00am to 4.30pm over a period of one week. Each subject was required to read the instruction sheet prior to performing the trials, and was allowed to familiarise themselves with the test vehicle for about 3 minutes. Subjects then performed the tasks according to the assigned test condition. The results were recorded on specially designed checklist and evaluation forms. A whistle was used to provide the cue for start-off or to serve as a warning to subjects if they committed errors. In this regard, subjects were allowed to repeat the trial once and the best time was taken as the test score.

Having completed the experimental trials, subjects were asked to complete the questionnaire which measured their attitudes towards the use of test helmets. On the whole, the two sessions spanned 30 minutes. The data were analysed with SPSSx using ANOVA and t-tests. Post hoc analyses were performed on the data using Student's Newman-Keul test.

2.6. Questionnaire reliability and validity

The questionnaire was tested for its reliability and validity in a pilot study and also on the final data. Actual reliability scores, following the Alpha-Cronbach test, on the importance of use, suitability and comfort, ranged between 0.85 to 0.86 for full face helmet, and 0.86 to 0.87 for open face helmet. The Pearson Correlation was used to test the validity of scores, and 21 test items from a total of 24 were significant at the 1% probability level. The remaining three items were insignificant at the 5% level. These items were still included in the final analysis as excluding them did not affect the significance level. Overall, it can be concluded that the questionnaire was reliable and valid for use in the study.

3. RESULTS

3.1. Effects of helmet wear on performance

The results showed highly significant effects of helmet wear on response time, with full face helmet users unable to perform all three tasks in the 'criterion' time. In Test 1 (body balance and control), there was a significant effect of helmet wear, ($F(2, 141)=4.68$, $p<0.05$); while Newman-Keul's test showed mean performance for full face helmet (mean=13.69) to differ significantly from the baseline condition (mean=15.39) but not with the open face helmet (mean=14.84). That is, the use of full and open face helmets hindered the subject's ability to balance and control while riding on the plank, relative to not wearing the helmet. In terms of performance decrement, the use of the full face helmet deteriorated the task performance as much as 11.05% compared to not wearing, and only about 3.51% decrement when using the open face helmet

Similarly in Test 2 (skill manipulation), the use of a helmet affects performance ($F(2, 141)=5.45$, $p<0.01$). The Newman-Keul's test produced similar results mean for full face helmet (19.92) differed significantly from the baseline (18.85) but not with open face helmet use (19.22). Again, the use of helmets affected subject's skill at manipulating the vehicle while riding between the pylons. The time taken to perform the task was slightly longer than not wearing the helmet at all. The decrement in performance was about 1.96% for open face and 5.68% for full face, relative to no helmet wear condition. That is, the use of full face helmet affects skill manipulation considerably.

Also, in performing the curve negotiation test (Test 3), the mean performance of subjects wearing the helmets was significantly different from not wearing ($F(2,141)=14.89$, $p<0.001$). The results of post hoc analysis revealed both helmet use differed significantly from the condition in which subjects did not use any helmet, and that the use of full face helmet differed significantly from open face helmet wear. In other words, subjects had difficulty in negotiating curves while using the full face helmet as opposed to the open face helmet. The time taken to complete the task was relatively longer (full face = 4.40; open face = 4.12; not wearing = 4.05). In this instance, performance deteriorated by 8.64% when using the full face helmet relative to not wearing, and by 1.73% when using the open face helmet.

3.2. Effects of helmet wear on user acceptability

The results of t-test analysis showed no significant effect of helmet wear on the importance of use ($t(46)=-0.47$, $p>0.05$). That is, all subjects agreed that the use of motorcycle helmets was important to their safety. However, the use of helmets produced significant effects on suitability ($t(46)=12.28$, $p<0.001$) and comfort ($t(46)=10.38$, $p<0.001$). Further analysis of the data showed that subjects tended to rate higher the design of the open face helmet (mean=30.58) compared to the full face helmet (mean=22. 12). Similarly, the mean ratings for open face helmet on comfort (30.54) was greater than full face (23.40), suggesting that subjects preferred the open face helmet in terms of its design and comfort.

In order to establish whether this difference is a function of experience, comparisons were made between the experienced group (> 3 months experience in using a full face helmet) and inexperienced. It was revealed that experience did affect user acceptability significantly, particularly on design suitability ($t(47)=-2.91$, $p<0.01$) and comfort ($t(47)=2.67$, $p<0.05$). The experienced group, relative to the inexperienced, found the design of the open face helmet better, while the full face helmet was deemed more comfortable.

4. DISCUSSION

This small-scale exploratory study produced three important findings. First, the use of helmets deteriorated the performance of three types of task -- body control and balance, skill manipulation and curve negotiation. The decrement is greater with full face than open face helmets. This perhaps is attributable to the restriction of the vertical visual field as documented in previous studies, although the decrement is much lower (+6% - +11%) than that found by Hayward and Marsh (1988), about 38% as plotted mechanically on a Goldman Perimeter. Thus, in this study subjects experienced difficulty in perceiving and identifying stimuli in the test environment due to the presence of a physical 'obstacle' which presumably led to slower response times in tests 2 and 3, as explained by Wickens' (1984) information processing model. Also, the role of peripheral vision in detecting and placing objects of significance on the fovea may be further reduced in the case of full face helmet relative to open face. In this regard, the helmet may be conceived as an obstacle in the interface between the user-task-vehicle-environment.

Second, the results also showed that the performance decrement is not necessarily a function of task complexity. The first task which is less complex than the remaining tasks, given the nature of task characteristics, suffered greater decrement because its performance is associated with the use of the subject's vertical visual field rather than the other tasks which involved greatly the use of the lateral visual field. This further supports the claim that the restriction of the vertical visual field is an important issue in safe riding.

Third, the design of the open face helmet in terms of suitability and comfort was found to be better than the full face helmet as established by experienced users. In ergonomic terms, both usability measures are crucial in ensuring safety. Studies by Mauritzson-Sandberg (1991) found that prolonged use of full face respiratory protective devices was not comfortable to children. Similarly, subjects in this study complained that full face helmets required greater adaptibility skills on the user's part than the open face. As such, all users possessed both helmets for different purposes, the full face for long distance travel while the open face was used for near/short distance travel. This raises the importance of experience and skill in reducing re-adaptation problems when switching between helmet types.

In addition, full face helmet users complained of the restriction of peripheral vision and hearing from the rear, as well as the tendency for the device to impinge on the user during high temperature and in high traffic density situations. During prolonged use, the helmet is said to cause stressing in the neck region due to its weight. Besides, the full face helmet is considered by subjects as not suitable for night riding due to the further restriction of the effective visual field. Also, its bulky feature renders it not easily portable, nor safe to be left with the vehicle.

4.1. Implications on design and standards

Clearly from the foregoing discussion, the design of full face helmets need re-consideration. In re-designing full face helmets, the following should be considered:

- using foam material that enables humidity absorption to increase comfort;
- introducing more respiratory holes to input/output air;
- providing effective internal respiratory lining;
- providing effective auditory system interface;
- using light-weight helmet material;
- using a non-reflective, scratch-and damage-proof visor shield.

Ooi (1993) suggests the modification of the internal structure of the helmet, in particular increasing the area for the lateral visual field and to provide better protection to the mouth/chin area using a durable chin-guard facility. This feature in fact distinguishes full face from open face helmets. To further strengthen the most vulnerable mouth/chin area, he recommended adding an internal backbone support.

In addition, designers and manufacturers should aim at designing helmets that are aerodynamic, safe and resistant. Therefore, the standardisation of helmet design is crucial in meeting safety and quality standards. The Singapore Standard (1983) specifies the colour of the helmet surface should always be visible and bright, and that less than 50% of the surface area may be in black, enabling better detection in different climatic and day/night conditions.

5. CONCLUSION

Inefficient enforcement of standards have resulted in safety helmets that do not meet the desired specifications nor ergonomics criteria. Some of these helmets have found their way into the local market giving rise to concern. Given that safety helmets are meant to be protective devices, their modifications should take into account some of the suggestions derived from this study. Clearly full face helmets require enhancement so as to increase both lateral and vertical visual fields, and to provide value added protection to the mouth and chin region. On this note, there is a clear role for the Standards and Industrial Research Institute of Malaysia (SIRIM) in undertaking further R&D efforts on the usability and safety aspects of motorcycle helmets.

REFERENCES

Chen, C.Y. (1985). The Incidence of Fatalities and Injuries from Motorcycle Accidents in Kuala Lumpur, University of Malaya, Kuala Lumpur.

Halimahtun M. Khalid (1983). Kemerosotan Prestasi Penglihatan Periferi Akibat Desakan Tug as Utama: suatu Sangkalan terhadap Ide Penyempitan Persepsi, Akademika, 23, 65-82.

Hayward, J.M. and Marsh, R.J. (1988). Visual Field Restriction Caused by Motorcycle Helmets. In Gale, A.G., Freeman, M.H., Haslegrave, C.M., Smith, P. and Taylor, S.P. (Eds.) Vision in Vehicles II, Amsterdam: North-Holland.

Mauritzson-Sandberg, E. (1991). Psychological Effects on Prolonged Use of Respiratory Protective Devices in Children, Ergonomics, 34 (3), 313-319.

Mclean, A.J., Chen, C.Y., Wong, T.W. and Ukai, T. (1990). Comparative Study of Motorcycle Accidents, Research Report No. 2, NHMRC Road Accident Research Unit, University of Adelaide.

Ooi, P.C. (1993). Evaluation on the Usability and Acceptability of Safety Helmets among Motorcyclists, Unpublished BA(Hons) Thesis, Department of Psychology, Universiti Kebangaan Malaysia, Bangi, Selangor, Malaysia.

Radin Umar R. Sohadi (1993). Research Report No. 4, Research, Evaluation and Development Committee, Road Safety Council of Malaysia, Kuala Lumpur.

Radin Umar, R. Sohadi and Aminuddin Adnan (1991). System Diagnosis Kemalangan Jalanraya. Paper presented at the 32nd Annual General Meeting, Road Safety Council Malaysia, Kuching, Sarawak.

Road Accidents Statistical Report (1991). Royal Malaysia Police, Kuala Lumpur.

Ross, B.C. (1989). Noise Exposure of Motorcyclists, Annals of Occupational Hygiene, 33 (1), 123-127.

Schoone-Harmsen (1990). A Design Method for Product Safety, Ergonomics, 33 (4), 431-437.

Singapore Standard (1983). Specification for Protective Helmets for Motorcyclist, No. 9, SIRIR, Singapore.

Wickens, C.D. (1984). Engineering Psychology and Human Performance, C.E. Merrill, Ohio.

VISION IN VEHICLES - V
A.G. Gale et al. (Editors)

THE VISIBILITY AUDIT: A CONCEPTUAL FRAMEWORK FOR THE ASSESSMENT OF VISIBILITY AROUND TRUCKS AND INDUSTRIAL VEHICLES

D. GIGUÈRE and C. LARUE
Safety-Ergonomics Program, IRSST,
505 de Maisonneuve Blvd. West, Montréal (Québec), H3A 3C2, Canada

Abstract

The Visibility Audit is proposed as a framework to further structure research and development in the field of visibility offered by vehicles to their users. This conceptual tool is being designed to help quantify visibility around vehicles in order to reduce occupational accidents. Like the financial audit, it subtracts any structural, accessory or environmental impediments to vision (liabilities) from openings in the cab and supplemental visibility offered by some devices (assets). As a demonstration, a Visibility Audit was carried on the mock-up of a straight-body truck. The openings and structures of the cab were measured and transferred to a computer-assisted drawing software. The projection of a light source, located at the driver's cyclopean eye location, on a hexahedral screen is simulated by computer. Visibility is expressed as the surface area totalling all the lighted areas on all sides of the screen. The audit calculated a loss of 44% in visibility following the installation of a 22 foot long cargo box to the rear of the cab. Installing large (600 cm^2) flat mirrors on the cab subtract 29 m^2 from the available visibility on the sides, but allows a supplemental 113 m^2 of reflected visibility from the rear. The Visibility Audit can be a simple and powerful tool to assess visibility around trucks and other heavy vehicles providing it is integrated in an ergonomic approach.

1. INTRODUCTION

Many studies have been carried out to tackle, in different ways, the problem of visibility around vehicles: (Reiss *et al.* (1972); Burger *et al.* (1980); Case *et al.* (1980); Hulbert (1984); Jankovsky *et al.* (1987); Village (1989); Hella *et al.* (1991); Rebiffé *et al.* (1991)). These studies are all sound and valuable but the authors wish to propose a unifying concept, the Visibility Audit, to further help in structuring the research and development efforts invested in this field The objective of this paper is to propose this conceptual framework and to exemplify it with a theoretical case.

2. PRESENTATION OF THE FRAMEWORK

2.1 Limit of the framework

This proposed framework is valid within the proposition (Giguère *et al.*, 1992) that the following distinction should be made while studying any visibility problem around vehicles: i) vision is considered as human anatomical and physiological characteristics; ii) the processing of visual information by drivers or operators is a cognitive characteristic of humans, and iii) visibility is made available to drivers or operators through the structural characteristics of the vehicles. Of course, these characteristics are closely inter-related and are simultaneously necessary to correctly and safely manoeuvre a vehicle. The framework proposed in this paper only applies to the third and last one and is limited, for the moment, to straight-body trucks.

2.2 Rationale

The proposed concept evolved from an observation that, in eastern Canada, sometimes many additional mirrors are found on trucks besides the ones made mandatory by the Canadian Motor Vehicle Safety Act. This observation might be an indicator that rearview mirrors that meet legal requirements for highway use may not give the relevant information to drivers or operators during non-highway use of their vehicles. Examples of such situations are the frequent changes of direction of compactors or bulldozers, or the manoeuvring in tight spots in the presence of other workers or pedestrians in a truck delivery yard or on a construction site.

2.3 The Visibility Audit

The Visibility Audit is being designed to help quantify the visibility offered by a vehicle to its driver or operator in order to reduce occupational accidents. It has in mind the ergonomist or the occupational health and safety practitioner who has, for example, to evaluate visibility as a buying criterion for a new vehicle, or the benefits of installing blind area reduction devices (BARD) on an existing one.

Table 1.
Components of the Visibility Audit

Audit item	Element	Example
Assets	Openings	Windshield, side and quarter windows, back window, ...
	Standard BARD*	Rearview mirrors mandatory by law, ...
	Accessory BARD	Fresnel lens, convex mirrors, CCTV, ...
Subtotal Asset	***Total enhancement***	
Liabilities	Structural impediments	Cab pillars, engine hood, rearview mirrors, parts of dash, cargo type, ...
	Accessory impediments	Communication equipment, exhaust stacks, wind deflectors, ...
	Environmental impediments	Mud, snow, fogging, specular reflections on glass surfaces, ...
(Subtotal Liability)	***(Total impediments)***	
Total	**Enhancement - (impediments) = visibility offered to operator**	

***BARD : Blind Area Reduction Device**

The Visibility Audit is based on the accounting concept of the audit, a model based on the financial sciences, that allows the financial value of a company to be quantified by subtracting its debts (liabilities) from what it owns (assets). Likewise, the Visibility Audit (see Table 1) subtracts any structural, environmental or accessory impediments of a vehicle cab (liabilities) from openings in the cab plus the supplemental visibility offered by BARDs (assets). Doing a Visibility Audit also allows specific elements that contribute to or reduce visibility to be identified.

3. DEMONSTRATION OF THE FRAMEWORK

In order to exemplify the proposed concept, we carried out a Visibility Audit of the mock-up of a truck cab. The cab is made up from the measurements of relevant features from existing vehicles without specifically representing any of these.

3.1 Method and material

As in some ISO standards (Tisserand and Englert, 1983; Tisserand and Schouller, 1983), and following an extensive literature review (Giguère and Larue, 1992), we choose to simulate, on a computer, the principle of the projection of light on a screen. The field of visibility offered to a driver or operator then corresponds to lighted zones, while shadowed areas correspond to blind areas generated by obstacles in the path of the light. The light source is placed inside the cab mock-up at a position corresponding to the cyclopean eye location of a 50th percentile driver. The surfaces of the lighted zones projected on the screen are then measured under the two following conditions: i) the "cab only" condition, i.e., the cab on its wheeled frame only, which is the closest situation to the design stage, and ii), the "equipped cab" condition, which is the same as i) but with mandatory mirrors, accessories and payload installed, and considering the supplemental visibility offered by any BARDs. This situation is closest to the operational use of the cab.

The visibility Audit is constructed with measurement data originating from these two conditions. Visibility is expressed as the amount, in square metres, of visible surface available to a specific driver or operator around the vehicle.

Table 2

Results of the Visibility Audit

Element	Projection side	Assets (m^2)	Liabilities (m^2)	Subtotals (m^2)
"Cab only"	Ground	1 040.83		
	Side surfaces	1 386.95		
Subtotal "Cab only"		*2 427.78*		*2 427.78*
22 foot cargo box	Ground	0.00	- 538.53	
	Side surfaces	0.00	- 547.16	
Subtotal cargo box		*0.00*	*- 1 085.69*	*- 1 085.69*
"Driver side" mirror	Ground	53.59	-11.84	
	Back surface	33.93	0.00	
	Left surface	0.00	-14.45	
Subtotal "Driver side" mirror		*87.52*	*-26.29*	*61.23*
"Helper side" mirror	Ground	15.87	0.00	
	Back surface	9.45	0.00	
	Right surface	0.00	-2.83	
Subtotal "Helper side" mirror		*25.32*	*- 2.83*	22.49
Total offered visibility		**2 540.62**	**- 1 114.81**	**=1 425.81**

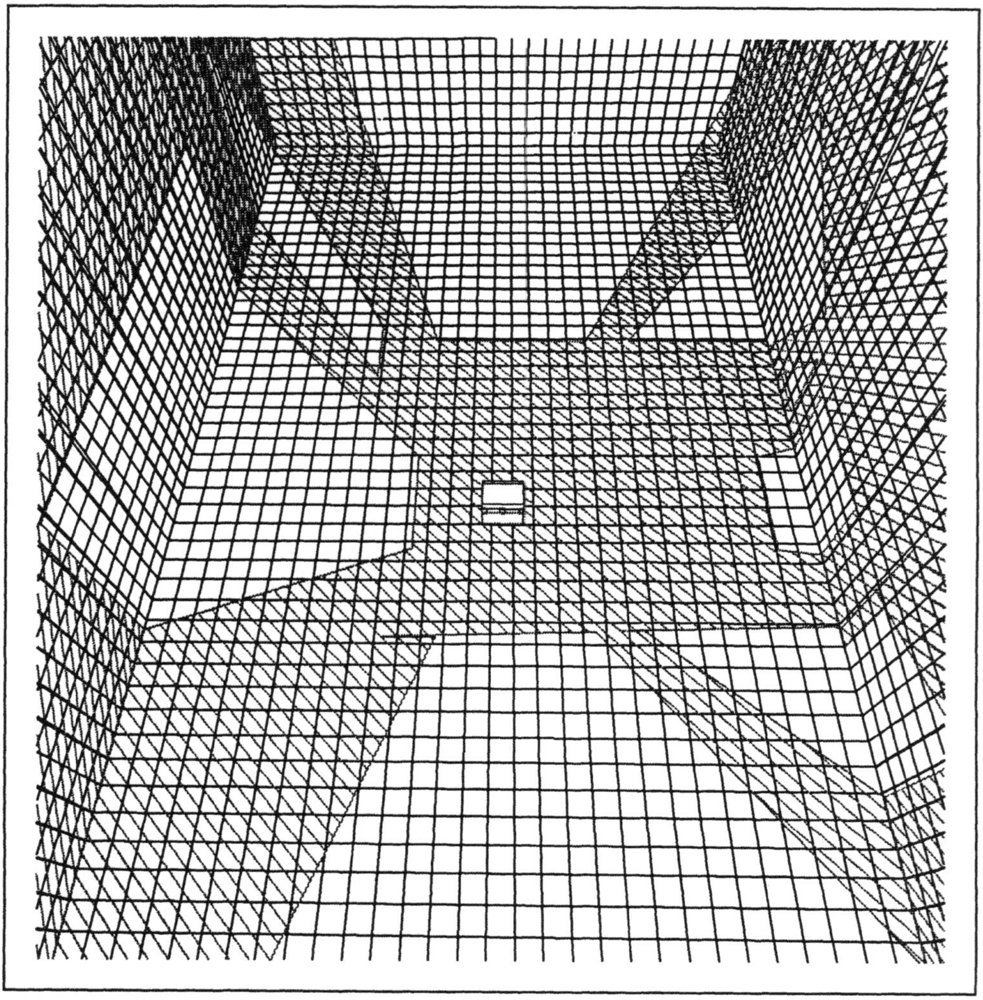

Figure 1 - Field of visibility in the "Cab only" condition. Field of visibility offered to a 50th percentile (height and weight) driver, in the left-hand drive truck cab mock-up. The hatched areas are not visible from the cyclopean eye location. Eye-to-ground vertical distance is 0.95 m and eye-to-windshield horizontal distance is 0.88 m. The grid mesh is one square metre. The view is from the upper rear of the hexahedral screen (front of cab pointing upward). The total visible area (ground plus all sides) is 2427.78 m^2.

Figure 2 - Field of visibility in the "Equipped cab" condition. Field of visibility offered to a 50th percentile (height and weight) driver, in the left-hand drive truck cab mock-up equipped with a 22 foot long cargo box and "West coast" type flat rearview mirror on each side. The hatched areas are not visible from the cyclopean eye location. Cross-hatched area corresponds to the field of visibility made available by the left rearview mirror. Eye to ground vertical distance is 0.95 m and eye to windshield horizontal distance is 0.88 m. The grid mesh is one square metre. The view is from the upper rear of the hexahedral screen (front of cab pointing upward). The total visible areas (ground plus all sides) is 1425.81 m^2, a loss of 1114.81 m^2 compared to the "Cab only" condition.

For the benefit of the demonstration, we have built a full size mock-up of the aforementioned cab. It is equipped with a real adjustable truck seat and with flat rearview mirrors as per the Canadian Motor Vehicle Safety Act (two "West coast" type mirrors each having 600 sq cm of surface area). The perimeter of each structural element of the cab, as well as of the openings and the rearview mirrors, is measured with a portable co-ordinate measuring machine (Faro Technologies CMM, Model IND-01) offering a precision of ±0,0635 cm in a one-metre radius half-sphere. The position of the "H-point" and of the cyclopean eye of an anthropomorphic manikin (50th percentile height and weight) are measured with the CMM with the seat at its furthest aft position and the backrest straight. These spatial coordinates are transferred to a drawing software program (AutoCAD r. 12). The numerical representation of the cab is then positioned inside a hexahedral virtual screen having 30 m width, 60 m depth and 60 m height (Porter *et al.*, 1980). For this particular set-up, the distance between the bottom surface of the screen and the vertical cyclopean eye location added up to 0.95 m, and the horizontal distance between the front windshield and the horizontal cyclopean eye location was measured at 0.88 m. A computer routine then simulates the projection of a light source located at the cyclopean eye point. The surfaces of the lighted (asset) and shadowed (liability) zones are measured on all sides of the screen and the values thus obtained are used to construct the Visibility Audit.

3.2 Results

Table 2 shows the numerical results obtained for this cab mock-up and for this specific eye location in it. Beginning with the visibility offered in the "cab only" condition (2 427.8 m^2), one can observe that the installation of a 22 foot (6.7 m) long cargo box on the frame diminishes the visibility by 1 085.69 m^2, including 538.53 m^2 on the ground. As can be seen in Figures 1 and 2, the losses are mostly in the rear and on the right hand side ("helper" side in North America).

Concerning rearview mirrors; adding a large (15 cm by 40 cm) flat device on the "driver side" further limits the visibility by 29.12 m^2 but adds 112.84 m^2 of supplemental visibility in the rear. From the driver's eye location, adding the same device on the opposite side of the cab only diminishes the visibility on that side by 2.83 m^2, but yields a mere 25.32 m^2 of reflected information in return. All the mirrors in this case are flat, but one can infer the benefits of using semi-spherical mirrors.

4. DISCUSSION

The results that were obtained clearly identify the amount and the location of blind areas around the simulated vehicle and highlight the impact of adding equipment to the original design of this cab. The performance of rearview mirrors in terms of the masking effects they impose (liability) against the added visibility they confer (asset) is also well demonstrated, and can be extended to other types of BARDs.

The results obtained here are valid only within a projection system similar to ours. Indeed, any change in the dimension of the screen will modify the projection surfaces, and it is important to keep to the same system if one wants to compare several different cab designs on the same basis. The precision of the measurements is also of great importance since an error of one degree at the eye location equates to a 17.45 cm displacement 10 m away. Also, even if using a CMM and a CAD software is not absolutely necessary in carrying out an audit, the use of a computer makes it easier to model special situations or proposed solutions. Calculating the field of visibility of drivers of different height, or adopting different postures, thus becomes possible without redoing all the measurements each time.

Further than the mere quantification of visible square meters around a vehicle, the Visibilty audit can be a valuable complement in different types of studies regarding visibility offered by vehicles. Applications in ergonomics can include, for example, the combination of an audit's results with interviews or with the detailed analysis of the work of truck drivers in order to rank and weight the portions of the field of visibility that are most important for driving on roads or higways, and which portions are most important for manoeuvring on construction sites or delivery yards. Correlations would also be possible with detailed accident analysis data (Zlotnicki *et al.*, 1980) to determine blind areas which represent risks for occupational or traffic accidents. Information from a Visibility audit should also be welcomed by vehicle designers, and could be integrated with other design tools such as the one developed by Ziedman (Ziedman *et al.*, 1987). For example, in this theoretical case study, the benefits of installing semi-spherical rearview mirrors, which is a small liability compared to the asset it can provide, could easily be quantified The benefit could also be proportional to the amount of risk-sensitive information hidden in the area to be covered.

The usual *caveat* thus applies: settling a visibility problem on a vehicle cannot be based solely on a Visibility audit: It also depends on the type of work that has to be done with the equipment and on how drivers or operators take up the necessary visual informations to perform their work safely.

5. CONCLUSION

The authors believe that the Visibility Audit can be a simple and powerful tool for assessing the visibility around trucks and other related equipment, provided that it is integrated into an ergonomic approach. It also shows some promise as a practical and standardizable way of evaluating the visibility offered by vehicles and equipment to their drivers or operators.

ACKNOWLEDGEMENT
The authors wish to thank Mr. Patrick Léveillé. co-op student from the École de Technologie Supérieure in Montréal for his programming of the visual representation of the data. The work presented here is part of the research and development efforts of the Safety-Ergonomics Research Program of the IRSST (Québec's Occupational Health and Safety Research Institute), a non-profit organization funded by the Province of Québec Worker's Compensation Board (CSST).

REFERENCES
Burger, W., Mulholland , M., Smith, R. and Bardales, M., (1980). Measurement of blind areas on the right front of heavy trucks. U.S. Department of Transportation report HS-805-636, Washington, DC, USA.

Case, K., Porter, J.M. and Bonney, M.C., (1980). "Design of mirror systems for commercial vehicles." Applied Ergonomics, 11(4): 199-206.

Giguère, D., Hella, F., Robert, J-M.and Tisserand, M. (1992). "Prévention des risques liés aux restrictions de visibilité dans les poids-lourds et les véhicules industriels". Actes du XXVIIième congrès de la SELF, Lille, pp. 227-230.

Giguère, D. and Larue, C. (1992). "Field of visibility evaluation of industrial and road vehicles: an ergonomic review". Proc. XXVth Conference of the Human Factors Association of Canada / Association canadienne d'ergonomie, Hamilton (Ontario), pp 7 -12.

Government of Canada. Motor Vehicle Safety Act. Statuts révisés du Canada, chapt. 40, 1988.

Hella, F., Tisserand, M., Schouller, J.F. and Englert, M., (1991). "A new method for checking the driving visibility on hydraulic excavators." International Journal of Industrial Ergonomics, 22 : 135-145.

Hulbert, S.F. (1984). Human Factors Consideration for Heavy Vehicles. *in:* Proc. 1984 International Conference on Occupational Ergonomics, Toronto, pp. 141-153.

Jankovsky, F., Chapet, R. and Benetti, A., (1987). Analyse des champs visuels des conducteurs de poids lourds. Rapport Aract des pays de la Loire, Angers, 37 pages.

Porter, J.M., Case, K. and Bonney, M.C. (1980). "A computer-generated three-dimensional visibility chart." *in:* Human Factors in Transport Research, Oborne and Levis eds., Academic Press, pp. 365-373.

Rebiffé, R., Guillien, J. and Trasbot, J. (1991). "Évaluation des conditions de vision à bord des voitures particulières". *in:* Actes du congrès international "Les composantes de l'habitacle automobile", Paris, 4-5 décembre 1991, pp. 11-15.

Reiss, M.L., Luhnenfeld, H. and Morton, G.W., (1972). Field of view requirements directly behind large trucks and buses. Report PB 209-256, NHTSA, US Dept. of Transport, Washington, DC, 188 pages.

SAE, (1990). SAE Handbook vol. 4: On-highway vehicles and Off-highway machinery. SAE Handbook. SAE, Warrendale, Pa. 400 pages. ISBN-0-89883-895-9.

Tisserand, M. and Englert, M., (1983). Exigences minimales de sécurité au poste de conduite des chariots élévateurs. Rapport 1151/RE, Centre de recherche de l'INRS, Nancy, 26 pages.

Tisserand, M. and Schouller, J.F., (1983). Visibilité au poste de conduite des pelles hydrauliques. Rapport 1152/RE, Centre de recherche de l'INRS, 11 pages.

Village, J., (1989). "Ergonomic and environmental assessment of haulage trucks for design improvements." Comptes rendus de la 22 ième conférence annuelle de l'Association canadienne d'ergonomie / Human Factors Association of Canada, ACE/HFAC, pages 125-130.

Ziedman, K., Burger, W.J. and Smith, R.L., (1987). The development of figures of merit for vehicle visibility and conspicuity systems. SAE Transactions SP-699, 96(2): 42-51.

Zlotnicki, J., Hutchinson, T.P. and Kendall, D.L., (1980). Some problems and prospects with commercial vehicle safety, illustrated by case reports of accidents involving ergonomic factors. Proc. International Conference on Ergonomics and Transportation, Swansea (UK), Academic Press, pages 151-159.

9: AROUSAL AND VISUAL PERFORMANCE

VISION IN VEHICLES - V
A.G. Gale et al. (Editors)

Saccadic Eye Movements and Blinks During Long-Term Driving on the Autobahn with Minimal Alcohol Ingestion

Niels Galley[a] & Gabriele Andrès[a,b]

[a] Psychological Institute, University of Cologne, D-50923 Köln, Germany

[b] ASS, Universitätsstraße 5, D-50937 Köln, Germany

1. INTRODUCTION

One major problem in long-term driving on the autobahn is drowsiness with the risk of falling asleep. As alcohol is effective on the GABA-receptor in the same manner as barbiturates and benzodiazepines (Olsen et. al. 1986), a main action of minimal doses could be to increase the natural tiredness in response to monotony and/or circadian rhythm. Additionally, there continues to be interest in the development of effective (Akerstedt et al. 1991) as well as practicable indicators of sleepiness. In the laboratory decreases in saccadic velocity (Galley 1989) and increases in blink rates (Carpenter 1948, Luckiesh & Moss 1937) were claimed to be good indicators of fatigue, we examined therefore in a field study these and other parameters of saccades and blinks.

The increase in blink rate (in our data the decrease in the mean blink interval) as a sign of fatigue seems to contrast with most time parameters which slow down when vigilance decreases. Therefore we include the fixation durations, i.e. to prove the interval between successive saccades, if due to fatigue this succession is increased as blinks or decreased as mental performance times. We looked at the mean saccadic amplitudes as well, because spatial parameters of behavior could be more resistent to vigilance decrements. These latter parameters were seldom used in this respect (Galley 1993), but had shown their significance as indicators of changing information processing.

We expected a) differences in our parameters between the city driving situation and the autobahn driving, b) a time on task effect, i.e. the longer people drive the more should their vigilance decline, c) a difference in the parameters due to the subjective awakefulness vs. tiredness, d) a further decrease in vigilance due to the low dose of alcohol, and e) a circadian effect, because all drives took place from the forenoon until the afternoon thus avoiding night driving. Because this study is still in progress, this paper is to be seen as a preliminary report.

2. METHODS AND SUBJECTS

We carried out on-line registrations of saccadic eye-movements and blinks on 15 drivers. They drove at least six hours on the autobahn, and we analyzed the effects of task, tiredness, and alcohol. Subjects drove as their own controls and were fully informed: The first day without alcohol, and on another day subjects drove after consuming a minimal dose of alcohol (less than .5 per mille) at the beginning of the second of five periods which were approximately one hour long. Every period of driving was followed by a pause of ca. 15 minutes. Saccades and blinks were identified on-line from the electrooculogram (with the equipment of PAR-ELEKTRONIK, Berlin and a program by Königstein 1989) and registered in files over a length of five to ten minutes. Storing such a file on a hard disk took just a second and registration went on immediately. The subjects scored their tiredness or awakefulness on a ten-point scale whenever they became aware of a change and told this to the experimenter who typed in these and other relevant information about weather, illumination, traffic density and so on. Alcohol concentrations were measured in the breath by the ALCOTEST instrument (manufactured by DRÄGER, Köln). The route of driving was the same for all subjects, and included an initial and final period of city driving which was roughly ten minutes in duration.

Collected data were grouped mainly in the five one-hour periods of the journey framed with the two city driving epochs. Another grouping took together all files of subjectively scored 'awakefulness' or 'tiredness' leaving out the middle values as neutral. Group means of 'awakefulness' and 'tiredness' were calculated only in the periods two to five (i.e. with and without minimal ingested alcohol). Mean saccadic velocities had to be standardized because different amplitudes show different velocities, in general. Therefore all velocities are recalculated as if they had had the same amplitude of 20 degrees following a formula of Becker (1989) :

saccadic velocity = 608 / 1.64 * saccadic amplitude / (7.6 + saccadic amplitude).

For a discussion of different standardization procedures see Galley (1989). In all groupings the individual medians were calculated from a lot of saccades and blinks, usually several hundreds of events. Next the median of all the subjects' medians was determined and then analyzed with parameter free statistics (Wilcoxon rank comparisons).

3. RESULTS

Mean *saccadic amplitudes* (see figure 1,2) show a decrease, i.e. a narrowing of the gaze behavior, from the first city driving period to the first autobahn period and a further decrease to the second period. The curves of the second day show lower values. In subsequent periods values remained stable at the first day, but increased on the second day. Both curves reached roughly the same values during the concluding city driving period. The bar graphs show a nonsignificant increase in the group mean of the 'waking' vs the 'tired' condition on day 1 and 2. Most curves are seen to reach initial values (i.e.those of the initial city driving period) at the concluding city driving period after often showing slight or clear increases in period 4 and 5. There is an additional second day effect, i.e. lowered values at the inital periods when still no alcohol is consumed. To rule out the second day effect which is confounded with a possible alcohol effect in this data presentation we recalculated all individual means as differences with respect to the values in period 1 which was defined as one hundred percent. This is shown in figures 2, 4, 6, 8, and 10.

Now in relation to the period 1 the city driving effects remain stable and significant and all other effects are non significant.

The mean *fixation durations* also show strong effects of city driving which are shorter in this condition than during autobahn driving. Additionally one can see some increases from period 1 to 2 .

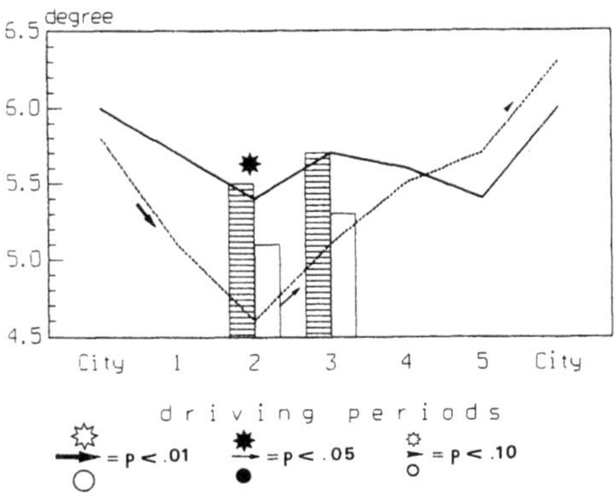

Figure 1. Mean saccadic amplitudes of 15 subjects driving on the first day without alcohol and on the second day from period 2 with a small dose of alcohol. The bar graphs show first the 'awake' and then the. 'tired' condition on day 1 and 2 (with alcohol). Stars indicate significant changes from the first day to the second, arrows from one period to another

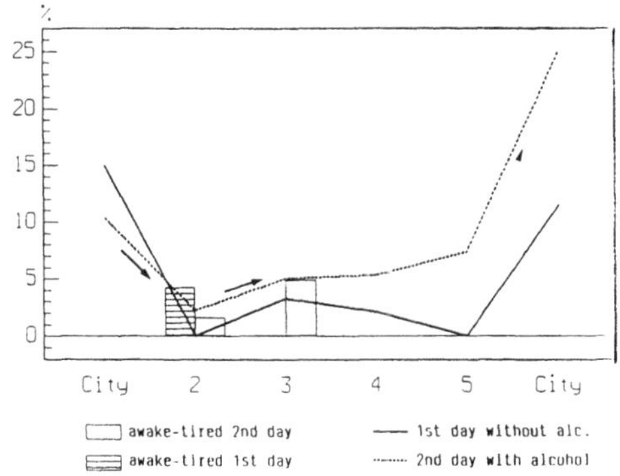

Figure 2. The same data recalculated as differences to period 1. One sees that the city driving effects persist, but effects of time on task, tiredness, and alcohol are marginal for the best.

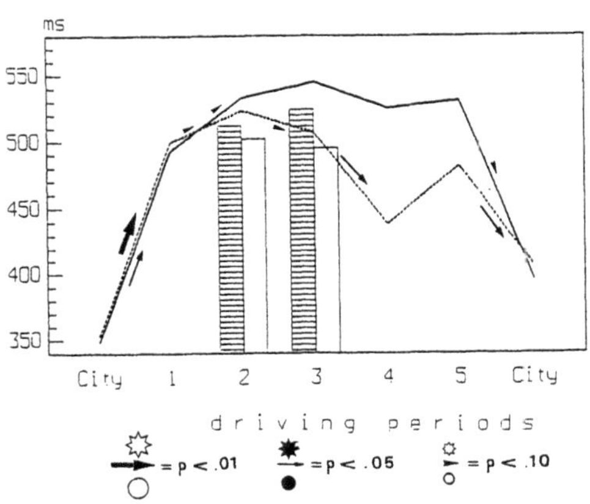

Figure 3. Fixation durations were considerably longer on the autobahn and increase from period 1 to 2. On the second day they began to decrease afterwards. No tiredness and alcohol effect are to be seen.

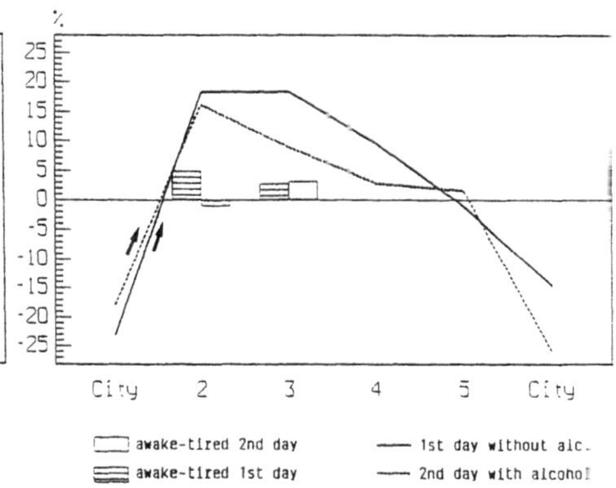

Figure 4. In relation to period 1 the fixation durations remained longer in the period 2 to 4. There is no fatigue and alcohol effect.

Again group mean effects due to alcohol and tiredness are small or absent.

In the mean standardized *saccadic velocities* (see figure 5,6) which are often claimed as valid vigilance indicators we see the usual decrease at the beginning and also in the second period, but no further decreases as expected. The 'tiredness'-effect is small and no further decrease due to alcohol is to be seen.

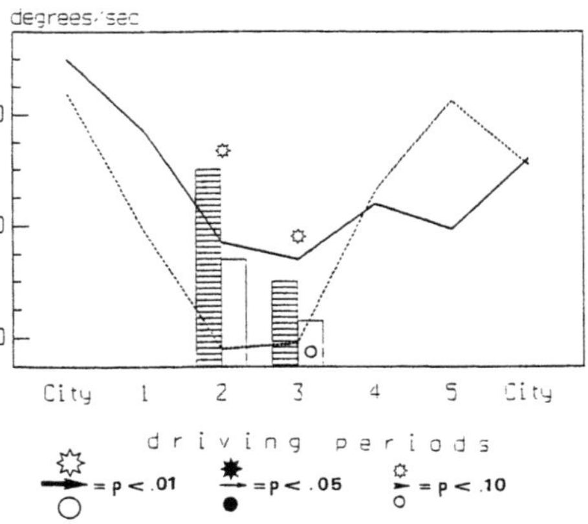

Figure 5. Mean saccadic velocities show lower values on the second day, a decrease from period 1 to 2 and small effects of fatigue.

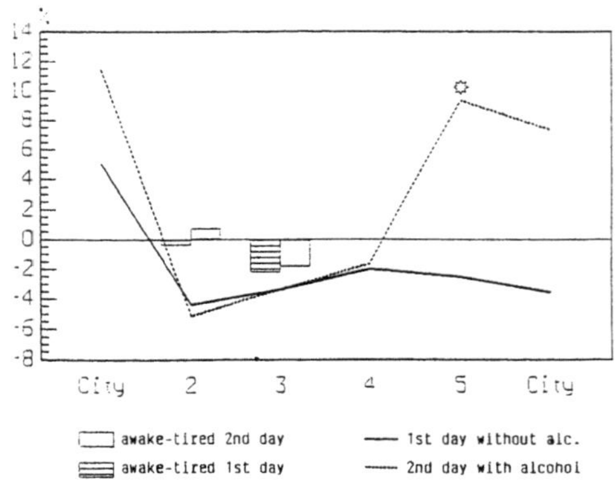

Figure 6. in relation to period 1 the values in period 2 to 4 are only a little bit slower. No alcohol effect is seen.

In then mean *velocities of the eyelid closure* (see figure 7,8) a second day effect, the initial decrease due to leaving the city and on the second day the increase at the end of driving are to be seen.

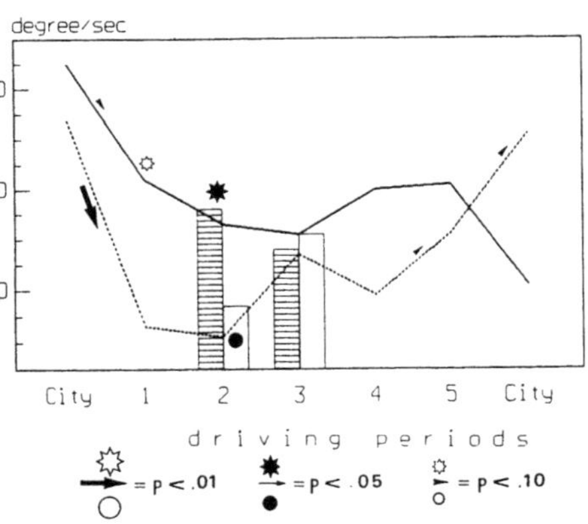

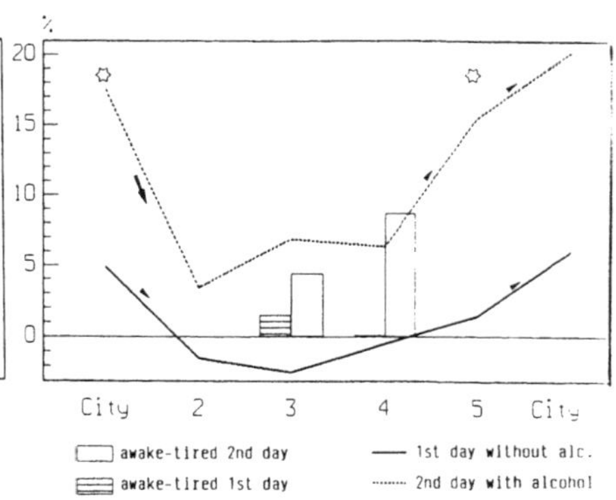

Figure 7. Mean velocities of eyelid closure show lower values on the second day, a decrease from period city to 1, and on the second day an increase at the end of driving.

Figure 8. In relation to period 1 the values of the second day are greater. Alcohol shows an paradox increase in the fatigue condition.

In the mean *blink intervals* (see figure 9, 10) one can find decreased values - i.e. increased blink rates ! - going out from the town and a further decrease in the long term driving. There are small fatigue and alcohol effects which persist in figure 10.

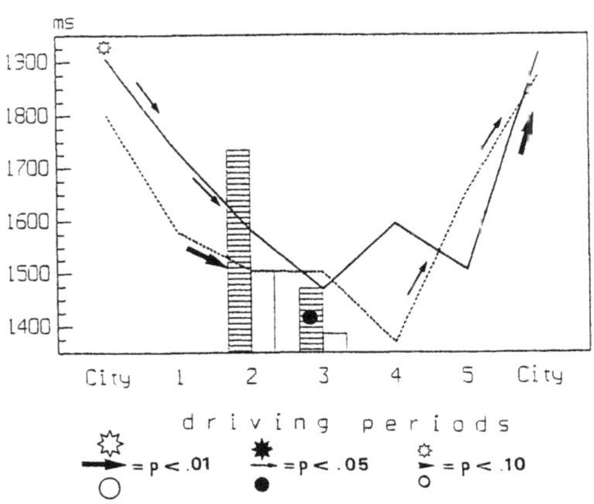

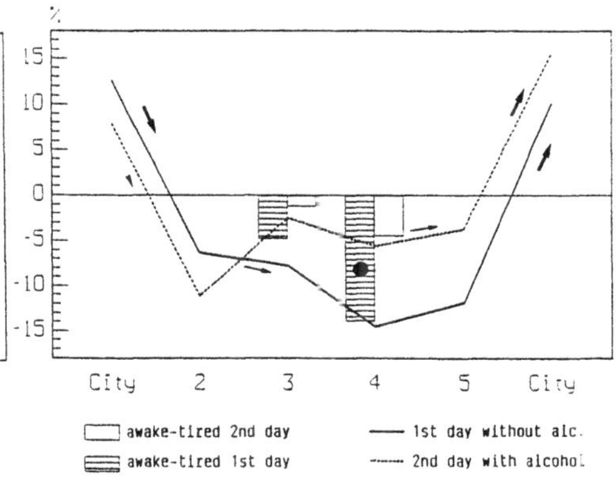

Figure 9. Blink intervals were considerably shorter on the autobahn and show decreases from period 2 to 3. Small tiredness and alcohol effects can be seen.

Figure 10. In relation to period 1 the blink intervals remained shorter in the period 2 to 5. The fatigue and alcohol effect persist.

4. DISCUSSION

On most measures we found a clear effect of *city vs. autobahn driving*, i.e. a significantly higher value in the mean saccadic amplitude, the saccadic velocity, the eylid closure velocity, the blink interval, and a lower value in the mean fixation duration while driving in the city. The mean for the looking amplitude appeared to be broadened for city driving and narrowed for autobahn driving. Regarding the broader functional visual field during city driving, this effect could be expected. However, to our knowledge this is the first claim that such a simple measure as the median of all saccadic amplitudes can indicate such a complex behavioural structure as the functional visual field. Fixation durations are more than 100 ms shorter during city driving. It seems to be a different visual task with more objects and locations to look at. Blink intervals are also lengthened dramatically by more than 300 ms in the city. This is another sign of the visual load. The increase in the saccadic velocity has been claimed to be a sign of effort (Galley 1989), and the comparable increase in the velocity of eylid closure adds to the view that city driving is a task with more visual load than autobahn driving.

Three effects of decreasing vigilance had been expected in the oculomotoric parameters: First a *time on task* effect over the five periods of autobahn driving, second a effect of feeling '*fatigue*' vs 'alert' , and last an effect of *alcohol*. Unexpectedly we found two additional effects: A habituation effect of *driving at the second day* which diminish most values, and an increase on most parameters between period 4 to 5; this letter effect we would prefer to interpret as a *circadian* related increase in vigilance at the late afternoon.

During driving for hours on the autobahn, most parameters show a small decrease in vigilance from period 1 to 2, but seldom to 3. These effects can be interpreted as a time on task effect. But in most curves we found an increase towards the later periods, mostly from period 4 to 5. Thus we never found a continous decrease over the five periods due to continously driving as expected with time on task as the most effective influence. It may be that the short pauses between the periods played a role to counteract the time on task effect.

Unexpectedly we found a clearcut second day effect, i.e. most parameters showed decrements or increments in the sense of some habituation when subjects drove the same tour for the second time; significant were the smaller saccadic amplitudes, the shorter blink intervals, the slower velocities of saccades and eyelid closures. These habituation effects were seen mostly in the first periods, and seldom persisted to the late periods of driving. Our idea was to avoid the double load of driving with EOG cables and alcohol on the first time. But this habituation effect may be now confounded with a possible alcohol effect. It necessitates the recalculating of our data as a change in baselines. This is seen in figures 2, 4, 6, 8, and 10. Accordingly a second day effect should have been eliminated. But a more rigorous conclusion may be to run more habituation tours as well as more alcohol tours: experimental driving should become as 'normal' to the subjects as their all day driving.

The 'fatigue' effect was unexpectedly small, when we compared the subjectively most tired with the most awakened situation, i.e. the pooled data files when the subjects score themselves as more awake or more fatigue. Significant was the shorter blink interval on the first day and the slower saccadic velocity on the second day. A number of studies in the laboratory show a decrease of saccadic velocity in response to fatigue as well as a dose dependent slowing in response to sedatives (for a review see Galley 1989). We had expected a clearcut evidence for a strong relation of this parameter to subjectively scored fatigue as well as time on task. The following causes may be responsible for this small or missing effects: 1. There are big interindividual differences, some subjects seem susceptible to monotony, others do not, 2. the subjective scala seems to be not constant, 3. the subjective feeling of being tired may be associated with a tonic deactivation process, but the objective indicators as saccadic velocity may measure the sum of tonic deactivation and phasic self-activation processes, 4. 'sleepiness' seems to be a phasic short term event (Akerstedt et al.1988) and our data grouping interval of 8-10 minutes may be too long not showing such a brief episode. The data are currently being analysed to examine these possibilities.

Significant alcohol effects were absent. Sometimes there were small paradoxical effects of increasing vigilance. Normally, a negative effect should not be interpreted. But we believe, that the indicators are sensitive enough, when city driving could be discriminated from autobahn driving, when the second day show habituation effects, when time on task was effective. Thus alcohol had had a chance to be effective, but it wasn't. In our opinon this does not mean that alcohol in such small doses has no detrimental effect on vigilance in normal driving, but has no direct effect on the brainstem arousal centers. Because the GABA receptors on which alcohol is acting are mostly located in the cortex and the limbic system, but not in the brainstem (Möhler et al. 1978), one can suppose that indirect effects like decreasing motivation or anxiety decrease the relevance of the environment which normally leads to fatigue. In our experimental situation the subjects could feel that the alcohol has an effect and therefore compensated with more effort thus counteracting the more central effects. Paradoxical performance benefits of alcohol are often seen in the laboratory with small doses (Krüger et. al. 1990). Therefore alcohol is unlikely to be effective directly on brainstem centers where saccadic velocity is generated (Fuchs et al. 1985). This would argue against earlier views of the saccadic slowing (Franck & Kuhlo 1970).

Looking at the oculomotor parameters as indicators of all the influencing factors one can say: Saccadic amplitude show a broadening of .5 to 1 degree due to city driving, a small second day decrease due to habituation, but a small increase due to fatigue, and a small decrease due to alcohol. Thus the spatial monitoring behavior seems to be insensitive for fatigue, monotony and alcohol but sensitive for the visual load, i.e. a perceptual variation. Fixation duration show a dramatic shortening (140 ms) due to city driving but a further lengethening of 50 ms due to time on task. However, the effects of fatigue and alcohol are only marginal on this parameter. Thus again the mean interval between two saccades seems to be more sensitive to perceptual variation than to fatigue and sedation, in contrast to the mean interval between two blinks. The velocity of eyelid closure shows a behavior that is similar to that of the saccadic velocity. Blink intervals are shortened in autobahn driving and also due to fatigue, thus confirming the known effect of an increasing blink rate in fatigue as well as a decrease due to visual load. Blink behavior show a second day effect as well as an effect of time on task. Altogether the blink interval was the most sensitive indicator for all identified influences in this study. The interpretation of blink rates has two aspects: On the one side there are good reasons to believe that higher rates indicate higher levels of dopaminergic arousal (Karson 1989) in different subjects, but on the other side evidence shows that the blink is positioned at a time when a 'cognitive sequence is ending' (Stern et al. 1984, Galley 1993). Thus one had to postulate a central inhibition for the undesired interruption of vision by the blink, increasing when the visual load increases and decreasing when the central facilities ('wish for monitoring the world' for example) decline. If this interpretation is correct, the marginal facilitating effect due to alcohol would suggest again a central compensation of a suspected central effect of alcohol.

In conclusion, a design to study alcohol and monotony effects in the field should allow more habituation thus eliminating the heightened self-monitoring and concentrating effects of experimental driving. Our pilot study showed the sensitivity of oculomotor parameters to different aspects of the drivers task.

REFERENCES

Akerstedt, T., Kecklund, G., Sigurdsson, K., Anderzén, I., & Gillberg, M. (1991). Methodological aspects on ambulatory monitoring of sleepiness. In A. Gundel (Ed.), Proceedings of the workshop 'Psychophysiological Measures in Transport Operations.' (Interne Berichte der DLR IB-316-91-01). Köln: DLR.

Akerstedt, T., Torsval, L., & Gillberg, M. (1988). Ambulatory measurements of vigilance. In J. P. Leonard (Ed.), Vigilance: Methods, Models, and Regulation. Frankfurt/Main: Peter Lang.

Becker, W. (1989). Metrics. In R. H. Wurtz & M. E. Goldberg (Eds.), The Neurobiology of Saccadic Eye Movements. Amsterdam: Elsevier.

Carpenter, A. (1948). The rate of blinking during prolonged visual search. Journal of Experimental Psychology, 38, 587-591.

Franck, M. C., & Kuhlo, W. (1970). Die Wirkung des Alkohols auf die raschen Blickzielbewegungen (Saccaden) beim Menschen. Archiv für Psychiatrie und Nervenkrankheiten, 213, 238-245.

Fuchs, A. F., Kaneko, C. R. S., & Scudder, C. A. (1985). Brainstem control of saccadic eye movements. Annual Review of Neuroscience, 8, 307-337.

Galley, N. (1989). Saccadic eye movement velocity as an indicator of (de)activation. A review and some speculations. Journal of Psychophysiology, 3, 229-244.

Galley, N. (1993). Traffic relevant behavior monitored by the electrooculogram (EOG) as a psychophysical measuring instrument. In A. G. Gale, et al. (Eds.), Vison in Vehicles IV (pp. 189-196). Amsterdam: Elsevier.

Karson, C. N. (1989). Blinking. Bulletin of Society of Belgian Ophtalmologists, 237, 443-457.

Königstein, A. (1989). Die On-Line-Identifizierung sakkadischer Augenbewegungen aus dem Elektrookulogramm (Diplomarbeit). Bonn: Fachbereich Informatik der Universität zu Bonn.

Krüger, H.-P., Kohnen, R., Diehl, M., & Hüppe, A. (1990). Auswirkungen geringer Alkoholmengen auf Fahrverhalten und Verkehrssicherheit (Bericht zum Forschungsprojekt 8707 der Bundesanstalt für Straßenwesen). Bergisch Gladbach: Bundesanstalt für Straßenwesen.

Luckiesh, M., & Moss, F. K. (1937). The eyelid reflex as a criterion of ocular fatigue. Journal of Experimental Psychologie, 20, 589-608.

Möhler, H., Okada, T., Heitz, P., & Ulrich, J. (1978) . Biochemical identification of the site of action of benzodiazepines in human brain by 3H-Diazepam binding. Life Sciences, 22, 985-996.

Olsen, R. W., Wamsley, J. K., Lee, R. J., & Lomax, P. (1986). Benzodiazepine/ Barbiturate/ GABA Receptor-Chloride Ionophore complex in a genetic model for generalized epilepsy. In A. V. Delgado-Escueta, A. A. Ward Jr., D. M. Woodbury, & R. J. Porter (Eds.), Epilepsy, Molecular and Cellular Approaches. (Advances in Neurology Vol. 44). New York: Raven Press.

Stern, J. A., Walrath, L. C., & Goldstein, R. (1984). The endogenous eyeblink. Psychophysiology, 21, 22-33.

VISION IN VEHICLES - V
A.G. Gale et al. (Editors)

Performance in Detecting Traffic Signs With and Without Alcohol Ingestion (A Laboratory Study)

L. Nunes[a], M. Peralbo[b], A. Risso[c] y P. Vieiro[b]

[a]Area de Formación y Comportamiento de Conductores, Dirección General de Tráfico, Josefa Valcárcel 28, 28027 Madrid, Spain

[b]Dpto. de Psicología Evolutiva y de la Educación, Universidad de La Coruña, Campus de La Zapateira, 15071 La Coruña, Spain

[c]Dpto. de Psicología, Universidad de La Coruña, Campus de La Zapateira, 15071 La Coruña, Spain

Abstract

The purpose of this work was to examine performance in detecting traffic signs when subjects had drunk alcohol as compared to when they had not. Five drivers (undergraduate students) performed a detection task with and without ingesting alcohol. The amount of alcohol was close to the legal blood alcohol limit in Spain (until 0.8 gr/l for non professional drivers).

Forty-eight computerized stimuli were presented on a colour screen; half of them were pictures of traffic signs and the other half were signs showing irrelevant objects. A point was centred on the screen and preceding each picture, which was displayed peripherally somewhere around the central point. Subjects were instructed to locate the stimulus and to say 'yes' or 'no' depending on whether the given stimulus was a traffic sign or not. A record of eye movements using an NAC-EMR 600 allowed us to obtain measures of the time required to locate the stimulus (eye movement velocity from the previous fixation point at the centre of the screen), as well as measures of the duration of eye fixation on the target.

Data analysis compared movement velocity and duration of fixation separately for traffic and non-traffic signs in each group of subjects. The results showed that performance is slightly deteriorated after consuming alcohol.

Interesting consequences concerning vision during driving were found from these data. If alcohol ingestion affects a very simple task like this, the implications regarding its influence on a highly complex task like driving must obviously be much more important.

1. INTRODUCTION

Many studies have confirmed the influence of alcohol ingestion on driving. However, public service announcements and legal limits do not discourage many people from driving under the influence of alcohol effects. In fact, there is a dangerous perception that driving after drinking is only risky beyond a certain point, and an individual is not always aware of this point. The aim of this study, then, is to examine the effects of alcohol consumption up to the established legal limit of blood alcohol concentration (BAC) in Spain on eye searching movements and on detection of relevant and non-relevant traffic signs.

As Avant, Bowes, Tepin and Kerwin (1991) point out, data about the influence of different BAC levels on drivers' visual behaviour do not always agree. Nevertheless, there are several interesting facts known: alcohol ingestion tends to reduce the velocity of saccade and ocular movements of smooth pursuit, to increase the latency of saccade movements, to produce nystagmus, and so on (see Stapleton, Guthrie & Linnoila, 1986). All these make the processing of visual information difficult. In addition, the degree of effects seems to depend on the BAC level (Levett & Hoeft, 1977; Tong, Knott, McGraw & Gillian, 1974). Our experiment was an attempt to verify our hypotheses that BAC levels close to the established legal limit in Spain affect both the duration of ocular fixation on the target stimulus and the velocity of the eye searching movements.

During driving, the rapid discrimination of relevant and non-relevant stimuli is essential. Discrimination and processing of traffic signs, as different from other irrelevant signs, can be an example. There are several studies (Avant et al., 1991; Linfield & Dunne, 1988) which lead us to suppose the existence of differences in duration of eye fixation on traffic and non-traffic signs; moreover, those differences may be affected by alcohol ingestion. The same types of differences are expected to be found in the velocity of eye searching movements from the centre to the periphery of the screen.

2. METHOD

2.1. Subjects

Initially, twenty undergraduate students of both sexes (age range 19-23) participated in this study; all had normal vision and none used glasses or contact lenses, because their use was incompatible with the equipment. However, eleven of the subjects withdrew from the experiment at the end of the first session, for two reasons: a) discomfort from the equipment; b) they changed their mind about drinking alcohol. With another four subjects there were interferences in the recording of their eye mark data so they had to be eliminated.

2.2. Stimuli

Some stimuli were specially designed for this study, and others were taken from traffic signs. The group of relevant stimuli consisted of 24 coloured traffic signs; the group of irrelevant stimuli consisted of 24 coloured representations of several non-traffic objects. These objects were shown inside standard triangular, circular and square sign-type shapes; the traffic and non-traffic objects had the same format and size. For the present study, three danger signs and two irrelevant signs with the same shape were taken into account. These five selected signs appeared in the upper left square of the screen.

2.3. Apparatus

An NAC-EMR 600 was used. This is a portable system for registration of eye movements. It can sample eye mark data of both eyes with an accuracy of 0.17 degrees at the maximum data sampling rate of 600 Hz. It uses the CPU board and calibration frame (for calibration chart) for rapid semiautomatic calibration which is required to eliminate the effects of different subjects and the distortion of optics on measurement. It provides an analog OUT terminal so that the coordinate data after eye mark calibration can be outputted as 30 Hz sampling data for realtime processing. Data for both eyes movements (right eye and left pupil) were recorded on video (NTSC system). In addition, special software was used to analyze eye movements and fixations and to project the eye movement trajectory over the video image. A field viewing angle of 30 degrees was best suited for this experimental situation.

In NAC EMR-600, a fixation point is the centre of the range in which the eye mark remains for a certain time or more in a particular range. The time and range are specified at fixation point data creation. The minimum time duration was 66.66 milliseconds and the range was 5 degrees. The selected sampling rate was 30 Hz. The distance from the camera sensor to the viewing plane was 70 cm.

The centroid mode was used to determine the fixation points. This centroid was obtained sequentially and used as the reference to set the fixation point.

2.4. Design

The design was intrasubject and multivariate. The levels of the independent variable were: traffic signs and non-traffic signs. The dependent variables were: a) ocular movement velocity from the last fixation point, in the centre of the screen, to the first point of fixation on the selected stimuli; and b) ocular fixation time on the stimulus target.

2.5. Procedure

Firstly, the subject's headmotion was controlled by fixing the head on a specially designed headrest. Secondly, we fixed the goggle unit with the help of guide LEDs cables. Thirdly, we pointed them towards the cornea and calibrated them using a calibration frame placed 70 cm from the eye. Finally, we fixed the parallax: the subject's sight had to be fixed on the centre of the screen (to correct the initial deviation along X and Y axes and to give an accuracy of ± 1 degree). The subjects were given instructions to begin the task and we began the experimental session.

The stimuli (each shown for 2000 msec) were presented randomly on a colour screen; but the central point (shown for 2000 msec) appeared before the display of each stimulus. The subjects had to answer "yes" or "no", according to circumstances ("yes" if the stimulus was a traffic sign and "no" if it was a non-traffic sign). Responses were recorded by hand; at the same time we recorded the left eye image and the movements of the right eye.

Each subject had two experimental sessions, the first one without having drunk alcohol, and the second having had a quantity which resulted in a BAC level of approximately 0.7 gr/l (calculated from the height, weight and age of the subjects) one hour before reinitiating the experiment. This second session took place one week after the first one.

The eye marks of the right eye and its calibration data were recorded on video.

3. RESULTS AND DISCUSSION

The means of the eye fixation times and the velocities of the eye searching movements are shown in Table 1 and Figures 1 and 2. They include the results for the traffic and non traffic signs under the two conditions: with and without alcohol.

Table 1
Results of mean durations of eye fixations and velocities of eye searching movements.

SUBJECTS	TRAFFIC SIGNS		NON-TRAFFIC SIGNS	
	MEANS OF FIXATION DURATIONS (MILLISECONDS)			
	WITHOUT ALCOHOL	WITH ALCOHOL	WITHOUT ALCOHOL	WITH ALCOHOL
1	670	1620	400	670
2	660	1080	720	850
3	1020	920	1080	700
4	1440	1430	1170	1150
5	1260	1260	700	980
	MEANS OF EYE MOVEMENT SPEED (DEGREES/SECOND)			
	WITHOUT ALCOHOL	WITH ALCOHOL	WITHOUT ALCOHOL	WITH ALCOHOL
1	138.33	217.00	242.00	237.50
2	210.00	314.67	282.00	291.00
3	398.00	215.33	453.00	250.50
4	296.00	236.33	298.00	254.50
5	231.67	231.00	220.50	234.00

Student's t-test for related samples was used for the statistical analysis.

Results showed that under the non-alcohol condition there were no differences between the traffic and non-traffic signs for the fixation point duration (t_4=1.67; p>.10), or for the velocity of the searching movements from the centre of the screen to the upper left square t_4=-2.05; p>.10).

Alcohol produced a significant increase in the durations of the fixation points when dealing with traffic signs instead of non-traffic signs (t_4=2.78; p<.05). But differences were not found regarding the velocity of the eye movements (t_4=-1.06; p>.10).

The comparison of the fixation times for the traffic signs with and without having ingested alcohol did not reveal significant differences (t_4=-1.28; p>.10).

The same was found when comparing the velocity of movement from the centre of the screen (t_4=0.23; p>.10). Nevertheless, the fixation durations tended to be higher under the alcohol condition.

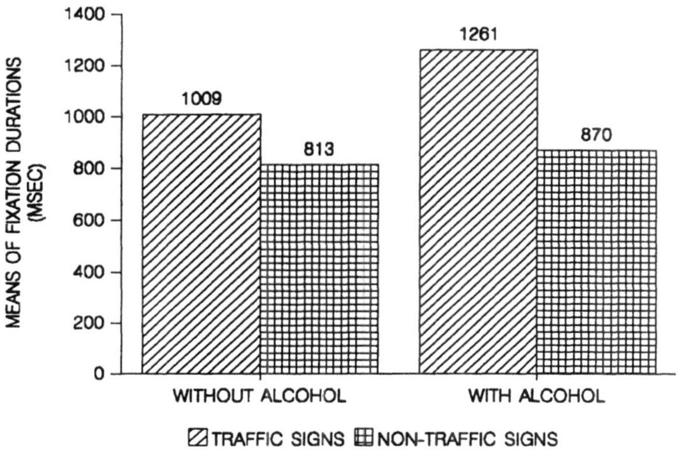

Figure 1. Means of fixation durations on traffic and non-traffic signs with and without alcohol ingestion.

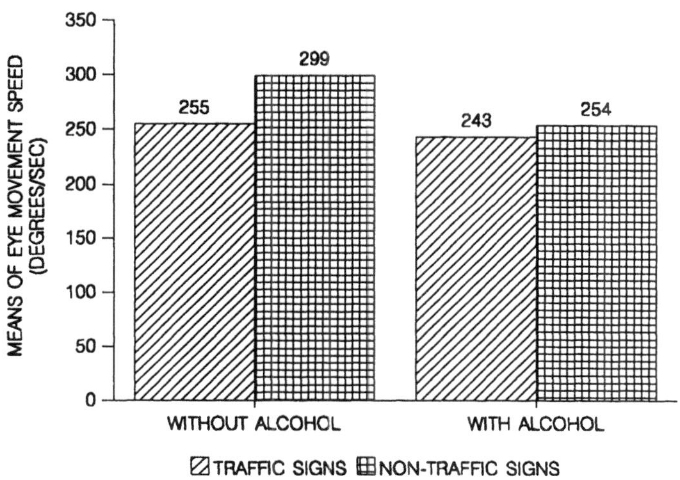

Figure 2. Means of velocity of eye movements from central point to upper left traffic and non-traffic signs with and without alcohol ingestion.

Similar results appeared when analyzing eye movements for non-traffic signs under the two conditions (alcohol and non-alcohol). Results were not significant but the fixation times tended to be higher in the alcohol condition (t_4=-0.46; p>.10). Moreover, the velocity of eye movement to the non-traffic signs seemed not to be affected by alcohol (t_4=1.12; p>.10).

Considering these data, it could be said that the legally permitted dose of alcohol in Spain has some effect on the control of the exploration eye movements and on the discrimination of traffic signs. It shows that alcohol increases the time that is needed for proper stimulus recognition. These findings coincide with other results indicating an increase in eye fixation durations after drugs and alcohol abuse (Stapleton, et al., 1991; Fuster, Wiley & Riley, 1985; Moscowitz, Ziedman & Sharma, 1976).

From our point of view, these results lead to thinking that, even within legal limits of alcohol ingestion, a driver's visual performance is, indeed, affected by alcohol. So, the legal interdiction of alcohol consumption for drivers seems well justified for traffic safety.

REFERENCES

Avant, L.L., Bowes, M., Tepin, M. and Kerwin, K. (1991). Alcohol and visual detection of traffic signs. In A.G. Gale et al. (Eds.): *Vision in Vehicles III.* Amsterdam, Elsevier Science Publishers B.V., 291-298.

Fuster, J.M., Willey, T.J. and Riley, D.M. (1985) Effects of ethanol on eye movements in the monkey. *Alcohol, 2(4)*, 611-616.

Levett, J. and Hoeft, G. (1977). Voluntary eye movements and alcohol. *Aviation, Space and Environmental Medicine, 48*, 612-614.

Linfield, P.B. and Dunne, M.C.M. (1988). The effects of alcohol induced binocular instability on a driver's ability to correctly identify road direction signs. In A. G. Gale et al. (Eds.): *Vision in vehicles- II.* Amsterdam, Elsevier Science Publishers B.V., 75-83.

Moscowitz, H., Ziedman, K, Sharma, S. (1976) Visual search behavior while viewing driving scenes under the influence of alcohol and marihuana. *Human Factors, 18(5)*, 417-431.

Stapleton, J.M., Guthrie, S. and Linnoila, M. (1986). Effects of alcohol and other psychotropic drugs on eye movements: Relevance to traffic safety. *Journal of Studies of Alcohol, 47(5)*, 426-432.

Tong, J.E., Knott, V.J., McGraw, D.J. and Gillian, L. (1974). Alcohol, visual discrimination and heart rate: Effects of dose, activation and tobacco. *Quarterly Journal of Studies on Alcohol, 35(3-A)*, 1003-1022.

AUTHOR INDEX

SUBJECT INDEX

www.ingramcontent.com/pod-product-compliance
Ingram Content Group UK Ltd.
Pitfield, Milton Keynes, MK11 3LW, UK
UKHW020230290926
15470UKWH00002B/450

9 780444 814777